Also by John Hope Mason
and available from Quartet Books

The Indispensable Rousseau

John Hope Mason was a Scholar in History at Corpus Christi College, Cambridge, where he took a First in the Anglo-Saxon and Old Norse Tripos. He has since worked in theatre and opera, both as a writer and director, as well as in the history of ideas. His first book, *The Indispensable Rousseau*, was published in 1979.

THE IRRESISTIBLE DIDEROT

JOHN HOPE MASON

QUARTET BOOKS
LONDON MELBOURNE NEW YORK

First published by Quartet Books Limited 1982
A member of the Namara Group
27/29 Goodge Street, London W1P 1FD

Copyright © 1982 by John Hope Mason

British Library Cataloguing in Publication Data

Mason, John Hope
  The irresistible Diderot.
  1. Diderot, Denis—Criticism and interpretation
  I. Title
  194   B2017

ISBN 0-7043-2277-3

Typeset by MC Typeset, Rochester, Kent
Printed and bound in Great Britain by
Mackays of Chatham Limited, Kent

Contents

Preface

Diderot is one of the most attractive, original and little-read writers of modern Europe. This book sets out to show the nature of his achievement and make it more accessible than it has been up to now.

Since the new edition of his *Oeuvres complètes*, now in course of publication, will run to thirty-two volumes, there is clearly much that must pass without mention in a mere 400 pages. This book makes no claim to be either comprehensive or exhaustive. Many of the actual texts of Diderot's writings present complex problems – uncertainties about exact dates of composition and/or revision, the conflicting evidence of different manuscripts, and the particular circumstances in which manuscripts have come down to us – all these have been excluded from this study. Instead my aim has been to present the principal works, indicate the interest of other writings, and show why they remain of compelling interest today. The first step to enjoying and appreciating Diderot is to understand how he thought, rather than what he thought, and this also I have tried to explain.

The book has a broadly chronological framework (with certain obvious exceptions). However, the reader coming to Diderot for the first time would do best, I believe, not to read the chapters in this sequence. After the introductory chapters (1 and 2) he or she should turn to *Rameau's Nephew* (9) and *D'Alembert's Dream* (10), which are devoted to Diderot's two most individual achievements; these should provide the quickest and surest way to understanding why his writings evoke such interest and enthusiasm. Thereafter the reader can pick and choose among the other chapters devoted to different aspects of his work, ending, in due course, with the *Conclusion* (15).

There are some omissions among Diderot's writings that I particularly regret. I would like to have devoted much more space to his art criticism, the *Salons*. To do them justice, however, they need a book to themselves, with appropriate illustrations. I hope that some publisher may produce such a book, like that which already exists for the art criticism of Stendhal. I would also like to have given more space to *Jacques le fataliste*, but that work and the fictional writings in general are least suited to treatment in extracts.

An immense amount of work has been done on Diderot in the last thirty years or so and this book has benefited from much of it. Most of the translations are my own but I have made use of some other versions; I am grateful to a number of publishers for permission to reprint these. Lawrence and Wishart gave permission to quote from J. Stewart and J. Kemp's translations of the *Rêve de d'Alembert* and the *Supplément au Voyage de Bougainville* (originally printed in *Diderot: Interpreter of Nature*); Macmillans gave permission to quote from D. Coltman's translations of the *Pensées sur l'interprétation de la nature*, *Entretiens sur le Fils naturel*, *Paradoxe sur le comédien* and *Réfutation d'Helvétius* (originally printed in *Diderot: Selected Writings*, edited by L. G. Crocker); New York University Press gave permission to quote from J. Robert Loy's translation of *Jacques le fataliste*; and Columbia University Press gave permission to quote from J. H. Ginn's translation of the *Discours sur la poésie dramatique* (originally published in *Dramatic Essays of the Neoclassic Age*, edited by H. H. Adams and B. Hathaway). I have made minor alterations to all of them for the sake of fluency and consistency. Details of translations for each chapter are given in the Notes (where no translator is given the translation is my own); likewise the references for the page numbers printed in the margins. Throughout the book square brackets [ ] indicate an insertion by the author or translator.

I would like to thank Professor Peter France, Dr Robert Wokler and Christopher May for reading the book in manuscript and making a number of valuable suggestions. I am also grateful to my mother and father for their support in difficult times; it is to them that I would like to dedicate this work.

The Irresistible Diderot

1

Introduction

I

The eighteenth century is not what it was. Admired for its lucidity and envied for its calm, it once had the character of a picturesque bay, sheltered from the dense forests of the sixteenth and seventeenth centuries and the turbulent seas of the nineteenth and twentieth centuries. It was seen as a time of order, an age of reason, when 'the wealthy and educated of Europe must have enjoyed almost the nearest approach to earthly felicity known to man'.[1] A century when tours were grand, gardens were landscaped and music was Mozart; when the intellect had broken free from centuries of serving the Church but had not yet grown heady with Hegelian, Marxist or Nietzschean excess. Not everyone admired these qualities; to some the century was 'the natural era of compromises and half-convictions',[2] a period which displayed 'an incapacity of producing deep or strong feelings',[3] a 'winter of the imagination'.[4] It lacked the exuberant splendour of the Renaissance, the vivid extravagance of Romanticism, the restless invention of modern times. But the century such critics looked down on was the same as that which others admired – a century of clarity, rationality and comparative calm.

All that has gone. For the clarity cast deep shadows, the calm was illusory. 'A level of disorder existed in eighteenth-century England,' a leading historian wrote recently, 'which if it occurred today would certainly result in the declaration of martial law.'[5] Through the clear surface strange and unexpected life-forms have been seen; behind the glittering couplets of Alexander Pope, no less than behind the sonorous judgements of Dr Johnson, there was an agitated uneasy mind. What was once regarded as melancholy or sardonic humour has assumed the dimensions of metaphysical panic. Voltaire's work is no longer dismissed as 'a chaos of clear ideas'[6] but seen as a sombre struggle against the spectre of a world without meaning; he has been called 'a great poet of anxiety'.[7] Rousseau's writings were not an exhibition of facile paradoxes and paranoid ravings but the sustained development of profound insights into man's place in society and the world. The eighteenth century, in fact, was as aware of fundamental problems, contradictions and tensions as our own bewildered century. And it was equally ready to face such problems and make what sense it could of them. That sense was not achieved through simple rationality but by means of a rationality that existed alongside, and within, more complex patterns of mind.

In this new perspective the writings of Diderot have come to occupy a central place. Diderot's importance, his status as a major figure in the eighteenth century, has never been in doubt. His immense achievement – editing almost singlehandedly the *Encyclopédie*, the twenty-eight folio volumes which seemed to embody the Enlightenment's ambition and achievement – was sufficient to ensure that; quite apart from the other works which in their different ways won the admiration of Goethe, Stendhal, Hegel, Comte, Carlyle, Sainte-Beuve and so on. But Diderot's writings taken as a whole seemed to raise so many problems, his contradictions seemed so pervasive, his inconsistencies so habitual, that it was difficult to see how they could all emerge from one mind and remain valid. For one person to hold apparently irreconcilable opinions may not be uncommon, but prominent writers and thinkers owe their prominence precisely to the fact that their ideas are coherent. Diderot seemed a case of being all exceptions and no rule.

But now that we are more aware of the complexities of his time we can appreciate better the particular merits of his work. We can see how large a part of its value lies in the attempt to go beyond common assumptions and accepted categories. In his most search-ing works Diderot operated on and over the borders of rationality; he valued clarity but he was conscious of how it could fall short of a comprehensive grasp of living reality and he valued that compre-hension more. A preoccupation that underlay much of his work, though never explicitly formulated, was that his writing should convey the whole experience of the living moment; that it should be both precise enough and flexible enough to describe the world as it is, in all its richness, density and variety. Hence the extraordinary openness, mobility and directness of his best work. At the same time, however, much of his thought remained rooted in the general assumptions of the period; although individual insights may have called these into question, Diderot never outgrew them or discarded them. The result is the strange and idiosyncratic nature of his work, in which the conventional and the audacious, the commonplace and the original, exist not only side by side but in a curiously symbiotic relationship.

Once this is realized Diderot's writings can be seen for the achievement they are, displaying the individuality, versatility and brilliance which those who knew him well say he possessed in person. To read him now is to recapture some of the excitement which his friends felt in his presence. 'This astonishing, universal, perhaps unique genius',[8] wrote Rousseau; a man, according to Grimm, who 'seemed inspired, stirred up by the demon of enlightenment and truth . . . [who] encompasses everything he comes near.'[9] 'When I remember Diderot,' wrote Meister, 'the immense variety of his ideas, the astonishing range of his knowledge, the rapidity and warmth and impetuous tumult of his imagination, all the charm and disorder of his conversation, I am tempted to compare his mind to nature as he saw it himself, rich, fertile, abounding in seeds of every kind, gentle and wild, simple and grand, good and sublime.'[10]

II

The generation who reached maturity around the middle years of the eighteenth century in France came into a rich intellectual inheritance. In the preceding 150 years several powerful intellectual systems had either been built or sketched out by Bacon, Descartes, Spinoza, Newton, Locke and Leibniz. Despite the specifically Renaissance flavour of Bacon's writings, and the sense of human limitations stressed by Locke, despite the errors soon revealed in Descartes' physics and the unsolved problem arising from Newton's key notion of attraction, despite the obscurity or unavailability of much of Spinoza and Leibniz, these thinkers handed on to those who came after a striking confidence in the ability of the human mind to understand the world. They had stepped forward out of the brilliant confusion of the Renaissance into a world which we can recognize as modern; a world, that is, which regarded truth as a matter of evidence and examination, the result of human thought, rather than a matter of belief, tradition or supernatural revelation. A hundred years before Kant's celebrated summary of the Enlightenment – *Sapere aude*, Dare to know – Fontenelle had written: 'You must be daring in every activity.'[11]

Such daring needs freedom to explore and toleration to survive. Although all the above thinkers did in their different ways believe in God, many of their ideas were anathema to the Churches. Since in France one of the monarchy's claims to legitimacy, the divine right of kings, rested on a religious foundation, there were additional restrictions to freedom. The expulsion of the Protestants, by the Revocation of the Edict of Nantes in 1685, and the stricter operation of government censorship in subsequent years, meant that much intellectual activity had to be conducted abroad, as was the case with Bayle, or was driven underground, as was the case with the large number of writings which, in the early part of the century circulated clandestinely, usually in manuscript. Some critical works were published openly, notably Montesquieu's *Lettres persanes* (1721) and Voltaire's *Lettres philosophiques* (1734), but these were exceptions. The more searching works remained unpublished. These developed bold lines of thought about such forbidden questions as the existence of God, the immortality of the soul and the nature of the world. A few, of which those by Jean Meslier became best known later in the century, went a stage further in questioning the existence of privilege, the (apparent) eternity of oppression and the nature of society. This marked a significant change of emphasis, a change made consciously in a short work, first published anonymously in Amsterdam in1743, entitled *Le Philosophe*.

Le Philosophe was, in effect, the first of a number of manifestos around the middle of the century which proclaimed the importance of free enquiry not merely in metaphysics or ethics, for the good of the soul, but in matters specifically concerned with the good of society. (Most of the essay later appeared as the article 'Philosophe' in Volume Twelve of the *Encyclopédie*.) The role of the philosopher was being redefined; he was becoming what we would call an intellectual. Instead of conducting his thought in isolation, shut away from the world, he was now among his fellow men and like-

minded thinkers, *la république des lettres*. *Le Philosophe* attacked
religion for its concern with the next world rather than this world,
and it attacked the asceticism of the Stoics. For the *philosophe* 'civil
society is, so to speak, the only divinity he recognizes on earth';[12]
he 'does not believe himself to be an exile in this world', he wants
'to please and make himself useful'.[13] His activity can change the
way things are: 'This love of society, so vital to the *philosophe*,
makes plain the truth of the comment by the Emperor Antoninus –
"How happy the people will be when kings are *philosophes* or when
philosophes are kings!" '[14]

This conception of their place at the centre of their society was
shared by all Diderot's fellow *philosophes*. He himself, in his last
published work, gave a striking example of their ambition:

> The magistrate executes justice; the *philosophe* teaches the
> magistrate what the just and unjust are. The soldier defends his
> homeland; the *philosophe* teaches the soldier what a homeland
> is. The priest advises the people to love and respect the gods; the
> *philosophe* teaches the priest what the gods are. The sovereign
> commands everyone; the *philosophe* teaches the sovereign
> about the origin and limit of his authority. Every man has duties
> to fulfil in his family and in society; the *philosophe* teaches each
> person what his duties are[15] . . . . I love to see the wise man on
> display, like the athlete in the arena; a man only recognizes his
> strength when he has opportunities to show it.[16]

In short, as he wrote elsewhere, 'Man is born for action.'[17]*

This active practical spirit animated all Diderot's public writing.
The publication of the *Encyclopédie* was undertaken, carried out
and sustained against innumerable obstacles and discouragements
precisely in order 'to change the general way of thinking' (see
p. 107). Ideas must be communicated. 'The priest tight-fisted with
his money and the *philosophe* tight-fisted with his discoveries, are
both stealing from the poor. What is more, I think discoveries are
only valuable and secure when they circulate among the general
mass of people; I am impatient to take them there.'[19]

---

* Voltaire, a generation older than Diderot, had expressed the same idea in his
Lettres philosophiques.[18] His handling of his own career, particularly his astute
financial dealings, showed that this was more than a rhetorical flourish, a stick
with which to beat Pascal. In his later years, moreover, from the late 1750s, he
displayed as energetic a concern for practical issues as any of Diderot's generation.

Foremost among these ideas were the beliefs held in common by Montesquieu, Voltaire and the author of *Le Philosophe* (probably Dumarsais),[20] and the younger generation responsible for the important works which began to appear around the middle years of the century: Condillac in his *Essai sur l'origine des connaissances humaines* (1746), Buffon in the first volumes of his *Histoire naturelle* (1749), Turgot in his *Tableau philosophique des progrès* (1750), and the work that is often seen as a summation of all these, D'Alembert's *Discours préliminaire* to Volume One of the *Encyclopédie* (1751). These ideas were that man has no innate knowledge, learning about the world empirically, through his senses; that however the world may have been created it now obeys laws which we can discover through observing facts and exercising our reason; that human beings are naturally sociable and reasonable, and from these capacities have developed common ideas of justice and morality; that human nature is not fallen or sinful, the emotional and passionate aspects of our personality being as valuable and essential to us as our minds, brains or souls; that intellectual freedom is a necessary prerequisite for the discovery of the truth – which makes it, wrote Diderot, 'the finest prerogative of mankind' (see p. 103) – and toleration must follow as an obvious corollary.

All these works conveyed a remarkable sense of confidence, a firm belief in human potential. There was a sense that change was at hand and that these works were helping to bring about that change. However, it is wrong to suppose that this was synonymous with a faith in progress.* Turgot, it is true, did state that 'the overall mass of the human race is continually moving, though slowly, by good and evil, calm and unrest in turn, towards greater perfection'.[21] But this was not the attitude of Diderot or D'Alembert. For them improvement and advance were possible and in the short term very probable, but they were not inevitable and would never be continual. 'The fate which rules the world wants everything to pass away. The most fortunate condition of a man or a State has its limit. Everything carries within it a secret seed of destruction.'[23]

---

* Also, the fact that the Enlightenment thinkers believed that all kinds of human activity would benefit from being examined and analysed does not mean, as is often supposed, that they had a bland belief that universal laws could one day operate in ethics or politics as they had been shown to operate in physics. Helvétius attempted 'to treat morality like all the other sciences'[22] but his work was severely criticized by Turgot and Diderot, as well as by Rousseau.

There were always upheavals (see pp. 105 and 354) and there were always limits to the spread of enlightenment: 'the bulk of a nation will always remain ignorant, afraid and consequently super-stitious'.[24] This should not surprise us; there were few reasons for them to suppose otherwise. It was quite different for those who succeeded them and were able to see the transformations that were beginning to occur later in the century.

The fact remains that, judged in the light of their own time, the men of this generation displayed great self-assurance and an invigorating belief in human nature. 'I love the philosophy that exalts humanity,' wrote Diderot.[25] Human beings belong in the world and in the final analysis it is their existence alone that gives this world meaning. 'If man . . . was banished from the earth's surface the sublime and moving spectacle of nature would become no more than a silent, desolate scene. The universe would be dumb; night and silence would take hold of it. Everything would be transformed into an immense solitude where unobserved pheno-mena would occur dimly and unheard.' (see p. 106).

The practical spirit was not confined to such general attitudes. It extended to almost all human activities: 'The spectacle of human industry is in itself great and satisfying.'[26] There was a constant emphasis on experience, facts, things: 'to speak informatively about bakery you have got to have put your hands in the dough.'[27] Diderot's short work on scientific method, *Pensées sur l'inter-prétation de la nature* (published in 1754) was remarkable for its awareness of the place of intuition and inspired conjecture in scientific discovery; but he gave equal weight to the need for experiments and the factual confirmation which alone could vali-date such discoveries. One of his principal concerns in the *Encyclopédie* was to change people's attitudes to what were termed 'the mechanical arts'. He himself wrote in detail and with great care about such subjects as the manufacture of stockings and steel, activities which were not only useful but could be beautiful as well (see p. 91). The main reason for collecting the huge variety of plates which filled the final eleven volumes of the work was to supplement such descriptions and show as clearly as possible how things were made, what processes, skills and techniques were involved. It is those who work in such activities who make us not 'think we are happy' but make us actually 'happy in fact' (see p. 90). Manufacturing, he wrote elsewhere, is 'the state which sets you free',[28] because it does not depend on seasonal fluctuations, like agriculture. (Which is not to say that manufacture, which at this date meant mostly small-scale industry, was being in any way promoted at the expense of agriculture; the latter was still the basis of every economy and recognized as such.) This belief in the value of technology was the most original feature of Diderot's contribution to the *Encyclopédie* and of obvious historical importance.

Besides the awareness of practical benefit there was a strong humanitarian impulse. 'It is good to know how the different contributions each person makes relate to the general benefit of society.'[29] Diderot always had a keen sense of the effects of poverty; he had himself spent a number of precarious years in Paris before the editorship of the *Encyclopédie* brought him a regular income, and he argued vehemently against Helvétius when the latter suggested that the labouring poor enjoyed a happier existence than the bored rich.[30] This humanitarian concern was evident in many articles in the *Encyclopédie*. It was one manifestation of the moral impulse that was an integral part of the practical spirit. To spread ideas, to change people's attitudes, to call attention to poverty and injustice was necessary in order to make people not only happier or more comfortable, but to make them better.

Indeed, for Diderot and his generation the concept of happiness was essentially linked to the idea of goodness. Given two of their premises – the empirical basis of knowledge (if everything is learnt through the senses moral ideas must develop through pleasure and pain), and man's natural sociability – this association was no surprise. Moreover, ethical naturalism of this kind – the belief that man's moral character owes nothing to divine guidance or any innate ideas – had been a feature of the seventeenth-century revival of interest in the ideas of Epicurus, particularly associated with Gassendi and evident in many clandestine manuscripts. The promotion of Locke's ideas in the first part of the eighteenth century had provided additional support for this point of view; (even though Locke's own treatment of the subject was ambivalent, since despite his empirical premises he did refer to man's moral awareness as 'a candle of the Lord').[31] But these ideas took on a new practical emphasis in the mid-century. Diderot said of himself that he was 'a man who loves to moralize',[32] everyone has his '*tic* . . . mine is to moralize'.[33] A moral impulse informed all his public writings.* When he turned his attention to writing plays it was not simply through the desire to succeed in a prestigious literary activity, or to reform the dramatic conventions of the time, though both these motives did apply; it was also because of a belief that the theatre when used in the right way could be morally beneficial. This was not a new idea, to be sure, but Diderot's persistent advocacy of the theatre as a means of moral instruction, in his *Entretiens sur le Fils naturel* (1757) and the *Discours sur la poésie dramatique* (1758), was influential. His faith in the idea survived, despite set-backs and evidence to the contrary, because he believed that 'there is a trinity against which the gates of hell will never prevail: the true which brings forth the good, and emerging from both of these the beautiful'.[34]

The self-assurance of the 1750s did not last. Major disagreements arose among the *philosophes*, and despite all that they did achieve – and were conscious of having achieved, as Diderot showed in 1769[35] – their analyses and remedies did not match up to the serious problems that were developing. France's defeat in the Seven Years War, with the loss of most of her colonies, aggravated an already bad economic position. An archaic and grossly unjust tax structure, which exempted the rich, the aristocracy and the clergy, from paying taxes, was reinforced by an archaic and inflexible political structure, which allowed little scope for reforming initiatives and no expression for general grievances. The monarchy and the privileged were locked into an increasingly bitter conflict which would eventually destroy them both.

For a number of reasons Diderot had neither an aptitude nor an inclination for political thought. But the growing seriousness of the crisis in France (first perceived as a crisis with Maupeou's so-called coup in 1771, when the Parlement of Paris was exiled and the judiciary replaced by hand-picked men), and his journey to Russia in 1773–4 to meet his benefactress Catherine II, made him turn his attention more fully to political matters. Most of his political writing was not published till long after his death but one important work did appear in his lifetime, Raynal's *Histoire des Deux Indes** which appeared in three editions in 1770, 1774 and 1780, and to which Diderot made a large number of contributions.

---

* He also 'moralized' in his unpublished writings, but that was in the sense of reflecting on moral issues rather than of promoting morality.

* The full title was *Histoire philosophique et politique du commerce et des établissements des Européens dans les deux Indes*, but it will be referred to throughout in its better-known abbreviated form.

These contributions were anonymous and it was only thirty years ago, with the discovery of the collection of Diderot manuscripts known as the Fonds Vandeul, that it became possible to identify what exactly they were; only in the last few years has this knowledge become generally available. The result has been a reappraisal of Diderot's political ideas and a widespread belief that at the end of his life he was a radical, if not a revolutionary. However, this view is not supported by a rigorous examination of the evidence. There are many striking and forceful passages among Diderot's writings for the *Histoire*; there is a sense of outrage and indignation, we read impassioned protests at injustice, eloquent affirmations of liberty. But there is no vision of a new order, no call for or belief in popular or particular revolt in any European context, not even a properly developed political theory. Nor do the occasional references to the possible need for extreme measures show evidence of a revolutionary temperament; they relate to a different matter, the old and well-established tradition that justifies tyrannicide.

Diderot's outrage and indignation were sincere, and they were more acute in so far as they clashed with no less strongly held convictions about the cyclical patterns of history and about the basic contradictions in human nature – he saw man as a 'bizarre combination of sublime qualities and shameful weaknesses',[36] both 'a truthteller and a liar, cheerful and sad, wise and mad, good and bad',[37] not as intrinsically wicked as Hobbes might have suggested, but neither as intrinsically innocent as Rousseau might have suggested (see p. 112). And Diderot did not complain about this. On several occasions he asserted that the good qualities people displayed were essentially linked to the bad,[38] and he also said that in society generally speaking 'everything balances out (*tout se compense*)'.[39] Moreover, his attitude to how human nature was formed, more the result of heredity than environment or social conditioning, provided him with no alternative to accepting these contradictions; it precluded him from envisaging any transition to a new order. Above all, his imagination was not of the kind that is fired by general concepts or visionary schemes. Diderot's contributions to Raynal's *Histoire* were important; in several respects they amount to the culmination of the work that had occupied the later years of his life. But they do not reveal a new ability in handling political problems. This should neither surprise us nor disappoint us. For Diderot's limitations as a political thinker were essentially linked to his brilliance in other areas. A thorough considcration of the reasons why he was not a revolutionary brings us face to face with the characteristics that constitute his true originality. This was evident less in any of the works published in his lifetime, than in those that were only published after his death.

III

Diderot's writings took two forms, a public form and a more confined, intimate and private form. To understand his work it is necessary not only to know this but also to realize that neither form was for him more 'true' or more 'real'. Both forms had their value and Diderot was equally committed to them both, even when they displayed contradictory impulses.*

Although he complained at times of the burden of editing the *Encyclopédie* and although his output in the years following the publication of the last volumes of text in 1765 was prodigious, he was willing nevertheless in 1774 to undertake another *Encyclopédie* for Catherine II, and he made no particular effort to publish those morc private works which he had written in the meanwhile. We may be pleased that he did not devote the rest of his life to another *Encyclopédie* and that he was able to give time to completing, improving or writing the othcr works which we now value more. But it is vital to understand that Diderot himself thought otherwise, because the published works were the public structure within which he lived, which provided the necessary conditions without which the more private works could never have been written. This was not merely the social fact of identity, definition, occupying a place in the world; it was also a mental fact, a peculiarity of his own temperament and intellectual character.

---

* Diderot's attitude to language was an example of this. On the one hand he had a firm belief that if words were more clearly defined there would be an immense step forward in human understanding: 'logic and metaphysics would be very close to perfection if the dictionary of language was well done'.[40] Hence his interest in definitions in the *Encyclopédie* and his concern to improve this aspect of the work if he undertook a second edition.[41] On the other hand he was convinced that the language people use was only an approximation of their real feelings, that common terms always omitted the individual sense, and that disagreements about the meanings of words were not accidental but inevitable. He was both fascinated and haunted by this problem – 'the mystery of daily conversation'[42] – all his life.

The beliefs Diderot shared with his fellow *philosophes* did not form a precisely worked-out system; they were a body of ideas which to some extent owed their force to what they opposed. The process of enlightenment had obvious imperatives and the confidence of the 1750s was in part due to the shared sense of such imperatives being fulfilled. But what exactly was visible when the dark was cleared away? At this point disagreement set in, problems were admitted, difficulties became plain. The rich inheritance of the previous century was no longer sufficient to explain many aspects of the world that were then coming into focus. Many ideas retained their efficacy, but others were found wanting. It was in this confused and fluid context – the second half of the eighteenth century as it is now understood – that Diderot's most interesting work was done. In his unpublished works he explored the new problems and difficulties.

On one major issue Diderot made up his mind early: there was no God or spiritual being, either transcendent (like the Christian God or the God of the deists) or immanent (like the God of Spinoza or any of the occult, mystical or pantheist thinkers). He was assisted in coming to this decision by a crucial change of emphasis in scientific thinking which was taking place in the middle years of the century; this was a move away from a mechanistic view of nature, based on astronomy, physics and mathematics, towards a dynamic view based on biology, physiology and chemistry. The universe of Descartes and Newton was one in which matter was moved by forces external to it in accordance with certain fixed laws; the world that biological discoveries began to reveal was one in which living forms were animated by internal forces in a far less regular way. The former model would be grasped as a single entity, beautiful in its unity and simplicity; the latter seemed to manifest a prolific diversity, strikingly varied yet also bewilderingly elusive. These two models were not seen as being incompatible. The belief that there was an underlying unity, a basic natural order, and the Cartesian criterion that what was true could be formulated in clear distinct notions – these remained valid. But the new view of nature being in some way self-creating and continually changing was a growing challenge to all the arguments and beliefs based on the previous attitude.

Foremost among these were the arguments for the existence of God. The universe described by both Descartes and Newton contained matter which by itself was inert and therefore needed a God to set it in motion (and maybe keep it in motion as well). The laws of the universe discovered by Newton revealed an intelligence, design and sense of order which also seemed to need a God to explain them. But what if matter could somehow animate itself? And what if the order we see is only a temporary phenomenon, a momentary pattern, even perhaps only a projection of our minds? The evidence of biology and other life-sciences gave these questions overwhelming force and led Diderot to become an atheist.

However, it would be wrong to see this development as a purely intellectual matter. Diderot had ineradicably religious inclinations; that is to say, he always felt a sense of awe when he faced the ultimate questions of existence, and although he denied any essential purpose or finality to the universe he did believe that life was more than the mere play of chance. Rational arguments alone would not have converted him to atheism; emotional reasons were also necessary, and in his case they were central. There was a profound affinity between his temperament, his instinctive manner of being, and the view, then coming to prominence, of a nature that was neither stable, uniform nor simple. It is this affinity which more than anything else explains both the difficulty and fascination of his writing.

The first characteristic that strikes any reader of Diderot is the bewildering disorder and lack of focus that most of his writings display. Both the subject-matter and the viewpoint are continually shifting, there are endless interruptions and digressions, and the last page or a later work often seems to contradict or call into question what has gone before. Many critics have concluded that his remark about his fellow townsmen having 'the inconsistency of weathercocks . . . never fixed in any one direction',[43] must be seen as a fair comment on Diderot himself. He would not have disagreed with them completely – after this remark about his fellow townsmen he went on to admit that he had much in common with them – but he would not have regarded this entirely as a failing. What one of the characters in his last play called his *héracliterie*[44] – meaning his changeableness, his personal demonstration of Heraclitus' conception of reality as a state of constant flux – was not a quality which set him apart from the world but, on the contrary, showed how close was his response to it and his contact with it. 'Happy the person who has received from nature a sensitive and mobile soul!'[45] The most frequent criticism Diderot makes of other writers is that they impose an order or arrangement or symmetry on their material which that material does not itself have. They lack the 'apparent negligence',[46] 'the disordered manner'[47] which he admired in Horace[48] or Montaigne (see p. 120), not purely out of aesthetic preference but because it was closer to the truth as he saw it. He liked a writer who 'does not compose [but] pours out his mind and soul onto the paper; [who] does not wear himself out giving his phrase a [good] cadence . . ., [but] sounds the depth of his heart'.[49] He looked for a similar quality in painting – 'the effect of art should be a beautiful disorder'[50] – for truth emerges in a disorderly way. It would be a mistake to suppose that Diderot did not take care over his writing, because he did.[51] But it explains the apparent shapelessness of much of his work, and why he could say that a book could be 'a great obstacle to truth'.[52]

Nature is in a state of endless flux: 'the general order of nature changes unceasingly',[53] 'the whole [universe] alters continually'.[54] Since man is part of nature he too is in 'a state of continual vicissitude',[55] not only were no two men alike but no person was the same in any two consecutive moments, 'the condition of man varies unceasingly'.[56] Being so aware of this was both Diderot's delight and his torment. He was caught between the exhilaration of feeling in touch with the living moment and the despair of the intellectual relativism which this attitude could entail. This was why he valued a sense of immediacy and personal involvement so highly in his written work, and this is also why that work so often approached a form of conversation, as dialogue or letter or marginalia. What was spoken, or written down as speech, retained the ebb and flow of present time.

A remarkable aspect of this combined sense of immediacy and transitoriness was that it was not accompanied by any feelings of impatience or panic. Faced with the mutability of life Diderot did not exclaim, like so many writers before him or since, *Carpe diem*, Seize the day. He disliked the thought of extinction or the idea that he might be forgotten but the pleasure of the moment did not turn sour at the prospect of its passing. There are several reasons for this. One was that his quasi-religious sense of wonder at the mystery of existence survived his rejection of any belief in God; he could go so far on occasion as to imagine some form of life after the fact of physical death.[57] Another was his belief in a basic natural order; there was 'a natural interconnection, the law of unity',[58] everything was 'bound together, interconnected',[59] which gave it a kind of sense. Most important of all was the fact that his imagination was animated not by images of decay but by ideas of creation, generation and growth. Sexuality and reproduction were to him not only opportunities for pleasure but occasions for wonder and reverence at the renewal of life. Connected with all of these was Diderot's fascination with the uniqueness of the individual, his attention to the *petits phenomènes*,[60] his capacity to grasp the particular detail. He could capture the moment and transmit its immediacy and sensuality as though he was somehow immersed in the body of nature itself. (Sexual metaphors are entirely appropriate here: Diderot himself sometimes referred to his thought in sexual terms (see p. 000). And this was how he characterized genius: 'there is no intermediary between nature and genius'.[61]

Man and nature are one substance. When Buffon wrote, in his *Histoire naturelle*, 'It is . . . the way we are constituted, our life, our soul which in effect makes our existence. From this point of view matter is [only] an extraneous envelope', Diderot objected strongly: 'It is a constant fact that this despicable cocoon . . . has a prodigious influence on the sequence of thoughts which forms our being' (see p. 87). The soul 'is nothing without the body. I defy anyone to explain anything without the body.'[62] Anything that might be described as spiritual, such as a sense of virtue or a state of inspiration, had a physical explanation of some kind. Although this belief can be correctly described as materialist, and Diderot himself would have agreed with such a description, the word suggests something too narrow (and probably also too positivist) to be entirely accurate. This point was made shortly after his death by Meister: 'Although he was a passionate defender of materialism you could say that as far as his manner of feeling and living were concerned he was no less the most decided idealist; he was like that in spite of himself, as a result of the unconquerable aspiration of his character and imagination.'[63]

The material basis of all reality, the existence of only a single substance – these were unaltered features of Diderot's mature thought. The problems that arose from them were his constant preoccupations and form the subject-matter of some of his major works. How does life arise? How does inert matter become living matter? What forms our physical character? How do physical sensations develop into complex ideas? What is the difference between thinking and dreaming? These are the questions that produced the three dialogues known as *Le Rêve de d'Alembert*. In his answers to them Diderot threw out remarkable insights into evolution and the structure of matter but it is not the ideas alone that make this work a masterpiece; it is the extraordinary way in which Diderot presents them. What gives his ideas their force and conviction – for the evidence to support them had not yet been found – is the way they emerge from a living situation, the way the characters in the dialogues search for explanations, and lead us forward with them. We share both the excitement of discovery and Diderot's intense delight in relating all human experience to the natural world of which it is a part.

However, the conviction that we are part of nature, combined with what was for Diderot an equally fundamental belief that everything in nature is necessary (see p. 33), faced him with an acute problem, that of human freedom. If our ideas are determined by our physical state, then how can we be said to be free? And if we have no freedom, how can there be any morality? In *Le Rêve de d'Alembert* he denied that notions of virtue and vice could have any meaning. In subsequent writings, the three extended works of marginalia – the *Éléments de physiologie*, the *Réfutation d'Helvétius*, the *Commentaire sur Hemsterhuis* – and in his last novel *Jacques le fataliste* he turned over this question obsessively.

One reason why this issue troubled him so much was that he experienced it personally as a problem. He often felt he was the passive plaything of external forces. He saw himself at times in the same terms as the sultan Mangogul in his first novel *Les Bijoux indiscrets*: 'Isn't it true that we are only puppets?'[64] In a letter of 1769, in which he complained of being 'tangled up in a devil of a philosophy which my mind cannot resist confirming and my heart denying', he wrote: 'It is hard to abandon oneself blindly to the universal torrent, [but] it is impossible to resist it.'[65] This 'universal torrent' was experienced by Diderot in many forms; it could be the climate, the countryside, financial pressures, sexual impulses. In his last play *Est-il bon? Est-il méchant?* he depicted himself as someone constantly put upon by friends or acquaintances, 'I think I was born to do nothing of what suits me [but] everything that others demand',[66] and many contemporaries testify to this characteristic, though they saw it more as his willing generosity than as reluctant self-denial.

His intellectual character displayed similar features. Diderot was not alone in needing the stimulus of other writers to develop his own ideas, but he was unusual in the way his own writing so often borrowed, took over, or assumed characteristics of those who stimulated him. The tone of each of the three works of marginalia mentioned above differs according to the author and subject-matter in question. His exclamation in the *Réfutation d'Helvétius* 'I contradict you: therefore I exist'[67] reveals how central this dual function of stimulation and dependence was. A similar conclusion can be drawn from the amount of plagiarism in his writing. The number of authors who, frequently unacknowledged, provided him with ideas was legion; Diderot must be included among the great plagiarists of all time. Yet there is a certain innocence about his pillaging, a lack of either self-awareness or self-promotion. It was as though his attitude was like his attitude to property (derived from Locke); by his own labour he made the ideas his own.* He very often did put other authors' ideas to work in a new way and endow them with new perspective, vitality, a personal flavour. But he needed those other authors to build on in the first place.

The problem of human freedom also occupied a central place in Diderot's work because it arose at the point of intersection between the natural realm and the human realm. Being convinced that man and nature existed in a continuum, and not in conflict, Diderot then had to explain how and why men differed from the rest of nature, and how it was possible for them to have 'natural' impulses that were incompatible. This problem had also concerned Rousseau and his solution, first indicated in the *Discours sur l'inégalité* (1755), constituted one of the major intellectual achievements of the eighteenth century. However, Diderot neither adopted Rousseau's solution, nor was able to provide a solution of his own. Nature and culture, nature and society always existed for him within the same conceptual framework: 'All that is can neither be outside nature nor opposed to nature.'[69]

How is it then that human society has come to be in opposition to many of our needs or desires? Diderot could not answer this question. He stared at it again and again. In his fiction and his plays he depicted the problem in graphic detail, in dialogues like the *Entretien d'un père avec ses enfants* and the important *Supplément au Voyage de Bougainville* he tried to think his way through it; in one of his contributions to the *Histoire des Deux Indes* he made a

---

* There is a certain irony in the fact that so habitual a plagiarist should have written one of the earliest works formulating the idea of literary property, an author's right to the ownership of what he wrote.[68]

final attempt to provide an answer (see pp. 353-4). But instead of insights we find only anecdotes; the analysis degenerates into a mere episodic sequence of events.

The fact is that Diderot had an aversion to abstraction (apart from mathematics) and no special gift for conceptual thinking. 'The act of generalization tends to strip concepts of everything tangible (*sensible*) that they possess';[70] 'I [am] a physician [or] a chemist . . . who grasps the body in its material substance and not in my head.'[71] He believed that 'the wing of a butterfly, well described, would bring me closer to divinity than a volume of metaphysics'.[72] Abstract sciences, such as mathematics, could be like 'the fable of Daedalus. Men made the labyrinth and then got lost in it.'[73] Given this aversion he was not inclined to develop ideas in a logical, conceptual manner. But even when he was so inclined it must be admitted that he was out of his element. He never freed himself from mental patterns set down early in his life; this is why audacious insights that may logically alter the whole basis of an argument can be followed by the reiteration of an earlier position as if no such insights had been made, why his insights can be vivid but his theories pallid.

In one sense this aspect of Diderot's work is obviously a weakness, but in another sense that weakness is beside the point. For much of his writing is a complex and fascinating argument between his routine conceptual equipment and his spontaneous instinctive responses. Given the uncertainty of the latter and the weakness of the former he often lacked confidence in his own achievements; (this is one reason why so much of his best work was written for a small select audience or a circle of friends: 'O how vital my friends are to me! Without them my heart and my mind would be dumb'[74]). Given this lack of confidence he often fell back into either fixed ways of thought or into the scepticism that always hovered around the edge of his mind. But faced with a particular image, individual or event that fired his imagination Diderot could display remarkable brilliance.

Nothing illustrates this better than his art criticism, the *Salons*. Asked to write an account of the biennial exhibitions in the Grand Salon of the Louvre, he provided at first a workmanlike description of the paintings. He then became more interested and with each successive *Salon* his comments became longer and more penetrating. Painters are praised, castigated, asked for their advice or their intentions; pictures are taken apart, reassembled, or used as examples in a continuous discussion about the nature of art. Ideas are thrown up, asserted, offered to the reader: 'When one writes must one write everything? When one paints must one paint everything? Please, leave something for my imagination to provide.'[75] What Diderot demands of a painting he in turn exemplifies in his writing. He engages us in a conversation into which we are immediately drawn and which is resumed whenever we return to these pages. Furthermore, in giving free rein to his imagination he broke out of the restrictions within which his conceptual thinking usually operated. In the *Salon de 1767*, as in the *Paradoxe sur le comédien* (dealing with how actors operate), Diderot saw a clear distinction between nature and culture, he described an area of specifically human creation. These speculations about the nature of art, fragmentary though they are, occupy an important position in the development of romantic and modern ideas of what exactly art is.

There is a similar sense of freedom and a similar fascination with the individual detail in his last novel *Jacques le fataliste et son maître*. This is an extraordinary ragbag of a book which operates at three levels. Jacques and his master are travelling, and as they do so they discuss the problems of human freedom (Jacques being a *fataliste*, denying freedom exists); they also tell and are told stories; but both their journey and their stories are subject to endless interruptions from the author calling attention to the basic problem of fiction – is this story true? – and showing how arbitrary the events of the novel are. The achievement of the book is uneven but it is written with great verve and at its centre is a problem which Diderot experienced intensely; the relationship between our concepts, values and mental attitudes, and the actual dynamic and texture of our lives.

This problem is also at the heart of his best-known work, *Le Neveu de Rameau*. In this dialogue Diderot *in propria persona* meets an eccentric but brilliant character, the nephew of the composer Rameau, who confronts him with a manifest and, it seems, overwhelming denial of almost every value he upholds. As in *Le Rêve de d'Alembert* it is not the ideas as such that make this work a masterpiece, striking though those ideas are. It is rather the way they arise out of a particular situation, the two men meeting and arguing, the collision of their attitudes, the elemental force of the nephew's attack on Diderot, his unpredictability, brilliance and pathos. We do not know why, nor precisely when, Diderot wrote this dialogue; although it is now his best-known work there is not a single reference to it in any of his other writings nor those of any contemporary. Nor have critics been able to agree on the outcome of the work, on which of the two men gets the better of the argument, whether they are both vindicated or both shown to be wrong. All readers have agreed, however, about the vivid force of the dialogue and the disturbing cogency of the questions it raises. In other words, the fact that the conclusion remains in doubt does not affect the value of the work as a whole.

In this respect *Le Neveu de Rameau* could be taken as the epitome of Diderot's achievements as a writer. We do not read him for the clear articulation of particular problems, even less for conclusive answers. 'Who knows where the interconnection of ideas will lead me? *Ma foi*! not me.'[76] The person who writes good dialogue, he wrote, is the one who lets himself be carried away by his characters.[77] 'The spirit of invention is agitated, moved, and active in a disordered way; it seeks. The spirit of method arranges, orders and assumes that everything is found.'[78] Diderot was an inventive spirit who went in search and we read him most of all for the risks and delight he took in that search. We read him for the pleasure of being with such a lively, engaging, unpredictable person, a pleasure that brings the realization that where we arrive is less important than how we travel. This is not to say that there are no fixed points, or that sudden revelations cannot be caught, retained and then sent home on a postcard. Much of the excitement in reading Diderot comes from the fact that not only do these exist but that many of them are so modern: his ideas about materialism, the mind–body relationship, and what makes us specifically human; about scientific discovery, artistic creation, the value of poetry, the nature of fiction; most modern of all, his intimations that the ultimate nature of reality cannot be disentangled or defined apart from our own perception of reality.

But to be adequate to Diderot as he attempted himself to be adequate to reality we must try to see him whole. 'There is a poetic embroidery which is so closely bound up with its material that it is impossible to separate it without tearing the fabric.'[79] In his own time Diderot was criticized for his 'continual digressions',[80] and for the fact that his works seemed to be 'never finished'.[81] In our own time he has been acclaimed as a precurser of every conceivable intellectual fashion; particular insights have been bundled up into modern conceptual schemes and presented as the essence of his thought. Both these emphases seem to me misplaced. His writings do digress continually and his works are full of insights we can call modern, but they cannot be contained within either of these aspects or attitudes. The heart of Diderot's achievement lies rather in a quality of openmindedness, a persistent desire to do justice to whatever makes the individual detail what it is, to catch the living moment in all its mobility, and a wonderful ability to show how the life of the mind interweaves with the complex texture of our whole experience. He wrote at a time when a new world was beginning to emerge, when people were beginning to have new confidence in their powers and to be apprehensive with new fears. It was a time rich with a sense of potential and opaque with a sense of confusion. Diderot lived that potential and that confusion, openly, honestly and zestfully. His writings were true to his experience. That is why they remain so vivid today.

2

Life

Denis Diderot was born on 5 October 1713 in Langres, a moderate-sized town in Champagne about fifty miles north of Dijon. His father was a master cutler, an able man respected both for his skilled workmanship and his upright character. Of his mother we know little – Diderot rarely referred to her – but the home atmosphere seems to have been warm and stable during the years he was growing up. He did well at school and in 1728 or 1729 went to Paris to complete his education. Although his refusal to take up a secure career and his marriage later caused a bitter family quarrel, Diderot always remembered his father with great affection. The position of head of the family which the latter had filled so admirably was one which he not only dramatized in his play *Le Père de famille*, but one he prided himself on filling in his own later years. 'There is no doubt that a father inspires kinds of feeling which one has for no one else.'[1]

In 1732 he obtained a master of arts degree. At this stage or earlier it is possible that he thought of going into the Church; there is no evidence that he made a definite decision to do so but it does seem, from remarks both by himself[2] and by his daughter in her memoir of him,[3] that he gave the matter serious consideration. Three of his uncles occupied ecclesiastical posts, both his sisters and his younger brother later did likewise, and Diderot himself had a religious streak in his character (not that that was necessary for a career in the Church). At any rate the phase passed and with his father's approval he began to study to become a lawyer. Not for long. The prospect of years of training and the aridity of the subject-matter appalled the 'lively, ardent and crazy'[4] young man.

He threw up his position and faced an unknown future.

For the next twelve or so years he lived a precarious hand-to-mouth existence. He wrote sermons for clerics, gave lessons to children, devised ways of borrowing money. He thought of becoming an actor, he taught himself English and obtained work as a translator. He abandoned himself, wrote his daughter, 'to work, grief, pleasure, boredom and need; he was often drunk with happiness, more often plunged into the most bitter reflections'.[5] They were years of continual uncertainty but also of unexpected revelations and surprises; vivid memories of them often surfaced in Diderot's later writings.

In 1743 he married. His wife, Anne-Toinette Champion, was a seamstress and was three years older than him. The marriage was conducted in secret because Diderot's father, already exasperated at his son's wayward behaviour, opposed it and took steps to prevent it. Nor was it a success. The couple were not well matched and the combination of Diderot's infidelity and his wife's short temper soon soured the atmosphere. They remained together, despite that, and Diderot always upheld the ideal of a stable home, a loyal husband and a devoted father. In this last capacity his behaviour was exemplary: he was deeply attached to the one child who survived, the girl Angélique (born in 1753), and took trouble over her education and even more to secure her future. As far as the rest of the ideal was concerned, however, his own conduct was completely the opposite.

On occasion he blamed his marriage for forcing him to accept the editorship of the *Encyclopédie*.

> I arrive in Paris. I was going to take the fur and set myself up among the doctors of the Sorbonne. On my way I meet a woman of angelic beauty; I want to go to bed with her. I do so. I have four children by her. And here I am forced to give up the mathematics I loved, Homer and Virgil whom I always carried in my pocket, and the theatre for which I had some inclination; only too happy to undertake the *Encyclopédie*, to which I will have sacrificed twenty-five years of my life.[6]

There is some truth in this: Diderot needed the modest financial security which the work on the *Encyclopédie* gave him to meet his family commitments. But it seems likely that he would have taken on the work anyway. The project was a natural development from his previous work as a translator and it did not have, at the outset, the huge dimensions which it later developed.

His first translation, of Temple Stanyan's *History of Greece*, was published in 1743. Two years later came Shaftesbury's *Inquiry concerning Virtue or Merit*, and after that Robert James's *Medical Dictionary*, published in six folio volumes between 1745 and 1748, translated in collaboration with Toussaint and Eidous. The *Encyclopédie* was initially going to be no more than a translation of Ephraim Chambers's successful two-volume *Cyclopaedia*, first published in 1728, and reprinted several times since. However, from the *Essai sur le mérite et la vertu* onwards Diderot had shown a distinct independence of mind; he did not merely translate Shaftesbury, he 'filled himself with his spirit . . . Never has another writer been used with so much freedom to such good effect.'[7] This was an exaggeration, but the confidence displayed was revealing. The following year saw the (anonymous) publication of his bold *Pensées philosophiques*, which were condemned and burnt by the Paris Parlement, and in 1748 the (anonymous) publication of his salacious novel *Les Bijoux indiscrets*. Other writings at this time, the allegory *La Promenade du sceptique*, the short treatise *De la suffisance de la religion naturelle*, and the speculative *Mémoires sur différents sujets de mathématiques*, indicate his wide range of interest. It is not surprising, therefore, either that he should have been asked to collaborate on the *Encyclopédie* (initially in only a minor capacity) or that his involvement should have played a part in transforming the project from a straightforward translation of Chambers into the ambitious work it soon became.

Before the first volume was published, however, Diderot was arrested and imprisoned at Vincennes for the publication of his *Lettre sur les aveugles* (1749). This arrest may have been provoked more by a reference to the mistress of one of the king's ministers than by the actual content of the work, but the work itself was certainly audacious. It also came at a time of general unrest, largely because of opposition to a proposed new tax, the *vingtième*; the Bastille was full, which was why Diderot was sent to Vincennes.

The imprisonment lasted little over three months, and only the first four weeks were under strict conditions. His wife and friends were then able to visit him – on the way to one such visit Rousseau had his famous *illumination* – and he was able to have books he wanted. During his time there he translated Plato's *Apology* (Socrates' defence at his trial) and took notes from the first volumes of Buffon's newly published *Histoire naturelle*. But the experience shook Diderot badly. He referred later to the 'sudden and terrible effect of a spell in a dungeon',[8] 'the terrible anxiety'[9] it caused at the time, 'the bitter regrets . . . and the troubles that [could subsequently] last a lifetime'.[10] It seems plausible to attribute to this episode some of his later reluctance to publish his works: 'I do not have an ambition to be any kind of martyr.'[11]

The publishers of the *Encyclopédie* worked hard for Diderot's release and in November 1749 he was set free. In October 1750 the *Prospectus* for the enterprise was published and in June 1751 Volume One, then in January 1752 Volume Two. Sale was by subscription; over two thousand copies of the initial volumes were sold and this figure increased steadily till by the end it had almost doubled. The daunting scale of the work – Volume One took 900 double-column folio pages to deal only with the letter A – and the self-assured critical tone with which it treated many subjects, brought it immediate prominence and growing opposition. After Volume Two further publication was banned by the royal *Conseil* and one of the contributors, the Abbé de Prades, was attacked by the Church and threatened with arrest. However, it would be wrong to see this set-back simply as a straightforward conflict between old institutions and new ideas. Not all the ideas in the *Encyclopédie* were new, and the official institutions were not monolithic. The royal government, the Church and the Paris Parlement all had their own interests and internal differences, and within the government the *philosophes* had their friends; notable among these was the official censor, Malesherbes. It was partly due to him that the ban was lifted later in the year. In a contribution to the *Apologie de l'abbé de Prades* Diderot defended those ideas under attack and in his Preface to Volume Three (published in October 1753) his co-editor D'Alembert did likewise. In this way the work became the self-conscious agent of the process of enlightenment.

The publication of Volumes Four to Seven followed at annual intervals up to November 1757, but at no time did this work occupy Diderot exclusively. In 1751 he had published a short work on language and aesthetics, the *Lettre sur les sourds et muets*, in 1754 his speculative and methodological *Pensées sur l'interprétation de la nature*, and in 1757 and 1758 his two plays, *Le Fils naturel* and *Le Père de famille* with their important theoretical accompaniments, the *Entretiens sur le Fils naturel* and the *Discours sur la poésie dramatique.* In addition, he began to contribute to the *Correspondance littéraire*, a cultural newsletter then edited by his friend Grimm which regularly informed a small number of princes and monarchs in Germany, Sweden and Russia about intellectual life in Paris.

The confidence that informed these works, especially the *Pensées sur l'interprétation de la nature* and the important article 'Encyclopédie' in Volume Five (1755), did not last. The opposition to the *esprit philosophique* grew more vocal; D'Alembert's article on Geneva in Volume Seven led to further attacks and his resignation as co-editor. Diderot became disillusioned: 'Is it certain that [far from being useful to men] we are doing anything except amuse them and that there is any difference between the *philosophe* and the man who plays a flute?'[12] There were personal disappointments as well. His friendship with Rousseau, which had begun in 1742 and been of great significance to them both, ended in a bitter quarrel that Rousseau made public in 1758. Worse was to follow. The next year the Paris Parlement condemned the *Encyclopédie* and the government withdrew the *privilège*, the licence required for its publication, thus bringing the venture to a complete halt. In June Diderot's father died. In 1760 a comedy by Palissot, *Les Philosophes*, which ridiculed the *philosophes* in general and Diderot in particular, enjoyed a spectacular success at the Comédie-Française. The decade that had begun with such striking self-assurance ended in mockery and apparent failure.

But Diderot did not stop work on the *Encyclopédie*. Some, in particular Voltaire, suggested that publication should be continued outside France. The publishers and Diderot decided otherwise, and with the consent of Malesherbes it was agreed that the volumes of plates could be published openly (the first appeared in 1762), while the remaining ten volumes of text would be published all at once and unofficially, with *permission tacite* (a device by which the government withheld its approval but refrained from objection). When these volumes were completed, in 1765, a further condition laid down that they could not be distributed in Paris, so subscribers had to go and collect their copies outside the city. In the event these arrangements worked smoothly. The only set-back was internal – Diderot's discovery that the publisher Le Breton had censored some articles of his own accord. As far as the public was concerned the enterprise was completed with the same impressive confidence that had marked its beginning.

Diderot was sustained through these difficult years by a number of close friendships. In the mid-1750s he had fallen in love with Sophie Volland, the second (unmarried) daughter of a government official; exactly how intimate their affair was remains a matter of conjecture, but of Diderot's feelings for her there is no doubt. The letters he wrote to her, of which 189 survive, display a love that was passionate and affectionate in turn. They are the most personally revealing of all his writings. As his friendship with Rousseau faded and ended, that with Grimm became more important. Grimm was for a time the lover of Madame d'Epinay and it was in this circle that the idea arose which developed into Diderot's second novel *La Religieuse*, most of which was written in 1760. More important intellectually was his friendship with the Baron d'Holbach, who had contributed articles to the *Encyclopédie* on mineralogy and political subjects. Diderot often spent several weeks in the summer or autumn at the latter's country house at Grandval, not many miles south-east of Paris, and Holbach's town house was a regular meeting-place for like-minded *philosophes*: 'It is there that every honest and able person in the capital comes together . . . It is there that conversation is safe.'[13] Holbach was as thoroughgoing a materialist as Diderot and the (anonymous) publication of his *Système de la nature* in 1769 caused an uproar.

The completion of the volumes of text of the *Encyclopédie* left Diderot feeling exhausted: 'My head is tired. The burden I have shouldered for twenty years has so bent me double that I despair of being able to stand up again.'[14] But the ten years that followed saw an astonishingly productive output. The *Salon de 1765* and *Salon de 1767*, accounts of the biennial exhibitions at the Louvre which Diderot had been reviewing for the *Correspondance littéraire* since 1759, developed into book-length studies. His reflections on biology and the nature of matter produced *Le Rêve de d'Alembert* (1769), the *Principes philosophiques de la matière et le mouvement* (1770), and the *Éléments de physiologie* (*c*. 1765–*c*. 1782). A short-lived but passionate affair with Madame de Maux seems to have sparked off a number of works concerned with sexuality, the stories *Ceci n'est pas un conte* (1772) and *Madame de la Carlière* (1772), and the dialogue the *Supplément au Voyage de Bougainville* (1772). There were also other stories, the first versions of the *Paradoxe sur le comédien* and *Jacques le fataliste*, and the important commentaries on Helvétius and Hemsterhuis.

None of this work was published, and none of it was paid. As his

contract for the *Encyclopédie* came to an end Diderot had to find
another source of income. He received a modest rent from the
family property, after the death of his father, but it was not sufficient either to support his family or, a matter that became of
increasing concern to him, to provide a good dowry for his
daughter. To meet this need he decided to sell his library. (One of
the clauses of his contracts for the *Encyclopédie* had been that he
should keep possession of all books needed for the work.)
Catherine II of Russia, who had previously offered to print the
Encyclopédie in Russia, agreed to buy his library under very
generous terms: she made a large immediate payment, followed by
smaller annual amounts, and Diderot had the use of the books until
his death. This provided him with financial security for the rest of
his life.

In 1773, when the last volume of plates had been published and
Angélique safely married, Diderot set off to visit Catherine. He
spent two months in Holland on the way and arrived in St
Petersburg in October. His stay lasted five months and produced
his two most extended political works, a series of reflections and
memoranda on the situation in France and Russia, known as the
Mémoires pour Catherine II, and a commentary on Catherine's
proposed constitutional reforms, the *Observations sur le Nakaz*.
The first was based on conversations he held with the Empress
during the autumn of 1773; the second was written after his return
to France and only sent to her after his death. He also wrote out an
educational scheme for her, the *Plan d'une université*.

It is difficult to assess Diderot's exact feelings about what he saw
in Russia and learnt about Catherine. His daughter said that he
valued a ring which the Empress gave him with her portrait on it
'more than all the treasures in the world',[15] and he certainly had
reason to be grateful. Yet he was fully aware of the unscrupulous
way she had come to power and the despotic nature of her rule: 'the
Empress of Russia is certainly a despot'[16] he wrote in his
Observations. This ambivalence is characteristic not only of his
feelings about Catherine but of his attitude generally in his last
years; for Diderot was pulled in two contradictory directions. On
the one hand he wanted a certain level of social status and went to
considerable lengths to secure the advancement of his son-in-law,
Caroillon de Vandeul; on the other hand he became increasingly
aware of political problems. Even as he expressed his desire to see
his children 'rich . . . very rich'[17] he was writing some of his most

eloquent denunciations of greed and injustice for Raynal's *Histoire des Deux Indes*. For a man as concerned about morality, about the need to be moral, as Diderot, the contradiction in these attitudes was inescapable.

This problem haunted his last years. Much of his time was spent working for Raynal's *Histoire* and revising and having copied his unpublished writings; one collection was sent to Catherine after his death, another – the Fonds Vandeul – was left to his daughter; other copies were left to his friend and disciple Naigeon, who published the first proper edition of his works in 1798. But he also turned over this problem, briefly in a play, *Est-il bon? Est-il méchant?* and at length in a reflective commentary on Seneca, first published as the *Essai sur la vie de Sénèque* in 1778 and then in a longer version, the *Essai sur les règnes de Claude et de Néron* in 1782. Seneca too had received favours from tyrants, but was he not virtuous in spite of that? The first version of the book was not well received and Diderot's estimate of himself became still more uncertain.

> Am I a good man or a vile apologist? And should my attempt, whether apposite or misplaced, be praised or blamed? If someone had set out to undertake my defence as I have done Seneca's, would he have brought on himself scorn and universal indignation? Do I or do I not know my language? Can I set out an argument or only sophisms? Am I a writer of good faith or bad faith? Does my discourse have substance or am I only an empty windbag? Do I know logic and have ideas or do I not? Have I written a good book or a bad book? Which of the two?[18]

The questions remained unanswered.

Diderot was now tired and ageing. This last work, and the contributions to Raynal's *Histoire*, 'ruined and destroyed his remaining strength'.[19] After his return from Russia he spent less and less time in Paris, preferring to stay in the country. Increasing ill-health made it difficult for him to climb the stairs to his attic study in the Rue Taranne, and Catherine II rented an apartment for him on the Rue de Richelieu. Soon after he had moved in he died, on 31 July 1784. One of his last remarks, according to his daughter, was: 'The first step toward philosophy is disbelief.'[20]

The previous year D'Alembert had died and in his *Éloge de d'Alembert* Condorcet had paid tribute to Diderot:

a man with a comprehensive mind, a lively and brilliant imagination, who with a single glance covers the sciences, literature
and the arts all at once; a man with an equal passion for the true
and the beautiful, a man equally suited to penetrate the abstract
truths of philosophy, to discuss with subtlety the principles of the
arts, and to depict with enthusiasm their effects; a clever and
often profound philosopher, a writer both eloquent and agreeable to read, as bold in his style as in his ideas; who instructs his
readers, but who above all inspires them with the desire to learn
to think, and always makes them love the truth, even when,
carried away by his imagination, he has the misfortune not to
recognize it.[21]

Condorcet regretted those moments when Diderot was 'carried
away by his imagination'. For us they provide his most attractive
aspects, his most brilliant insights.

Diderot's death did not create the stir which the deaths of
Voltaire and Rousseau, six years earlier, had caused. But as his
unpublished writings began to appear, often in more unusual
circumstances than any that had accompanied his life, his reputation grew. From being a figure of purely historical interest he
became a writer of unusual and widespread appeal, a man in whom
the comparatively conventional and the strikingly original walked
hand-in-hand in a fascinating one-man partnership.

3

Atheism

Among the books Diderot translated from the English in the 1740s one work was of paramount importance – Shaftesbury's *Inquiry concerning Virtue or Merit*. The French version appeared in 1745 under the title *Principes de la philosophie morale ou Essai de M. S*** sur le mérite et la vertu avec Réflexions*. Its importance lay in the fact that Diderot found in Shaftesbury a kindred spirit; through Shaftesbury's words he was able to articulate ideas which were waiting to be formulated, and which, once formulated, remained permanent features of his thought.

As its title suggests the *Inquiry*, first published in 1699, dealt with virtue and the nature of morality. It set out to show, said Diderot, that man was virtuous 'when without any base or servile motive, such as the hope of a reward or the fear of a punishment, he compels all his passions to work for the general good of his species'.[1] Of the two elements in this definition, (virtue having no ulterior motive and being in harmony with the passions), the first may seem commonplace and the second implausible, but that is to leave out of account Shaftesbury's strong conviction that man's happiness lies essentially in social (rather than purely personal) activity. 'Out of these two branches (viz. Community or Participation in the pleasures of others, and Belief in meriting well from others) would arise more than nine-tenths of all that is enjoyed in life.'[2] 'To have the natural, kindly, or generous affections strong and powerful towards the good of the public is to have the chief means and power of self-enjoyment.'[3] Furthermore, we have a

natural inclination to prefer such a balance, because we have an
aesthetic preference for order and harmony: 'the Admiration and
Love of Order, Harmony and Proportion, in whatever kind, is
naturally improving to the Temper, advantageous to social Affection, and highly assistant to Virtue; which is itself no other than the
Love of Order and Beauty in Society.'[4] In one form or another
these beliefs in a natural identification of virtue and happiness, and
in a basic consonance between our moral and aesthetic faculties,
were to be constant elements of Diderot's ethical thought.

Another important aspect of the *Inquiry* was that it separated
morality from religion. The break was not complete, since
Shaftesbury's ethics were underpinned by metaphysical beliefs that
were religious in character and did not pretend to be otherwise. But
in stating that a 'religious conscience supposes moral or natural
conscience',[5] in defending human passions against Christian
detractors (a defence sharpened by Diderot in one of his notes[6]),
and in attacking Christianity for its anti-social emphasis
Shaftesbury made it clear that morality neither did nor could
depend on any particular religious faith. He stated in his opening
remarks that deism was the only belief compatible with the morality he was expounding; by deism he meant a belief that the world
was created by God and operated according to God's laws, both
physical and moral, but that God had not and would not intervene
in human affairs. For Shaftesbury the world manifested a divine
intelligence and purpose and everything related to an overall
harmony; every creature was part of a single whole. These views
could have obvious social implications and these were drawn by
Shaftesbury: to have a sense of the whole and behave in the light of
that was to act in accordance with nature itself – 'to have this entire
[as opposed to partial] affection . . . is to live according to nature
and the dictates and rules of supreme wisdom'.[7]

This idea of the unity of nature, of the interrelation of every
aspect within a single whole, was underlined by Diderot in one of
his notes: 'In the universe everything is united. This truth was one
of the first steps taken by philosophy . . . and all the discoveries of
modern philosophers agree in stating the same proposition . . .
The further we look into nature the more unity we see.'[8] This note
drew on another of Shaftesbury's works, *The Moralists*, but the
desire to emphasize the point was Diderot's. For his conviction that
all living things are one was of fundamental importance to him; it
corresponded not merely to the way he made sense of phenomena

intellectually (there were in fact considerable problems in doing that), but to a deep-seated emotional need. The idea of an overall harmony in the terms put forward by Leibniz came to be widely held in the eighteenth century under the general name of optimism. Although Diderot rejected optimism as such, since he denied that the operations of the universe followed a divine purpose, he retained the framework on which that belief was constructed. 'Pope has proved very well, following Leibniz, that the world can only be what it is; but when he then concluded that all is well he said an absurdity; he should have been content to say that all is necessary.'[9]

Although Shaftesbury attacked Christianity for being harmful both to society and the individual he did in fact remain a Christian. He made a distinction between religion and superstition, the former being a quasi-Christian version of deism and the latter being the narrow, sectarian kind of Christianity which no humane, intelligent person could support or endorse. In so doing he made a distinction which became common in the eighteenth century between tolerant deist belief and the actual dogma and institutions of any particular Church. Diderot in his preface to his translation identified himself with this position: 'No virtue without religion; no happiness without virtue.'[10] Virtue and happiness depended on religion. In one of his notes Diderot stated: 'Atheism leaves honesty unsupported; it does worse, indirectly it leads to depravity.'[11]

Yet this same note continued: 'Nevertheless, Hobbes was a good citizen, parent and friend, and he did not believe in God. Men are not consistent . . . If there is any surprise it should not be an atheist who lives an upright life but a Christian who lives a bad life.'[12] In other words, Diderot had his doubts; his blunt denunciation of atheism was immediately followed, in characteristic fashion, by a reservation, a qualification that shifted his position.

The uncertainty which this note demonstrated led to Diderot's first original published work, the *Pensées philosophiques*, which appeared anonymously in 1746. It was a series of short reflections, sixty-two in all, on Christianity, deism, scepticism and atheism. Many of the thoughts are restatements or developments of Shaftesbury's ideas, sometimes closely based on his actual texts, but there is a new assertive tone; we are reminded more of the polemical writings of Pierre Bayle or some of the clandestine manuscripts. While Shaftesbury wrote with a certain detachment, a serene assurance, Diderot writes here in a more open, invigorating, combative way. While the attack on Christianity in the *Inquiry* was muted, here it is explicit. The points he makes are not original, but they are expressed with a freshness and sense of personal involvement which was new. He also throws out ideas (XIX, XXI, XXVI) which were both ambiguous and suggestive, and ends with conclusions (LVIII, LXII) which were far from conclusive. He wants to believe in God, but what kind of God? Or must he remain agnostic, a sceptic? The arguments vary, the emphasis alters. Here for the first time Diderot opens the door to the workshop of his mind. He tries out the implements that are ready to hand. What do they feel like? What results can they produce? Are such results satisfactory? His own inquiry has begun.

Pensées philosophiques

I write of God; I expect few readers and little acclaim. If these thoughts please no one they can only be bad; but I should regard them as contemptible if they were to please everyone.

I

People are continually declaiming against the passions; they attribute to them all the pain that man endures and forget that they are also the source of all his pleasure. They are an element in his constitution which cannot be spoken of too highly or too critically. But what annoys me is that they are only considered for the harm they do. It is thought an affront to reason to say a word in favour of its rivals. Yet it is only the passions, and strong passions, that can lift the soul up to great things. Without them there is nothing sublime either in behaviour or in art; the fine arts would return to their infancy and virtue would become petty-mindedness.

III

Dulled passions degrade remarkable men. Constraint destroys the grandeur and energy of nature. Look at that tree; it is to the luxury of its branches that you owe the coolness and breadth of its shade. You will enjoy it until winter strips it of its foliage. There will be no more excellence in poetry, painting and music, once superstition has brought us to a condition of old age.

IV

So it would be happiness, people will say to me, to have strong passions? Certainly, if they are all in harmony. Establish a just harmony among them and you need fear no disorders . . .

[Diderot then speaks out against religious excess, especially asceticism.]

VIII

There are people of whom we ought not to say that they fear God, but that they are afraid of him.

XII

Yes, I maintain that superstition is more offensive to God than atheism. 'I would rather,' said Plutarch, 'that people thought that a Plutarch had never existed, than that they thought of Plutarch as unjust, angry, capricious, jealous and vindictive . . .'

XIII

Only the deist is effective against the atheist. The superstitious person does not have his strength; his God is only a creature of the imagination. Apart from the intrinsic difficulties of the subject he is open to all those other difficulties which arise from the errors of his ideas. A C[udworth], a S[haftesbury] would have been a thousand times more troublesome to a Vanini, than all the Nicoles and Pascals of this world.*

XVI

One day somebody asked a man if real atheists existed. Do you think, he replied, that real Christians exist?

XVII

None of the nonsense of metaphysics has the force of an argument *ad hominem*. In order to convince it is only necessary sometimes to

---

* Vanini was an Italian thinker executed in 1619 at Toulouse for atheism, although his ideas would now be called pantheist. Nicole, like Pascal, was prominent among those philosophers and writers associated with Port-Royal, developing and propagating that dour form of Catholicism known as Jansenism.

rouse a physical or moral feeling. The sceptic was convinced by a stick that he was wrong in doubting his own existence . . .

XVIII

It is not from the metaphysician that atheism has received its heaviest blows. The sublime meditations of Malebranche and Descartes were less use in shaking materialism than one observation by Malpighi. If this dangerous hypothesis is wavering nowadays it is experimental physics that must take the credit. It is only in the works of Newton, Musschenbroek, Hartsoeker and Nieuwentyt that satisfactory proofs have been found of the existence and sovereignty of an intelligent being.* Thanks to the work of these great men, the world is no longer a god; it is a machine with a machine's wheels, cords, pulleys, springs and weights.

XIX

The subtleties of ontology have at best made sceptics: it was reserved for the knowledge of nature to make true deists. The discovery of germs alone has destroyed one of the most powerful arguments of atheism. Whether motion is essential or accidental to matter, I am now convinced that its effects are limited to developments; all experiments agree in demonstrating to me that putrefaction alone never produced any organism. I can admit that the mechanism of the lowest insect is no less marvellous than that of man; and I am not afraid of the inference that, as an intestinal agitation of molecules is able to produce the one, it is plausible that it has produced the other. If an atheist had maintained two hundred years ago that some day, perhaps, people would see men spring fully formed from the bowels of the earth, just as we see a mass of insects emerge from putrefying flesh, I would like to know what a metaphysician would have had to say to him.

XX

It was in vain that I tried scholastic subtleties against an atheist; he drew from the very weakness of those arguments a strong objec-

---

* Malpighi was an Italian biologist, Musschenbroek and Hartsoeker were Dutch physicists; Nieuwentyt wrote a popular work of Christian apologetics based on scientific discoveries, *L'Existence de Dieu démontrée par les merveilles de la nature*.

tion: 'A multitude of useless truths is proved to me without difficulty,' he said, 'but the existence of God, the reality of moral good and evil, the immortality of the soul, are still problems for me. What! Is it less important for me to be enlightened on these issues than to be convinced that the three angles of a triangle are equal to two right-angles?' While with his skilful rhetoric he made me taste all the bitterness of this reflection I joined battle again with a question which must have seemed odd to a man puffed up by his initial success. 'Are you a thinking being?' I asked him. 'How can you doubt it?' he replied in a self-satisfied way. 'Why shouldn't I? What have I seen to convince me? Sounds and movements. But the philosopher sees as much in the animal to which he denies the faculty of thought. Why should I allow you what Descartes refuses the ant? . . . You must agree it would be madness to deny your fellow men the faculty of thought.' 'No doubt,' [replied the atheist] 'but what follows from that?' 'What follows is that if the universe – why do I say universe? – if the wing of a butterfly offers me signs of an intelligence which are a thousand times clearer than the evidence you have that your fellow man is endowed with the faculty of thought, then it would be a thousand times more stupid to deny that a God exists than to deny that your fellow man thinks. Now, however that may be, I appeal to your knowledge, your conscience. Have you ever noticed in the arguments, acts and behaviour of any man more intelligence, order, wisdom and consistency than in the mechanism of an insect? Is the Divinity not as clearly stamped on the eye of a mite as the faculty of thought on the works of the great Newton? What! Does the world as it is demonstrate less intelligence than the explanation of that world? . . . I use against you only the wing of a butterfly, the eye of a mite, when I could crush you with the weight of the universe. Either I am completely mistaken, or this proof is easily worth the best that has ever come out of the schools. It is on this argument, and a few others of similar simplicity, that I believe in the existence of a God, and not on that mass of dried-up metaphysical ideas which are less suited to reveal the truth than make it seem like falsehood.'

XXI

I open the pages of a celebrated professor* and I read: 'Atheists, I grant you that movement is essential to matter; what conclusion do

---

* Rivard, teacher of philosophy at Beauvais.

you draw from that? That the world is the result of a fortuitous throw of atoms? You might as well tell me that Homer's *Iliad* or Voltaire's *Henriade* is the result of a fortuitous throw of written characters.' I would take care not to use that argument against an atheist; he would make quick work of the comparison. According to the laws of the analysis of chances [i.e. the calculation of probabilities], he would say, I ought not to be surprised that a thing happens when it is possible and when the difficulty of the result is compensated for by the number of throws. There is a certain number of throws in which I would back myself to bring a hundred thousand sixes at once with a hundred thousand dice. Whatever the finite number of letters with which I am invited to create the *Iliad* by chance, there is a certain finite number of throws which would give me a definite advantage; indeed, my advantage would be infinite if the number of throws allowed me was infinite. You are willing to grant me, he would continue, that matter exists from all eternity and that movement is essential to it. In return for this concession I will suppose, as you do, that the world has no limits, that the multitude of atoms is infinite and that this order which causes you astonishment nowhere contradicts itself. Now, from these mutual admissions there follows nothing else unless it is that the possibility of creating the universe by chance is very small but that the quantity of throws is infinite; that is to say, that the difficulty of the result is more than sufficiently compensated for by the multitude of throws. Therefore, if there is one thing which should be repugnant to reason, it is the supposition that – [given that] matter is in motion from all eternity and there is perhaps in the infinite number of combinations an infinite number of admirable arrangements – none of these admirable arrangements would have resulted from the infinite multitude of forms which matter took on successively. Therefore the mind ought to be more astonished at the hypothetical duration of chaos than at the actual birth of the universe.

XXII

. . . I pity genuine atheists; all consolation seems to me to be dead to them. And I pray God for the sceptics; they lack knowledge.

XXIII

The deist maintains the existence of God, the immortality of the soul and its consequences; the sceptic has not decided on these points; the atheist denies them. The sceptic, therefore, has one more motive for practising virtue than the atheist, and some reason less than the deist. If it were not for the fear of the laws, the tendency of a man's character, and the knowledge of the actual benefits of virtue, the honesty of the atheist would lack foundation, and that of the sceptic would be built on a 'perhaps'.

XXIV

Scepticism does not suit everybody. It presupposes profound and disinterested examination. He who doubts because he is not acquainted with the reasons for believing is no better than an ignoramus. The true sceptic has counted and weighed his reasons. But it is no easy matter to weigh arguments. Which of us knows their value with any exactness? Out of a hundred proofs of the same truth each will have its partisans. Every mind has its own telescope. An objection which is invisible to you is a colossus to my eyes, and you find an argument trivial that to me is overwhelming. If we dispute about their intrinsic value, how shall we agree about their relative importance? Tell me how many moral proofs are needed to balance a metaphysical conclusion? Are my spectacles at fault, or yours? If then it is so difficult to weigh reasons, and if there are no questions which do not have two sides, and nearly always in equal measure, how do we come to cut knots with such rapidity? How do we come to seem so convinced? Have we not experienced a hundred times how revolting dogmatic self-assurance is? 'I have been brought to detest things that are probable,' says the author of the *Essais*,* 'when they are foisted on me as infallible; I love words which soften and moderate the boldness of our propositions – *perhaps, not in the least, some people say, I think* and the like; and if I have to teach children I should train them to answer in this tentative and undecided way – *What does that mean*? *I do not understand; maybe; is it true*? – so that they would have kept the manner of apprentices at the age of sixty rather than having that of doctors at the age of fifteen.'

XXVI

People begin to speak to us of God too soon [i.e. at too early an

* Montaigne: Bk III, Chapter 11.

age]: another mistake is that his presence is not sufficiently insisted upon. Men have banished God from among them, they have confined him to a sanctuary; the walls of a temple shut him in, he has no existence outside. Fools that you are, break down these barriers that limit your ideas; set God free (*élargissez Dieu*); see him everywhere where he is, or else say that he does not exist. If I had a child to bring up I would make his God his companion in such a real sense that he would perhaps find it easier to become an atheist than to escape his presence. Instead of quoting as an example another man, whom he knows sometimes to be worse than himself, I would say to him bluntly: 'God hears you and you are lying.' Young people like to be led by the senses. So I would multiply around him signs indicating the divine presence. If for instance there were a gathering at my house, I would leave a place for God, and I would accustom him to say: 'There are four of us – my friend, my tutor, myself, and God.'

[In most of the remaining *Pensées* Diderot attacks religious enthusiasm, the belief in miracles, the fanaticism of the early Christians, and the unreliability of the scriptures. There must be good reasons for any belief.]

XXXI

What has never been questioned has not been proved. What has not been examined without prejudice has never been well examined. Scepticism is therefore the first step towards the truth . . .

L

A single proof affects me more than fifty facts. Thanks to the great confidence I have in my reason my faith is not at the mercy of the first trickster I meet. Priest of Mahomet, you may cure the lame, make the dumb speak, give sight to the blind, heal the paralysed, raise the dead, and even restore to the mutilated the limbs they have lost, a miracle hitherto unattempted, and to your great surprise my faith will not be shaken. Do you want me to become your proselyte? Then leave these prodigies and let us reason. I trust my judgement more than my eyes. If the religion which you proclaim is true, its truth can be demonstrated by unanswerable arguments. Find these arguments. Why plague me with prodigies when you only need a syllogism to convince me? Do you find it easier to make a cripple stand upright than to enlighten me?

LVII

It is agreed that it is of the greatest importance to use only sub-stantial reasons in defending a belief; nevertheless people allow those who work at denouncing bad reasons to be persecuted. What! Is it not enough to be a Christian? Is it more important to be one for bad reasons? Believers, let me warn you: I am not a Christian because St Augustine was one; I am one because it is reasonable to be one.

LVIII

I know the devout; they are quick to take alarm. If they come to decide that this work contains something contrary to their ideas I expect all the abuse they heaped on the thousand people who were of more consequence than me. If I am only a deist and a criminal I will have got off lightly. It is a long time since they condemned Descartes, Montaigne, Locke and Bayle; and I hope that they will condemn plenty more of such men. Nevertheless I declare to them that I do not pride myself on being a more upright man, or a better Christian, than the majority of these philosophers. I was born into the Roman Catholic Church; and I submit myself entirely to its decisions. I wish to die in the religion of my fathers, and I think that that religion is as good as any religion can be for someone who has never had any immediate contact with the Divinity and has never witnessed a single miracle. There is my profession of faith; I am almost certain that they will not be happy with it, even though there may not be one among them in a fit state to make a better.

LXI

It was during my search for proofs that I found difficulties. The books which contain the motives for my belief offer at the same time reasons for unbelief. They are arsenals available to all sides. I have seen the deist arm himself there against the atheist; the deist and the atheist attack the Jew; the atheist, the deist and the Jew gang up against the Christian; the Christian, the deist, the atheist and the Jew oppose the Muslim; the atheist, the deist, the Jew, the Muslim and a multitude of Christian sects attack the Christian; and the sceptic on his own against everyone. I was the umpire; I held the balance between the adversaries. It rose or fell in sympathy with the weight thrown into the scales. After long hesitation, the balance dipped in favour of the Christian, but [less through] its own weight [than] in reaction to the other side. I can bear witness to my own impartiality. I have not tried to make any case better than it is. I call God to witness my sincerity.

LXII

This diversity of opinions has led the deist to imagine an argument which is perhaps more curious than substantial. Cicero, having to prove that the Romans were the most warlike people in the world, cleverly extracts this admission from the lips of their rivals. Gauls, to whom, if any, do you yield the palm in courage? To the Romans. Parthians, after you, who are the most courageous men? The Romans. Africans, whom would you fear, if there was anyone you had to fear? The Romans. Let us interrogate other believers in the same way, say the deists. Chinese, what religion would be the best, if yours were not? Natural religion. Muslims, what religion would you embrace if you renounced Mahomet? Naturalism.* Christians, what is the true religion, if it is not Christianity? The religion of the Jews. But you, Jews, what is the true religion, if Judaism is false? Naturalism. Now those, Cicero goes on, to whom the second place is given by unanimous agreement, and who do not give first place to anyone, they are the ones who undoubtedly deserve that first place.

II

Although there was little in the *Pensées philosophiques* that was original the boldness of the expression brought upon it the condemnation which Diderot expected. The work was publicly burnt at the order of the Paris Parlement. But it was also reprinted several times and was the object of a number of refutations. For the questions it dealt with were central issues and the ambiguous way in which Diderot handled them was as unsettling as some of the more

* In this context naturalism is synonymous with natural religion.

emphatically materialist or atheist works then in circulation.

Over the next few years Diderot tried to answer some of the questions he had raised. He wrote a short treatise, *De la suffisance de la religion naturelle*, which was a development of *Pensée* LXII, and an allegory, *La Promenade du sceptique*. The latter takes the form of a discussion between a small group of philosophers as they walk through the avenue of thorns, which represents Christianity, the avenue of chestnut trees, where the philosophers feel at ease, and the avenue of flowers, which represents unthinking hedonism. The work is both unsatisfactory to read, since the allegory is banal and poorly realized, and difficult to interpret, since it is not at all clear where Diderot himself stands. Mostly he seems to align himself with the deist against the atheist, yet the atheist has strong arguments against the deist and a Spinozist has a strong case against the atheist.

In the *Pensées philosophiques* four arguments had been used or referred to in favour of a belief in the existence of God: the argument from first causes, a creator being needed to explain how the world came into being (XIX); the argument from design, the world displaying signs of a superior intelligence (XVIII, XX); the moral argument, without the threat or promise of an afterlife no one would be virtuous (XXIII); and the historical argument, all people having had some form of religious belief (LXII). In *La Promenade du sceptique* the moral argument is abruptly reasserted. When Atheos, the atheist, returns home after the discussion he finds 'his wife abducted, his children murdered and his house ransacked'; and he only had himself to blame since he had taught the man suspected of the crime 'to despise the voice of conscience and the laws of society'.[13] The peremptory way in which Diderot handles this episode betrays an unease which was sometimes to recur when he faced the problem of justifying morality without religion. But the episode should not be given too much prominence. The focus of the discussion is elsewhere, on the argument from design.

The success of Newtonian physics in explaining the movements of the planets, and the biological discoveries revealed by the use of the microscope, had given this argument overwhelming force in the first half of the century. Nature in its grandest dimensions and its smallest particular seemed to demonstrate irrefutable signs of intelligence, design and order. Christian apologists like the Abbé Pluche in *Le Spectacle de la nature* (the first volume of which was published in 1732) and the Dutch biologist Swammerdam with his *Bible de la nature* (1737) set out the case with eloquence and detail. In his *Pensées* XVIII and XIX Diderot based his deism on what had been learnt from 'experimental physics' and 'the knowledge of nature'.

During the 1740s new discoveries were made and new evidence put forward in biology and zoology which could still be used to support the argument from design, but in an altered form. The Swiss scientist Trembley showed that the freshwater polyp seemed to have properties of both an animal and a plant and to be able to generate itself. This discovery, in conjunction with other developments, led to the conception of nature as being in some way self-organizing, having its own internal dynamism; this was suggested by Maupertius in his *Vénus physique* (1745) and La Mettrie in *L'Homme machine* (1747). The implications of this view were that an intelligent force existed but that it animated or ordered the world not from outside but from within; in other words, there was an immanent God. This belief, frequently associated in the eighteenth century with Spinoza, though his works were little read, is advanced by the character Oribaze in *La Promenade du sceptique*.[14]

His argument is used less for its own sake, however, than to overcome arguments put forward by the atheist. In *Pensée* XXI Diderot had suggested that if it were conceded that motion was essential to matter (and matter was not, as Descartes, Newton and all deists maintained, intrinsically inert and set in motion only by God), then an atheist could maintain that the universe came about by chance. In *La Promenade du sceptique* the atheist repeats this argument,[15] stressing the inadequacy of our own knowledge in relation to ideas of infinity and eternity. In his *Lettre sur les aveugles*, published in 1749, Diderot developed this line of thought to a point of no return.

The problem of knowledge – how we come to have ideas, and what we can have ideas of – has been a major preoccupation of western philosophy since Descartes. In eighteenth-century France Locke's empirical view of knowledge came to replace Cartesian rationalism, or, more accurately, Locke's empiricism was adopted with some Cartesian elements retained. An important aspect of the empirical position was its emphasis on the limitations of human knowledge; there were certain questions which human beings were simply not equipped to answer. One of these, for Locke, was the purpose of existence; we cannot have any certain knowledge of why we exist. In his *Lettre sur les aveugles* Diderot extended the area of doubt by suggesting that we also cannot know how long the order we now see in nature has existed; we have no certain knowledge of either its universality or its permanence. Furthermore, the existence of monsters could be taken to show that such order as does exist is arbitrary rather than necessary. The argument was not new, it goes back to Lucretius' *De rerum natura*, and the presence of Lucretius can be felt behind several passages in the work. But Diderot gives it new force both by the way he presents it and by setting it within the contemporary debate on the nature of knowledge.

The *Lettre* revolves around one of the many problems with which the empiricists, from Locke onwards, had been faced. If all knowledge comes through the senses, in what way would a person deprived of one particular sense differ from a person endowed with all five senses? What would be the ideas of a man born blind? Also, if someone born blind were to have his sight restored, would he be able to use his sight to recognize objects previously known to him only through the sense of touch? This latter question, known as Molyneux's problem, had been dealt with in different ways by Locke, Berkeley, Voltaire, La Mettric and in 1746 by Condillac in his important *Essai sur l'origine des connaissances humaines*, a work which Diderot, a friend of Condillac, had helped to get published.

The *Lettre sur les aveugles* takes the form of a letter addressed to a woman who shared Diderot's interest in these issues and, like him, had been refused admission to an operation in which Réamur, the director of the Académie royale des Sciences, had removed the cataracts from a girl born blind. Unable to see how the blind girl had actually reacted Diderot turns to other evidence. He describes a visit to a blind man at Puiseaux, he gives an account of the blind English mathematician Saunderson, and he discusses and criticizes Condillac's treatment of Molyneux's problem. The subject under discussion alters constantly and we are continually reminded of the urgency that these apparently abstruse matters have for Diderot; he wants to know what it is possible for human beings to know because he craves certainty. Most of the letter is an even-tempered and imaginative discussion, but half-way through, in Saunderson's death-bed scene, it becomes something else, a *cri de coeur*, an impassioned outburst in which the argument is sustained as much by emotional force as by strength of reason.

This passage has been carefully prepared. In his description of the blind man of Puiseaux Diderot draws attention to the way certain of his responses, in particular to sounds and to atmospheric conditions, are more acute than those of other men, and how certain mental attitudes are also different. 'As I have never doubted that the conditions of our organs and senses has a great deal of influence on our metaphysical and moral ideas, and that our most purely intellectual ideas, so to speak, relate very closely to the structure of our bodies, I began to question our blind man about [his ideas of] vices and virtues.'[16] He then describes how the blind man had a different estimate of theft, and less sense of shame or pity. As for metaphysics, 'how many of their ideas are only absurdities for us, and vice versa . . . The great argument which is based on the wonders of nature is very weak for the blind . . . [and] as they see matter in a much more abstract way than us, they are less reluctant to believe that it thinks.'[17] (The possibility that matter could think was, of course, fundamental for atheists and anathema for Christians; shortly beforehand Diderot had made the equally provocative suggestion that 'one can scarcely doubt [that] an animal reasons'.)[18] A discussion of how the blind handle abstract ideas of geometry then leads to a detailed account of the 'palpable arithmetic' developed by the blind Cambridge professor of mathematics and Fellow of the Royal Society, Nicholas Saunderson. A consideration of this man's remarkable qualities leads into an account of his death, in 1739.

Lettre sur les aveugles

. . . I could add to this account of the blind man of Puiseaux and   118
Saunderson, that of Didymus of Alexandria, Eusebius the Asiatic, Nicaise of Mechlin and some others who, though lacking one sense, seemed so far above the level of the rest of men that the poets might without exaggeration have been able to maintain that the jealous gods had deprived them of that sense, through fear of mortals being equal to them. For what was Tiresias, who had read the secrets of the gods and possessed the gift of predicting the future, but a blind philosopher whose memory has been handed down to us by fable? But let us not stray from Saunderson; let us follow this remarkable

man to the grave.

When he was on the point of death a clergyman of great ability, Mr Gervase Holmes, was called to his side and they held a discussion about the existence of God, some fragments of which survive which I will translate as best I can, for they are well worth it. The clergyman began by arguing from the wonders of nature. 'Ah, sir,' said the blind philosopher, 'leave aside that beautiful spectacle which was never made for me. I have been condemned to spend my life in darkness, and you cite prodigies which I do not understand, and which are only proof for you and for those who see as you do. If you want me to believe in God you must make me touch him.'

'Sir,' replied the clergyman cleverly, 'touch yourself, and you will recognize the divinity in the admirable mechanism of your organs.'

'Mr Holmes,' answered Saunderson, 'I must repeat, all that does not appear so beautiful to me as it does to you. But even if the animal mechanism were as perfect as you suppose, and I dare say it is – for you are an upright man incapable of deceiving me – what does it have in common with a sovereign and intelligent being? If it surprises you, that is perhaps because you are accustomed to treat as miraculous everything which strikes you as beyond your own powers. I have myself been so often an object of admiration to you that I have a very low opinion of what surprises you. I have attracted people from the length of England who could not imagine how I could work at geometry; you must agree that such people did not have very correct notions of the possibility of things. We think a phenomenon beyond human power and we immediately say: "It is the work of a God." Our vanity is not content with anything less. Why can we not talk with a little less pride and a little more philosophy? If nature offers us a difficult knot to untie let us leave it for what it is and not use to cut it the hand of a being who immediately becomes a fresh knot, harder to untie than the first. Ask an Indian why the earth hangs suspended in the sky and he will tell you that it is carried on the back of an elephant. And what supports the elephant? A tortoise. And the tortoise, who will carry that? You pity the Indian, and one might say to you, as to him: "Mr Holmes, my friend, first admit your ignorance, and spare me the elephant and the tortoise."'

Saunderson stopped a moment, apparently waiting for the clergyman to reply; but how can anyone attack a blind man? Mr Holmes rested his case on the good opinion Saunderson had of his

119

120

honesty and of the abilities of Newton, Leibniz and some of his
fellow countrymen, men of the highest genius, who had all been
struck by the wonders of nature and recognized an intelligent being
as its author. This was undoubtedly the clergyman's strongest
argument against Saunderson. The blind man also agreed that it
would be rash to deny what such a man as Newton had not thought
it beneath him to admit; yet he showed the clergyman that
Newton's evidence did not count as much to him as the evidence of
the whole of nature had counted to Newton; and that Newton
believed on God's word while he [Saunderson] was reduced to
believing on Newton's word.

'Consider, Mr Holmes,' he added, 'what confidence I must have
in your word and in Newton's. I see nothing, yet I admit there is an
admirable order in everything. But I hope you will not demand
more. I grant you the current state of the universe in order that you
will allow me in return the liberty of thinking as I please about its
original, first condition, about which you are as blind as myself.
Here you have no witnesses to speak against me, and your eyes are
no use at all. Imagine, if you like, that the order which you find so   121
striking has always existed, but allow me to think otherwise, to
believe that if we went back to the birth of things and times, and
experienced matter moving itself and chaos untangling itself, we
should find [only] a few properly formed creatures among a multitude of unformed creatures. If I have nothing to argue against the
present state of things at least I can question you about their past
state. I can ask you, for example, who told you, Leibniz, Clarke
and Newton that in the first moments of the formation of animals
some were not without heads and others without feet? I could
maintain that some had no stomach, others no intestines, that
some, which through having a stomach, palate and teeth seemed
certain to survive, came to an end because of some fault in the heart
or the lungs; that monsters were destroyed one after another; that
all the faulty combinations of matter disappeared, and the only
ones to remain were those whose mechanism did not have any
serious contradiction and who were able to support themselves and
perpetuate themselves.   122

'Suppose, Mr Holmes, that the first man had his larynx blocked,
or had lacked suitable food, or had something wrong with the
organs of generation, or had failed to find a mate, or had propa-
gated in another species, what would have become of the human
race? It would still have been wrapped in the general clearing

(*dépuration*) of the universe, and that proud being called man, dissolved and dispersed among the molecules of matter, would have remained, perhaps for ever, among the number of mere possibilities.

'If there never had been unformed creatures, you would not fail to assume that there never will be any, and that I am throwing myself into fantastic hypotheses; but the order is not so perfect [even now] that monstrous productions do not appear from time to time.' Then, turning to face the clergyman, he added, 'Look at me, Mr Holmes, I have no eyes. What have we done to God, you and I, that one of us has this organ while the other has not?'

Saunderson uttered these words in such a true and sincere way that the clergyman and the rest of the company could not resist sharing his grief and they began to weep bitterly for him. The blind man noticed this. He said to the clergyman, 'Mr Holmes, I was aware of the kindness of your heart, and I am very touched by the expression of it you have just given; but if I am dear to you do not deprive me of the consolation as I die of never having caused any-one suffering.'

123

Then, continuing the conversation in a firmer tone, he went on: 'I conjecture, then, that in the beginning, when matter in ferment-ation brought forth this world, creatures like myself were very common. But why can I not assume of worlds what I believe about animals? How many disabled, incomplete worlds have been dis-solved, form again and perhaps dissolve at every moment in distant space which I cannot touch and which you cannot see, but where motion continues and will continue to combine masses of matter, until they have found some arrangement in which they may finally survive? O philosophers! Come with me to the edge of this uni-verse, beyond the point where I touch and you see properly formed creatures; survey this new ocean and search in its irregular agita-tions for some traces of that intelligent being whose wisdom you admire so much here!

'But what is the use of taking you out of your element? What is this world, Mr Holmes? A compound subject to cycles of change (*révolutions*), all showing a continual tendency to destruction; a rapid succession of creatures which appear one after another, flourish and disappear; a fleeting symmetry, a momentary order. A moment ago I reproached you for considering the perfection of things according to your own capacity, and I could accuse you here of measuring duration by your own existence. You judge of the

successive existence of the world as the ephemeral insect judges of
yours. The world is eternal to you just as you seem eternal to the
creatures of a day. And the insect is more reasonable than you.　　124
What a prodigious number of generations of insects bears witness
to your eternity, what a long tradition! Yet we shall all pass away
without being able to know the real amount [of space] which we
have occupied, or exactly how long we have lasted. Time, matter,
and space are perhaps only a point.'

During this conversation Saunderson became more excited than
his state of health would allow; an attack of delirium followed
which lasted several hours and he only emerged from it to cry out
'O God of Clarke and Newton, have mercy on me' and to die.

That was the end of Saunderson. You see, madam, that not even
all the arguments he had just put to the clergyman could reassure a
blind man. What a disgrace to men who have no better arguments,
men who can see and to whom the astonishing spectacle of nature,
from the rising of the sun to the setting of the smallest stars,
proclaims the existence and glory of its author! They have eyes,
which Saunderson was deprived of, but Saunderson had a purity of
behaviour and an uprightness of character which they lack.
Accordingly they lead the life of the blind, and Saunderson died as
if he had sight. The voice of nature made itself clear enough to him
by means of the senses he still possessed, and his evidence is even
more convincing against those who stubbornly shut their eyes and
ears. I would like to know if the true God was not more obscured
for Socrates by the darkness of paganism, than it was for　　125
Saunderson by lack of sight and the absence of the spectacle of
nature?

I am very sorry, madam, both for your sake and mine, that no
other interesting details of this eminent blind man have been
passed down. His answers would perhaps have afforded more
enlightenment than all the experiments that have been suggested.
Those around him cannot have been very philosophically minded! I
make an exception of his pupil Mr William Inchlif, who only saw
Saunderson during his last moments, and who assembled his last
works for us, which I should advise all who know English to read in
the original, printed in Dublin in 1747, entitled *The Life and
character of Dr Nicholas Saunderson, late Lucasian Professor of the
mathematics in the university of Cambridge; by his disciple and
friend William Inchlif, Esq*. They will find a charm, energy, truth
and gentleness not found in any other writing, which I do not

presume to have conveyed to you in spite of all I have done to preserve them in translation . . .

This passage marks a crucial stage in Diderot's development as a writer. The meandering form of the letter, unlike the concentrated *Pensées philosophiques* or the rigid *La Promenade du sceptique*, allowed him to pursue points which interested him, as the interest took him. He apologizes to the addressee for his digressions[19] but he does not avoid them, because he needed that freedom. He is then able to develop Saunderson's last moments in the imaginative way that he does. The scene is significant in a number of respects. To begin with, it is Saunderson who is speaking, or rather, Diderot impersonating Saunderson; this use of a character gave a stimulus and freedom which Diderot both needed and exploited. Likewise the extreme situation – a man close to death – made plausible the daring thought; it helped to cast light on what was barely glimpsed. In unusual states of mind we may grasp aspects of reality which otherwise elude us. Yet such states pass, and when they do the insights they bring often pass also. Diderot tries to prevent this, in a way, by his false attribution to William Inchlif. The reference is pure fiction, no such book existed, but Diderot hopes that by giving it he will make what has preceded seem true, authentic, verifiable. This desire was also to be a constant preoccupation. After the reference he returns to the discussion of the initial problem and when he comes to the last pages of the letter he is so far removed from the exciting ideas expressed by Saunderson that he ends in complete scepticism: 'Alas, madam, when human knowledge is put in the scales of Montaigne we are not far from adopting his motto. For what do we know? About what matter consists of? Nothing. About what mind and thought are? Even less. What movement, space, duration are? Nothing at all . . . . So we know almost nothing.'[20]

However, it is always a mistake to suppose that Diderot's last word is conclusive. In the moment of calm consideration he may admit that conjectures are not certain knowledge, but those conjectures still have value. Knowing the importance the issues had for Diderot, and the context in which the conjectures are made, we are not wrong to give them more attention than the final scepticism of the work. We should not forget the latter, but we should not take it to cancel out what has gone before.

In his speech Saunderson effectively destroyed the argument
from design. He also suggested that the universe could have developed out of chaos and that no creator was needed to explain its
existence. That does not mean that Saunderson was an atheist; his
very last words are ambiguous. But he has removed two major
reasons for needing to believe in God. In his concluding comments,
about Saunderson's pure and upright character, Diderot also
implies that morality does not need a religious underpinning.

Saunderson's view of nature is important not only for negative
reasons, however, but also for introducing a new dimension, time.
The universe does not function in fixed patterns according to
unchanging laws; it is in a state of constant change. This had been
Lucretius' belief and Diderot is clearly inspired by Lucretius when
he speaks of matter combining, dissolving, and recombining until it
finds a form in which it can survive.[21] But he was inspired not only
by Lucretius; or, perhaps more accurately, he could adopt
Lucretius' view because there was new evidence to justify it. In the
works by Maupertius and La Mettrie mentioned previously, and
others like De Maillet's *Telliamed* (1748) and the still unpublished
speculations of Buffon, which may have been known to Diderot,
the concept of evolution was gradually and hesitantly starting to
emerge.

Saunderson's speculations are important, finally, for what they
contribute to the specific subject of the *Lettre*, the problem of
knowledge. For Diderot did not accept Condillac's view that the
mind is passive, devoid of initiative or the capacity to generate
ideas: 'It is not enough that objects strike us, we must in addition
pay attention to the impression they made on us.'[22] 'How does a
man born blind form ideas of shapes?'[23] Diderot analyses the
process minutely and demonstrates how the man must not merely
associate memories or sense-impressions but actually 'form
(*compose*) . . . points, surfaces, solids'.[24] A magnificent example
of this ability of the mind is Saunderson's outburst. Our minds are
not mere recipients of information received, they are active and
imaginative instruments which can penetrate and grasp reality of
their own accord.

III

Diderot sent Voltaire a copy of his *Lettre sur les aveugles*. The latter took exception to Saunderson's pronouncements; he maintained that 'infinite relationships in everything' were still evident, indicating the existence of 'an infinitely able workman'.[25] This position, recently reasserted in *Zadig* (published in 1747), remained the basis of Voltaire's deist faith; it was later to be the subject of bitter disagreement between him and the next generation of *philosophes*, in particular Holbach. Diderot replied that the 'infinite relationships' and 'wonderful order' 'are metaphysical creatures which only exist in your mind'.[26] Nevertheless, he continued, 'I believe in God though I live quite happily with atheists'; the latter, however, were good men.

Whether or not Diderot did still believe in God may at this point be uncertain but it is clear that he had no need to do so intellectually. From 1748 onwards he had been moving steadily towards atheism. The sense of physicality which is so prominent in his writing gave him a natural inclination towards materalism; already in his novel *Les Bijoux indiscrets* the idea had appeared that the soul is not spiritual but purely physical.[27] Reports made to the police in 1746 spoke of him as being an atheist.[28] The ambiguity of XIX and XXI of the *Pensées philosophiques* was decisively cleared up in the *Lettre sur les aveugles*. In his *Pensées sur l'interprétation de la nature* (1754) the ideas of the emergence of life from chaos were developed further. The arguments from first causes and from design had been effectively discarded.

If Diderot still showed some reluctance to do without God altogether it was because there was a religious streak in his character. In two short pieces written probably in 1764, known under the title *Introduction aux grands principes*, he wrote: 'God speaks to me . . . through his works, through the heavens, through the earth, through the midge as through the elephant', and of 'the voice of my conscience [through which] God speaks to me . . . as he speaks in one way to all men'.[29] He went on: 'the image of annihilation (*néant*) makes me shudder; I lift up my mind to the supreme Being and I say to Him: Great God, you who have given me the happiness of knowing you, have you granted me that happiness only to enjoy it for a few fleeting days?. . . Having admired your wonderful works in this world, make another where I can find delight in contemplating the author of them both.'[30] He wrote on more than one occasion of how religious processions could move him,[31] and he told Catherine II: 'I do not believe in the divinity [but] I will perhaps believe as I die; it is a stiff neck which puts the most vigorous heads back on their pedestal.'[32]

These examples should be noted, because this aspect of Diderot's character is often forgotten, but they should not be overemphasized. There is no doubt that from the early or mid 1750s at the latest Diderot was an atheist and remained one until his death. Whatever conclusions are drawn from his *Lettre à Landois* (1756) it is clear from his *Réflexions* on Helvétius' book *De l'esprit* (1758) that he had arrived at an explanation for our moral sense which satisfied the only remaining doubt he might have had about getting rid of God. In these *Réflexions* he wrote: 'It is possible to find in our natural needs, in our life, our existence, our physical constitution and our *sensibilité*, which make us aware of suffering, an eternal foundation for [the ideas of] just and unjust.'[33] And in the *Introduction aux grands principes* he reiterated that belief which he had initially found in Shaftesbury and retained throughout his life, that 'the path to happiness is the very path to virtue. Ill-fortune may raise obstacles . . . but the virtuous man finds in his own heart abundant compensation for all that he suffers.' Virtue is accompanied by 'sweet delight, pure pleasure'.[34]

In 1762 Diderot added some *Additions* to his *Pensées philosophiques*, most of which were drawn from another work by an unknown author (who had himself drawn on the *Pensées philosophiques*). The *Additions* which were by Diderot himself add nothing to the position he had now arrived at, and the writing generally is undistinguished. For Diderot was never at ease with sharply anti-Christian polemic like his friends Holbach and Naigeon. He disliked their 'ugly, tedious and repetitious writings about Jesus Christ and his apostles'.[35] Moreover, he was aware that atheism could be 'very close to a kind of superstition almost as puerile as [religion]'[36] when it came to believing in astrology or similar incredible ideas, and atheism *per se* was no guarantee against 'fanaticism and intolerance'.[37]

His last considered treatment of the subject came in a dialogue entitled *Entretien d'un philosophe avec la maréchale de* ***, written in 1774 and published in 1777 with an attribution to Thomas Crudeli, an Italian writer who had died in 1745. The work takes the form of a relaxed, at times light-hearted conversation between Diderot and an unnamed Marshal's wife; it is possible that it was based on an actual meeting between Diderot and Madame de Broglie that could have taken place in 1771. Certainly the Maréchale is clearly characterized in a way that would not have been the case unless Diderot had a definite person in mind. She is a charming, intellectually unsophisticated, sincere Christian, and it is her delight and curiosity in meeting Diderot which sets the tone of the conversation: 'Aren't you M. Diderot?' 'Yes, madam.' 'So it's you who doesn't believe in anything?' 'That's me.' 'Yet your morality is that of a believer?' 'Why not, if he's a decent person?' 'And you practise that morality?' 'As best I can.' 'What! You don't steal or kill or plunder?' 'Very rarely.' 'What do you gain by not believing?' 'Nothing at all, madam. Does one believe because there is something to be gained by it?'[38] So the conversation continues. Diderot shows that he is not less moral or honest than a believer, and how few Christians, if any, actually carry out the teaching of the Sermon on the Mount. He indicates the harm religion has done: 'if a misanthrope intended to make the human race unhappy what better way could he have thought up than the belief in an incomprehensible being about which men would never have been able to agree, and to which they would have attached more importance than their own lives?'[39] Worst of all, 'the natural order of moral duties [was] subordinated to an imaginary order of duties'.[40] As for the problem of the creation of the world, 'if spirit makes matter, why could matter not make a spirit?'[41] To the Maréchale's persistent doubts about the possible consequences of unbelief, in the next world as much as this, Diderot is able to say 'I have been sincere to myself and that is all that can be demanded of me.'[42]

4

Discovery

In his *Lettre sur les aveugles* Diderot had made bold speculations about the emergence of the world and the evolution of man. In his article 'Animal' in Volume One of the *Encyclopédie* (1751) he was more hesitant; he doubted whether we would ever have adequate or accurate knowledge of certain facts: 'Experiments will always fall short and systems will always go too far, experience walking step by step and the spirit of system always going in leaps and bounds' (see p. 87). The speculations of the *Lettre sur les aveugles* were not supported by any factual evidence, and that work therefore ended in scepticism. Some of the ideas in the article 'Animal' were perhaps such that no factual confirmation would ever substantiate them. How should these problems be dealt with? What was, or should be, the relation of experiment to conjecture?

It was largely to answer these questions that Diderot wrote his *Pensées sur l'interprétation de la nature*. The work first appeared, under the title *De l'interprétation de la nature*, in November 1753; only one copy of this version has come down to us. Two months later, in January 1754, a revised version was published. The title was altered and there were a number of minor changes. The work consists of fifty-eight reflections, conjectures and questions about scientific method and specific scientific problems. It is a mixture of suggestion, advocacy and speculation, sometimes methodical, sometimes enthusiastic, sometimes obscure. It moves back and forth from general statement to particular example; this makes it difficult for the reader but this is how Diderot's mind worked, as he himself indicated in his opening remarks (I). Likewise, the general statements were not limited to theoretical problems, they tackle practical issues as well: scientific work needs financial support (XXVII), discoveries must be made public (XXXIX, XL). The whole work is suffused by a restless, adventurous spirit of enquiry.

There is also a polemical edge to several *Pensées*, attacking the status and value of geometry and what Diderot calls rational philosophy, by which he means Cartesian rationalism as opposed to experimental science or philosophy. It is sometimes suggested that this polemic was aimed at D'Alembert, and that the work was intended in some way as a correction to, or qualification of, the latter's *Discours préliminaire*. While it is true that there were intellectual and temperamental differences between the two men, on neither side were these differences so pronounced at this stage as to justify the tone adopted by Diderot. Also, it must be remembered that geometry held an enduring fascination for Diderot.[1] It therefore seems more likely that the polemic arose less from a need to attack a specific opponent than from the desire to promote the general cause in hand. It was a matter of feeling less the strength of the opposition than the uncertainty of his own position; in other words, it was part of the process of self-definition. 'We are approaching the moment of a great revolution in the sciences' (IV). What was this revolution? It was not the defeat of geometry and the Cartesian rationalism associated with it; that battle had been fought earlier in the century. The superiority of Newtonian over Cartesian physics had been demonstrated decisively, and that superiority rested precisely on the confirmation which the former had received from observation of the facts. The revolution, according to Diderot, would replace geometry with 'ethics, literature, natural history and experimental science'. The last of these was already being promoted by the *Encyclopédie*; Diderot's polemic in this work could be seen as underlining that concern and associating with it a concern for 'ethics, literature and natural history'. These subjects were, of course, his own main preoccupations – a large part of his subsequent work could be subsumed under these three headings – and some of the enthusiasm which the work displays can be attributed to a sense of moving in step with the times.

Ethics and literature, it might be thought, would have no place in a treatise on scientific method. But Diderot was unable to make categorical distinctions of this kind; almost all categories were to him relative and flexible. He was incapable of separating off one subject from another, something which can be seen as either a chronic failure or as one of his most stimulating and attractive features. It is no surprise, therefore, to find ethical concern in the *Pensées*. This takes both an explicit and implicit form; explicit in the practical admonitions – for scientific discoveries to be made generally available (XXXIX, XL), or on the moral objections that adventurous minds always have to face (LV) – and implicit in the case that is made for experimental science. Diderot's emphasis on 'the knowledge of things' (XVII), his continual reiteration of the importance of facts, has a moral flavour. It is not just that facts alone determine the truth, but the process of testing ideas, of experiment, of observing facts, is one that takes the individual out of his own mind, it engages him with reality as it is. It is a process of evaluation similar to that which we conduct in the moral realm.

We touch here on the aspect of the *Pensées* that was both most personal and most original. Diderot realized that there was a mental activity involved in scientific discovery that was neither as internally consistent as rational analysis nor as shapeless and passive as the simple collecting of facts. We would call this activity intuition. Diderot did not use this word, probably because its use at this time was mainly theological;* instead he called it a *pressenti-ment*, an *esprit de divination* (XXX). It was not in any respect supernatural, as he was at pains to indicate here and in his article 'Théosophes' (see p. 122). It was an ability to sense, glimpse, or in his own vivid term 'smell out' hidden connections by pursuing 'vague ideas, slight suspicions, deceptive analogies, and even . . . the fantasies which the mind when excited easily takes for [accurate] pictures'.[2] It was 'a habit of folly (*déraison*)',[3] a 'philo-sophical delirium',[4] which occurred in a 'kind of dream'.[5] He had given one example of this activity in Saunderson's speculations, he was to give a further example in *Le Rêve de d'Alembert*.

We would call such intuition an imaginative faculty. Although at one point Diderot did write of 'conjectures formed by the imagi-nation'[6] he generally refrained from so describing it. This may have been because the imagination was still to some extent seen in the poor light cast over it by Descartes, Pascal and Malebranche. Diderot did not share their view; on the contrary, one of his notable

---

* *Intuition* had been used as a secular epistemological term by Descartes (*Règles pour la direction de l'esprit*, XII.425) and Pierre Coste in his translation of Locke's *Essay on Human Understanding* (IV.II.1), but the 1762 edition of the *Dictionnaire de l'Académie française* defined it solely as 'a theological term. It describes the clear and certain vision which the blessed have of God.' The adjective *intuitif* was similarly defined in Volume Eight of the *Encyclopédie*.

achievements was the way he reinstated the importance of the imagination and brought new insights to its working. But he was anxious to avoid any suggestion that this faculty might be either non-human, i.e. magical or supernatural, or less than rational, i.e. a matter of chance or luck. To him it was a human capacity that was operated with unconscious skill, the ability to see or sense *analogies*, 'that delicate awareness (*ce tact fin*) which we get from the sustained observation of phenomena and which makes us conscious of a secret liaison, a necessary interconnection'.[7] This description occurs in the *Essais sur la peinture*, and similar remarks occur in the *Salons*.[8] People endowed with this faculty, these kind of antennae, were 'creative genuises' (VI, XV), and they were found working in both the arts and the sciences.

An essential prerequisite for discovery, and, indeed, all experimental work, was an openness of mind. 'Experimental science knows neither what will turn up nor what will not turn up',[9] but it 'is always content with what appears'.[10] 'Chance . . . is more fruitful than shrewdness',[11] 'experiments must be allowed their freedom'.[12] Equally necessary was persistence: 'nature operates in a slow and stubborn way',[13] and we should proceed 'in a manner similar to nature'.[14] It was for Diderot the mark of a man of genius that his mind operated in direct contact with nature (see p. 270). He shared the general assumption that there was a fundamental order which could be discovered – 'chaos is an impossibility, there is an order which is essentially in keeping with the primitive qualities of matter',[15] 'the absolute independence of a single fact is incompatible with the idea of the whole; and without the idea of the whole there would be no more philosophy'.[16] He envisaged the outcome of these assumptions and precepts as a continual process of conjecture and experiment combined (IX, XVIII), always remembering that facts alone could decide the truth (VII). The method, in short, was one of 'observation of nature, reflection and experimentation' (XV). The true scientist needed 'perspective, imagination, shrewdness [and] resources'.[17]

In the course of the work Diderot made some conjectures himself about a variety of subjects – reproduction, electricity, metallurgy, dynamics and, most of all, natural history. In the summer of 1753 Maupertius, the President of the Berlin Academy of Sciences, had been in Paris. We do not know whether Diderot met him in person, but he did become acquainted with an important work by Maupertius, the *Dissertatio inauguralis metaphysica de universali* *naturae systemate*. This had been published in 1751 under the pseudonym of Baumann as if it was a dissertation for a doctorate at Erlangen University.* It was a work of major importance in the development of the theory of evolution, 'the first complete formulation of a general theory of transformism',[18] and it fired Diderot's imagination. In Maupertius' ideas about the self-organizing capacity of matter Diderot saw new possibilities for explaining the emergence of life (L, LI), and in the idea of the 'prototype' which undergoes 'successive metamorphoses' (XII) a possible account of evolution. Much is still unclear, and Diderot ends with a series of questions which have to be answered, but there is a strong feeling that answers will be found along the lines suggested by Maupertius, and by the method advocated by Diderot.

Maupertius' ideas occupy such an important place in the work that they may well have been the main reason Diderot wrote it. The general attitude of the work, however, and the actual title, derive from Francis Bacon; many of the *Pensées* express views about method and research that had previously been formulated by Bacon. In this respect the work was an extension of that intellectual debt which Diderot had already acknowledged in his *Prospectus* and his article 'Art'. While he made use of Bacon, he was not always in agreement with him. His stress on the need for people with exceptional gifts of intuition was quite different to Bacon's conception of scientific advance coming about through the general collection of facts.

Diderot prefaced the work with some remarks 'to young people who are interested in the study of natural philosophy'. He indicated that his intention was less 'to instruct than to exercise [the mind]'; the *Pensées* should be regarded more as speculations than as conclusions. And he added a warning, to avoid confusion: 'Always bear in mind that nature is not God; that man is not a machine; and that a hypothesis is not a fact.'[19]

---

* The work appeared in French in 1754 under the title *Essai sur la formation des corps organisés*, and then under the title *Système de la nature* in the 1756 edition of Maupertius' *Oeuvres*.

Pensées sur l'interprétation de la nature

I

It is about nature that I am going to write. As I do so I will let the ideas take their own course in the very order that the subjects offer themselves to my reflection; because that way they will represent more closely the movement and workings of my mind. They will be either general views about experimental science or particular views about a phenomenon which seems to concern all our *philosophes* and divides them into two kinds. It seems to me that some have many instruments and few ideas; others have plenty of ideas and no instruments. The interests of truth require . . . that all our efforts should be brought together at the same time and directed against the resistance of nature, and that in this kind of philosophical brotherhood everyone should do what suits him.

II

One of the truths that has been proclaimed in our time with the greatest courage and force, a truth that no good physicist will ever lose sight of, and one that will certainly have the most beneficial results, is that what are taken to be rigorous truths in the purely intellectual sphere of mathematics lose that advantage absolutely when brought down to the world in which we live. It has been concluded from this fact that it is the task of experimental science to rectify the calculations of geometry, and this conclusion has been accepted even by the geometricians. But what good does it do to correct geometrical calculations with experiments? Is it not simpler to content ourselves with the results of the latter? . . .

III

. . . One day someone asked: what is a metaphysician? A geometrician replied: it is a man who knows nothing. Chemists, physicists, naturalists and all those devoted to experimental science, no less bold in their judgements, seem to me to be on the point of avenging metaphysics and of making the same comment about geometry . . . .

IV

We are approaching the moment of a great revolution in the sciences. Judging from the inclination that minds seem to have for ethics, literature, natural history and experimental science, I would almost dare to predict with certainty that in another hundred years there will not be three great geometricians left in the whole of Europe. Geometry will have stopped short at the point where men such as Bernoulli, Euler, Maupertius, Clairaut, Fontaine and D'Alembert left it. They will have erected the Pillars of Hercules. No one will go beyond . . .

VI

When we compare the infinite multiplicity of natural phenomena with the limitations of our understanding and the weakness of our organs and when we consider how slowly our work progresses, forever hampered by long and frequent interruptions and by the scarcity of creative geniuses, can we ever expect anything from it but a few broken and isolated fragments of the great chain that links all things together? . . .

Then what is our goal? The execution of a work that can never be completed and that would be far beyond the comprehension of human intelligence if it ever were completed. Are we not madder than those first inhabitants of the plain of Sennar?* We know that the distance separating the earth from the sky is infinite, and yet we do not stop building our tower. But is it to be presumed that a time will never come when our disheartened pride will abandon the operations? . . . Will men not be stopped by the confusion of languages, already acute and very awkward in natural history? Besides, utility sets bounds to everything. It is utility that in a few more centuries will call a halt to experimental science, just as it is on the point of doing with geometry. I grant the former study a few more centuries because its sphere of usefulness is infinitely greater in extent than that of any abstract science and because it is, beyond dispute, the basis of our genuine knowledge.

VII

As long as things are in our understanding only, they are our opinions, they are notions, which may be true or false, agreed with

---

* Builders of the tower of Babel.

or contradicted. They can acquire solidity only by being linked to external objects. This can be accomplished either by an uninterrupted chain of experiments, or by an uninterrupted chain of reasoning that is supported at one end by observation and at the other by experiment, or by a chain of experiments with gaps between them that are bridged by abstract reasoning, like a series of weights strung out along a thread that is supported at both ends. Without these weights, the thread would become a plaything for even the slightest motion of the air.

IX

Men have scarcely begun to be aware as yet how rigorous the rules are for the investigation of truth or how limited are the means at our disposal. Everything is reduced to going back from the senses to reflection, then from reflection back to the senses: a ceaseless going into ourselves and coming out of ourselves. It is the work of the bee. An area has been covered completely in vain if the bee does not return to the hive loaded with wax. A lot of wax will have been made in vain if it is not known how to make honeycombs.

X

Unfortunately, however, it is easier and quicker to consult oneself than to consult nature. Also, reason is inclined to stay within itself, and instinct to spread itself outside. Instinct constantly goes looking, tasting, touching, listening; and perhaps more could be learnt about experimental science from studying animals than from following a course of lectures by a professor. There is no nonsense about the way they proceed. They aim at their goal without bothering about what surrounds them; if they surprise us it is not because they mean to do so. Astonishment is the first effect of some great phenomenon; it is up to philosophy to dissipate it . . .

XII

Nature seems to take pleasure in varying a single mechanism in an infinite variety of ways. She never abandons any one kind of production until she has multiplied the individual examples to produce as many different aspects as possible. If we consider the animal kingdom and perceive that there is not a single quadruped whose functions and parts, above all the internal ones, are not entirely similar to those of another quadruped, would it not be easy to believe that in the beginning there was only one animal, a prototype of all animals, certain of whose organs nature has merely lengthened, shortened, transformed, multiplied or obliterated? Imagine the fingers of your hand joined together and the material of which the nails are made suddenly becoming so abundant that they spread and swell, enveloping and covering the whole extremity: instead of a hand you have a horse's hoof. When we see the successive metamorphoses of the prototype's outward form, whatever it may have been in the first place, bring one kingdom gradually and imperceptibly nearer to another kingdom and people the boundaries of those two kingdoms (if one may use the term 'boundaries' where there is no real division), and people, I repeat, the boundaries of those two kingdoms with uncertain, ambiguous beings, stripped to a great degree of the forms, the qualities and the functions of the one, and taking on the forms, qualities and functions of the other, is it not difficult to resist the belief that there was never more than one first being, a prototype of all other beings? But whether we accept this philosophical conjecture, as Dr Baumann [Maupertius] does, or reject it as false, as M. de Buffon does, we cannot deny that it must be accepted as a hypothesis essential to the progress of experimental science, to the progress of rational philosophy, and to the discovery and explanation of phenomena which depend on physical constitution. For we can clearly see that nature has been unable to maintain so great a similarity between the parts, while producing so great a variety of different forms, without often making perceptible in one animal's structure what she has contrived to conceal in another's. She is a woman who likes to disguise herself and whose different disguises, revealing now one part of her, now another, permit those who follow her assiduously to hope that one day they will know the whole of her person.

XV

There are three principal means of acquiring knowledge available to us: observation of nature, reflection and experimentation. Observation collects facts; reflection combines them; experimentation verifies the result of that combination. Our observation of nature must be diligent, our reflection profound and our experiments exact. We rarely see these three means combined; and for this reason, creative geniuses are not common.

XVII

Is there a shortage of men of genius in the universe? Not at all. Have such men failed to think and study? Even less . . . Why then do we have so little knowledge that is certain? . . . I have already given a reply to these questions. The abstract sciences have preoccupied the best minds too long and with too little result; either what should be studied has not been studied, or the studies have not been selective and have lacked perspective and method. Words have been endlessly proliferated, and the knowledge of things has remained backward.

XVIII

The true way to conduct philosophy would have been and would be to apply understanding to understanding; understanding and experiment to the senses; the senses to nature; nature to the investigation of instruments; instruments to the research and perfection of the skills, which would be shown to the people to make them learn to respect philosophy.

XIX

There is only one way to make philosophy truly desirable in the eyes of the people: to present it to them as something that is useful. The common man always asks, 'What's it good for?' and we must never find ourselves in the position of having to reply, 'Nothing.' He does not know that what enlightens the philosopher and what is useful to the mass of people are two very different things, since the philosopher's understanding is often enlightened by that which is harmful and obscured by that which is useful.

XX

Facts, of whatever kind they may be, are the true wealth of the philosopher . . .

XXII

Understanding has its prejudices; the senses, their uncertainty; memory, its limits; imagination, its dim light; instruments, their imperfection. The phenomena of nature are infinite; their causes are hidden; their forms perhaps transitory. In the face of so many obstacles, either within us or which nature sets up outside us, we have only gradual experiment, limited reflection. These are the levers with which philosophy undertakes to move the world.

XXX

The habitual practice of making experiments produces even in the most unrefined of workers involved with physical processes an intuition (*pressentiment*) that is akin to inspiration. It depends on the individual whether or not he makes the same mistake as Socrates and calls it a 'familiar daemon'. Socrates had such a remarkable habit of observing mankind and evaluating circumstances that even when confronted with the most intricate problems, an immediate and accurate series of combinations took place secretly inside him, followed by a prognostication that was scarcely ever belied by the event. He judged men as people of taste judge works of art: by feeling. The same is true of the instinct shown by our great investigators in the field of experimental science. They have watched the operations of nature so often and so closely that they are able to guess what course she is likely to take, and that with a fair degree of accuracy, even when they take it into their heads to provoke her with the most outlandish experiments. So that the most important service they can render to those they are initiating into experimental philosophy is not so much to teach them about procedures and results as to pass on to them that spirit of divination by means of which it is possible to *smell out* (*subodore*), so to speak, methods that are still to be discovered, new experiments, unknown results.

XXXI

How is this spirit communicated? The person who possesses it must go down into himself to see exactly what it is, to replace the idea of a familiar daemon with clear and intelligible notions, and explain these to others. If, for example, he finds that it is *an ability to imagine or perceive opposition or analogies, which derives from a practical knowledge of the physical qualities of creatures taken individually, or their reciprocal effects when taken together*, he will develop this idea. He will support it by a host of facts which his memory will provide; it would be a faithful account of all the apparently extravagant ideas which have passed through his head. I say *extravagant* for what other name can be given to that interconnection of conjectures which are based on contrasts or resemblances so remote, so imperceptible, that the dream of a sick man would not seem either more bizarre or more disjointed? . . .

[The next seven *Pensées* are a series of conjectures about specific problems: reproduction, electricity, dynamics, metallurgy.]

XL

It is not enough to reveal [i.e. make public]; it is even more necessary that the revelation is clear and complete. There is a kind of obscurity which could be termed the *affectation of great masters*. It is a veil which they like to draw between the people and nature . . . Let us hasten to make philosophy popular . . .

XLII

Once we have formed in our heads a line of thought that requires to be checked by experiments, we should neither persist in it stubbornly nor abandon it lightly. Sometimes we think our conjectures are false when we have not taken the correct measures to find them true. Indeed, stubbornness in such a case is less improper than the opposite excess. By dint of multiplying the number of our experiments, we may not find what we are looking for, but we may also find something better. Time spent investigating nature can never be entirely wasted. The extent of our persistence should be determined by the degree of probability. Completely outlandish ideas deserve only one trial. Those that seem a little more likely should be given rather more, and those that hold promise of an important discovery should be abandoned only when we have tried everything . . .

XLIV

Experiments should always be repeated, first in order to avoid uncertainty in matters of detail, second in order to establish their exact scope. They must be applied to different objects, permutated and combined in every possible way. While experiments still remain scattered, isolated, unconnected and irreducible to any other terms, then it is demonstrable, by means of that very irreducibility, that there are further experiments still to be made. In that case, we must attach ourselves solely to our object and torment it, so to speak, until the phenomena have been so linked that once one of them is given, all the others follow: we must work first at the reduction of effects; there will be time later to think about the reduction of causes . . . Any experiment that does not extend a law to a new case or that does not restrict it by some exception is meaningless. The shortest way of finding out the value of an experiment is to posit it as the premiss of an enthymeme* and to examine the consequent. Does it tell us nothing that has not already been proven by another experiment? Then we have discovered nothing; at the most, we have simply confirmed a discovery already made . . .

XLV

Just as, in mathematics, all the properties of a curve turn out upon examination to be all the same property, but seen from different aspects, so in nature, when experimental science is more advanced, we shall come to see that all phenomena, whether of weight, elasticity, attraction, magnetism or electricity, are all merely aspects of a single state. But how many intermediary phenomena still remain to be discovered, between the known phenomena already attributed to one of these causes, before we can form the links, fill in the lacunae, and so produce proof of this identity? That is what we are unable to determine. . .

XLVIII

When we are on the wrong road, the faster we walk, the more lost we become. And when the distance we have already covered is immense, how are we to retrace our steps? Exhaustion renders it impossible; vanity, without our conscious knowledge, is opposed to it; and an obstinate attachment to principles casts a spell on all the things around us that distorts them. We no longer see them as they are, but as we think they ought to be. At this point we find people who, instead of reshaping their ideas to conform with reality, seem to take it upon themselves to remodel reality in accordance with their notions. Among all the different kinds of philosophers, there is none more evidently dominated by this sort of madness than the classifier of natural history. As soon as one of these classifiers has placed man in his system at the head of the quadrupeds, he becomes unable to view him as a natural phenomenon other than as an animal with four feet. In vain does man's

---

* An enthymeme is, in logic, a syllogism in which one premiss is unexpressed. *Cogito ergo sum* is an enthymeme.

sublime gift of reason cry out against the label 'animal' or his physical structure contradict that of 'quadruped'; in vain has nature raised his eyes toward the heavens: this insistence on a category bends his body down again to earth. Reason itself, according to this argument, is only a more perfect kind of instinct; and its adherents seriously believe that it is only because he has lost the habit of walking on all fours that man is unable to use his legs properly when he decides to change his hands into two feet.

[Diderot then gives an example of this erroneous attitude in the work of Linnaeus.]

I.

In order to shake a hypothesis, it is sometimes not necessary to do anything more than push it as far as it will go. We are now going to try out this method on the hypothesis put forward by the Doctor of Erlangen [Maupertius], whose work, filled with singular and new ideas, is going to put our philosophers through a great deal of agony. The object of his study is the highest that the human mind can propose to itself: the universal system of nature. The author begins by giving a brief account of the opinions put forward by his predecessors and of the inadequacy of their principles to provide a general explanation of phenomena. Some had included only extension and motion. Others had thought it necessary to add impenetrability to extension and inertia to mobility. Observation of celestial bodies, or, more generally, the physics of large bodies, had proved the need to include also a force causing all parts of the universe to tend or weigh toward one another, in accordance with a specific law; whereupon attraction was admitted, acting in simple ratio to the given masses and in inverse ratio to the square of the distance between them. The simplest chemical experiments and the elementary physics of small bodies then forced other philosophers to have recourse to other attractions following other laws; and the impossibility of explaining the formation of a plant or an animal by means of these various attractions, inertia, mobility, impenetrability, motion, matter or extension has now led the philosopher Baumann [Maupertius] to postulate still other properties in nature. Dissatisfied with those plastic natures which have been put forward as the agents of all the marvels of nature, even though they lack both matter and intelligence; dissatisfied too with subordinate intelligent substances acting upon matter in an unintelligible way, and with the simultaneity of the creation and the formation of substances, which, since they are all contained the one within the other, develop in time through the continuation of an original miracle, and also with the extemporaneity of their production, which is nothing but a chain of miracles repeated at every instant of existence,* it then occurred to him that none of these rather unphilosophical systems would ever have been developed were it not for our unfounded fear of attributing extremely well-known modifications to a being whose essence, since it is unknown to us, may for this very reason, and despite our preconceptions, be perfectly capable of such modifications. But what is this being? And what are those modifications? Shall I say? Of course, Dr Baumann answers. The material universe is this being; the modifications are *desire, aversion, memory* and *intelligence* – in a word, all those qualities that we recognize in animals, that were included by the Ancients in the term *sensitive soul,* and that Dr Baumann accepts as being present, in due proportion to their forms and masses, in the smallest amount of matter as well as in the very largest animal. If there were any danger, he says, in allowing some degree of intelligence to material molecules, that danger would be no less if we allowed it to an elephant or to a monkey than if we allowed it to a grain of sand. Here the philosopher of the Academy of Erlangen uses every means at his disposal to avoid any suspicion of atheism; and it is evident that he supports his hypothesis, with some heat, only because it seems to him to embrace even the most recalcitrant phenomena without leading to materialism. His work should be read as an example of how to reconcile the boldest of philosophical ideas with the most profound respect for religion. God created the world, Dr Baumann says, and it is our task to discover, if possible, the laws according to which he willed it to continue in existence and the means he laid down for the reproduction of individuals. We are free to explore as we wish in this direction, and these are the doctor's principal ideas on the subject:

The seminal element, having been drawn from a part of the body similar to that which it must later form in the animal and also possessing powers of feeling and thought, will retain some memory

* These were all explanations for the existence of living creatures put forward in the previous hundred years which assumed that matter was inert and that life arose by some form of spiritual intervention. Maupertius himself believed that the world was created by God but that matter was not inert.

of its place of origin: hence the preservation of species and the resemblance of related creatures.

It may happen that the seminal fluid has either an excess or a deficiency of certain elements, that these elements are unable to combine from some deficiency of memory, or that extraordinary combinations of supernumerary elements may take place. This would explain both sterility and all the possible kinds of monstrous birth.

Certain elements will inevitably have acquired a prodigious facility for combining ceaselessly in exactly the same way. This will result, if the elements are dissimilar, in the formation of an infinite variety of microscopic animals or, if they are identical, in the formation of polyps, which may be compared to a swarm of infinitely small bees that have retained an active memory of only a single place of origin and therefore remain together, clinging to the situation that is most familiar to them. . .

What is to prevent elementary, intelligent parts that are capable of sensation from producing endless variations in the pattern that constitutes the species? [Nothing:] hence the infinite number of animal species that have sprung from the first animal, the infinite number of beings that have emanated from the first being. There was only a single act on the part of nature.

But will each element, as it continues to accumulate and combine, gradually lose the tiny degree of feeling and perception it possesses? Not at all, according to Dr Baumann. Those qualities are inherent in it. What will happen then? This: from the perceptions of all these elements, when they have been grouped together and combined, there will result a single power of perception, one proportionate to the resulting mass and its arrangement. This system of perception, in which each element will have lost all recollection of its self and will contribute to forming the awareness of the whole, will be the animal's soul. [Diderot then quotes, in Latin, Maupertius' statement to this effect. He continues:]

It is at this point that we are surprised to find either that the author did not realize the terrible consequences of his hypothesis or, if he had realized them, that he did not abandon it. It is here that we must begin to apply our method and examine his principles. I shall ask him, therefore, whether the universe, or the sum total of all molecules endowed with powers of thought and feeling, forms a whole or whether it does not. If he replies that it does not form a whole, then with a single word he is threatening the existence of

God by introducing disorder into nature; and he will also be destroying the basis of all philosophy by breaking the chain that links all phenomena together. If he agrees that it does form a whole, one in which the elements are no less ordered than the subdivisions (whether they be distinct in fact or only conceivably so) within an element or the elements within an animal, he will have to admit, as a necessary consequence of this universal copulation, that the world, like a vast animal, has a soul. He will also have to admit, since the world may be infinite, that this soul it possesses, I do not say is, but may be an infinite system of perceptions, and that the world may be God.

Let him protest as much as he wishes against these consequences, they will be none the less true; and no matter what light his sublime ideas may cast into the deeps of nature, those ideas will be none the less frightening. It was necessary only to generalize them in order to become aware of that. The act of generalization is to the metaphysician's hypotheses what the repetition of observations and experiments is to the experimental scientist's conjectures. Are the conjectures valid? Then the more experiments one makes, the more their validity is confirmed. Are the hypotheses true? Then the further one extends their consequences, the more truths they will embrace and the more certainty and force they will acquire. On the other hand, if the conjectures and hypotheses are fragile and ill founded, one will either discover a fact or run up against an opposing truth, upon which they will founder. Dr Baumann's hypothesis will explain, if you wish, the most unfathomable of nature's mysteries, the formation of animals or, more generally, that of all organized bodies; but the universal bond that links all phenomena and the existence of God will be the reefs on which it must be wrecked. But though we reject the ideas of the Doctor of Erlangen, we should have formed but a poor conception of how obscure were the phenomena he undertook to explain, of the richness of his hypothesis, of the surprising consequences that may be deduced from them, of the merit of new conjectures on a subject that has occupied the greatest men of all ages, and of how difficult it is to combat his conjectures with any success, if we failed to recognize them as the fruit of a profound meditation, a daring attempt to explain the universal organization of nature, and the undertaking of a great philosopher.

LI

On the Impulse of a Sensation

If Dr Baumann had restricted his system within just limits and had applied his ideas to the formation of animals only, without extending them to the nature of the soul (for I think I have proved it against him that if they can be carried that far, they can also be extended to the existence of God), he would not have rushed headlong into the most seductive kind of materialism by attributing desire, aversion, feeling and thought to organic molecules. He ought to have been satisfied with supposing in them a degree of *sensibilité* a thousand times less than that which the Almighty has granted to those animals closest to non-living matter. As a result of this muted *sensibilité* and of the varying configurations of all organic molecules, it would then be clear that there could be only one situation in nature for which each of them was properly fitted. Each molecule would therefore have been impelled, by an automatic and constant feeling of anxiety, to seek out the situation proper to it, just as we see animals move about in their sleep, when the use of almost all their faculties is in abeyance, until they have found the position most suited for repose. The use of this principle, with no further help, would have embraced, quite simply and without any dangerous implications, all the phenomena he was undertaking to explain, as well as all those numberless marvels that keep our observers of insects in such a perpetual state of amazement; and it would have provided him with the following general definition of an animal: a system of different organic molecules that have combined with one another, under the impulse of a sensation similar to an obtuse and muffled sense of touch given to them by the creator of matter as a whole, until each one of them has found the most suitable position for its shape and comfort.

[In the remaining paragraphs Diderot indicates how little is known about the nature of matter.]

5

Encyclopaedia

Diderot's success in translating from English first Temple Stanyan's *History of Greece*, then Shaftesbury's *Inquiry concerning Virtue or Merit*, led to his being involved in two much larger projects, the translation of Robert James's *Medical Dictionary*, undertaken with two collaborators and published in six folio volumes between 1746 and 1748, and then the projected translation of Ephraim Chambers's *Cyclopaedia*. Chambers's work had first appeared in two folio volumes in 1728; it had met with considerable success and three further editions were published, the fourth appearing in 1741. The idea of translating this into French was put to the Paris printer and publisher Le Breton in 1745 and he obtained the necessary official permission, the *privilège*, to do this. His initial plan did not materialize, however, and the following year he obtained another *privilège* to publish the work in conjunction with three other publishers, under the editorship of a brilliant but eccentric mathematician, Gua de Malves. In 1746 Diderot began to receive some payments for work as a translator; then, in 1747, Gua de Malves's contract was terminated and Diderot and D'Alembert were put under contract as editors. From the outset Diderot was the dominant partner in the collaboration, being paid more than twice the amount D'Alembert received.

It seems probable that Le Breton always intended something more than a straight translation of Chambers, since his original *privilège* was for five volumes of text and one of plates, but in Diderot's hands the project grew with the amazing and alarming speed of a fairy-tale forest. The *Prospectus* in 1750 invited subscriptions for ten volumes of text and two of plates, then Volume One took over 900 double-column folio pages to deal with the letter A alone, which suggested that more than twenty volumes would be needed. In the event there was a total of seventeen volumes of text, amounting to about twenty million words, and eleven volumes of plates. Despite this awesome and forbidding size the *Encyclopédie* was a notable commercial success for the publishers. A thousand subscriptions were taken up before Volume One was published; a year later, after the publication of Volume Two, this number had doubled. Two years later, in 1754, it had doubled again, so that over 4000 copies of each volume were printed. Unfortunately no list of the subscribers has survived (or has yet been discovered); it has been suggested that as many as half, or more, may have been outside France. However that may be, the fact that the enterprise was so successful commercially was important in ensuring that publication continued. There was money and employment at stake, as well as ideas, and the government looked as favourably on the former as it did equivocally on the latter.

Opposition to the work soon became evident, from three different sources: the Paris Parlement, the Church and the royal government. After Volume Two appeared a decree by the royal *Conseil* forbade further publication, and the Church made its antagonism plain when the Faculty of Theology at the Sorbonne condemned a thesis by the Abbé de Prades. The latter was a contributor to the *Encyclopédie* and his thesis had drawn heavily on D'Alembert's *Discours préliminaire*, with ideas about natural religion, the empirical basis of knowledge, the natural equality of men and so forth. The thesis was violently attacked by the Bishop of Auxerre, who reaffirmed the doctrines of original sin, the fall and the need for grace, as well as the need for subordination in society and obedience to the monarchy. Diderot came to the Abbé's defence and wrote a section of his *Apologie*. This controversy over the Abbé's thesis revealed the major points at issue between the Church and the *Encyclopédie*.

These issues were fairly clear because one subject on which most of the contributors were agreed was their hostility to the Church, to its intolerance, privilege and obscurantism. As far as the government was concerned the matter was more complex. A number of contributors were in government service, the official censor, Malesherbes, was in sympathy with the work, and at the court itself there were people in favour, among them Madame de Pompadour. Diderot wrote to her asking for her support – 'the building is taking shape and all Europe admires it'.[1] While his article 'Autorité politique' may have been outspoken in places, it had ended with an unequivocal statement that subjects should obey their legitimate king, who was Louis XV; and to the crucial question of why his rule should be legitimate Diderot stated that that depended not on actions he performed or failed to perform but on his right as legitimate heir in the direct line from Hugh Capet. (This point was reaffirmed at the start of Volume Three.)[2] Generally speaking the *Encyclopédie* did not put forward either original or radical political ideas; an article like Rousseau's 'Economie politique' in Volume Five (1755) was an exception.

In 1753 the ban on publication was lifted and Volume Three appeared. The controversy surrounding the work had increased interest and further copies of the first two volumes were printed to meet the demand. The next four volumes came out over the following four years; D'Alembert was elected to the Académie française and Diderot's article 'Encyclopédie' in Volume Five 'won the admiration of everyone in Paris'.[3] Criticism continued but success seemed more certain. Criticism in fact served a useful purpose because in making extracts from the work and highlighting particular articles it made the material more widely available. However, the publication of Volume Seven in 1757 precipitated a new crisis.

The crisis initially arose over D'Alembert's article on Geneva which suggested that the Genevans took such an enlightened view of Christianity that they scarcely believed in Christ's divinity, a suggestion to which the Genevan Church reacted with outrage and fury. But this issue was only the prelude to a more serious storm. Two events, in 1757 and 1758, gave a new impetus to the *Encyclopédie*'s critics: the attempted assassination of Louis XV by Damiens and the publication of Helvétius' *De l'esprit*. Helvétius' book cast a cold (and rather dull) analytical eye over human nature, society and education. Its premises were materialist and its implications were what would now be called behaviourist; it reduced all actions to self-interest and all human characteristics to the result of education. It epitomized all that the opponents of the *Encyclopédie* most feared. The fact that Helvétius was not associated with the work was irrelevant. Likewise the fact that Damiens had no connection with any of the *philosophes*; his action proved what the critics had said – such ideas were subversive. The work was denounced by the Paris Parlement, D'Alembert resigned as co-editor, and in March 1759 the official *privilège* was revoked. In other words, further publication was forbidden.

Diderot's commitment to the project did not waver. In the difficult weeks of 1758 he wondered whether the enterprise justified the enormous effort needed,[4] but he dismissed Voltaire's suggestion that publication should be continued outside France. He had the support of the publishers and Malesherbes also wanted to see the work completed. The result of his commitment, the publishers' persistence, and discreet official goodwill, was that unofficial permission, *permission tacite*, was granted for the remaining volumes. Three months after the *privilège* was revoked Diderot was hard at work – 'I am encyclopaedizing like a galley-slave'[5] – and this continued for another six years. A final crisis occurred when he discovered that Le Breton had censored some articles in the last ten volumes, but while his immediate reaction was one of acute bitterness[6] it seems that the deletions were not that drastic. In his Preface to Volume Eight he asked his colleagues to bear in mind that 'the materials for these last volumes have been assembled in haste and set out in difficulty'.[7] By the end of 1765 the volumes had all been printed, without Diderot's name on the title page and with a false attribution to a printer in Neuchâtel. They were not allowed to be distributed in Paris but had to be collected, by the subscribers, from a warehouse outside the city. Publication of the plates had been given official permission; the first of these appeared in 1762 and the eleventh and final volume in 1772.

Diderot was conscious of the extent to which the work fell short of its high ambitions: 'When I look at our work impartially I see that there is perhaps not a fault of any kind which we have not committed and I am forced to admit that barely two-thirds of a true encyclopaedia can be glimpsed in this *Encyclopédie*.'[8] This was written in 1755, before adverse circumstances had taken their effect. Nevertheless, it was an astonishing achievement and was recognized as such. Within fifteen years of the completion of the volumes of text there were three folio reprints, in Geneva, Lucca and Leghorn, a quarto edition in thirty-six volumes (which was then reprinted twice), and an octavo edition in thirty-six double volumes (later reprinted once), as well as a five-volume selection of articles, *Esprit de l'Encyclopédie*, printed in Paris in 1768, and four additional volumes of new articles, the *Supplément*, printed in Paris in 1776–7. Without doubt the *Encyclopédie* was one of the major intellectual events of the century.

Its success can be attributed to many factors. There had been a number of ambitious dictionaries printed in the previous half-century. Diderot's *Prospectus* referred to Thomas Dyche's *New General English Dictionary* (1737) and John Harris's *Universal English Dictionary of Arts and Sciences* (1704–10), as well as Chambers's *Cyclopaedia*. There had been Savary-Desbrulons' *Dictionnaire universel de commerce* (1723–30), Bourreau-Deslandes' *Histoire critique de la philosophie* (1737), Zedler's sixty-four volume *Universal-Lexicon* (1732–50). But no previous publication had brought together as the *Encyclopédie* did such a wide range of subjects, in particular the combination of philosophical ideas and technical information. It was as though the critical examination of ideas carried out by Pierre Bayle in his *Dictionnaire historique et critique* (1697) was combined with Fontenelle's fluent exposition of scientific matters, with the customary concern of dictionaries to define words,* and with a new emphasis on technical achievements. The *Encyclopédie* was inspired by a clear sense of purpose, ideas mattered as technical advances mattered, and despite the bewildering variety and unevenness of the articles that sense of purpose was clear, forceful and explicit.

This sense of purpose was all the stronger for being shared; the work was essentially a collective enterprise. It was written, proclaimed the title page, by a 'society of men of letters'. A hundred and thirty of them were named, some well known, like Montesquieu and Voltaire (though their contribution was very slight), some becoming well known, like Rousseau, Turgot and Holbach, many about whom we know little, and some about whom we know nothing. They included doctors, lawyers, scientists, government servants, ecclesiastics (for the first two volumes), *littérateurs*, skilled craftsmen and friends of the editors, almost all of them unpaid. One friend of Diderot, the Chevalier de Jaucourt, threw himself so wholeheartedly into the work that his eventual contribution amounted to over 17,000 articles, more than a quarter of the entire text; he had to sell a house to pay his secretaries and he sold it, ironically, to Le Breton, who was growing as rich on his profits as the Chevalier was growing hollow-eyed from his labours.

---

* Was Diderot's dedication *A Posterité* (see p. 85) a self-conscious reference to, and redefinition of, the dedication that always headed the dictionaries of the Académie française, *A L'Immortalité*?

The 'society of men of letters' was to some extent like a model for human society as a whole – open, tolerant and free. 'Everyone has his individual way of thinking and writing,' wrote Diderot in his article 'Éditeur', 'and he should not be asked to sacrifice that in an association which he has entered into on the tacit understanding that he would retain all his freedom.'[9] By the same principle the editors did not object to criticism.* 'We believe,' wrote D'Alembert in his Preface to Volume Three, 'that the democracy of the republic of letters should extend to all, even to the extent of allowing and putting up with the worst criticism, providing there is nothing personal about it. It is enough that this freedom should produce some good criticism.'[10]

'It is principally by the *esprit philosophique*,' wrote D'Alembert in the same Preface, 'that we will endeavour to make this dictionary distinct.'[11] By *esprit philosophique* – the characteristic feature, according to Voltaire, of a man of letters[12] – D'Alembert meant an enquiring, critical and rational frame of mind. Men should not rely on authority or tradition but use their own minds, and theories should be subjected to the evidence of facts. Freedom of thought and toleration were essential for human advance. The Church was the target of many articles not necessarily for its doctrines, some of the contributors were Christians and many were deists, but for the way it taught and defended these doctrines. Since education was largely in the Church's hands its influence was widespread and powerful.

The *Encyclopédie* was equally concerned with economic freedom. Different articles attacked the malign influence of guild monopolies and government intervention, suggestions were made for more equitable and efficient taxes, and new economic ideas were put forward – notably in articles by Turgot and Quesnay, in favour of free trade, especially of grain, and articles on commerce by Véron de Forbonnais, promoting competition and free trade generally. The contributors to these articles, and the *Encyclopédie* as a whole, were so diverse, they came from such a wide range of backgrounds, that these ideas cannot be ascribed to any single class interest. But the contributors did share a general sense of hostility to the many forms of privilege, restriction and prejudice which were stifling the economic life of France.

---

* That was the principle. In fact there were attempts to silence some of their opponents.

There was less emphasis on politics. Different articles drew on Montesquieu and the natural law philosophers, and significant ideas were advanced by Diderot, Holbach and Rousseau, but generally speaking they occupied only a minor place in the work. To some degree this was obviously a reflection of the conditions of publication, but it also stemmed from a certain non-political outlook. There was more concern with ideas than with institutions, more desire to change attitudes in the belief that reforms would then follow naturally. A strong humanitarian strain runs through the work, particularly evident in articles on poverty, slavery and the judicial use of torture, but it generally remained a moral matter and did not assume a political dimension.

In this respect, as in most others, the work reflected Diderot's own position. Diderot's personal contribution to the *Encyclopédie* was immense, yet difficult to assess exactly. We know very few precise details about his work as editor and there are many articles which may have been written by him but which cannot be attributed to him with certainty. At the outset the range of his articles was enormous. In Volume One, for example, he wrote or contributed to over 2000 articles, from midwifery and the manufacture of steel, to the use of asparagus in cooking, the superstitious belief that a tree could produce wool, and an article on agriculture which gave a brief summary of attitudes to the subject in the past, a survey of agricultural activities through the year, and an account of Jethro Tull's new method of raising crops. Like many other contributors he drew heavily on other sources – a frequent criticism of the work was its plagiarism – and the quality of his articles was uneven, another reason for criticism. But they were rarely routine; as a rule they conveyed a sense both of pleasure and purpose in conveying information.

There were four areas Diderot was particularly concerned with. 'He is the author,' wrote D'Alembert in his *Discours préliminaire*, 'of the most extensive and important part of this *Encyclopédie*, the part most desired by the public and, I would dare to say, the most difficult to carry out: the description of the [mechanical] arts.'[13] As Diderot explained in his *Prospectus* and his article 'Art', one of the main intentions of the work was to raise the status of, and general interest in, technical achievements. He did not carry out the research for these articles but he did take great pains gathering and checking the information and presenting it with clarity; likewise the volumes of plates which showed in fine detail the operations of innumerable skills and techniques.* There was no suggestion in these articles of the economic transformation that would occur in the next hundred years but there was a definite sense of the importance of these activities to human prosperity and well-being.

Another special area of interest to Diderot was the definition of words. He was concerned with making clear both technical terms, eradicating unnecessary obscurities or jargon, and words in general usage. As far as the latter were concerned he drew heavily on the *Synonymes françaises* by the Abbé Girard, 'a little masterpiece of originality, *finesse*, good taste and morality'.[15] Those who contributed to the *Encyclopédie* should make a rule of 'defining everything, without exception'.[16] The operation and use of language was a constant preoccupation for him and in this respect, as in many others, he was the ideal editor for a work of this kind.

After the difficulties of 1752 the contributors who had undertaken the articles on the history of philosophy, the Abbés de Prades and Yvon, left the project and Diderot took over these articles. He derived most of his material from the five-volume *Historia critica philosophiae* by the Lutheran pastor Jacob Brucker, published in Leipzig between 1742 and 1744. Brucker's work was wide-ranging and well informed; it was also an important work in the writing of the history of philosophy since it excluded religion as a philosophical subject. In the later volumes Diderot paid as much attention to these articles as he did to the technical articles in the early volumes, and his borrowings from, and adaptation of, Brucker were spiced with many personal reflections. The articles were significant not only for the information they contained but also for demonstrating the importance the *Encyclopédie* gave to history as such. There were few articles about specifically historical subjects, and very few biographies, but there was a general desire to provide perspective and background, to show how things were and have been.

The final main area that concerned Diderot was the general theory and approach of the work as a whole. In his *Prospectus* (most of which was incorporated by D'Alembert in the last section of his *Discours préliminaire*) and in his articles 'Art' and 'Encyclopédie' he set out the general principles of the work; in

* Since much of the detail of these articles is now remote none of them has been included in the extracts below. Those interested in the history of technology should consult the recent two-volume selection of plates, which shows vividly what was aimed at and achieved.[14]

many small articles and additions to other people's articles, as well as in his overall editorial activity, he demonstrated those principles. Foremost among them was the idea of *enchaînement*, by which was meant the interconnection and concatenation of the different subjects; all were interconnected in one way or another. The full title of the work was *Encyclopédie ou dictionnaire raisonné des sciences, des arts, et des métiers par une société de gens de lettres.* The dictionary was *raisonné*, that is to say, systematic or analytical, both in its treatment of individual subjects and in its bringing them all together in a single work. Cross-references between articles provided some interconnections, their inclusion in the overall structure provided others. In this way the work was an image of the world, an image that both represented the world and made sense of it, like a Renaissance memory-theatre. But unlike a memory-theatre it was open, accessible, public. 'In time this work will certainly bring about a revolution in men's minds,' wrote Diderot, half-way through the enterprise; 'we shall have served humanity.'[17] There were many respects in which the *Encyclopédie* failed to realize its high ambition – the attention given to various subjects was erratic, the quality of the articles was uneven, the editorial principles were carried out inconsistently – but inasmuch as it conveyed that sense of ambition, and showed that such confidence was neither arrogant nor unfounded, it could be said to have fulfilled Diderot's prediction.*

Encyclopédie

PROSPECTUS (1750)

[We wish to inform the public of the nature of this work and the methods used to carry it out.]

   . . . It cannot be denied that since the revival of letters among us   V.86 some of the general enlightenment which has spread through society has been due to dictionaries; likewise the grain of science which, unnoticed, prepares men's minds for more profound knowledge.

---

* Given the size and range of Diderot's contributions it is very difficult to make a representative selection of extracts. The emphasis in choosing the passages below has been to include some of the most characteristic and to indicate something of their variety. A comprehensive selection would need a complete book.

How important it is, then, to have a book of this kind which could be consulted on all subjects, which would be as useful to guide those bold enough to work on educating others as to enlighten those who are only educating themselves. 87

That is one advantage we suggest, but it is not the only one. Putting all that concerns the sciences and the arts into one dictionary was even more a question of making evident the mutual light they throw on one another. [We want] to make use of the links to reveal the [underlying] principles more forcefully and the results more clearly; to indicate the close or distant connections [that exist] between the beings which form nature, and which have concerned men; to show by the interweaving of roots and branches how impossible it is to know well some parts of the whole without going up or down many others; to form a general map of the efforts of the human mind in all activities, over all the centuries; to present these subjects clearly, to give each of them the right amount of space, and if possible to vindicate our epigraph by our success: *Tantum series juncturaque pollet, tantum de medio sumptis accedit honoris!**

Up to now no one has envisaged a work as large as this; or at least no one has carried it out . . .

[Chambers's *Cyclopaedia* was good but was still inadequate in many ways.] We have looked at the whole of Chambers, in translation, and we have found an immense number of things lacking in the sciences; in the liberal arts there was a word where a page was needed; in the mechanical arts everything was missing. Chambers read books but he had scarcely seen men at work; however, there are many things that are only learnt in the workshops . . . 89

[We have divided our work among many people, finding whoever was most appropriate for each subject.] The different hands we have employed have stamped each article, like the seal of their individual style, with the manner suitable to that aspect of the subject in question . . . Each item has its own colour; to reduce them all to a uniform colour would be to mix up different shades. A lucid style, clarity and precision are the only qualities that can be common to all the articles, and we hope that they will be in evidence . . . 94

The realm of the sciences and the arts is remote from the ordinary 96

* These lines, taken from Horace's *Ars Poetica* (242–3) may be translated: 'So great is the power of order and arrangement, so much honour can be added to commonplace terms!' They formed the epigraph to the whole *Encyclopédie*.

world; every day people make discoveries, yet accounts of them are very strange. It has been important to confirm those that were true, to avoid those which were false, to make plain the positions from which people set out, and in this way to make possible the research for what remains to be done. Facts are given, experiments compared and methods envisaged simply in order to stimulate men of genius to open up unknown routes, to move on to new discoveries, to regard the place where great men have stopped as the first step. That is also the goal we put forward in giving together with the principles of the sciences and liberal arts an account of their origin and their subsequent development. If we have achieved this, good minds will no longer spend time looking for that which was already known . . .

[There will also be many articles on the use of language.] We   97
believe we can be certain that no known work will be as complete
and as instructive as ours will be on the rules and use of the French   98
language, and even on the nature, origin and philosophy of
languages in general . . .

Let posterity say when opening our dictionary: such was then the
state of the sciences and fine arts. Let them add their discoveries to
those we have catalogued and let the history of the human mind   99
and its productions go from age to age until the most far-off
centuries. Let the *Encyclopédie* become a sanctuary where men's
knowledge is protected from time and upheavals . . . Let us do for
the centuries to come that which we are sorry the past centuries did
not do for us . . .

Too much has been written [before now] on the sciences; not
enough has been written well on most of the liberal arts; almost
nothing at all has been written on the mechanical arts. . . . We
have spoken to the most accomplished workers in Paris and the
kingdom. We have taken the trouble to go to their workshops, ask
them questions, write down what they said, develop their thoughts,   100
find out the particular terms they used, draw up lists of these and
define them; we have talked with those who have obtained
accounts, and – a vital precaution – by long and frequent conversations with some to correct what others had imperfectly, obscurely
and sometimes inaccurately explained . . . There are some crafts so
individual and some work so intricate that it is difficult to talk about
it precisely without doing it oneself – operating a machine with your
own hands and seeing the work taking shape under your own eyes.
It has therefore been necessary on several occasions to obtain

machines, to put them together, set to work, make oneself an apprentice, as it were, and produce some bad results in order to teach others how to produce good results.

In this way we have become convinced of the ignorance which surrounds most of the objects of our life and the necessity to escape from this ignorance. . . . [For this reason the *Encyclopédie* will include illustrations and diagrams as well as descriptions.]

Despite the help and assistance we have described we state 103 openly, on behalf of our colleagues and ourselves, that we will always be ready to admit our inadequacy and to benefit from any information sent to us. We will receive it with gratitude and make use of it without protest, so aware are we that the complete perfection of an encyclopaedia is the work of centuries. Centuries have been needed to begin, more will be needed to finish, but TO POSTERITY, AND THE BEING WHICH DOES NOT DIE . . .

[There follows an elaborate 'System of Human Knowledge', based on the system of Francis Bacon, which categorizes subjects under three headings – Memory, Reason, Imagination.]

VOLUME ONE (1751)

Adorer. To adore, to honour, to revere; these three verbs are used 277 in both religious and civil worship. In religion you adore God, honour the saints, revere the relics and images. In civil life you adore a mistress, honour upright people, revere those who are illustrious and distinguished . . .

Aius Locutius. God of speech, whom the Romans honoured with 315 this bizarre name . . . Works produced by non-believers should not be feared except for their effect on the masses and the faith of simple people. Those who think know very well the basis for their thought; a pamphlet is not going to divert them from a path they have chosen with care and which they follow by preference. It is not absurd or petty arguments which persuade a philosopher to abandon his God. So impiety is only fearful for those who allow themselves to be led astray. But a way of reconciling the respect we owe to the faith of the people, and to national religion, with the freedom of thought which is so highly desirable for the discovery of the 316 truth – and a way also of keeping the public calm, without which there is happiness neither for the philosopher nor for the people – would be to forbid all writing against government and religion in the vernacular, to take no notice of those who write in a scholarly language, and only to prosecute translators. It seems to me that if that were done the absurdities written by authors would do no harm to anyone. Moreover, the freedom obtained by this method is the greatest, in my opinion, that one can grant in a well-ordered society . . .

Animal. What is an animal? This is a question which becomes   381
more perplexing the more philosophy and knowledge of natural history you have . . . If it is true, as can scarcely be doubted, that the universe is a single and unique machine in which everything is connected and in which beings rise above or fall below one another by imperceptible degrees, so that there is no break in the chain . . . it will be very difficult for us to fix the two limits between which animality, if it can be so termed, begins and ends. A definition of animal will be too general, or not extensive enough; it will include   382
beings which should perhaps be excluded and vice versa. The more you examine nature the more you become convinced that to express yourself exactly you need almost as many different terms as there are individuals . . .

Nevertheless, what is the animal? It is, according to M. de Buffon, living and organized matter which feels, acts, moves itself, nourishes itself and reproduces itself. Consequently, the vegetable is living and organized matter which nourishes itself and reproduces itself, but which does not feel, act or move itself. And the mineral is dead or inert matter which neither feels, acts, moves itself, nourishes itself nor reproduces itself. From which it follows that feeling is the principal differentiating mark of the animal. But is it quite certain that there are no animals without what we call feeling?. . . Does not man himself sometimes lose feeling without ceasing to live or be an animal?. . . Let us listen to M. de Buffon explaining himself at greater length . . .

[Buffon writes, in his *Histoire naturelle*:] Our general ideas are   384
only artificial methods which we have constructed to collect a large amount of subjects under a single heading:. . . they can never cover everything. They are even contrary to the activity of nature, which is uniform, unconscious (*insensible*) and always individual . . . We imagine that a word is a line that can be drawn between the productions of nature, that everything above that line is really animal and everything below it can only be vegetable . . . But these lines of separation do not exist in nature; there are beings that are neither animal nor vegetable nor mineral . . . [He gives as examples Trembley's polyp and the moving bodies in seminal fluid or ripe

cheese.] The activity of nature occurs in subtle and often imper-   385
ceptible degrees; it passes from the animal to the vegetable by
imperceptible stages. The passage from vegetable to mineral, however, is abrupt . . .

[For Buffon there is a clear distinction between animal and
vegetable matter, on the one hand, and inanimate mineral matter,
on the other; though not all mineral matter, he points out, may be
equally inanimate: 'it could be said that there are some minerals
which are less dead than others'. Diderot, however, is less categorical. He writes: Just as we see] the degree of this faculty of   388
thinking, acting and feeling to be more pronounced in some men,
and less so in others, [so it could] get weaker as we descend the
chain of beings and die out at some very remote part of   389
the chain, somewhere between the animal and mineral realm, a
point to which we will get closer and closer by observations but
which will always elude us. Experiments will always fall short and
systems will always go too far, experience walking step by step and
the spirit of system always going by leaps and bounds.

[Although we have common bonds with matter in general,
Buffon continues, they do not have any effect on us within.] It is
our physical constitution, life, the soul, which actually makes our
existence. Considered from this point of view matter is less the
subject than the accessory; it is an extraneous envelope which
unites with us in an unknown way and is present in a harmful way,
and that sequence of thoughts which forms our being is perhaps
quite independent of it. [Diderot disagrees:] It seems to me that
here the natural historian grants much more to the metaphysicians
than they would dare ask him. Whatever may be the way we will
think when our soul is freed of its envelope and leaves the state of a
chrysalis, it is a constant fact that this despicable cocoon in which it
is trapped for a while has a prodigious influence on the sequence of
thoughts which forms our being; and in spite of what are sometimes
the very troublesome results of this influence it does not display any
less evidence of the wisdom of Providence [since Providence]
makes use of this spur to remind us continually of our self-
preservation and the survival of our species. [On the previous page
Diderot had written in awe of 'that procreative virtue . . . which is
to us, when we consider it in itself . . . a mystery, the depths of
which it seems we will never be allowed to sound'.]

[Among the other comments he makes on the passages taken
from Buffon Diderot writes:] The soul can be seen to be subject to   390

inertia, so that it would remain perpetually applied to the same thought, perhaps to the same idea, if it was not drawn away from that by something external which affects it without however overriding its freedom. It is by this latter faculty that it stops or passes lightly from one contemplation to another. When the exercise of this faculty ceases it remains fixed in the same contemplation, and perhaps the state of someone going to sleep or even being asleep is like that, likewise someone who meditates very profoundly. If the latter should deal with different subjects in succession, this succession does not occur as a result of an act of his will, but as a result of the connection between the subjects themselves. I know of nothing so mechanical as a man absorbed in a profound meditation, except for a man immersed in a deep sleep.

[On the question of what defines an animal, Diderot concludes:]   399
The more observations you make the more convinced you become that the Creator has put no fixed term between animals and vegetables, that these two kinds of organic being have many more properties in common that real differences . . . and that the living and the animate, instead of being a metaphysical degree of being, is   400
a physical property of matter . . .

Ansico. [An African country where the inhabitants were said to   401
be cannibals.] We should suspect every ordinary traveller and historian of exaggerating things somewhat . . . The principle on which I base this suspicion is that people do not like to take up their pens to tell commonplace adventures . . .

Antédiluvienne. [This article is about the state of philosophy before the Flood. Adam had some knowledge, writes Diderot; he knew about God and about himself and above all about practical things, which he needed for his happiness.] But what has [this kind   404
of knowledge] in common with that philosophy produced by curiosity and wonder, the daughters of ignorance? The philosophy which is only acquired by the painful work of reflection and only improved by the conflict of opinions? The wisdom with which Adam was created is that divine wisdom which is the product of grace and which God puts into even the most simple souls. That wisdom . . . is very different from the wisdom the mind brings forth and to the growth of which centuries have contributed . . .   405

Arithmétique politique. [Political arithmetic, i.e. statistics] is that   475
arithmetic which is aimed at those areas of research useful to the art of governing people, like the number of men who live in a country, the amount of food they must eat, of work they can do, how long

they live, how fertile the land is, how many ships are wrecked, etc. It can readily be imagined that such discoveries and many others of the same kind, acquired by calculations based on well-founded research, could provide an able minister with a host of ideas about improving agriculture, internal and external trade, colonies, the flow and use of money, etc. But often ministers think they have no need to make use of arithmetical devices and calculations, (not that there are no exceptions). Many suppose they are endowed with great natural ability which absolves them from so slow and troublesome an activity . . .

Art. Abstract and metaphysical term. People began by making observations of nature, the activity, function and quality of beings and their symbols; then they gave the name of 'science', 'art' or 'discipline' in general to the centre or meeting-point to which the observations were related, thus forming a system with rules or instruments, and with rules leading to a single goal; for this is what 'discipline' in general is. For example: people reflected on the use and function of words and then invented the word 'grammar'. Grammar is the name of a system of instruments and rules relative to a specific object; and this object is the articulated sound, the signs of a word, the expression of a thought and all that relates to it. Likewise the other arts and sciences. 495

Origin of the arts and sciences. It is man's industry applied to the productions of nature – either for his needs or his luxury, amusements or curiosity – which gave birth to the arts and sciences. These meeting-points of our different reflections have been termed 'science' or 'art' according to the nature of their formal object, as logicians say. If the object is practised, the collection and technical arrangement of the rules by which it is practised is called an 'art'. If the object is only contemplated under different aspects, the collection and technical arrangement relative to that object is called a 'science'. Thus metaphysics is a science and ethics is an art. It is the same with theology and pyrotechnics.

Theory and practice of an art. It is evident from what has been said that every art has its theoretical and its practical aspect. Its theory consists simply of unapplied knowledge of the rules of the art; its practice is simply the habitual and instinctive use of these rules. It is difficult, almost impossible, to go far in practice without theory and likewise to grasp the theory without the practice . . . 496

Distinction between liberal and mechanical arts. If you examine the products of different arts you will see that some are more the work of the hand than the mind, and with others it is the opposite. That is, to some extent, the origin of the preference that is given to some arts over others and of the distinction that is made between 'liberal arts' and 'mechanical arts'. This distinction, although basically sound, has had the bad effect of degrading very useful and estimable people and of encouraging in us a natural laziness, which has already led us too easily to think that a steady and close application to experiments and to individual material things is unworthy of the dignity of the human mind; that to practise, or even study, the mechanical arts is to lower oneself to things which it is laborious to research, undignified to meditate, difficult to describe, dishonourable to trade in, impossible to enumerate, and of infinitesimal value . . . This prejudice had tended to fill towns with arrogant intellectuals and useless contemplatives, and the countryside with petty tyrants who are ignorant, idle and full of themselves. This was not the opinion of Bacon, one of the great geniuses of England, or of Colbert, one of France's greatest ministers, nor of men of intelligence and wisdom in all ages . . . More praise has   497 been given to men occupied in making us think we are happy than to those occupied in making us [actually] happy in fact. A bizarre way of judging things! . . .

Aim of arts in general. Man is only the minister and interpreter of nature. He can understand or accomplish only as much as he knows, either from experience or by reflection, from the beings which surround him. His bare hand, however strong, tireless and skilful it may be, can only achieve little. To achieve great things men need the help of tools and rules . . . Tools and rules are like additional muscles to his arms and new faculties to his mind. The aim of all art in general . . . is to print well-defined forms on a base given by nature; and this base is either matter or thought or some function of the mind or some product of nature. In the mechanical arts, which I particularly emphasize because others have neglected them, 'men's power is limited to bringing together or separating natural objects' . . .*   498

[Diderot then outlines a project for a treatise on the mechanical arts. He recalls how much progress there has been, often resulting from chance discoveries, and he reflects on the present.]

In what physical or metaphysical system will one find more intel-   505
ligence, shrewdness or consistency than exists in machines for

---

* A quotation from Bacon's *Novum Organum* (I.iv).

spinning gold thread, or making stockings, or the crafts of lace-making, gauze, clothwork or silk-work? What mathematical proof is more complex than the mechanism of certain clocks, or the different processes through which hemp passes, or the silkworm's cocoon before it provides a workable thread? What projection is more beautiful, delicate and distinct than that of a design on the cords of a loom, and from the cords of the loom to the threads of a weft? Has anyone, in any activity whatever, imagined anything more subtle than the colouring of velvets? . . .

[He then discusses three inventions: the art of printing, the discovery of gunpowder and the compass.] These three arts have almost changed the face of the earth. Let us at last give artisans their due. The liberal arts have spent enough time singing their own praises; they could now use what voice they have left to celebrate the mechanical arts. It is for the liberal arts to lift the mechanical arts from the contempt which prejudice has kept them in so long. It is for the patronage of kings to protect them from the poverty which they still suffer. Artisans have considered themselves contemptible because they have been subject to contempt; let us teach them to think better of themselves. It is the only way to obtain better products from them. Let some man come out of the academics and go down into the workshops, to collect information about the arts and set it out in a book which will persuade artisans to read, philosophers to think usefully, and the great to make at last some beneficial use of their authority and wealth . . .

We invite artisans for their part to take advice from scientists and not to allow their discoveries to die with them. Let them know that to keep useful knowledge secret is to be guilty of a theft from society, and that it is as bad in these cases to put private interest before public interest as it is in a hundred others where they would not hesitate to speak out. If they are communicative many prejudices will be discarded, above all the idea that their art has reached the highest possible degree of perfection. Their lack of information often leads them to regard as the nature of things a fault which is only in themselves. Obstacles seem insuperable as long as they know no way of overcoming them. Let them make experiments and let everyone share his experiments. Let the artisan contribute his manual skill, the academician his knowledge and advice, and the rich man the cost of materials, time and trouble; and soon our arts and manufactures will be as superior to other people's as we could want . . .

506

507

508

Autorité politique. No man has received from nature the right to   537
command others. Liberty is a gift from heaven, and every person of
the same species has the right to enjoy as much liberty as he enjoys
reason. If nature has established any authority it is paternal power;
but that has its limits and in the state of nature it would finish as
soon as the children were in a state to look after themselves. All
other authority comes from some other origin than nature. Look at
the matter closely and you will always come down to one of two
sources: either the strength and violence of the person who has got
hold of it, or the consent of those who have submitted to it by a
contract, actual or presumed, between them and the person on
whom they have confirmed authority.

Power acquired by violence is nothing but usurpation and only
lasts as long as the person in command has more strength than
those who obey; so that if the latter become in turn the strongest
and shake the yoke they do so with as much right and justice as the
person who imposed that yoke on them. The same law which has
given authority takes it away: it is the law of the strongest.

Sometimes the authority established by violence changes its
nature, namely, when it lasts and is supported by the explicit
consent of those who have been subjected. But in that case it comes
under the second category I shall describe, and the person who
takes on that authority, by becoming a prince, ceases to be a tyrant.

The power which comes from the consent of the people necessarily presupposes conditions which make its use legitimate, useful
to society, advantageous to the republic, and which determine it
and restrict it within limits. For a man neither should nor can give
himself entirely and without reserve to another man, because there
is one supreme master above everyone to whom man entirely
belongs. That is God, whose power over his creatures is always   538
direct, a master as jealous as he is absolute, who never gives up his
rights and never transfers them. For the common good and the
maintenance of society he allows men to establish a hierarchy
between them, so that they obey one man among them. But he
wants this [power over others] to be reasonable and moderate, not
blind or unrestrained, so that the person [with power] does not take
for himself the rights of the Creator. Any other submission is pure
idolatry . . . To hand over heart, mind and conduct without reserve
to the will and caprice of a simple created being, to make him the
single and final referee of what is done, is without question a crime
of divine *lèse-majesté* to the Lord.

True and legitimate power is thus necessarily limited . . . The prince derives from his own subjects the authority he has over them; and that authority is limited by the laws of nature and of the State. The laws of nature or the State are the conditions under which the subjects have submitted, or are deemed to have submitted, to the prince's government. One of these conditions is that as his power and authority over them only arise from their choice and consent the prince can never use that authority to break the act or contract by which that power has been bestowed on him; he would then be acting against himself, since his authority can only exist by virtue of the title which established it. What cancels the one cancels the other. The prince can therefore dispose neither of his power nor of his subjects without the nation's consent . . . 539

Besides, the government, although hereditary in one family, and put in one person's hands, is not an individual possession but a public possession which can therefore never be taken away from the people; it belongs essentially and wholly to them . . . It is not the State which belongs to the prince but the prince who belongs to the State. But it is for the prince to govern in the State because the State has chosen him for that . . . In a word, the crown, government and public authority are possessions of which the body of the nation is the owner and princes are occupants, ministers and depositaries . . . 540

The deposition of authority is sometimes only for a limited period, as in the Roman republic, sometimes for the life of a single man, as in Poland, sometimes as long as a family lasts, as in England, sometimes as long as the male line of a family lasts, as in France. This deposition is sometimes entrusted to a certain rank in society, sometimes to several people chosen from every rank, and sometimes to a single individual.

The conditions of this pact are different in different States. But everywhere the nation has the right to maintain the contract it has made despite all opposition; no power can change it; and when it no longer exists the nation has the right and complete freedom to make a new contract with whom it pleases and how it pleases. That is what would happen in France if, by the greatest misfortune, the entire ruling family down to the last heir should die out. Then the sceptre and crown would return to the nation. It seems that only slaves whose minds were as narrow as their hearts were base could think otherwise . . .

The observation of the laws, the preservation of freedom and the 541 love of the country (*patrie*) are the fertile sources of all great things and all fine actions. In them is found the happiness of peoples and the true fame of the princes who govern them. With them, obedience is glorious and command is noble. On the other hand, flattery, self-interest and a servile mentality are the origin of all the evils which overwhelm a state and all the cowardliness which dishonours it. There subjects are wretched and princes hated, . . . submission is shameful and domination is cruel. If I regard France and Turkey from the same point of view, I see on one side a society of men whom reason unites, whom virtue animates, and whom a leader both wise and glorious governs according to the laws of justice, on the other a herd of animals brought together by habit, set in motion by the law of the stick, and led by an absolute master at his whim.

[Diderot then cites as an example of good political authority a speech made by Henry IV in 1596: 'That is how a monarch should address his subjects when he evidently has justice on his side.' As for the subjects, he concludes, talking of France, they should be obedient, so long as the reigning king is the legitimate heir.]

If it ever happened that they had an unjust, ambitious and violent   544
king, they should use only one remedy against this misfortune; they should calm him by their submission and persuade God by their prayers, for this is the only legitimate remedy, by virtue of the contract of submission sworn to the prince previously reigning and to his descendants by the male line, whoever they may be. They should consider that all those motives which are believed to justify resistance, when closely examined, are only subtly phrased excuses for disloyalty; and with such action princes have never been corrected, nor taxes abolished, and the misfortunes which were reason for complaint only became still worse. These are the foundations on which people and those who govern them should be able to establish their reciprocal happiness.

VOLUME TWO (1752)

Beau. [Diderot summarizes the ideas of previous writers – Plato, Augustine, Wolff, Crousaz, Shaftesbury – about beauty, and pays particular attention to Frances Hutcheson and Père André. He finds the latter the most perceptive but inadequate in so far as he did not explain clearly the empirical basis of all ideas, including those of beauty. He then sets out his own concept.] Beautiful is a word which we apply to an infinite number of creatures; but what-   VI.156

ever difference there may be between these creatures, . . . there must be one quality in them all to which the word beautiful refers . . . [But] which quality shall we choose? It seems clear to me that it can only be the one which when present makes them all beautiful; the one which is more or less beautiful according to its frequency or rarity, . . . in a word, the one which produces beauty and increases it, variously alters it, decreases it or lacks it. Now, the notion of relationships (*rapports*) is the ony one that can have these results. I therefore call beautiful external to myself all that contains within itself whatever produces the idea of relationships in my understanding, and beautiful with respect to myself all which arouses this idea . . . It is necessary to distinguish clearly the forms which are in the objects and the notions which I have of them . . . [For] although there is no absolute beauty, there are two kinds of beautiful in relation to us, a real beauty and a perceived beauty.   157

[Diderot then makes further distinctions between real and relative beauty, and perceived and intellectual or fictitious beauty. Despite the assurance with which he makes these distinctions he admits that judgements on beauty are nevertheless very varied. He therefore devotes the rest of the article to explaining this variety; it may be a matter of aptitude, ability, education, circumstances, mood, association, etc.]

Beaucoup, Plusieurs. A great deal, several . . . For a state to be   173
well governed we say that it needs a single leader, several ministers, and a great deal of enlightenment and justice.

Besançon. French town, capital of Franche-Comté. [Not far   177
from the town is a large cave, described in various learned journals and regarded by the peasants as being a reliable indication of the weather; when the cave is full of vapour it will rain next day.] We invite our credulous readers to examine these [accounts]; less to learn about the particulars of this cave, which are not that extraordinary, as to learn to doubt. . .

Cadavre. . . . To discover the causes of illnesses by the opening   245
of corpses a superficial examination was not enough; it was necessary to delve into the viscera and note carefully the effects produced in each one and in the whole physical mechanism . . .
The preservation of men and the development of the art of curing   246
them are such important matters that in a well-ordered society priests should not receive corpses except from the hands of the anatomist, and there should be a law forbidding the burial of a corpse before its autopsy. What a host of knowledge would be

acquired in this way! How many phenomena [may exist] which we
do not suspect and we will never know because only the frequent
dissection of corpses can bring them to light!

Caucause. Range of mountains which begins above Colchides   286
and ends at the Caspian Sea. It is there that Prometheus, chained
up, had his liver torn by a vulture or an eagle. If Philostrates is to be
believed the inhabitants of this country took this story literally and
made war on the eagles, hunting out the young and shooting them
with sharp arrows. Or, according to Strabo, they interpreted the
story as a fable of the unhappy condition of mankind, going into
mourning at the birth of their children and rejoicing at their
funerals. Any Christian who truly believes in his religion should
imitate the inhabitants of the Caucasus, and be happy at the death
of his children. Death guarantees a newly born child eternal happiness; the fate of the man who appears to have led the most holy life
is not as certain. How terrible and consoling our religion is!

Cérémonie. . . . Representations which affect the senses, what-   310
ever form they take, have a prodigious effect on most people.
Antony's eloquence never achieved as much as Caesar's robe.

VOLUME THREE (1753)

Chaos . . . Ancient philosophers understood by this word a con-   358
fused mixture of particles of every kind without form or regularity,
which they presumed had an intrinsic movement and to which as a
result they attributed the formation of the universe . . . They
regarded the creation as a fantastic and contradictory idea . . .

[Diderot then sets out an ironic defence of the account of the
creation in Genesis, and continues:] To imagine as some thinkers   360
do that in the beginning God only made a vague and indeterminate
matter, in which movement gradually brought forth by internal
agitations, reductions and attractions, a sun, an earth and the
whole panoply of the world . . . is to abandon history to indulge in
dreams, and to substitute implausible opinions for the eternal
truths which God vouched for through the mouth of Moses . . .

Today philosophy agrees that matter was created and that God   362
endows it with movement; but [philosophy] wants that movement,
of its own accord, to be able to operate all the phenomena of the
visible world. A philosopher [Descartes] who dares to explain by
the laws of movement alone the mechanism and even the first
formation of things, and who says: give me movement and matter

and I will make a world, should first show (which is quite easy) that existence and movement are not essential to matter. Otherwise this philosopher, thinking incorrectly that he can see nothing in the wonderful spectacle of this universe which movement alone could not have produced, is in danger of falling into atheism . . .

Citoyen. The person who is a member of a free society of several 463 families which share the rights of that society and enjoy its immunities . . . This title is not given to women, young children or servants, except as members of the family of a citizen properly speaking; but they are not really citizens. [Diderot describes citizenship in the ancient world, and as conceived by Hobbes and Pufendorf. He concludes:] The closer the citizens approach an 467 equality of aspirations and wealth the calmer the State will be . . . But even in the most perfect democracy complete equality between the members is a fantasy, and that is perhaps the cause of this kind of government's dissolution, unless it is corrected by all the injustice of ostracisms. With government as with animal life, each step in life is a step towards death. The best government is not that which is immortal but that which lasts longest and most peacefully.

Conjecture. Judgement based on proofs which have only a certain 485 degree of plausibility, that is to say, on circumstances whose existence does not have a close enough connection with the thing which is thought about it for it to be positively certain that given the one the other will or will not be. But what makes this connection evident? Only experience . . .

There is a certain imperceptible point when we cease to conjecture and we become positively certain. All other things being equal, this point varies from one man to another and from one moment to another in the same man, according to the interest taken in the event, the character, and a multitude of things of which it is impossible to give an account . . . [However,] in everything there is a unity which should be the same for all men since it is based on experience, and which perhaps is not the same either for two men or two actions in life, nor for two moments. This real unity would be that which would result from a calculation made by a completely stoical philosopher who, counting himself and all his surroundings for nothing, would have regard only for the natural course of things. An at least approximate knowledge of this true unity, and the conformity of feelings and actions in ordinary life to that knowledge, are two things virtually indispensable to constitute 486 the philosophical temperament. The knowledge of the unity would constitute the theoretical moral philosophy; the conformity of feelings and actions to this knowledge the practical moral philosophy.

VOLUME FOUR (1754)

Croire . . . It is as rare as it is difficult to feel content in yourself if   522
you have not made use of your reason, or, if you have, made bad use of it. Anyone who believes he has found the truth without having any reason to believe will always feel guilty of having neglected the most important prerogative of his nature . . . Anyone who is deceived after he has used his mental faculties to their fullest extent bears witness to himself that he has fulfilled his duty as a reasoning creature . . . So any assent [to a belief] will be appropriate if you have listened to the voice of your conscience and your reason. To act otherwise is to sin against your own intelligence   523
and abuse the faculties which have been given to us for no other end than that of following the clearest evidence and most likely probability . . .

   Délicieux. This term is applied to the organ of taste. We say of a   VII.9
dish or a wine that it is delicious when the palate has been tickled as pleasantly as possible. The delicious is the highest pleasure of the sense of taste. Its use has been generalized, and we say of a stay somewhere that it is delightful when everything that we meet has awakened the most attractive ideas or aroused the most agreeable feelings. The most delightful smell is the fragrant. Rest also has its delight, but what is a delightful rest? Only someone whose organs are sensitive and delicate has experienced its inexpressible charm. Someone, that is, who has received from nature a tender soul and a sensual temperament, who enjoys perfect health, is in the prime of life, whose mind is not troubled by a single cloud nor his soul disturbed by too lively an emotion, who is emerging from a sweet and gentle tiredness and experiences in every part of his body a pleasure so evenly diffused that he cannot relate it to any one particular spot. In this moment of enchantment and weakness there is no trace of memory of the past, or desire for the future, or anxiety for the present. Time has ceased to pass for him because he exists entirely in himself; his feelings of happiness only grows weak in conjunction with the feeling of existence itself. He passes imperceptibly from waking to sleep; but in the midst of this unnoticed transition, in the midst of this exhaustion of all his faculties he is still

awake enough, if not to think any distinct thought then at least to feel the whole sweetness of his existence. But he enjoys it with a purely passive enjoyment, without being attached to it or reflecting on it or being glad because of it or being happy about it. If you could fix in thought this condition of pure feeling where all the faculties of the body and soul are alive without being active, and attach to this delightful passivity the idea of immutability, you would form the idea of the greatest and purest happiness that men can imagine.

Distraction. The application of our mind to a different subject 14 from the one with which the present moment would demand us to remain occupied. Distraction has its source in an excellent quality of the understanding, an extreme facility among ideas to arouse one another. It is the opposite of stupidity, which remains fixed to the same idea. The distracted man follows all ideas indistinctly according to how they present themselves to him; they get hold of him and lead him away from his goal, unlike the person who, master of his own mind, throws a glance over ideas which are foreign to his subject and only takes up those which belong to it. A good mind should be capable of distractions but should not be distracted . . . [Distraction is a 'debauchery (*libertinage*) of the mind', a 'frenzy (*délire*)', an oblivion to what is going on around.]

VOLUME FIVE (1755) 2/4408

Dranses. The former people of Thrace . . . According to them, 24 birth was the beginning of misery and death the end of it. The Dranses regarded life as an evil and it is very hard to think that they felt obliged to thank the gods for this gift. However that may be, the general opinion a people has on the unhappiness of life is less an injury due to Providence than a very harsh judgement on the way they have been governed. It is not nature but tyranny which imposes on men such a burden that they groan and detest their condition . . .

Droit naturel. This phrase is used so frequently that there is 27 scarcely anyone who is not convinced in himself that he knows what it means. [However, the matter is in no way straightforward. In order to establish a basis for natural right Diderot considers the extreme case of whether a man has a natural right to take another man's life if he is then prepared to give up his own life. He concludes that such a right cannot exist.]

VI. But if we take away from the single individual the right of deciding what is just and unjust, where will we answer this great question? Where? In the presence of the whole human race. It is to that alone that this decision belongs, since the good of all is the only passion which concerns it. Individual wills are suspect, they can be good or evil; but the general will is always good, it never has and never will be deceived . . .

VII. It is to the general will that the individual must address him-   28
self to know how he should be a man, citizen, subject, father, child, and when he should live or die. It is for the general will to fix the limits of all duties. You have the most sacred natural right to everything which is not contested by the whole human race. It is the general will which will enlighten you on the nature of your thoughts and desires. All you envisage, all you contemplate, will be good, great, noble, sublime, if it is of common and general interest. The one attribute which is essential to the whole human race is that which you demand from your fellow men for your happiness and theirs . . . Therefore never lose sight of it; or else you will see the notions of goodness, justice, humanity and virtue unclear in your mind. Say to yourself often: I am a man, and I have no other truly inalienable natural rights except those of humanity.

VIII. But, you will say, where is the general will kept? Where can I consult it? In the principles of law written down by all civilized nations, in the social practices of savages and barbarians, in the tacit conventions – among themselves – of the enemies of the human race, and in [the feelings of] indignation and resentment, those two passions that nature seems to have placed even in animals to supplement the lack of social laws and public retribution.

IX. If you consider closely all the above you will be convinced (1) that the man who only listens to his individual will is the enemy of the human race; (2) that the general will in each person is a pure act of the understanding which reasons when the passions are silent on what a man can demand of his fellow man and on what his fellow man is entitled to demand of him; (3) that this consideration of the general will of the race and of common desire is the rule for behaviour between individuals of the same society, between an individual and that society of which he is a member, and between that society (of which he is a member) and other societies; (4) that submission to the general will is the bond of all societies, not excepting those which are formed by crime. Alas, virtue is so beautiful that robbers in the very depths of their caves respect the

image of it! (5) that laws should be made for all, not for one . . .; (6)   29
that since of the two wills, general and particular, the general will
never errs, it is not difficult to see to which of them legislative
power should belong, and what respect we owe to the august
mortals whose individual will unites both the authority and the
infallibility of the general will; (7) that if you envisage the possibility of different races being in a state of continual change, the
nature of natural right would not change, since it would always be
relative to the general will and the common desire of the whole
race; (8) that equity is to justice as cause is to its effect, or that
justice can never be anything except equity made plain (*déclarée*);
and (9) finally, that all these consequences are clear to the person
who reasons and that the person who does not wish to reason
renounces his quality as a man and should be treated as an unnatural creature.

Éclairé, Clairvoyant. [Enlightened, Perceptive.] Terms which   35
relate to the intelligence of the mind. Enlightened is used of
acquired intelligence, perceptive of natural intelligence. These two
qualities are, one to another, like science and insight . . . The
enlightened man knows what is going on, the perceptive man
guesses what will happen; the first has read widely in books, the
second can read in minds. The enlightened man decides according
to the authorities, the perceptive according to reasons . . . There
are a thousand educated men for a single enlightened man; a
hundred enlightened men for a single man of genius. The man of
genius creates things; the perceptive man deduces their principles;
the enlightened man applies that knowledge . . .

Éclectisme. The eclectic is a philosopher who tramples underfoot   36
prejudice, tradition, antiquity, general acceptance, authority, in a
word all that subjugates the majority of minds. He dares to think
for himself. He goes back to the most clear and general principles,
to examine and discuss them, and not allow anything except the
testimony of his own experience and reason. He makes a personal
and individual philosophy from all those he has analysed carefully
and dispassionately; . . . because the eclectic's ambition is less to
be the teacher of the human race than its disciple, less to reform
others than to reform himself . . . He is not a man who plants and
sows, but one who gathers and harvests . . .

Chancellor Bacon had the honour [of being the founder of   38
modern eclecticism] because he felt and dared to say to himself that
nature had not been less generous to him than to Socrates,

Epicurus, Democritus, and she had given him too a head [to think for himself].

Eclecticism has been the philosophy of intelligent men from the birth of the world but it only became a sect and took a name towards the end of the second century AD. [This was 'reformed Platonism', the Alexandrian philosophy, i.e. Neo-Platonism: the response of a small number of men, faced with the rise of Christianity, to find a generally acceptable system to which all philosophers could belong.] The God of the Christians was in three people – the Father, Son and Holy Ghost. The eclectics also had their trinity – the first principle, the divine understanding and the soul of the world. The world was eternal, according to Aristotle; Plato said it had been brought forth (*engendré*); according to the Christians, God had created it. The eclectics made it an emanation of the first principle, an idea which reconciled the other three systems and which did not prevent them from supposing, as previously, that nothing was made of nothing . . . Were they materialists, or were they not? That is not something which is easy to determine today. There was something very similar to Leibniz's monad in the tiny intelligent spheres they called *yunges* . . . These resemblances [of the early eclectics to Leibniz] would be much less surprising if people were more aware of the disordered progress and aberrations of poetic genius, of enthusiasm, of metaphysics and the systematic spirit.

[Diderot gives a short history of the leading eclectics – Potamon, Plotinus and Porphyry, who was given to enthusiasm.] I must point out here, in passing, that it is impossible to produce anything sublime in poetry, painting, eloquence or music, without enthusiasm. Enthusiasm is a violent movement of the soul by which we are carried away into the midst of the subjects we have to portray; then we see a whole scene take place in our imagination as if it were outside us . . . If this condition is not madness it is very close to it. That is why great intelligence is needed to balance enthusiasm . . . If enthusiasm is dominant in a work it spreads throughout it an exaggerated, heightened, unbelievable quality. If it is a habitual disposition or a natural (or acquired) inclination, the speech is alternately incoherent and sublime and actions are bizarrely heroic, at one and the same time noble, powerful and unhinged . . .

[After the fall of the Roman Empire eclecticism] was forgotten until the end of the sixteenth century. Then nature, inert for such a long time as if in a state of exhaustion, made an effort and produced

39
41
45
46
56
78

several men who were jealous of the finest prerogative of mankind, 79
the freedom to think for oneself. The eclectic philosophy was
reborn under Giordano Bruno, Girolamo Cardano, Francis Bacon,
Tommaso Campanella, Thomas Hobbes, René Descartes, Leibniz,
Thomasius . . . Malebranche . . . These men proposed nothing less 81
than to find again the portfolio of the great architect and the lost
plans of this universe . . .

There are two kinds of eclecticism: the experimental, which
consists in collecting known truths and given facts and increasing
their number by the study of nature; and the systematic, which is
concerned with comparing the known truths with one another and
combining the given facts, to derive from them the explanation for
a phenomenon or the idea for an experiment. Experimental eclecticism is for hard-working men; systematic eclecticism is for men of
genius. The person who combines the two will see his name alongside that of Democritus, Aristotle and Bacon . . .

Up to now eclecticism has scarcely been used except for philo- 84
sophical subjects. But it is not difficult to foresee that with the
[current] activity of human minds it will become more widespread.
Not that I think, or perhaps that it is desirable, that its first effects
should be immediate. Because those who are skilled in the practice
of the arts are not sufficiently reflective, and those who have the
habit of reasoning are not sufficiently instructed, or disposed to be
instructed, in the mechanical part. If the thing is done with haste it
could easily happen that the desire to correct everything would
spoil everything. The first impulse is to take things to extremes. I
invite philosophers to distrust that impulse. If they are prudent
they will resolve to become pupils of many forms of activity before
wanting to be masters; they will advance a few conjectures before
laying down principles . . .

[Diderot concludes by suggesting that an academy should be
formed to assist and promote the mechanical arts.]

Encyclopédie. This word means interconnection of knowledge; 174
it is made up of the Greek preposition *en*, in, and the nouns *kyklos*,
circle, and *paideia*, knowledge.

In fact the aim of an encyclopaedia is to collect the knowledge
that is scattered across the earth, to reveal its overall structure to
our contemporaries, and to pass it on to those who will come after
us, so that the work of past centuries may be useful to the centuries
to come, so that our children, becoming more informed, may
become at the same time more virtuous and happy, and so that we

ourselves will not die without having earned the gratitude of the human race . . .

A systematic universal dictionary of the arts and sciences cannot 178 be the work of one man alone [like Chambers's *Cyclopaedia*. Nor can it be produced by an academy, since academies always limit themselves to certain subjects] . . . Such a work can only be carried out by a society of men of letters and artisans, working in different 180 places, each concerned with his particular subject, bound together only by the general interest of humanity and a sense of mutual goodwill . . .

Such a work will not be completed if a government becomes 181 involved. A government's influence should be limited purely to giving assistance. A monarch may with a single word make a palace rise up in a field; but a society of men of letters is not like a gang of workmen. An encyclopaedia is not produced to order . . . [Then there are the uncertainties that accompany all matters affected by royal patronage, the fact that sovereigns are concerned more with glory than utility, and above all the fact that any delay would be fatal to such a work.] An encyclopaedia, like a dictionary, must be 182 started, carried through and completed within a certain space of time . . . Revolutions are almost as swift in the sciences as they are in language . . . Opinions grow old and disappear as words do . . . 183 The revolution may be less dramatic and noticeable in the sciences and liberal arts than in the mechanical arts, but it has taken place. If you open dictionaries of the previous century you will not find 'aberration' in them, nor anything of what our astronomers understand by this word; there will be only a few lines full of wrong ideas and old prejudices about 'electricity', that very fruitful phenomenon. The same could be said of many terms of mineralogy and natural history . . . Observation and experimental physics continu- 184 ally increase the number of phenomena and facts, and rational philosophy, by comparing and combining them, continually extends or narrows the limits of our knowledge. As a result the accepted use of words also varies . . .

But what above all will make the work seem out of date, and bring it into disrepute, is the revolution which will occur in the minds of men and the national character. Today philosophy advances with giant strides; it brings under its influence all the subjects it tackles, its tone is pervasive. The yoke of authority and tradition begins to give way to the laws of reason. There is now scarcely a work on basic dogma with which people are completely satisfied. Such works are recognized as being based on the products of men, not the truth of nature. We dare to have doubts about Aristotle and Plato, and the time has come when works that still enjoy the highest reputation will begin to lose some of their eminence or even fall into complete neglect. Certain literary forms will fall into disuse for lack of a foundation in living reality and current behaviour; they will no longer have a permanent aesthetic validity. Other genres will remain, sustained by their intrinsic value, but they will take an entirely new form. Such is the effect of the progress of reason, a progress which will topple many statues and will raise up others – previously cast down – to those rare men who came before their time. We had our contemporaries, if they can be so termed, in the time of Louis XIV . . .

[Despite his confidence, however, Diderot does not believe that progress is unlimited.] We do not know how far the human race   186 would go, or of how much it would be capable, if it was not stopped in its progress. But revolutions are necessary; they always happen and always will happen. The maximum interval between one revolution and another is fixed. This is the only limit to the extent of   187 our achievements. There is in the sciences a point beyond which it is hardly permissible to go.* When this point is reached what survives of the progress that has been achieved is forever a marvel for all mankind . . .

The most glorious moment for a work [like this encyclopaedia]   188 would be immediately after some great revolution which had halted the advance of science, interrupted the work of the arts and plunged some part of the globe once again into darkness. What gratitude the generation coming after this troubled time would have for those who, alarmed about the future, and foreseeing the havoc, had safeguarded the knowledge of past centuries!

[All knowledge is conveyed through language and Diderot deals with this subject at length. He then turns to the question of how items would be set out in the *Encyclopédie*.]

There is an infinite number of points of view by which both the   211 real world and the world of ideas (*l'univers soit réel soit intelligible*) can be represented, and the number of possible systems of human knowledge is as great as the number of such points of view . . . [In

* Elsewhere Diderot wrote: 'Poetry, painting and music have a fixed point which the genius of language, the imitation of nature, and the *sensibilité* of our organs will determine; they will reach that point by slow steps and can never go beyond it.'[18]

choosing a system] one consideration above all should be borne in   212
mind. It is that if man, or the thinking and contemplative creature,
was banished from the earth's surface the sublime and moving
spectacle of nature would become no more than a silent, desolate
scene. The universe would be dumb; night and silence would take
hold of it. Everything would be transformed into an immense
solitude where unobserved phenomena would occur dimly and
unheard. It is the presence of man which makes the existence of
creatures interesting, and what better consideration can we adopt
in dealing with the history of such creatures? Why should we not
put man in our work as he has been put into the universe? Why not
make man the centre point of it? . . . This is what made us decide to
locate the general organization of our work in the principal faculties of man [i.e. memory, reason and imagination] . . . Man is the   213
particular point from which you must set out and to which you must
lead everything back if you want to please, interest and affect
people even in the most abstruse matters and the driest details . . .

[This system will not necessarily be neat and tidy. The editor will
not lay down a general method which all contributors must follow.
The only general rule would be to avoid] the boredom of uni-   217
formity. The encyclopaedic order will from time to time produce
bizarre arrangements, and the alphabetical order will provide
amusing contrasts . . . Making an encyclopaedia is like building a   218
large town. All the houses should not be built in the same way . . .

On all matters it is of the greatest importance to set out clearly   220
their fundamental principles (*la métaphysique des choses*) or their
first and general reasons. Then all the rest becomes clearer and
more definite in the mind. All those supposed mysteries, so criticized in some sciences and so alleged by others to compensate for
criticism, vanish like the ghosts of the night at the approach of day
when they are discussed at a fundamental level . . . It is therefore
necessary to make a point of giving the [basic] reasons, when they
exist; to indicate causes, when they are known; to show effects,
when they are certain; to resolve difficulties by the direct application of the [relevant] principles; to demonstrate truths, unmask
errors and skilfully to discredit prejudices; to teach men to doubt
and to learn; to weaken ignorance and to demonstrate the value of
human knowledge; to distinguish the true from the false, the true
from the plausible, the plausible from the fantastic and unbelievable . . . to know the general course of events and so take each
thing for what it is. In such a way we hope to inspire a taste for

science, a horror of lies and wickedness, and a love of virtue. For   221
everything which does not have happiness and virtue as its final end
is worthless.

[Another way of casting light on disparate subjects will be the use
of cross-references – 'the most important aspect of the encyclopaedic order'. These will not only relate a subject to those similar to
it or with an affinity to it, but they will also] have the opposite
effect; they will oppose ideas, they will contrast principles, they will
attack, shake and secretly overthrow ridiculous opinions which one
does not dare insult openly . . . There would be great skill and
infinite benefit in these cross-references. The whole work should
gain an inner strength and a secret purpose from them, the effects
of which would inevitably be felt in time . . . If these cross-
references, confirming and refuting, are thought out in advance   222
and carried through with skill they will give an encyclopaedia the
character which a good dictionary should have: that of changing
the general way of thinking . . .

We have come to see that this encyclopaedia could only be under-   232
taken in a philosophical century, and that such a century has
arrived . . . This is because such a work needs much bolder thinking   233
than is the rule in those faint-hearted centuries that are concerned
with taste. Everything must be examined, everything must be
aired, without exception and without fuss. We must dare to see, as
we are beginning to become aware, that literary genres, like the
codification of laws and the building of towns, owe their birth to
some freak chance, to some odd event, or sometimes to a moment
of human genius. Those who have followed after the first inventors
have mostly been their slaves; works which should have been seen
as the first step were blindly taken as the last word, and instead of
leading an art to its perfection they have merely retarded it by
reducing other men to the servile condition of copyists. As soon as
a name was given to a composition of a particular type it became
necessary to model all others rigorously on this sketch . . . All
these puerile old ideas must be trampled underfoot. Any barriers
not set up by reason itself must be overthrown. The arts and
sciences must be given the freedom which is so vital to them, and
the admirers of the classics must be told: call *The London Merchant**

---

* *The London Merchant or the History of George Barnwell* by the English
playwright George Lillo made a powerful impression on Diderot. However, this
play did not observe the accepted conventions of tragic drama, hence Diderot's
concern for a new freedom among literary genres.

whatever you like, provided you agree that this play shines with
sublime beauty. A reasoning age was needed [for these changes],   234
when people did not look for rules in writers but in nature, and
could distinguish the true from the false in so many arbitrary
aesthetics. I take the word aesthetic (*poétique*) in its widest sense,
as a system of rules for any form of activity according to which you
must operate in order to succeed.

[This encyclopaedia has also not been too exclusive.] It is some-   242
times important to mention absurdities. They should be treated
lightly and in passing, merely to show the history of the human
mind, which reveals itself better in certain particular oddities than
in the most reasonable action. These oddities are for the moralist
what the dissection of a monster is for the natural scientist: they are
more use to him than the study of a hundred individuals who are all
alike . . .

The person charged with writing about the mechanical arts will   248
not fulfil his task satisfactorily, either for himself or for others,
unless he has studied in depth natural history and especially
mineralogy, unless he is expert in mechanics and informed about
theoretical and experimental physics, and unless he has taken
several courses in chemistry. [If this is the case he will know about
the materials used by artisans, what their properties are, how they
do function and how they might function.] Armed with this knowledge he will begin by introducing some order into his work, by   249
relating the arts to the natural materials. This is always possible
because the history of the arts is nothing other than the history of
nature put to work. [He will ask the artisan to give him a description of his craft, which he will compare and check with his own
account. In addition:] he must show the origin of an art and follow   250
its development step by step, when this is known. If it is not known
he must substitute conjecture and a hypothetical history for the
actual history. We can be sure that in this matter the fiction
(*roman*) will often be more instructive than the truth . . .

I would describe the general character of the style of an encyclo-   254
paedia in two words – *communia, proprie; propria, communiter.**
In following this rule general things will always be elegant and
particular and individual things will always be clear. A universal

* This is an allusion to Horace – '*Difficile est proprie communia dicere*' (*Ars
Poetica*, 128) – which might be translated: 'It is difficult to be individual in
presenting subjects of general interest.'

dictionary of the arts and sciences should be seen as an immense landscape covered with mountains, plains, rocks, water, forests, animals and all the things which make up the variety of a landscape. The light from the sky shines on them all but it illuminates them all differently . . .

[An editor] will think of the world as his school and the human   258
race as his pupil, and he will give lessons in such a way that intelligent men will not lose precious time and the mass of ordinary people will not be put off. There are only two kinds of men, almost equally small in number, who should be equally neglected – transcendent geniuses and imbeciles, neither of whom need teachers . . .

Épicuréisme ou Épicurisme . . . No philosophy has been less   267
understood or more vilified than that of Epicurus. This philosopher was accused of atheism, although he admitted the existence of gods . . . and was regarded as an apologist of debauchery, although during his life he practised all the virtues, especially moderation . . . [Epicurus' moral philosophy was that] happiness is   279
the end of life. It is the secret admission of the human heart and the evident purpose of our actions, even those which seem distant from it. The man who kills himself regards death as a good. It is not a question of reforming nature but of directing its general inclination
. . . Pain is always evil, pleasure always good; yet there is no pure   280
pleasure. The flowers grow at our feet and you must at least bend down to pick them. Nevertheless, O pleasure! It is for you alone that we do all that we do. It is never you whom we avoid but the pain that too often accompanies you. You warm up our cold reason; it is your energy which makes our soul resolute and our will strong . . . If we think well of our fellow men we will find pleasure in fulfilling our duties, because that is a sure way of being thought well of by them . . . Everything should lead to the practice of   281
virtue, the preservation of life and liberty, and contempt for death
. . . What is called natural right is only the symbol of general utility. Common consent and general utility should be the two main rules of our conduct . . . Friendship is one of the greatest goods in life
. . . These are the fundamental doctrines of Epicurus, the only ancient philosopher who could reconcile his ethics with what he took to be the true happiness of man, and reconcile his advice with the appetites and needs of nature. Thus he did have and will always have a large number of disciples. You can make yourself a Stoic, you are born an Epicurean . . .

VOLUME SIX (1756)

Exiger. [To demand] is to ask for something which you have a right   295
to obtain and which the person whom you are asking is reluctant to
grant. We say, he demands the payment of that debt. One can
demand, even from a minister of State, that he is scrupulously
honest.

Fin. End [as a term in morality], is the last of the reasons we   305
have for acting, or that which we regard as such. Thus we ask a
man, to what end have you done this action? What end would you
propose in this situation? Press a man from motive to motive and
you will find that his individual happiness is always the last end of
all his considered acts.

VOLUME SEVEN (1757)

Grecs. [An account of Greek philosophy under three headings –   328
mythical, political and sectarian. Diderot begins with some Greek
myths, among them that of Prometheus.] I share the opinion of
those who see in this former lawgiver a benefactor of the savage
inhabitants of Greece; he led them out of the barbarism in which
they were immersed and made the first rays of the light of the arts
and science shine among them. And the vulture which continually
eats him I see as an emblem of solitude and profound meditation. It
is in this way that one tries to draw the truth out of fables, though
the large number of explanations only shows how uncertain such
explanations are. There is a poetic embroidery so closely bound up
with its material that it is impossible to separate it without tearing
the fabric . . .

[Diderot then discusses the political figures of early Greece and
asks:] How did most of the wise men of Greece come to have so   343
great a name when they had done so little? . . . Is it that general
utility, constantly altering, also causes our judgements to alter as
circumstances do? What was it that the Greeks needed when they
emerged from barbarism? Intelligent men who were resolute in the
practice of virtue, aloof from the seduction of wealth or the terrors
of death; and that is what their wise men were. Today, however, it
is other qualities which will ensure you a reputation after your
death: it is genius, not virtue, which makes great men. Among us
virtue wins little attention and there is only a narrow sphere in
which it can be practised. It is only a privileged creature, the
sovereign, whose virtue can influence general happiness; other

good people die and are spoken about no more. Virtue had the same fate among the Greeks in the following centuries . . .

VOLUME EIGHT (1765)

Preface

When we began to undertake this enterprise, perhaps the largest 350 ever conceived in literature, we only expected the difficulties which would arise from the extent and variety of its subject-matter. This was a passing illusion, however; we did not have to wait long to see the mass of physical obstacles which we had expected increased by an immense number of moral obstacles for which we were quite unprepared. The world grows old in vain, it does not change. The individual person may improve but the race as a whole gets no better or worse. The amount of harmful passions remains the same and there are as many innumerable enemies of everything good and useful today as there used to be . . . [However, the work is now completed, and whatever its faults – which Diderot is well aware of] it cannot be disputed, I think, that our work is up to the level of our 353 century, and that is something. The most enlightened man will find in it ideas which were unknown to him and facts which are unfamiliar. May general education advance so quickly that in twenty years' time there will be scarcely a line in a thousand of our pages which will not be popular! It is for the masters of the world to hasten this happy revolution. It is they who extend or restrict the extent of enlightenment. Happy the times when they will have understood that their safety lies in commanding educated men! . . .

Hobbisme. [An account of the philosophy of Hobbes] . . . Seeing 381 laws trampled underfoot, the throne wavering, men carried away as if by a general frenzy to commit the most terrible acts, [Hobbes] thought that human nature was bad, and from this [he derived] his whole fable or history of the state of nature. Circumstances made his philosophy; he took some passing moments to be the unaltering rules of nature and so became the aggressor of humanity and the apologist of tyranny . . .

[Nevertheless, Diderot admires Hobbes, not only for his materialism, but because he] had received from nature a boldness in 406 thinking . . . a profound, penetrating, precise and wide-ranging mind . . . Even his errors have contributed more to the progress of human thought that a host of works full of common truths. He had the failing of systematic minds, of generalizing from particular facts and skilfully bending them to fit his hypotheses. To read his works you must be a mature and careful person . . . Take care not to go beyond his first principles if you do not want to follow him everywhere he wants to lead you.

The philosophy of M. Rousseau of Geneva is almost the inverse of that of Hobbes. The first thinks man naturally good and the other thinks him wicked. For the philosopher of Geneva the state of nature is a state of peace; for the philosopher of Malmesbury it is a state of war. It is laws and the formation of society which have made man better, if you follow Hobbes, and which have depraved him, if you follow Rousseau. One was born in the midst of tumults and strife; the other lived in the world among men of learning. Different times, different circumstances, different philosophies. M. Rousseau is eloquent and moving; Hobbes is austere, dry and powerful . . . They were both extreme. Between their two systems there is perhaps another which is the true one: it is that although the condition of the human race may be in continual strife, man's goodness and wickedness remain the same, his happiness and mis-   407
fortune circumscribed by limits which he cannot go beyond. All artificial benefits are balanced by evils; all natural evils by good things . . .

Homme. [Man considered from a political point of view.] There   423
is no true wealth except man and land. Man is worth nothing without land and the land is worth nothing without man.

Man increases in value as his number increases. The more numerous a society the more powerful it is in peace and the more formidable it is in war. A sovereign will concern himself seriously with the multiplication of his subjects . . .

But it is not enough to have men, they must be industrious and   424
vigorous. They will be vigorous if they conduct their lives well and if it is easy for them to achieve and maintain a degree of comfort. They will be industrious if they are free. The worst possible administration would be that in which, through lack of freedom in trade, abundance became as much a scourge to a province as famine . . .

The number of workers employed in luxury [trades] and domestic [service] should be decreased. There are circumstances where luxury does not employ men profitably enough; there are no circumstances where domestic service does not employ men at a loss. The latter should be taxed, to the benefit of agriculture.

If the men who work in agriculture, who have the most exhausting work, are the least well provided for they will get fed up with their condition or die in it. To say that [too much] comfort would make them move away from their work is to be both uninformed and cruel.

No one hastens to go into an occupation except in the hope of a pleasant life. It is the enjoyment of a pleasant life which attracts people to it and keeps them in it. A job is only good when the profit exceeds the cost of wages. The wealth of a nation is the product of the sum of its work which is in excess of its costs. The greater and more equally divided the net product is, the better is the administration. A more equally divided net product is preferable to a larger but less equally divided net product which would divide the people into two classes, one wallowing in wealth and the other expiring in poverty . . .   425

Humble . . . We say that the proud palaces of kings are only maintained by the work of the person who lives in a humble cottage. It is by overworking and underfeeding the unlucky that the great achieve their momentary splendour.   442

Jesus Christ . . . Strictly speaking, Jesus Christ was not a philosopher: he was a God. He did not come to offer opinions to men but to announce oracles to them; he did not come to make syllogisms but miracles; the apostles were not philosophers but inspired men. Paul ceased to be a philosopher when he became a preacher . . .   478

Illicite. [Unlawful], that which is prohibited by law. An unlawful thing is not always bad in itself. The fault of almost all legislation is to have increased the number of unlawful actions by bizarre prohibitions. Men are made wicked by the opportunities of becoming law-breakers. And how will they not become law-breakers when the law prohibits them something to which they are continually driven by the constant and unconquerable impulse of nature? And when they have trampled underfoot the laws of society how will they respect the laws of nature? Especially if the order of moral duties had been turned upside down and if prejudice has made them consider acts that are virtually harmless to be atrocious crimes? . . .   499

Immortalité. . . . Names pass away with empires without the voices of the poet and the historian which span the interval of time and place and teach those names to all ages and peoples. Great men are only immortalized by men of letters, [but] the latter can be immortalized without great men. If there are no famous deeds, the man of letters will sing of the activities of nature and the relaxation   502 (*repos*) of the gods, and he will be heard in the future. So the man who despises the man of letters is also despising the judgement of posterity, and he will rarely rise up to something worthy of being handed down to them . . .

Imparfait. . . . There is nothing imperfect in nature, not even   504
monsters. Everything is linked together, and the monster is as necessary an effect of nature as the perfect animal . . .

Inné. [Innate], that which is born with us. Only the faculty of   529
thinking and feeling is innate; all the rest is acquired . . .

Intolérance. The word intolerance is usually understood to mean   541
that violent passion which leads people to hate and persecute those who are in the wrong. But so as not to get different things mixed up, two kinds of intolerance should be distinguished – ecclesiastical and civil.

Ecclesiastical intolerance consists in regarding as false every other religion except your own, and in proclaiming this religion from the roof-tops without any inhibitions of fear, respect for others, or even concern for one's own life. This article will not be concerned with this kind of heroism which has made so many martyrs in the Church's history.

Civil intolerance consists in breaking all relations with other men and in pursuing, by every kind of violent means, those who have a way of thinking about God and his worship different from our own. A few lines taken from Holy Scriptures, the Fathers and [Ecclesiastical] Councils, will be enough to show that the intolerant person taken in this sense is a wicked man, a bad Christian, a dangerous subject, a bad politician and a bad citizen . . . [Diderot quotes various Christian authors in support of this view and then itemizes lines of argument against intolerance:] In an intolerant state the   543
prince would be simply a torturer under the sway of the priest. The prince is the common father of his subjects, and his mission is to   544
make all of them happy . . .

If your truth proscribes me, then my error, which I take for the truth, will proscribe you.

Cease to be violent or cease to reproach the pagans and Muslims for being violent.

When you hate your brother* and preach hate to your neighbour is it the spirit of God which inspires you?

---

* Much of this article was based on an impassioned letter Diderot had written to his brother the Abbé, who was often very sour and narrow-minded in his dealings with the *philosophe*. [18]

Christ has said: my kingdom is not of this world, and you, his disciple, you want to tyrannize over this world! . . .

Which is the way of humanity? Is it that of the persecutor who   546
strikes or that of the persecuted who cries out? If an unbelieving prince has an undeniable right to demand obedience from his subject, an unbelieving subject has an indisputable right to demand protection from his prince. It is a reciprocal obligation . . .

Intolerant men, men of bloodshed, see the consequences of your principles and tremble at them. Men whom I love, whatever your views, it is for you that I have collected these thoughts which I beg you to contemplate. Think about them and you will renounce an atrocious system which agrees neither with an honest mind nor the happiness of the heart.

Bring about your own salvation. Pray for mine, and recognize that everything you allow yourself beyond that is an appalling injustice in the eyes of God and men.

Jordanus Brunus. [Giordano Bruno] . . . Whatever opinion you   558
may hold of his philosophy and his mind you cannot refuse him the glory of having been the first to dare to attack the idol of the schoolmen and break free of the despotism of Aristotle, and by his example and his writing to encourage men to think for them-selves . . .

If you reflect carefully on [his ideas] you will find in them the   561
seed of sufficient reason, the system of monads, optimism and pre-established harmony; in a word, the whole Leibnizian phil-osophy . . . If you collect what is scattered through his works on the nature of God little will be left of Spinoza's thought that can properly be called his own . . .

There are few philosophers who could be compared with this   562
man if the impetuosity of his imagination had permitted him to put his ideas in order . . . But he was born a poet . . .

Jouissance. [The word is used of sexual pleasure, and it is this   575
usage that Diderot describes] . . . Tell me, you who have a soul, if among the objects which nature offers us on every side for our desires, there is any more worthy of pursuit – or the possession and enjoyment of which can make us so happy – as those creatures who   576
think and feel like us? Those creatures, that is, who have the same ideas, experience the same warmth and the same excitements, who offer their tender and delicate arms to embrace us, and whose caresses will be followed by the existence of a new creature who will resemble one or other of you, who in its first movements will look

for you to hold it, whom you will nurture beside you, and love together, who will protect you in your old age, respect you for ever, and whose happy birth has already reinforced the bond which united you? . . .

If there is any perverse man who can be offended by the praise I have given to the most noble and universal of all our passions, I would call up Nature before him and make her speak. She would say: why do you blush to hear aloud the name of a pleasure whose attraction you do not blush to experience under cover of night? Do you not know its aim and what you owe to it? Do you think your mother would have risked her own life giving you life if I had not given an inexpressible charm to the affectionate attentions of her husband? Be silent, you unhappy man, and reflect that it is pleasure which brought you forth out of nothingness . . .

Irregularité. Fault against the rules. Wherever there is a system   581
of rules which it is important to follow there can be deviations from these rules and consequently irregularity.

There is no human production that is not susceptible to irregularity. Sometimes the works of nature can even be accused of irregularity. But there are two considerations which should make us very cautious about that: the absolute necessity of nature's laws, and small extent of our knowledge of nature's variety and her way of working.

Irreligieux . . . You can only be irreligious in the society to which   582
you belong. A Muslim who scorned the law of Mahomet would not commit any crime in Paris, nor a Christian who forgot his worship in Constantinople. It is not the same with moral principles, they are the same everywhere. To neglect them is reprehensible in all places and at all times . . . [Morality] is the universal law which the hand of God has engraved on every heart. It is the eternal precept of *sensibilité* and common needs. Immorality and irreligion should not be confused. Morality can exist without religion and religion can exist, and often does, with immorality.

Without taking the matter beyond this life, there are a host of reasons which can demonstrate that, all things considered, to be happy in this world a man need do nothing more than be virtuous. Sense and experience alone will show that there is no vice which does not entail some misfortune and no virtue which is not accompanied by some happiness; that it is impossible for the wicked to be completely happy and for a good man to be completely unhappy, and that, in spite of self-interest and the attraction of the moment, there is nevertheless only one path to follow . . .

VOLUME NINE (1765)

Législation. The art of giving laws to peoples. The best legislation is 677
that which is simplest and closest to nature; it is a matter not of
opposing men's passions but rather of encouraging them by applying them to public and individual interests. By this means the
number of crimes and criminals would be reduced and there would
be only a very small number of laws.

Leibnitzianisme . . . [Leibniz] saw matter as simple extension, 683
indifferent to movement and to rest, and he came to think that to
discover the essence of matter it was necessary to conceive of a
particular force . . . Aristotle's entelechy, [Leibniz's] system of
monads, *sensibilité* as a general property of matter, and many other
ideas which currently concern us, are here very close . . .

In general physics he had another distinct idea, which was that
God had made what was most perfect and best with the greatest
possible economy; he was the founder of optimism, or that system
which seems to make God an automaton in his decrees and acts,
and to bring back under another name and a spiritual form the fate
of the ancient world, or that necessity in things to be what they
are . . .

Locke. [At Oxford Locke came across the works of Descartes, 710
which stimulated his own thought.] He passed from the study of
Cartesianism to that of medicine, that is to say, he learnt anatomy,
natural history and chemistry, and considered man from an infinite
number of interesting points of view. It is only someone who has
practised medicine a long time who can write on metaphysics . . .

[Locke] renewed the ancient axiom: there is nothing in the 712
understanding which was not previously in the senses, and he
concluded from this that there was no innate speculative faculty or
moral idea. From this he could have drawn another very useful
conclusion: that every idea, when completely broken down, should
be represented in a palpable (*sensible*) form, and that since everything which is in our understanding has come by way of sensation,
everything which goes out of our understanding is fanciful
(*chimérique*) unless – in going back by the same route – it finds a
palpable object outside us to which to attach itself. From this
follows a major rule in philosophy: that every expression which
does not find a palpable object outside our mind to which it can
attach itself, is devoid of meaning . . .

In spite of all that Locke and others have written on ideas and the   713
signs of our ideas I believe the subject to be quite new and the
untouched source of very many truths, the knowledge of which
would greatly simplify the machine called mind and prodigiously
complicate the science called grammar . . .

Malebranche . . . One page of Locke contains more truths than VIII.2
all the volumes of Malebranche; but one line of the latter shows
more subtlety, imagination, *finesse*, and perhaps genius, than the
whole of Locke's thick book . . .

VOLUME TEN (1765)

Métaphysique. [Metaphysic] is the science of the reasons of things.   32
Everything has its metaphysic and its practice; the practice without
the reason for it, and reason without the practice make only an
imperfect science . . .

Modification, Modifier, Modificatif, Modifiable . . . Man,
whether free or not, is a modifiable creature . . . There are no   33
causes without effects; there is no effect which does not modify the
thing on which the cause acts. There is not one atom in nature
which is not exposed to the action of an infinity of different causes;
there is not one of these causes which is active in the same way at
two different points in space; there are therefore no two atoms
strictly alike in nature. The less free a creature is the more certain
one is of modifying it, and the more the modification will necessarily affect it. The modifications which have been imprinted on us
change us permanently, both in the short term and for the rest of
our life . . .

Multitude . . . Mistrust the judgement of the multitude. In   47
matters of reasoning and philosophy its voice is that of wickedness,
stupidity, inhumanity, folly and prejudice. Mistrust it also in things
which depend on either being informed, or on having a developed
sense of taste. Mistrust it in morality; it is not capable of strong and
generous deeds; it is more astonished by them than approving of
them; heroism is almost madness in its eyes. Mistrust it in matters
of feeling; is refinement of feeling so common a quality that it must
be granted to the multitude? On what subject then, and when, is
the multitude right? In everything, but only after a very long time,
because then it is an echo which repeats the judgement of a small
number of sensible men who form in advance the judgement of
posterity . . .

VOLUME ELEVEN (1765)

Naître . . . Strictly speaking you are not born, you do not die; you 47
were from the beginning of things and you will be till their very end.
A point which was alive has grown and developed to a certain
extent by the successive juxtaposition of an infinite number of
molecules. Beyond this extent it declines and dissolves into
separate molecules which will be dispersed in the general and
common mass . . . Life is an essential and basic quality of the living 48
creature; it is not acquired or lost. Inert life must be distinguished
from active life. The two are like a dead force and a live force; take
away the obstacle and the dead force becomes live force; take away
the obstacle and inert life becomes active life . . . There is nothing
absolute about the terms life and death; they only indicate successive states of the same creature . . .

Naturaliste. A person who has studied nature and is versed in the 49
knowledge of natural things, particularly those concerning metals,
minerals, stones, vegetables and animals . . . The name naturalist 50
is also given to those who do not admit there is a God but who
believe that there is only one material substance, clad (*revêtu*) in
different qualities which are as essential to it as length, breadth,
depth, and as a result of which everything occurs necessarily in
nature, as we see it. Naturalist in this sense is synonymous with
atheist, spinozist, materialist etc.

VOLUME TWELVE (1765)

Perfectionner. To correct your faults, advance towards perfection, 64
make less imperfect. You improve yourself, you improve a work.
Man is composed of two main organs, the head, organ of reason,
and the heart, under which is included all the organs of passion –
the stomach, the liver, the bowels. In the state of nature the head
would have almost no influence on our behaviour. It is the heart
which is the source of that, the heart by which the animal man does
everything. It is art which has improved the organ of reason;
everything about its operations is artificial. We have not achieved
the same control over the heart; it is a stubborn, deaf, violent,
passionate, blind organ. In spite of our efforts it has remained what
nature made it: hard or sensitive, feeble or indomitable, cowardly
or bold. The organ of reason is like an attentive teacher which
never stops preaching to it; while it, like a child, never stops crying.

It wears out its teacher who finally abandons it to its own inclination . . . Improving yourself is a long process.

VOLUME THIRTEEN (1765)

Pyrrhonienne, ou Sceptique. [An article about scepticism] . . . The   141
main principle [of scepticism] is that there is no reason which
cannot be counterbalanced by an opposing reason of equal weight
. . . [Among the sceptics must be included Montaigne] author of   152
those *Essais* which will be read so long as there are men who love
truth, strength and simplicity. Montaigne's work is the touchstone
of a good mind. Anyone who gets no pleasure from reading him
must have some fault in his heart or his mind. There is scarcely a
subject which this author has not worked over, for and against, and
always in the same persuasive way. The contradictions of his work
are the faithful image of the contradictions of human understanding. He follows quite naturally the interconnection of his ideas. It
does not matter to him at all where he sets out from, how he
proceeds, or where he ends up. Whatever he says is how it strikes
him at that moment. He is neither more coherent or disconnected
when he writes than when he thinks or dreams. Now it is impossible
that, thinking or dreaming, a man can be completely incoherent
. . . There is a necessary link between any two thoughts, however   153
disparate; this link is either in the senses, in the words, or in the
memory, either within or outside the person. There is a rule to
which even the mad in their most extreme disorder are subject. If
we had a complete account of everything that was happening inside
them, we would see everything held together in them just as in the
wisest and most sensible man. Although nothing may be so varied
as the order of subjects set out by [Montaigne] and though they
seem to be brought together by chance, nevertheless in one way or
another they are connected; and although the subject of public
stage-coaches is rather far from the harangue the Mexicans
delivered to the Europeans when they set foot for the first time in
the New World, nevertheless we arrive in Cuzco [in Peru] from
Bordeaux* though in a rather roundabout way, without any break
in his train of thought. As we go along he reveals all aspects of
himself, some good, some base, sometimes compassionate, sometimes vain, now incredulous, now superstitious . . . But whatever
he says is interesting and instructive.

* A reference to Montaigne, *Essais* (Bk III, Ch. 6).

However, among the ancients and the moderns, scepticism did not have a more formidable defender than Bayle . . . He had few equals in argument, perhaps none superior. No one could get hold of the weakness of a system more subtly; no one could show the value of its benefits more forcefully . . . Although he piles up doubt upon doubt he always proceeds with order. He is a living polyp who divides himself into so many more polyps, always alive; he brings them forth from one another. 158

[Despite his admiration for Montaigne and Bayle, however, Diderot does not wish to endorse scepticism, and his final paragraph is an attack on the extreme scepticism put forward by Berkeley.]

Réfugié. This is the name given to the French Protestants forced to leave France by the Revocation of the Edict of Nantes . . . There is no good Frenchman who has not groaned for years at the thought of the deep wound the kingdom received by the loss of so many useful subjects . . . The spirit of persecution should be stamped out by every enlightened government . . . 216

VOLUME FOURTEEN (1765)

Ressusciter. [To raise from the dead.] Jesus Christ raised Lazarus from the dead. He himself was raised from the dead. There are resurrections in all the world's religions, but only those of Christianity are true. All the others, without exception, are false . . . 218

VOLUME FIFTEEN (1765)

Spinosiste. Follower of the philosophy of Spinoza. Modern spinozists should not be confused with early spinozists. The general principle of the former is that matter is sensitive, which they demonstrate by the development of the egg, an inert body which by the mere application of gradual heat passes to a state of a live and feeling creature; also, by the growth of every animal which in its origin is only a point and which by the nutritive assimilation of plants, . . . becomes a large body feeling and living in a great space. From which they conclude that there is only matter and that matter is sufficient to explain everything. As for the rest, they follow the early Spinozism in all its consequences. 328

VOLUME SIXTEEN (1765)

Théosophes. This is perhaps the strangest kind of philosophy. 365

Those who have professed it looked on human reason with pity;
they had no confidence in its dark and deceitful light. They
supposed that they were illuminated by a supernatural and divine
inner faculty which shone within them . . . [Diderot is referring to
Paracelsus, Robert Fludd, Jacob Boehme, Cabbalists and Rosi-
crucians. Mention of an inner voice leads him first to discuss
Socrates and his daemon.] Can I say a word in favour of the daemon   366
of Socrates and the theosophists? We all have intuitions (*pressenti-
ments*) and these intuitions are sharper and more accurate the more
insight and experience we have. They are sudden judgements
which certain very subtle circumstances produce in us. There is no
fact that is not preceded or accompanied by some phenomena.
However brief, slight and transient these phenomena may be, men
endowed with great *sensibilité* – which is struck by everything and
which nothing escapes – are affected by them but often at a
moment when they give no importance to them. Such men receive
a crowd of these impressions. The memory of the phenomenon
passes but the memory of the impression will be aroused when an
opportunity occurs. Then they announce that such an event will
take place. It seems that a secret voice is speaking to them in the
depth of their heart and warning them. They believe they are
inspired and in effect they are, not by some supernatural or divine
power but by a particular and remarkable foresight (*prudence*). For
what is foresight if not a supposition by which we are led to regard
different circumstances in which we find ourselves as possible
causes of reasons for fear or hope in the future? Now it happens
that this supposition is sometimes based on a large number of slight
things which we have seen, noticed, felt, which we cannot describe,
either to ourselves or to others, but which have a no less necessary
or less strong link with the object of our fear or our hope. It is a
crowd of atoms each of which is imperceptible but which together
form a substantial body which affects us without our knowing why.
God sees the order of the whole universe in the smallest molecule
of matter. The foresight of certain privileged men is a bit like this   367
attribute of the divinity . . .

[After an account of various theosophists, Diderot reflects on
their general character.] I conjecture that these men with their   390
sombre and melancholy temperament only owed their extraordinary and almost divine insight – which was seen in them from
time to time and which led them to ideas which were both mad and
sublime – to some regular disturbance of their physical constitu-

tion. They believed then that they were inspired and they were mad; their fits were preceded by a kind of stupor which they regarded as man's condition in a state of depraved nature. Drawn out of that lethargy by the sudden rush of humours rising up in them, they imagined that it was the divinity coming down, visiting them, working in them . . . Like those who have experienced the delicious rapture and enchantment which the use of opium brings the imagination and the senses, they were happy in their intoxication, dull in the interim. Tired, exhausted, overwhelmed, they found that ordinary life disgusted them. They sighed for the moment of exaltation, inspiration, alienation. Calm or excited they fled the company of men, unbearable both to themselves and others.

O how close genius and madness are! Those whom heaven has marked favourably or unfavourably are subject more or less to these symptoms. They are shut up or chained up, or else statues are built to them. They make prophecies, from thrones or theatres or pulpits; they captivate their audiences. They are listened to, followed and admired, or insulted, ridiculed and stoned. Their fate does not depend on them but on the circumstances in which they appear. It is times of ignorance and great disasters which produce them. Then men, thinking they are being pursued by the divinity, gather around these kinds of madmen, who order them about. They order sacrifices, and these are made; prayers, and people pray; fasts, and people fast; murders, and people slaughter; songs of delight and joy, and everyone is decorated with flowers, all 391 dance and sing; temples and they are built; the most desperate enterprises, and they succeed. When such men die they are worshipped. Pindar, Aeschylus, Mahomet, Shakespeare, Roger Bacon and Paracelsus must be included in this category. Change the period and the person who was a poet would have been a magician, or a prophet or a lawgiver. O men! to whom nature has given this great and extraordinary imagination – which cries out, which subdues, by which we are counted wise or idiotic – who can predict your destiny? You were born to walk between the earth's applause or its ignominy, to lead people to happiness or to misfortune, and to leave behind you feelings of praise or detestation . . .

Vice . . . A difference has grown up between a failing and a vice, as　443
a result of usage. Every vice is a failing but every failing is not a vice.
A man who has a vice is presumed to have some freedom which
[therefore] makes him guilty in our eyes. A failing is generally
attributed to nature: the man is excused, nature is accused.

When philosophy discusses these distinctions with care and precision it often finds them to be empty of sense. Is a man more
responsible for being cowardly, indulgent or angry than squint-
eyed, hunchbacked or lame? The more that is attributed to physical
constitution, education, national customs, climate, to the circumstances which have affected our life . . . the less vain you are of the
good qualities you have and which you owe so little to yourself, and
the more indulgent you are for the failings and vices of others; the
more careful you are in using the words vicious and virtuous–which　444
are never spoken without hate or love – and the more inclined you
are to substitute for them the phrases happily or unhappily born,
phrases which are always accompanied by a feeling of pity. You
have pity for a blind man; and what is a wicked man if not a man
who is short-sighted and does not see beyond the moment he acts?

Voluptueux. A person who loves sensual pleasures. In this sense　446
everyone is more or less sensual. Those who preach [otherwise are]
bilious men who should be shut up in a madhouse . . . According to　447
them we cannot have enough pain and grief. They would like
suffering to precede, accompany and follow every need; they think
they humour God by doing without the things which he has
created. They do not see that if such denial is good then God did
wrong in creating them . . .

6

Theatre

I

As a young man Diderot had a passion for theatre. He even thought of becoming an actor. His novel *Les Bijoux indiscrets* devoted two chapters (XXXVII and XXXVIII) to a critical examination of the contemporary French theatre and much of this criticism was later included by Lessing in his *Hamburg Dramaturgy*. His editorial work on the *Encyclopédie* then seems to have replaced the theatre as his consuming interest, for Diderot did not write the articles on theatre himself but had them written by Marmontel. However, in the article 'Encyclopédie' published in 1755 there are signs of a reawakened interest. 'Call *The London Merchant* whatever you like, provided you agree that this play shines with sublime beauty' (see pp. 107-8); if there was no existing literary genre to describe it then a new genre must be invented. The following year Diderot undertook that task.

In the summer of 1756 he wrote a play *Le Fils naturel*, which was published early in 1757 together with a Prologue and the *Entretiens sur le Fils naturel* which together provided 'the true history of the piece'.[1] The *Entretiens* were three discussions about the play conducted by Diderot and Dorval, the leading character in the play. The play itself, subtitled *The trials of virtue*, was about a conflict between friendship and love experienced by Dorval. The latter was illegitimate, the *fils naturel* of the title, but the arrival of his father in the last act reveals that Rosalie, the girl he was in love with, is in fact his sister. However, he had already sacrificed his love for the sake of his friendship – his best friend Clairville also being in love with Rosalie – so virtue had already prevailed. This unremarkable plot owed something to a Goldoni play, *Il vero amico*, and Diderot was accused of plagiarism; but while the initial situation was very similar the style and development of the play were quite different. Goldoni's play was light, Diderot's was serious, not to say earnest.

The most interesting feature of *Le Fils naturel* is Diderot's concern to make it realistic. His principal criticism of the contemporary theatre was its exaggerated artificial manner, 'a thousand leagues from what is natural'.[2] The events of *Le Fils naturel* are presented as a re-enactment of real events. In the Prologue Diderot explains how, when staying in the country, he had heard about Dorval, how he had met him and was told about what had happened; how Dorval's father had suggested that an account of these events should be written down and the people concerned should re-enact it once a year. Diderot himself had been present at the first such occasion. In other words, the play is fact, not fiction. One of the characters in *Les Bijoux indiscrets* had said that 'the perfection of a play consists in such an exact imitation of an action that the spectator . . . imagines he is present at the action itself'.[3] These criteria, ultimately deriving from Aristotle, had been lost sight of. Diderot wanted to give them new life.

It was for this reason that the *Entretiens* were published together with the play. By examining the play, criticizing it, justifying what had been written and suggesting ways in which it could be rewritten, Diderot gave clear indications of the kind of theatre he desired. The *Entretiens* were to be the *Ars Poetica* of the new theatre, and it is evident that he had Horace's example in mind; there are both direct quotations from and indirect references to Horace's text. The work conveys that strong sense of a new beginning that is also evident in the early volumes of the *Encyclopédie*. Just as in the latter there was a continual emphasis on facts and things, so in the *Entretiens* there is a concern for real events: 'daily experience'[4] must be the yardstick, 'abandon the boards [of theatre stages], come back into the living-room',[5] 'only the real world pleases reason'.[6] Diderot disliked both the artificial conventions of the Comédie-Française and the exaggerated knockabout of the popular theatres.[7] He wanted a kind of theatre that corresponded to the lives of the predominantly middle-class audience who were coming to constitute the bulk of theatre audiences and with whom he felt the closest sympathy. This theatre he called the 'serious genre', 'serious comedy', 'domestic tragedy', 'bourgeois tragedy', or, the term by which it came to be generally known, simply '*le drame*'. Serious plays at that time were meant to conform to the conventions of the classical theatre; that is to say, they had to be written in verse, to obey the unities of time, place and action, and to treat an elevated subject. Diderot wanted to widen or loosen these conventions so that plays written in prose, treating domestic subjects, were regarded as being no less worthy of critical respect than classical tragedy. George Lillo's *The London Merchant* had pointed the way ahead.

Diderot was not the first to turn away from the themes and form of classical tragedy towards serious domestic drama. Nivelle de la Chaussée and Gresset had earlier written plays in these terms and Voltaire's *Nanine* (1749) had been based on Richardson's novel *Pamela*. But no one before him had articulated so comprehensively or forcefully a new aesthetic. On some issues Diderot's position was ambiguous. He had great respect for the classical tradition and saw the new drama as being complementary rather than an alternative. He was also drawn in opposite directions, on the one hand to extreme situations displaying violent emotion, and on the other hand to sober situations showing everyday concerns; we find similar tendencies in his writing about art. But as is so often the case it is the abundance of his ideas, rather than their consistency, that is impressive. (He even envisages a theatre which seems like a reflection of his own mind, in which several scenes overlap and happen at the same time.) One of the most notable and influential of these ideas was that of plays concentrating on people's social function (*les conditions*); by this he meant the social rather than personal aspect of character, people as representatives of a social type.

Besides these theoretical concerns there is a personal element in the play and the *Entretiens* which both strengthens the play and clouds the theoretical issues. Shortly before Diderot sat down to write the play Rousseau had moved out of Paris to live at the Hermitage in Montmorency. This move was a symptom and a cause of the growing estrangement between the two men. Dorval's character owes much to Rousseau and the longest and most convincing scene in the play, Act IV Scene 3, is that in which Clairville's sister pleads with Dorval not to go away. Rousseau was not wrong to take offence at this scene, since Diderot clearly had him in mind. It is his absence that Diderot laments in his introduction: 'I no longer see Dorval, I no longer hear him. I am alone, among the dust of books, in the darkness of a study, writing cold, sad, feeble lines.'[8] And it is his presence which he evokes at the opening of the second *Entretien*.

Entretiens sur le Fils naturel

[Most of the first *Entretien* is concerned with the priority of making
stage action true to nature, and how that relates to theatrical
conventions. The second *Entretien* opens with a portrait of Dorval.]

   The next day, I made my way back to the foot of the hill. It was a   97
wild and solitary spot. In the distance, a few hamlets could be seen,
scattered across the plain; beyond them, an uneven ridge of jagged
mountains, partly shutting off the horizon. There were oak trees
providing shade, and the muffled sound of an underground stream
flowing nearby. It was that season of the year when the earth is
covered with the fruits it grants to men as a reward for all their
sweat and toil. Dorval had arrived before me. I drew near without
his seeing me. He was absorbed in the natural spectacle before him.
His chest was thrown out. He was breathing deeply. He was examining everything in the scene with an attentive gaze. I could follow
on his face the various impressions he was receiving, and I was just
beginning to share his ecstasy, when I exclaimed, almost without
meaning to, 'He is under the spell.'

   He heard me and answered in a voice filled with emotion, 'It is
true. This is a place where one can truly see nature. This is the
sacred haunt of enthusiasm. If a man has been endowed with
genius, then he will leave the city and its inhabitants. Following the
impulse of his heart, he loves to mingle his tears with the crystal
waters of a spring, to place flowers upon a grave, to tread with light
feet upon the tender meadow grasses, to move with slow footsteps
through fertile fields, to contemplate the toil of men, to escape into
the depths of woods. He loves their secret horror; he wanders, he
seeks a cave that will inspire him. Who mingles his voice with the
torrent tumbling down the mountainside? Who senses the sublime
in some lonely spot? Who listens to himself in solitude and silence?
[The man of genius.] Our poet lives on the shores of a lake. His   98
eyes wander over the waters, and his genius unfolds. It is there that
he is possessed by the spirit – tranquil one moment, violent the next
– that agitates his soul or calms it as it will . . . O Nature, everything
good is contained in your heart! You are the fertile source of every
truth! Nothing in this world but truth and virtue are worthy of my
concern . . . Enthusiasm is born of some natural object. If the mind
has seen it from various and striking aspects, then it is filled,

agitated, tormented by it. The imagination takes fire, the passions are aroused. We are successively astonished, moved, outraged, angry. Without enthusiasm, either the true idea does not present itself or, if by chance, we do encounter it, then it proves impossible to pursue it. The poet feels the moment of enthusiasm coming upon him; it follows a period of meditation. Its onset is heralded by a quivering that begins in his breast, then flows deliciously and rapidly out to the ends of his limbs. Soon it is no longer a quivering but an intense and lasting fire that sets him aflame, makes him pant, consumes him, kills him – but also endows whatever he touches with a soul and life. If this fire were to flame even higher, then phantoms would multiply before his eyes. His passion would be raised almost to the point of madness. He could experience no relief except by pouring out a torrent of ideas, crowding one against another, thrusting one another aside, driving one another out.'

Dorval was himself experiencing this state as he described it. I made no reply. A silence fell between us, during which I saw that he was growing calmer. Soon, like a man emerging from a deep sleep, he asked me, 'What have I been saying? What was it I had to tell you? I no longer remember.'

MYSELF   You were going to explain some ideas that Clairville's   99
scene of despair had suggested to you concerning the passions: how they should be expressed, what kind of delivery and gestures the actor should use.

DORVAL   The first is that a writer should never make his characters witty, but that he should know how to place them in situations that lend them wit . . .

Dorval then sensed, from the rapidity with which he had just uttered these words, that his soul was still in a state of some agitation. He broke off; and in order to give himself time to regain his calm or, rather, to counteract this inner disturbance with a more violent though fleeting emotion, he told me the following story:

DORVAL   A peasant girl who lived in the village whose roofs you can see above the tree-tops, over there between those two mountains, once sent her husband to visit her relatives, who lived in a neighbouring hamlet. While he was there, this unfortunate man was killed by one of his brothers-in-law. The following day, I visited the house where the accident had taken place. I have never forgotten the spectacle I beheld there, nor the words I heard. The dead man was lying on a bed. His bare legs were dangling over the side of it. His wife was lying in distraction on the floor. She was clasping her husband's feet, and she said, breaking into a flood of tears and making a gesture that drew tears from all the others present, 'Alas! When I sent you here, I did not think these feet were bearing you to your death.' Do you believe that a woman of any higher rank could have expressed herself with greater pathos than that? No. The same situation would have drawn forth the same words, her soul would have existed only in that moment; and what the artist has to discover is what everyone would say in a like case, the emotion that no one will be able to hear without instantly recognizing it in himself.

Great interests, great passions. Those are the well-springs of noble speech, of true speech. Almost all men speak well when they are dying.

What I like about Clairville's scene is precisely that it contains nothing except what passion inspires when it is extreme. Passion   100 attaches itself to one principal idea. It falls silent and then it returns to that idea, almost always by means of exclamations.

The scene also employs mime, and though mime is an art that has been badly neglected in this country, you yourself saw how success-ful it was in this case.

There is too much talking in our plays; consequently, our actors do not act enough. We have lost an art whose effectiveness was well known in classical times. At one time, mime plays depicted all conditions of men – kings, heroes, tyrants, the rich, the poor, city dwellers and country folk – selecting from every rank the trait that was peculiar to it and from every action its most striking aspect . . .

What this scene also made me see is that there are moments that   101 should be left almost entirely to the actor. It is his right to use the text of the scene as he sees fit, to repeat certain words, to return to certain ideas, to cut out some and to add others. In a *cantabile* passage, the composer will allow a great singer freedom to exercise his own taste and talent; he will be satisfied to provide no more than the principal intervals of a beautiful tune. And the poet should do likewise when he knows his actor well. What is it that moves us when we see a man animated by some great passion? Is it his words? Sometimes. But what never fail to stir us are cries, inarticu-late words, a broken voice, a group of monosyllables with pauses in between, a murmur, impossible to describe, deep in the throat or between the teeth. As the violence of the emotion cuts off the breath and fills the mind with unease, so the syllables of words become dis-   102 jointed, and the man jumps from one idea to another; he initiates a great many different lines of thought but does not finish any of them; and though there are a few sentiments he succeeds in expressing during the onset of his passion, and to which he returns again and again, the rest is merely a sequence of confused and feeble noises, of fading sounds, of stifled cries – all things about which the actor knows far more than the poet. The voice, the tone, the gestures, the stage movements – these are what belong to the actor. And these are the things that strike us, especially in the portrayal of great passions. It is the actor who provides the written text with energy. It is he who conveys to our ears the force and the truth of a character's words . . .

[This concern for truthfulness stems from a belief in the moral value of theatre.] I used to feel bitter when I went to the theatre and compared the usefulness of theatres with the little care that is taken in training actors. Then I used to say to myself: 'Ah my friends, if we should ever go to Lampedusa to found a small colony of happy people, far away, in the middle of the sea, these actors would be our preachers; and we would certainly select them according to the importance of their ministry. Every people has its sabbath, and we would have ours. On these solemn days a fine tragedy would be performed which would teach men to fear the passions, or a good comedy which would instruct them in their duties and inspire them with a taste for fulfilling them.' 105

[The two men then continue discussing the merits of *Le Fils naturel*.]

MYSELF   Then you think your play would not be successful on the stage? 112

DORVAL   There would be difficulties. It would mean either cutting out certain sections of the text or else changing our methods of staging plays.

MYSELF   What do you mean by changing our methods of staging plays?

DORVAL   I mean clearing all those things off the stage itself that are at present making such a small area even smaller still;* introducing scenery; being able to present different stage pictures from the ones we've been looking at for the past hundred years; and, in short, transporting Clairville's drawing room to the theatre just as it is . . .

---

* Diderot is referring to the seating of privileged spectators on the stage, a custom that was abolished two years later.

What a moment of terror and pity is that when we hear the prayer   114
and the groans of the unfortunate Orestes as they pierce through
the shrieks and frightful gestures of the cruel beings who are
hunting him down!* Could we execute such a scene on our stages?
No, for we can present only single actions, whereas in nature there
are almost always several occurring simultaneously, and the
concomitant representation of these, each action lending force to   115
the others, would produce terrible effects in us. Then we should
tremble indeed at the thought of going to the theatre – and yet be
unable to prevent ourselves from going. Then at last, instead of all
the petty, passing emotions, the lukewarm applause, the scanty
tears with which our present-day poets content themselves, they
might overwhelm people's minds, bring confusion and fear into
their souls, and we should see the prodigies of ancient tragedy, so
possible and so little believed, renew themselves in our time. In
order to appear again, they are only waiting for a man of genius
who is able to mingle mime with speech, combine a spoken scene
with a silent one, and take advantage of the moment when they
come together, especially of that instant, whether it be frightening
or comic, when we see, as we always would, that the two scenes are
on the point of merging.

[After further discussion Dorval appeals to Voltaire to regener-
ate the theatre by writing in the new genre he envisages:]

'O you who still possess all the fire of your genius at an age when   119
others have nothing left but cold reason, why can I not be at your
side like one of the Eumenides to scourge you forward? I would
give you no peace. You would write it for us, this work . . . And
then, in disappearing from among us, you would not leave us still
longing for a genre that you had the power to create.'

MYSELF   And what will you call this new genre?

DORVAL   Bourgeois and domestic tragedy. The English have
The London Merchant and *The Gamester*, their prose tragedies.   120
And Shakespeare's tragedies are half in verse, half in prose. The
first poet who made us laugh with prose introduced prose into
comedy. The first poet who makes us weep with prose will have
introduced prose into tragedy.

But in art, as in nature, everything is linked; if we approach
nearer to the truth in one way, then we shall find other ways of
approach opening up to us as well. Then we shall see those natural

* Dorval is talking about Aeschylus' *Eumenides*.

situations portrayed upon the stage that propriety, ever the enemy of genius and great effects, has outlawed from it. I shall never tire of shouting to our fellow countrymen: Truth! Nature! The Ancients! Sophocles! *Philoctetes*! For Sophocles, in his play about Philoctetes, showed him, lying at the entrance to his cave, dressed in tattered rags. He writhed on the ground, racked by a fit of pain; he let out cries, he made inarticulate noises. The setting was primitive; the action unfurled without the help of machinery. Real clothes, real speech, and a simple and natural plot. Our taste would be completely corrupt if such a spectacle did not affect us more than that of a richly dressed man, tricked out in finery . . .

[The third *Entretien* develops this discussion of the serious genre.]

After a few general remarks on the way events occur in real life   135 and the way they are imitated on the stage, he said to me:

DORVAL   We can divide every moral matter into a middle and two extremes. It appears then, since every dramatic action is a moral matter, that there should exist a central genre and two extreme genres. We already have the last two; they are comedy and tragedy. But man is not always in a state of grief or joy. Therefore   136 there must be a point that bisects the distance between the comic genre and the tragic genre.

Terence has written a play [of this kind, his *Hecyra*] . . . How would you classify this particular play? Is it comedy? There isn't a funny line in it. Tragedy? There is no point at which it arouses terror or pity or any of the great passions. Yet it holds the interest; and any dramatic composition, even though it contains no absurdity to make us laugh or perils to make us shudder, will always hold the interest if the poet adopts the tone that we ourselves use in serious matters, and if the action evolves through a series of perplexities and hindrances. And since such actions are the ones most commonly met with in real life, it seems to me that the genre taking these as its object will be the most useful and the most comprehensive. I shall term this the serious genre.

Once this genre has been established, there will be no rank in society and no important actions in life that we cannot relegate to some part of the dramatic system.

Would you like to enlarge this system to its greatest possible extent? Would you like to see it include truth as well as fantasy, the world of imagination as well as the world of reality? Then add burlesque below comedy and the fantastic above tragedy.

MYSELF   I understand what you mean: burlesque . . . comedy   137
. . . serious drama . . . tragedy . . . fantastic drama.

DORVAL   It is the advantage of the serious genre, being placed
midway between the other two, that it can draw its resources from
both above and below itself. This is not true of the tragic and comic
genres. All the nuances available to comedy are comprised in the
region between itself and the serious genre, and all those available
to tragedy between the serious genre and the tragic genre . . .

If you need to be convinced of the danger that lies in crossing the   138
barrier nature has placed between the genres, then push things to
excess: take two widely separated genres, such as tragedy and
burlesque, and put them together; the result will be a scene in
which a grave senator indulges in the vilest debauchery at the feet
of a courtesan being immediately succeeded by another in which a
band of conspirators discusses its plans for destroying a republic.*

The subject [in the serious genre] should be important, the plot   139
simple, domestic, and close to everyday life.

I want to see no valets in serious drama. Right-thinking people
do not admit valets to a knowledge of their affairs, and the scenes
will be the more interesting for taking place entirely between
masters. If a valet speaks on the stage as he does in real life, he is
tedious, if he speaks in any other way, he is false. The nuances
borrowed from the comic genre must never be too strong. If they
are, the work will make us laugh and cry, and it will lack both unity
of interest and unity of tone.

The serious genre contains soliloquies. From this, I conclude
that it is nearer to tragedy than to comedy; for in comedy, soliloquies are infrequent and always short.

The moral content of a serious drama should be general and
strong . . .

A great deal of attention should be paid to mime. All *coups de
théâtre* whose effect is momentary should be eliminated, and tableaux invented in their place . . .

But, above all, remember that there is no general principle: there   140
is not one of the rules I have just set forth that could not success-
fully be infringed by a man of genius . . .

MYSELF   But what material will it use, this serious kind of   152

* See Otway's *Venice Preserved*, Shakespeare's *Hamlet*, and most plays of the
English theatre. (Note by Diderot.)

comedy that you look upon as a new branch of dramatic literature? There are only a dozen or so clearly defined and truly comic types in the whole of human nature.

DORVAL   I agree.

MYSELF   The minor differences observable in men's characters   153
can never be used to such good effect as clear-cut humours.

DORVAL   Again I agree. But do you know what follows from that? It follows that we should no longer be portraying characters, properly speaking, in our plays, but rank or station (*les conditions*). Up till now, character has always been the main object of comedy, and station only accessory. Now the social function must become its principal object, and character merely accessory. The entire plot used to be built from the character. Generally speaking, we tried to find a set of circumstances that would bring it out, then linked those circumstances together. But it is social station – its duties, its advantages, and its difficulties – that should serve as the basis of our plays. In my opinion, this is a more fruitful, more comprehensive, and more useful source of material than characters. A character need only be slightly exaggerated for the spectator to be able to say to himself, 'I'm not like that.' But he cannot deceive himself in this way when it is his social function that is being portrayed before him; he cannot fail to recognize his duties. He is compelled to apply what he hears to himself.

MYSELF   It seems to me that some of these subjects have already been treated.

DORVAL   No, they haven't. Make no mistake about that.

MYSELF   But we have financiers in our plays, don't we?

DORVAL   Certainly we do. But the social role of the financier has never been explored.

MYSELF   It would be difficult to cite a play without a father in it.   154

DORVAL   True, but the father as a social function has not been done. I would like you to consider, in a word, whether the various social functions, their duties, their disadvantages, and their dangers, have ever been depicted on the stage; whether they have ever formed the basis for the plots and moral arguments of our plays; and whether these same duties, advantages, disadvantages and dangers do not daily provide us with the spectacle of men enmeshed in the most complicated situations.

MYSELF   So you want us to enact the man of letters, the philosopher, the merchant, the judge, the lawyer, the politician, the citizen, the magistrate, the financier, the great lord, the *intendant*.

DORVAL   Yes, all those plus the fundamental family relationships: what it means to be a father, a husband, a sister, or a brother.
A father! What a subject that is in an age such as ours, when no one
seems to have the slightest idea of what it means to be the father of
a family!

Remember that new social roles are coming into being every
day. Remember that there is possibly nothing we know less about
than social functions, and nothing that should interest us more. We
each of us have our own place in society, but we all have to deal
with men of every other station.

Social function! Think how many important details such a source
will yield! How many public and domestic themes! How many
unknown truths! How many fresh situations! Are there not the
same contrasts between social roles as between characters? Will
the writer have any difficulty in producing conflicts between
them? . . .

[After a discussion of opera and ballet Dorval then lists the
reforms to be carried out:]

Bourgeois and domestic tragedy to be created.   167
The serious genre to be improved.
Man's social function to be substituted for characters, perhaps in
    all the genres.
Mime to be related closely to the dramatic action.
Scenery to be changed; tableaux to be substituted for *coups de
    théâtre*, a new source of invention for the poet and of study for
    the actor . . .
Real tragedy to be introduced into opera.
Dance to be shaped into the form of a true poem, to be written
    and distinguished from all other imitative arts . . .

II

Although *Le Fils naturel* was declared unplayable by Grandval,
one of the leading actors of the Comédie-Française, it was well
received by most of Diderot's friends. He had announced in the
Entretiens his plans for another play, *Le Père de famille*, and

encouraged by the reception of the printed text of *Le Fils naturel* he now wrote this. It was published, together with another theoretical essay, the *Discours sur la poésie dramatique*, in November 1758.

Le Père de famille demonstrates 'what it means to be the father of a family', that is to say, it is about the social function of fatherhood, rather than a particular father; the leading character is known only as The Father, he is never given a name. In this way the play fulfils one of the requirements Diderot had suggested for *le drame*. This stemmed not only from a desire for plays to relate to, and reveal, social circumstances; it also arose from Diderot's concern that plays should not be confined to their time and place but be true for all men. 'A writer who wants to ensure that his works have an enduring attraction . . . [will show those features of nature and those] passions of men which are always the same. Such will be the truth, conviction and permanence of his style that his works still astonish the centuries to come.'⁹ This preference for the general rather than the individual was a recipe for dull theatre and *Le Père de famille* is a dull play. Its best moments are those involving Saint-Albin, the son who is in love with a girl his father thinks an unsuitable partner. This character owes much to the youthful Diderot. 'The only way to succeed,' says Hardouin, the central character in *Est-il bon? Est-il méchant?*, 'is to turn the matter into something personal.'¹⁰ When Diderot acted according to this precept he was invariably interesting; in his public writings on the theatre, however, he wanted to achieve a kind of objective authority which transcended personal inclinations. The results were influential but, in some respects, disappointing.

The *Discours* that was appended to *Le Père de famille* deals with the same matters as the *Entretiens sur le Fils naturel* but in a more organized way. As is usually the case with Diderot organization was achieved at the expense of interest; the most vivid passages are those where he digresses from the main subject to discuss the nature of imagination, the demands of poetry, or, at the very end, how objective values can be achieved. 'O you who make general rules, how little you know about art,'¹¹ he exclaims, but most of his *Discours* deals precisely with general rules. He is anxious that the kind of theatre he is advocating shall belong to a clearly defined genre – he criticizes the English theatre for its indifference to this concern – but his striving for definition only makes matters more opaque. 'It is true that I have little knowledge of the theatre,'¹² he admits ingenuously at one point, and reading his laborious discussion of writing plays – should you pay more attention to the plot or the dialogue? – we are inclined to agree.

One aspect of *le drame* which is given much more attention than previously is the moral aspect. In the *Entretiens* Dorval had said that 'the moral content of a serious drama should be general and strong' and in a work of art 'the spirit of the century should be evident'.[13] In *Le Fils naturel* Constance proclaims that 'the times of barbarism are passed. Our century has become enlightened. Reason has become refined. Almost the only works people read are those which inspire men with a general benevolence,'[14] and Clairville sings the praises of commerce.[15] The central thrust of the play was the triumph of virtue. But this aspect received less emphasis in the *Entretiens* than the need for more realistic subjects and presentations. In the *Discours* however Diderot leaves his reader in no doubt about the purpose of *le drame*. It is to be no less serious or elevated than the greatest plays of previous epochs.

The *Discours* was dedicated to Grimm, who had done much to encourage Diderot in writing his plays, and whom Diderot addresses in the course of the work. Its epigraph was taken from Horace's *Ars Poetica* (304–5): 'I will take the part of a grindstone, which sharpens steel without itself having the ability to cut.'

Discours sur la poésie dramatique

I. ON DRAMATIC GENRES

If a nation had only ever had one kind of play, pleasant and light, and someone suggested to them another kind, serious and moving, do you know, my friend, what they would think of it? Unless I am very much mistaken, men of sense, having considered the possibility, would say, 'What use is this kind of play? Does life not bring us enough real afflictions, without inventing imaginary ones? Why should we admit melancholy even into our amusements?' They would speak as if foreign to the pleasure of being moved to pity and of shedding tears.

Habit holds us captive. Has a man with a spark of genius appeared and produced some work? At first he astonishes and divides opinion; gradually he unites it; soon he is followed by a crowd of imitators; the models multiply; observations are

189

collected, rules created; the art springs up, and its limits are fixed; and everything which is not included in the narrow limits that have been outlined is pronounced bizarre and bad: these are the pillars of Hercules; to go beyond them is to go astray. 190

However, nothing prevails against truth. The inferior passes, despite the praise of imbecility, and the superior remains, in spite of the indecision of ignorance and the cry of envy. The exasperating thing is that men obtain justice only when they are no more . . . What is to be done, then? Remain inactive, or submit to a law to which better men than we have been submissive? Woe to him who labours, if his work is not the source of his sweetest moments, or if he does not know how to content himself with little approval. The number of good judges is limited. O my friend, when I have published something, whether it be the rough outline of a drama, a philosophical idea, a bit of ethics or literature – because my mind is refreshed by variety – I shall come to see you. If my presence does not disturb you, if you meet me with a satisfied air, I shall wait without impatience for time and justice, which time always brings, to appreciate my work.

If one form exists, it is difficult to introduce another. If it is introduced, another prejudice arises: soon people imagine that the two adopted forms are neighbours and are connected.

Zeno denied the reality of movement. As a complete answer, his adversary began to walk, and if he had merely limped, he would still have answered.

I tried, in *Le Fils naturel*, to give the idea of a drama which was between comedy and tragedy.

Le Père de famille, which I promised, and which continual distractions have delayed, is between the serious genre of *Le Fils naturel* and comedy.

And if I ever have the leisure and the courage, I do not despair of writing a drama which comes between the serious genre and tragedy. 191

Whether some merit is recognized in these works, or none is admitted, they will none the less demonstrate that the gap which I have discovered between the two established genres was not illusory.

II. ON SERIOUS COMEDY

Here, then, is the system of drama in its whole extent: light comedy, which has for its object ridicule and vice; serious comedy, which has for its object virtue and the duties of man; the kind of tragedy which would have for its object our domestic afflictions; and tragedy which has for its object public catastrophes and the afflictions of the great.

But who shall depict the duties of man for us convincingly? What would be the qualities of the poet who gave himself that aim? He should be philosophically minded, should have examined himself, have observed human nature, be profoundly instructed in the conditions of society, and know its workings and consequences, its drawbacks and advantages . . .

If the circumstances of men provide us with plays like Molière's *Les Fâcheux*, that is already something; but I believe that we could go further.

The obligations and difficulties of a nation are not all of the same importance. It seems to me that one could seize the principal problems, make of them the basis of the work, and leave the rest in the details. That is what I tried in *Le Père de famille*, where the social position of the son and the daughter are my two central pivots. Chance, birth, education, the duties of fathers toward their children and of children toward their parents, marriage, celibacy – everything that relates to the condition of a father of a family is brought out by the dialogue. Let another writer take up his pen, let him have the talent which I lack, and you will see what his drama will become.

192

The objections raised against this genre prove only one thing: that it is difficult to handle, that it cannot be the work of a child, and that it presupposes more art, more ideas, more seriousness and mental force than those who devote themselves to the theatre usually have.

To judge a work well, one should not compare it to another work . . . Whether or not there are existing models is of no importance. There is a rule behind everything, and the poetic reason was there before there were any poets; otherwise, how could one have judged the first poem? Was it good because it was pleasing, or was it pleasing because it was good?

The duty of man is as rich a basis for the dramatic poet as his follies and vices; and sincere serious plays will succeed everywhere, but more certainly among a depraved people than elsewhere. It is in going to the theatre that they will preserve themselves from the company of the wicked by whom they are surrounded; it is in the theatre that they will find those among whom they would like to live; it is there that they will see humanity as it is, and become reconciled with it. Good men are rare, but they do exist . . .   193

Virtue and virtuous men must always be kept in mind when one writes. It is you, my friend, whom I evoke when I take up my pen; it is you whom I have before my eyes when I work. It is Sophie whom I wish to please. If you have smiled at me, if she has let fall a tear, if you have both liked me better, I am repaid.

When I heard the peasant scenes in *Le Faux généreux*,* I said, 'There is something which will please all the world, at all times; there is something which will make them melt in tears.' Fact has confirmed my judgement. That episode is entirely in the sincere, serious genre.

It will be said, 'The example of one happy episode proves nothing. And if you do not break up the monotonous discussion of virtue by the brawling of some ridiculous, and even slightly forced characters, as everyone else has done, I still believe that you will   194
bring out nothing but cold, colourless scenes; boring and unhappy morality; and sorts of sermons in dialogue.'

Let us run through the parts of a drama, and let us see. Is it by the subject that it must be judged? In the sincere, serious genre, the subject is no less important than in light comedy, and it is treated in a truer fashion. Is it by the characters? They may be as diverse and as original, and the poet is forced to portray them more strongly. Is it by the passions? They are shown with proportionately more energy, as the interest is greater. Is it by style? It will be more vigorous, graver, more elevated, more violent, more susceptible to what we call sentiment, the quality without which no style speaks to the heart . . .

I call forth the beautiful passages of Terence, and I ask in what genre his scenes of fathers and lovers are written.

If, in *Le Père de famille*, I did not know how to respond to the importance of my subject; if the progress of it is slow, the passions long-winded and didactic; if the characters of the father, his son, Sophie, the Commander, Germeuil and Cécile all lack comic vigour, is that the fault of the genre, or is it mine?

Let someone try to put on the stage the circumstances of a judge; let him plot his subject in a way that is suitable to him and which I understand; let the man be forced by the duties of his position   195
either to lose the dignity and sanctity of his post, and to dishonour

---

* *L'Orpheline, ou le faux généreux*, a comedy by Antoine Bret (1758).

himself in the eyes of others, or sacrifice himself to his passions, his tastes, his fortune, birth, wife and children – and then they may say, if they like, that sincere, serious drama is without warmth, colour and strength . . .

I repeat therefore: the sincere, the sincere. It touches us in a more intimate and sweeter way than that which excites our scorn and laughter. Poet, are you sensitive and refined? Strike that chord, and you will hear it answer or vibrate in every soul.

'Is human nature good, then?'

Yes, my friend, and very good. Water, air, earth, fire – everything is good in nature: the hurricane, which rises at the end of autumn, shakes the forests, and hitting the trees against each other, breaks off and separates out the dead branches; and the storm, which strikes the waters of the sea and purifies them; and the volcano, which spills waves of glowing matter from its opened side, and carries into the air the vapour that cleanses it.

It is miserable conventions which pervert man, and not nature which we must accuse. In fact, what affects us like the recounting of a generous action? Where is the unhappy soul who can listen coldly to the plea of a good man?

196

The audience of a comedy is the only place where the tears of the virtuous man and the wicked man are mingled. There, the evil-doer is angry at the injustices he would have perpetrated, feels the wrongs he would have occasioned, and becomes indignant at a man of his own type. But the impression is made; it remains with us, in spite of ourselves; and the evil-doer leaves the theatre less disposed to work evil than if he had been reproved by a severe, harsh orator.

The poet, the novelist and the actor strike at the heart in an oblique fashion, and in so doing, strike the soul the more surely and strongly, so that it lays itself out and offers itself to the blow. The troubles by which they move me are imaginary, agreed; but they do move me. Every line of *L'Homme de qualité retiré du monde*, of *Le Doyen de Killerine*, and of *Cléveland***** excites in me a stirring of interest in the misfortunes of virtue, and causes me to shed tears. What art could be more deadly than one which would make me a party to vice? But also what art could be more precious than one which would imperceptibly involve me in the fate of a good man, which would take me out of the calm and quiet situation which I enjoy, to make me walk with him, plunge me into the caverns

---

* Novels by the Abbé Prévost.

where he has taken refuge, and associate me with all the misfortunes with which it pleases the poet to try his steadfastness?

O, what good would be restored to man if all the imitative arts should take up a common subject and unite one day with the laws to make us love virtue and hate vice! It is up to the philosopher to invite them; it is up to him to speak to the poet, the painter, the musician, and forcefully to ask them, 'Men of genius, why has heaven made you gifted?' If he were here, soon pictures of debauchery would no longer cover the walls of our palaces, our voices would no longer be organs of crime, and taste and behaviour would gain by this . . .

III. ON A TYPE OF MORAL DRAMA

I have sometimes thought that in the theatre one could discuss the most important moral points, and do it without standing in the way of the violent and rapid development of the dramatic action. How would it actually be done? By arranging the poem so that the things should be brought about like the abdication of the empire in *Cinna*. It is thus that a poet would treat the question of suicide, honour, a duel, fortune, dignity and a hundred others. Our poems would take on a gravity which they do not have. If a certain scene is necessary, if it is fundamental, if it is anticipated and the spectator wishes to see it, he will give it all his attention, and he will be much more affected by it than by those farfetched little sentences with which our modern works are stitched together.

It is not words that I want to carry away from the theatre, but impressions. He who says of a play, from which many detached thoughts are quoted, that it is a mediocre work is seldom mistaken. The excellent poet is the one whose effect stays long with me.

O dramatic poets! The applause which you ought to aim for is not that clapping of hands which is suddenly heard after a brilliant line, but that profound sigh which escapes from the soul after the constraint of a long silence, and brings relief. There is a still more violent impression, which you will understand if you were born for your art, and if you are aware of all the magic of it: it is to put people as if on the rack. Their minds will be troubled, uncertain, floating, lost, and your spectators will be like those who in an earthquake see the walls of their houses tremble and feel the earth disappearing beneath their feet.

197

198

IV. ON A TYPE OF PHILOSOPHICAL DRAMA

[Diderot suggests a play which would be written about the death of Socrates.]

V. ON SIMPLE DRAMAS AND COMPLICATED DRAMAS

For my part, I think more of a passion, or a character, which 199
develops little by little, and ends by showing itself in all its strength,
than I do of those combinations of incidents from which are formed
the tissue of a play where the characters and the spectators are kept
equally in suspense. It seems to me that good taste disdains them,
and that great events are not suited to them. That, however, is what
we call action. The Ancient writers had another idea of it. A simple
plot, an action taken right to its conclusion, so that everything was
at its extreme limit; a catastrophe continually imminent and always
delayed by a simple, believable circumstance; energetic speeches;
strong passions; tableaux; one or two forcefully drawn characters:
there is all their material. Sophocles needed no more to astound the
mind. He who has been displeased by reading the Ancient writers
does not know how much our Racine owes to Homer . . .

[Diderot then discusses burlesque drama, plot and dialogue, and
the subject matter of plays.]

X. ON THE PLOT IN TRAGEDY AND COMEDY

. . . The question arises whether the plot of a comedy or a tragedy 212
is more difficult to write.

There are three kinds of subject. History, where the facts are
given; tragedy, where the poet adds to history whatever he
imagines can increase the interest; comedy, where the poet invents
everything.

From which we can conclude that the comic poet is the poet *par
excellence*. He is the one who makes. In his sphere he is what the
supreme Being is in nature. It is he who creates, making something
out of nothing. But with the difference that while in nature we see
only an interconnection of effects whose causes are unknown to us,
the action of a play is never obscure; and if the poet hides some of
his ingredients to heighten the drama, he always reveals them
sufficiently in the end to satisfy us.

'But if the comedy is an imitation of nature in all its aspects, does
the poet not have a model to which he must adhere, even when
constructing his plot?'

Undoubtedly.

'Then what is this model?'

Before answering I will ask: what is a plot?

'A plot is a fantastic story, constructed according to the rules of the dramatic genre; a story which in tragedy is partly invented by the poet and in comedy is entirely invented by the poet.'

Very good. Then what is the foundation of dramatic art?

'Historic art.'   213

Nothing is more certain. Poetry has been compared to painting, and to some purpose. But a much more useful comparison, one which would produce more truth, would be that between history and poetry. That would enable us to form exact notions of the true, the plausible and the possible; and to fix a clear and precise idea of the fantastic (*merveilleux*), a common property of all poetic genres, and which few poets have been able to define.

All historical events are not suitable for tragedies, nor all domestic events suitable for comedies . . .

There sometimes happens in the natural order of things a sequence of extraordinary events. It is this same order that distinguishes the fantastic from the miraculous. The rare cases are fantastic; the cases which are naturally impossible are miraculous. Dramatic art rejects miracles.

If nature never brought about events of an extraordinary kind everything which the poet imagined beyond the cold and simple uniformity of common things would be unbelievable. But this is not so. What then does the poet do? Either he makes use of the extraordinary events [which occur naturally] or he imagines similar events. But instead of our being unaware of the relation between events, as is often the case naturally, . . . the poet makes sure that a visible and credible relation prevails throughout his work. So that   214
he is less true and more plausible (*vraisemblable*) than the historian . . .

The Ancient writers had tragedies which were entirely the invention of the poet. History did not even provide the names of the characters. And what does that matter, as long as the poet does not go beyond the true limit of the fantastic?

What is historical in a play is known to very few people; nevertheless, if the poem is well written it holds everyone's interest, and perhaps the ignorant spectator more than the educated. For the former everything is equally true, while for the latter there are episodes which are only plausible. These are lies mixed up with truths with so much skill that there is no revulsion in accepting them.

Domestic tragedy will have the problems of both genres: it will have to produce the heroic effect of tragedy and to invent the whole plot like comedy . . .

[Diderot then discusses the nature of imagination and various dramatic devices, like the use of monologue, the exposition of a plot, the relation between character and situation, the division into acts, etc. He then comes to the question of how a theatre relates to its society.]

XVIII. ON MORALITY

. . . Every people has prejudices to destroy, vices to prosecute,   259
abuses to prevent and [therefore] needs theatres, but theatres which are appropriate [to that people]. What a way, for a government which knows how to use it, to prepare an alteration of a law, or the termination of some custom! . . .

To attack the theatre on account of the way it is abused is to be opposed to all kinds of public instruction . . .

Any one people is not suited to excel equally in all dramatic genres. Tragedy seems to be more appropriate to the republican genius: and comedy, especially light comedy, more suited to the monarchical character . . . Among an enslaved people everything is debased . . . Then poets are like the fools at the royal court; they   260
owe the freedom they are allowed to the contempt with which they are regarded . . .

We have comedies. The English have only satires, full of energy and humour it is true, but with no morality or taste. The Italians are reduced to burlesque.

Generally speaking, the more civilized and refined a people are the less poetic [i.e. suitable for poetry] is their behaviour . . . What does a poet need? Nature civilized or untamed, peaceful or dis-   261
turbed? Will he prefer the calm clear day to the horror of a dark night, when the intermittent whistling of the wind is mixed with the murmuring rumble of distant thunder? . . . Will he prefer the sight of a calm sea to that of restless waves? The mute cold facade of a palace to a walk among ruins? . . . Poetry wants something tremendous, barbaric and wild.

It is when the fury of civil war or fanaticism puts swords in men's hands, and blood flows in great waves on the ground, that the laurels of Apollo are shaken and become green. They want to be watered. They fade away in times of peace and leisure. The golden age may produce a song or an elegy. Epic and dramatic poetry require other circumstances . . . 262

All times have their geniuses. But the men who have genius remain dumb unless extraordinary events inflame the mass [of men in their society] and cause their genius to appear. Then feelings build up and work away inside them, and those who have a faculty feel the pressure to speak; they use their faculty and are relieved . . .

[The remaining chapters deal with scenery, costumes, mime and, finally, the role of critics. The last chapter ends with an examination of how values can be established. Diderot puts this discussion into the mouth of a character he calls Ariste.]

I am forty years old. I have studied a lot, I am called the 283
philosophe. But if someone came to me and said: Ariste, what is the true, the good and the beautiful, would I have a ready answer? No . . . [So Ariste] began to think out the origin of these ideas so fundamental to our conduct and our judgements. And this is how he proceeded to argue with himself.

There are perhaps, in the whole human race, no two individuals who have even an approximate likeness [given the variety of physical types, mental formations, social and cultural circumstances] . . . So would it be possible for any two men to have exactly the same taste, or the same notions of the true, good and beautiful? . . . Nor is that all. In the same man everything is in a state of continual flux, whether he is considered physically or morally; pain follows pleasure, pleasure pain; health sickness, sickness health. It is only on account of memory that we are a single individual for others and for ourselves. At my age now there is perhaps not a single molecule in my body that I had when I was born . . . So how would it be possible for anyone among us to keep throughout his 284
existence the same taste, and make the same judgement on the true, good and beautiful? The changes brought about by disappointment and by the wickedness of men would alone be enough to alter his judgements.

Is man then condemned never to be in agreement with his fellow men, nor with himself, about the only objects which it is important for him to know – truth, goodness and beauty? Are they [only] fleeting, momentary, arbitrary things, words devoid of sense? . . .

Here Ariste paused. Then he resumed. It is certain that there will be no end to our arguments while everyone takes himself as model and as judge . . . That makes it sufficiently evident for me to feel the need to look for a measurement, a yardstick, outside myself. Until this is done most of my judgements will be false and all will be uncertain.

But where shall I locate the unchanging measurement which I look for and lack. In an ideal man whom I will construct? . . . But this man will [also] be my work. Does that matter, if I create him according to fixed elements? But where are these fixed elements? In nature? All right, but how do you assemble them? The matter is difficult, but is it impossible? Does the fact that I could not hope to construct a perfect model absolve me from trying? No. Then let us try. But if the model of beauty to which the ancient sculptors related all their works cost them so much observation, study and trouble, what am I doing? . . . How much physical, natural, moral knowledge must be acquired! I cannot think of any science or art with which I will not need to be thoroughly acquainted. And would I then have the ideal model in all its truth, goodness and beauty? This ideal general model is impossible to construct, unless the gods grant me their intelligence and their eternity. Here I am once again fallen back into the uncertainties from which I intended to escape.   285

Ariste stopped here, sad and thoughtful.

Then, after a moment's silence, he continued. Why should I not imitate the sculptors? They made a model suitable to their situation, and I have my own situation. Let a man of letters make an ideal model of the most accomplished man of letters, and it will be by the mouth of that man that he will judge his own productions and those of others. Let the *philosophe* follow the same plan. All that seems good and beautiful to that model will be so. All that seems bad, false and ugly will be so . . . The more comprehensive one's knowledge the greater and more strict the model will be. There is no one, and there can be no one, who judges equally well on all matters about the true, good and beautiful. No. And if a man of taste is taken to be someone who bears within him the ideal general model in all its perfection, that man is a chimera.   286

How will I use this ideal model which is suitable to my situation as a *philosophe*, since that is what people wish to call me? In the same way that painters and sculptors use theirs. I will modify it according to circumstances. This is the second area of study to which I must devote myself . . . It is the study of passions, behaviour, character, and customs which teaches the man who paints men to alter his model and reduce it from the situation of man [in general] to that of a good, bad, calm or angry man.

It is thus that from a single image an infinite variety of different representations will emerge which will fill the stage and the canvas . . .

After this discussion with himself Ariste realized that he still had much to learn. He returned home and shut himself up there for fifteen years. He devoted himself to history, philosophy, ethics, the sciences and the arts; and at the age of fifty-five he was a good man, an informed man, a man of taste, a great author and an excellent critic.

287

At intervals in the *Discours* we see Diderot beginning to break out of the traditional terms of reference which cramp most of his writing on the theatre. The Aristotelian, or pseudo-Aristotelian, tradition of dramatic conventions exercised no less strong a hold over him than over most of his contemporaries, as the early chapters of the *Discours* demonstrate; most of Chapter X derives from Aristotle's *Poetics* and the moral concerns of Chapters II and III were a regular feature of the pseudo-Aristotelian tradition.

Even as Diderot was writing these pages Rousseau was making an acute and penetrating criticism of this tradition in his *Lettre à d'Alembert*, which was published two months before Diderot's *Discours* and which made final the breach between the two men. Rousseau attacked the moral pretensions of the theatre as it was then organized or as it was envisaged by Diderot. He demonstrated what little ground there was to suppose that plays taken to be morally beneficial really were so. The wedge that Rousseau drove between our aesthetic appreciation and how we behave as morally responsible people struck one of Diderot's most cherished beliefs, the unity of our aesthetic and moral faculties, and that hurt.

Diderot never replied to Rousseau's *Lettre à d'Alembert*, but already in the *Discours* he had unwittingly undermined his own position. His claim that 'poetry needs something tremendous, barbaric and wild' was in direct opposition to the bland assurance in Chapter II that virtue and sincerity are sufficiently rich material for effective theatre. In the *Salons* he developed this line of thought and in *Le Neveu de Rameau* he took it to the extreme. It is also interesting to read, in two letters of 1772, some of the same criticism of French theatre that Rousseau had made in his *Lettre*.[16]

But Diderot did not stop believing in the reforms he proposed or in the moral efficacy of such a reformed theatre. In reply to criticism of his *Discours* by Madame Riccoboni, wife of Luigi Riccoboni who ran the Théâtre Italien, he defended his call for realism against the need for dramatic artifice.[17] He worked on a translation of Edward Moore's play *The Gamester* and enthused over Aaron Hill's *The Fatal Extravagance* which, he maintained, had 'an effect a thousand times more terrible than that of *Oedipus*'.[18] He wrote a preface[19] for an (unpublished) volume that would bring together four examples of *le drame* – *The Gamester, The London Merchant*, Landois' *Sylvie* and Lessing's *Miss Sara Simpson*; he also wrote an *Éloge sur Terence*, the one dramatist of the ancient world to have written plays of the kind he advocated, in which he insisted on the moral benefits that would result from these plays being read or performed.[20] He suggested to Catherine II that she should use the theatre as a form of public instruction and moral teaching.[21] But his own best play, *Est-il bon? Est-il mechant?*, was neither public nor moral. And that fact, of course, contained its own moral.

7

Fiction

I

'A novel, up to now, has meant a tissue of frivolous and fantastic events which it was dangerous to read for [its effect on] both your taste and your behaviour.'[1] With these words Diderot opened his *Éloge de Richardson*, written in 1761 after the death of the English novelist and published in 1762. His statement describes the generally low view in which novels were held. Since there had been virtually no novels in the ancient world there existed no classical doctrine about them; they were therefore regarded as some kind of hybrid, illegitimate or other low genre. They had neither the edifying purpose of drama, nor the claims to be true like history. (In *La Promenade du sceptique* Diderot asserted he was a 'historian' not 'an author of a novel'.)[2] When these attitudes were taken together with the inclination of novelists to omit no aspect of human experience, the idea that novels had a corrupting effect was no surprise.

Diderot's statement could be taken as a description not only of the general attitude to novels but also of his own first novel *Les Bijoux indiscrets*, for that was frivolous, fantastic and salacious. The plot of the novel revolves around a magic ring which can make women's vaginas (the jewels of the title) speak; so that while a woman may say one thing, her sex may say another, and what her sex has experienced may be not at all what the woman wants (or can allow herself) to admit. As a comic device this palls, as a pornographic idea it lacks invention. Yet the narrative is not without merit. Apart from the incidental interest of the reflections on dreams or theatre there is a central tension that holds the book together, namely, whether or not the king who has the ring (a mild caricature of Louis XV) will use it to test his intelligent and independent-minded mistress. In the end he does, and she is shown to be faithful. A happy ending; the novel stays true to type.

Les Bijoux indiscrets showed that Diderot could write a novel with a fair degree of competence. As far as the critics were concerned it only confirmed their contempt for the form. But for Diderot and the critics a revelation was at hand in the works of Samuel Richardson. These were translated into French by the Abbé Prévost – *Pamela* in 1742, *Clarissa Harlowe* in 1751, *Charles Grandison* in 1755; the translations were poor, and often abridged, but together with other translations from the English they generated a new interest in the possibilities of the novel. Diderot, who read *Clarissa Harlowe* in the original and was overwhelmed by it, described these possibilities in his *Éloge de Richardson*. The English novelist dealt with a wholly realistic world. 'He does not carry you off to distant lands . . . The action is set in the world in which we live; the basis of his drama is true; his characters are as real as it is possible to be; they are taken from the middle ranks of society.'[3] In other words, they met the same aesthetic demands that Diderot required of the theatre. In addition, Richardson had a gift for showing the 'fleeting circumstance . . . Painters, poets, people of taste and of morality, read Richardson; read him continually. Know that it is through this mass of little things that the illusion works . . . It is by means of all these true details that the soul is prepared for the strong impression which great events make.'[4] The cumulative effect was that the reader experienced in all its force, 'in action', the moral teaching that Montaigne, La Rochefoucauld and others had shown 'in maxims'.[5] The moral effect of these books was such that they should be called something other than a novel;[6] it would be more accurate to call them poems;[7] they belonged to the same level as the works of Moses, Homer, Euripides and Sophocles.[8]

The desire to make the events they described seem true, to escape the pejorative sense of 'fiction', had made novelists use the device of presenting their books as memoirs, or in the form of letters between (supposedly) real people. The year before he wrote his *Éloge de Richardson* Diderot himself had written another novel, *La Religieuse*, which was the supposed memoirs of a nun. The book grew, we are told, out of a hoax. A friend of Diderot and Grimm, the Marquis de Croismare, had retired to his estate in Normandy; his friends missed his company and thought up a way to bring him back to Paris. Before he had left the city he had taken a keen interest in the case of a nun who had tried to have her vows annulled, so the friends decided to impersonate another nun writing to him for help. The trick worked in so far as the Marquis believed in the nun's existence, but it did not bring him to Paris. Instead he invited her to come to Normandy where she could stay with his daughter. Embarrassed by his generous invitation the hoaxers had to kill the nun off.

These events took place in the spring of 1760, but the matter did not end there. The case of the nun fired Diderot's imagination, partly perhaps because one of his sisters who had entered a convent had died mad before she reached the age of thirty. During the summer of 1760 he wrote up the nun's history and this became the novel. Or rather, this was the basis of the novel, for at this stage it remained unfinished. In 1770 Grimm printed the hoax letters, with the Marquis's replies, in the *Correspondance littéraire* explaining the circumstances in which they had been written and how they had led Diderot to write a 'work of genius'[9] which 'only ever existed in fragments',[10] and those fragments he supposed were now lost. But Grimm was wrong, they were not lost, and in 1780 Diderot revised them and brought the novel to a finished state. At the same time he revised the hoax letters so as to relate the novel more immediately to the circumstances which gave rise to it:[*] in one of the letters the Marquis is told that the nun has written 'a long letter'[11] about herself, and after her death there is a 'history of her life'[12] found among her papers. These hoax letters, with their replies, form what is known as the *Préface-Annexe* to the novel.

The novel itself describes how the girl Suzanne Simonin is put into a convent by her parents because she is illegitimate; once she has taken the vows, at the age of sixteen, she can make no claims on the family property. She lives in three convents before she finally escapes, and the convents become progressively more hostile. In the second convent she is subjected to cruel punishments and humiliations, and in the third she becomes the object of a lesbian Mother Superior's attentions. Eventually she is enabled to escape by the help of a sympathetic priest who comes to hear the nuns' confessions.

Despite his hostility to the Church Diderot does not primarily

---

[*] Or, to make a plausible story out of the supposed hoax and its sequel. There are a number of curious features about the relation of these letters to the completed novel which suggest that the latter may have grown out of less straightforward circumstances than the letters, and Grimm's account of the hoax, suggest.

attack religion as such in the novel. Suzanne is described as 'pious, but not bigoted'[13] and one of the reasons for the book's success lies precisely in the sympathy with which her religious feelings are depicted. At one stage she experiences a feeling of religious exalt- ation,[14] at another she is convinced of the 'profound wisdom'[15] of the Christian faith. Her first Mother Superior is a good woman and a saintly person, and most of the ecclesiastical officials from outside who become involved in Suzanne's case are reasonably fair- minded. The novel is aimed less at religion than at the unnatural conditions of convent life.

> Does God, who created man sociable, approve of people shut- ting themselves away? Can God, who created man so fragile and changeable, authorize the boldness of these vows? Can these vows, which go against the general inclination of nature, ever be properly observed except by some ill-formed creatures in whom the elements of feeling have been extinguished?[16] . . . To make a vow of poverty is to commit yourself by oath to be an idler and a thief; to make a vow of chastity is to promise God the constant violation of the wisest and most important of his laws; to make a vow of obedience is to renounce the inalienable prerogative of man, freedom. If you observe these vows you are a criminal; if you do not observe them, you are a perjurer. The monastic life is [only fit] for a fanatic or a hypocrite.[17]

These words are spoken by a lawyer, M. Manouri, who takes up Suzanne's case; in this context they are plausible. Elsewhere, when similar feelings are expressed by Suzanne herself,[18] they overburden the narrative and strain the effect.

This lapse is one instance of the principal weakness of the book, a certain confusion in the presentation of Suzanne's character. Since she is writing after the events have taken place her innocence can seem forced; she also vacillates from being completely weak to being resolutely strong, from extreme passivity and ignorance to active resistance and awareness. Similarly, the time-scale alters between events seen in the past and events being lived through as if happening now. Nevertheless, the narrative does achieve a high level of fluency, so that the suspense is maintained, and despite a certain blandness in her character we do care about Suzanne. The book is tautly written, with a single-mindedness that is unusual in Diderot. His successive revisions of the novel were aimed at making the events more plausible and the focus of the scenes sharper. The results were effective and helped give the novel the moderate success it has enjoyed.[19]

II

The concern to write about what is here and now, the concern to achieve the realism he admired in Richardson's novels, is also evident in a number of short stories Diderot wrote in the early 1770s. One of them, *Les Deux Amis de Bourbonne*, was written in part as a rejoinder to a story by Saint-Lambert, *Les Deux Amis, conte iroquois*, set in 'distant lands', among the North American Indians. Diderot wanted to show that 'greatness of soul and noble qualities are found in all situations and in all countries . . . and you do not have to go as far as the Iroquois to find two friends'.[20]

The story is unusual among Diderot's work in that it deals exclusively with the poor. It is set among the smugglers, charcoal-burners and other social outcasts who lived their lives in conflict with, and defiance of, the law-enforcing authorities or tax-gathering officials. The conditions of their existence were dangerous and unpredictable but their very poverty was a cause of their generosity, which in the case of Felix and Olivier, the two friends of the title, went so far as giving up their lives for one another. At the end of the story Diderot attaches what he calls 'a bit of morality'.

> Felix was a beggar who had nothing; Olivier was another beggar who had nothing; you could say the same about the charcoal-burner, and his wife, and the other characters in this story. And you can conclude from that that there are scarcely any complete and reliable friendships except among people who have nothing. Then a man is all his wealth to a friend, and vice versa.[21]

At the end of this story Diderot also included a short reflection on writing fiction. He was concerned with how stories can be made to seem true. Once again, as in the *Éloge de Richardson*, he sees the principal way to achieve this being to 'sprinkle the narrative with small circumstances so related to the matter, with details so natural and simple – and yet so difficult to imagine – that you will be forced to say to yourself '*Ma foi*, that is true. Things like that are not made up.'[22] He then goes on to give an example of this in the way a painter might add a scar or a wart to a portrait. Nevertheless, although this is the method he advocated, Diderot's stories are notable for their lack of physical descriptions or similar individual details. He himself adopted other means to make his stories convincing. One of these was his concentration on the narrative, treating the material in a very direct and forceful style. Another was the use of a framework within which the story was set. In *Les Deux Amis de Bourbonne* the framework took the form of a story the narrator had heard which is then amplified by an account given by a local official, the sub-delegate to the *Intendant*. This is then confirmed by a comment by a local curate who attacks the 'two brigands'[23] and denies them his charity because their virtues were 'pagan and natural' not Christian.[24] The two accounts, from differing standpoints, give the story a sense of verisimilitude.

Another kind of framework was to introduce the reader. 'When you tell a story there is someone who listens to it; and for the short while that the story lasts it is unusual for the storyteller not to be interrupted sometimes by his listener. That is why I have introduced into the narrative you are going to read . . . a character who takes on more or less the role of the listener.'[25] With these words Diderot opens *Ceci n'est pas un conte*. The story is framed within a discussion between the storyteller and his listener. The same applies to *Madame de la Carlière*. Both these stories were related to the *Supplément au Voyage de Bougainville* (which is also framed by, and much of it conducted as, a dialogue between two characters, A and B). They deal with the problem of the inconstancy of human affection. In the first story two episodes are recounted in which first a woman, then a man, falls out of love with her/his partner and cruelly rejects him/her. In the second, two lovers, both mature and experienced people, are cautious about making any long-term commitment to one another; they eventually do so only after the woman, Madame de la Carlière, has warned the man, Desroches, that she will publicly denounce him to all their friends if he is unfaithful. And their friends agree to break with Desroches if he fails her. In public Desroches swears 'eternal fidelity and devotion'[26] to her, and they are married. But the inevitable happens, Desroches is publicly humiliated and left a broken man.

In this story the public as well as the lovers are involved, and the former's approval of Madame de la Carlière's action is partly blamed by Diderot for the disaster that befalls Desroches. 'Public judgement on our individual actions'[27] aggravates what might not otherwise be, he suggests, such an intractable problem. But Diderot's comments are uncertain and unclear. There is no moral to either of these stories, in the ethical sense of the word. They do not set out to demonstrate a given value or point of view. They arc more like enquiries, simple statements of facts which ask questions, rather than suggest answers. And the impact of the stories ultimately derives from their initial basis in fact. These events had actually happened.

A story (*conte*) remained for Diderot a pejorative term.[28] When he wrote, in the *Salon de 1767*, 'let us always tell stories. When you are telling a story you feel happy, nothing annoying enters your mind',[29] he did not mean fiction, for he went on to recount real events that had happened. He was referring rather to that transformation of raw experience which literary composition must provide if that experience is to be conveyed to a third party with all the immediacy it had for those who initially experienced it. The problem of retaining the sense of immediacy was always of central importance for Diderot; he was fascinated by the contingency of the present moment. At the same time he was greatly concerned about the nature of morality. Out of these two interests came his preoccupation with human inconstancy. This is why these stories, both in their theme and in the form they took, reveal more about Diderot than their brevity and restricted scope suggest at first sight. It is no accident that those who know Diderot well find them so attractive.[30]

III

The main features of the stories – a fascination with exceptional characters, with changeablencss, with the author–reader relationship – play a large part in Diderot's longest and most original novel, *Jacques le fataliste et son maître*. This is how the book begins:

How had they met? By chance, like everyone else. What were their names? What does it matter to you? Where had they come from?

From the nearest possible place. Where were they going? Do we ever know where we're going? What were they saying? The master said nothing and Jacques said that his captain had said that everything that happens to us down here, good or bad, was written up above.

The Master: That's saying a lot.

Jacques: My captain added that every [musket-]ball that left a gun had its billet.

The Master: And he was right.

After a short pause Jacques cried out: 'The devil take the tavern-keeper and his tavern!'

The Master: Why send your neighbour to the devil? It's not Christian.

Jacques: It's just that while I am getting drunk on his bad wine I forget to take our horses to the watering-trough. My father notices and becomes angry. I shrug my shoulders; he picks up a stick and beats me with it on the shoulders rather hard. A regiment was passing on its way to camp before Fontenoy. Out of spite I join up. We arrive and the battle is on.

The Master: And you receive the musket-ball with your name.

Jacques: You have guessed it – wounded in the knee. And God only knows the good and bad adventures brought on by that shot. They hold together neither more nor less than the links of a bridle-chain. For example, without that shot in the knee, I don't think I should ever have been in love, nor lame.

The Master: So you were in love, then?

Jacques: Was I not!

The Master: And because of a musket shot?

Jacques: Because of a musket shot.

The Master: You never told me a word about it.

Jacques: I dare say I have not.

The Master: And why not?

Jacques: Because it couldn't have been told any sooner or later.

The Master: And the time to tell of your loves has now come?

Jacques: Who knows?

The Master: Well, in any case start on them.

Jacques started the story of his love affairs. It was after dinner, the weather was sticky, and the master went to sleep. Night overtook them in the middle of the fields and there they are, lost. There is the master in a terrible rage, falling on his lackey with a whip, and that poor devil saying with each blow: 'That one, too, must have been written up above.'

You see, reader, that I am well on my way, and that it is completely up to me whether I shall make you wait one year, two years, or three years for the story of Jacques' loves, by separating him from his master and having each of them go through all the haphazard events that I please. What's to prevent my marrying off the master and making him a cuckold? Shipping Jacques off to the islands? Guiding his master to the same place? Bringing them back to France on the same ship? How easy it is to make stories! But I'll let them both off with a bad night and let you off with this delay.

Dawn arrived. They are back on their horses, and on their way – And where were they going? – Now that's the second time you ask me that question and the second time that I tell you: 'What's that to you?' If I get into the story of their travels good-bye to the story of Jacques' loves . . .[31]

We have here a completely different atmosphere, a new sense of playfulness. Diderot was shown the way to it by Laurence Sterne. He had enthused over the first books of *Tristram Shandy* – 'the maddest, wisest, most entertaining of books'[32] – when he read them in 1762, and the remark 'every ball has its billet' and the wound in the knee are taken from Book VIII, published in 1765. In Chapter XIX of that book Corporal Trim tells how he was wounded at the battle of Landen and how that wound led him, as he explains in Chapter XXII, to fall in love with the girl who nursed him. Diderot uses these events – the story of the wound and the falling in love – to frame his own narrative; and at the end of *Jacques le fataliste*, as he introduces the story of the falling in love, he acknowledges his debt to Sterne, in an appropriately playful tone.[33]

The example of Sterne's masterpiece seems to have released something in Diderot, enabling him to write with an unprecedented detachment from his material. We do not know exactly when the novel was written, though it was long enough in 1771 for a reading of it to take a couple of hours.[34] It seems likely that he worked on it during the early 1770s, since apart from incidental references the main preoccupations relate closely to other works of that period. (It first appeared in the *Correspondance littéraire*, in instalments, from 1778.) In the *Réfutation d'Helvétius*, for example, Diderot wrote about fatalism (by which he meant determinism):

[Helvétius] has not considered that everything holds together in the mind as it does in the universe, and the most unlikely idea which seems to cut completely across my immediate thought has a very fine thread which connects it either with the idea I am concerned with or with some phenomenon occurring inside me or outside me . . . In the man who reflects there is a necessary interconnection among his ideas . . . In the man who acts there is an interconnection among the most significant events which is as inevitable as the rising of the sun. Double necessity specific to the individual, destiny woven from the beginning of time up to the instant I am now in; and it is the momentary forgetting [by Helvétius] of those principles . . . which makes a work riddled with contradictions. You are a fatalist, and at every step you think, speak and write as if you continued to believe in freedom, a belief you have been deluded with and which has produced an everyday language which you mumble and continue to use without seeing that it no longer agrees with our opinions. You have become a philosopher in your systems, and you remain an ordinary person (*peuple*) in your speech.[35]

Jacques has been taught by the captain, his previous master, that 'Everything is written up above.' 'He believed that a man was led as necessarily to glory or disgrace as a ball conscious of its own existence would follow the slope of a hill.'[36] That was his 'system'. But how did he behave?

According to his system you might imagine that Jacques neither rejoiced or was sad about anything. Such, however, was not the case. He behaved more or less as you and I do. He thanked the person who was good to him, so that he might be good to him again. He got angry with the unjust man; and when you pointed out to him that he was then like a dog biting the stone which had hit him, he said: 'Not at all. The stone bitten by the dog is not corrected; the unjust man is modified by the stick.' He was often as inconsistent as you and me, and as likely to forget his principles, except in a few situations where his philosophy clearly dominated him. It was then that he said: 'That had to be, for it was written up above.' He strove to prevent evil; he was prudent, yet had the greatest contempt for prudence. When an accident happened he returned to his usual refrain and that consoled him. As for the rest, he was a good man, frank,

straightforward, brave, affectionate, faithful, strong-willed,
even more talkative, and bothered, as you and I are, at having
begun the story of his love-affairs without almost any hope of
finishing it.[37]

In other words, he seems to be a *philosophe* in his system and
peuple in his behaviour.

But Jacques (unlike Helvétius) does not even suggest he is free,
he is continually seeing fate at work. 'We think we lead destiny, but
it is always destiny which leads us. And destiny, for Jacques, was
everything which affected him or came near him, his horse, his
master, a monk, a dog, a woman, a mule, a crow.'[38] Such a belief
was in some respects similar to Leibniz's concept of Providence
which had come to be known as optimism, the belief that everything that happens is for the best. Diderot himself had pointed out
the similarity in his article 'Leibnitzianisme' (see p. 117). (This
belief was parodied by Voltaire in *Candide* and from its first
appearance in 1796 Jacques has been seen by some as a reworking
of *Candide.)*[39] The trouble with the belief, as D'Alembert had
indicated in his *Discours préliminaire*,[40] was that it had the
supposed benefit of explaining everything, but in fact it explained
nothing; or rather, it was an explanation which we could never use.
It might have value in hindsight, as consolation, but never as
prediction, as a guide to live by. 'The great scroll' on which
everything was written could not be read by human eyes. And
Jacques is aware of this: 'the calculation we make in our heads, and
that which is decreed on the register up above, are two very
different calculations'.[41] This does not lead Jacques to abandon his
belief, and he is going to bring up his children according to it,[42] but
it puts an ironical, comic and ridiculous distance between his ideas
and his actions. 'I think in one way and I cannot prevent myself
acting in another.'[43]

This disparity between the idea of a deterministic world and the
occurrence of actual events is central not only to Jacques' behaviour
but to the narrative itself. The world through which Jacques and his
master move is characterized by the random and unpredictable;
what happens to them as they travel seems completely fortuitous.
Chance rules, everything is in flux. As they travel they tell stories
and are told stories; these stories are likewise instances of the
unexpected. Two of them – about Madame de la Pommeraye and
about Père Hudson – demonstrate kinds of human experience that

go beyond our normal terms of reference in other ways. The two protagonists in these stories are people who do exercise some control over events, (though the eventual outcome for Madame de la Pommeraye is unexpected), and in doing so they win our admiration. But they are also utterly ruthless and evil, they are like the renegade of Avignon in *Le Neveu de Rameau*. They show free will, undoubtedly, but what drives them is a primitive energy, as disturbing to contemplate as any notion of determinism.

In addition there is the relationship of the author and the reader. Diderot continually interrupts the narrative to address the reader. First, he wants to say that he is not writing a novel: 'It is obvious that I am not writing a novel because I leave out what a novelist would not have omitted.'[44] He is writing a history: 'I am making history . . . My intention is to be true; I have fulfilled it.'[45] Extraordinary things may be narrated, but 'nature is so varied, especially in [people's] instincts and characters, that there is nothing so bizarre in a poet's imagination for which experience and observation will not see a model in nature'.[46] But the interruptions are not only in this polemical vein. They are interruptions for the sake of interruptions, further demonstrations, on another level, of the unpredictable. They ambush the reader on his journey.

In this respect *Jacques le fataliste* is a work similar to *Le Neveu de Rameau*, it reveals the inadequacy of our mental concepts to grasp the nature of reality: 'My dear master, life is a series of misunderstandings (*quiproquo*).'[47] But while in *Le Neveu* the matter is treated in earnest, here it is dealt with in a consistently humorous way. We do not feel anything is at stake. There are other similarities between the two works. The fascination with evil is one, the character of Jacques is another. For like the Nephew Jacques is an *original*,[48] who has not been flattened or rounded by education,[49] and who has decided that whatever happens he will be himself.[50] But while Jacques and his master are contrasted in a manner similar to the Nephew and Diderot – the former being inventive, forceful and energetic and the latter being more detached, outwardly composed and bland[51] – the relationship between the two characters in each work is different. In *Le Neveu* the two men meet one afternoon and argue bitterly; the substance of their argument is of great importance but nothing holds them together. In *Jacques* the reverse is the case: the two men argue continually and to no avail, but the argument is incidental to their relationship. That is essentially a master–servant relationship, and as such it is one of mutual dependence. The master 'did not know what would become of him without his watch, his snuff-box and Jacques; they were the three main resources of his life, which was spent in taking snuff, looking at the time, and questioning Jacques, and these in all possible combinations'.[52]

At one point in the book a furious argument breaks out between the two men. They are staying at an inn where the hostess has told them the story of Madame de la Pommeraye. After the story the master asks Jacques to resume the story of his love-affairs; the latter, who feels he has been insulted, does not do so. The master orders him to go downstairs and be off; Jacques refuses. The hostess comes in to see what is causing the row and offers to arbitrate between them. The two men agree:

Then the hostess, seating herself at a table and assuming the tone and bearing of a very serious magistrate, announced: 'Having heard the deposition of M. Jacques and upon facts tending to prove that his master is a good, a very good, too good a master, and that Jacques is not at all a bad servant, albeit a little subject to confusing absolute and immovable possession with temporary and gratuitous concession, I abolish the equality which has become established between them over a period of time, and I immediately re-establish it. Jacques will go down and when he has gone down he will come back up. He will come back into possession of all the prerogatives he has enjoyed up to now. His master will offer him his hand and will say to him in a friendly voice: "Good day, Jacques, I am very happy to see you again." Jacques will reply: "And I, sir, am extremely happy to see you again." I further forbid that this affair ever come up between them again, and that the prerogative of either master or servant should ever again be disturbed. Let us hope that the one shall order and the other obey, each to the best of his ability, and that there be left, between what the one can do and what the other ought to do, the same obscurity as heretofore obtained.'

Upon finishing this pronouncement, which she had lifted from some contemporary work published on the occasion of a similar quarrel, and in which one heard a master cry from one extremity of the kingdom to the other at his servant, 'You will go down', and the servant cry from his side, 'I shall not go down', she said to Jacques:

'Come now, give me your arm without further argument (*sans parlementer davantage*).'*

Jacques cried out mournfully: 'It was written up above, then, that I should go down.'

The Hostess (to Jacques): 'It was written up above, that from the minute a man takes a master he will go down, go up, go forward, go backward, or stay, and all that without his feet being free to countermand the head's orders. Give me your arm, and let my order be carried out.'

Jacques gave his arm to the hostess, but scarcely had they passed the threshold when the master threw himself upon Jacques' neck and embraced him, left Jacques and embraced the hostess, and while embracing them both said: 'It was written up above that I should never be rid of that character, and that as long as I live he would be my master and I, his servant.' The hostess added: 'And that in all probability neither of you would be the worse off.'

The hostess, having settled this quarrel, which she took for the first and which was far more than the hundredth quarrel of this same sort, and having reinstated Jacques in his position, went about her business. The master said to Jacques: 'Now that we are cooled off and in a position to judge sensibly, don't you agree with me?'

Jacques: I agree that when you have given your word of honour you must hold to it, and that since we have promised our judge on our word of honour not to return to this matter, we ought not to speak any more about it.

The Master: You are right.

Jacques: But without coming back to this affair, couldn't we pre-arrange a hundred others by some reasonable agreement?

The Master: I consent to that.

Jacques: Let us stipulate then, that, first, since it is written up above that I am essential to you, and since I feel and know that you cannot get along without me, therefore I shall abuse these advantages at any and all times that the occasion permits.

The Master: But Jacques, no one has ever stipulated any such thing.

Jacques: Stipulated or not stipulated, that has always happened, happens today, and will happen as long as the world stands. Don't

---

* The allusion in this paragraph is to the quarrels between Louis XV and the Parlements, hence the pun in the last sentence.

you think that others, like yourself, have attempted to escape that decree? And do you think you will be cleverer than they? Get rid of that idea and submit to the law of necessity, from which it is not in your power to free yourself. Let us also stipulate second, that, since it is as impossible for Jacques not to realize his influence and power over his master, as it is for his master to be unaware of his own weakness and cancel his indulgence, therefore Jacques must of necessity be insolent and, for general peace, his master must not take notice. All that has been arranged without our knowledge; all that was sealed up above the moment nature made Jacques and his master. It was decreed that you would have the title and I should have the thing itself. If you tried to oppose the will of nature, you would only pass clear water.

The Master: But at that rate your lot is better than mine.

Jacques: And who's disputing that?

The Master: But under those circumstances I have only to take your place and put you in mine.

Jacques: Do you know what would happen? You would lose the title and you wouldn't have the thing. Let's stay as we are; we're both well off. And may the best of our life be passed in making a proverb.

The Master: What proverb?

Jacques: 'Jacques leads his master.' We shall be the first of whom it will be said, but it will be repeated about thousands of others who are worth more than you and me. . .[53]

The great diversity of material in *Jacques le fataliste* and Diderot's detachment from it, the open-ended quality of the book – no one arrives anywhere finally, neither Jacques nor his master learn anything as a result of what happens – have meant that the book has been subject to a wide range of interpretations. The above passage obviously lends itself to a Marxist analysis and other aspects of the book have been seen in the same light – Jacques' fatalism being a provisional acquiescence to the traditional social order which he shows he has the power to deny.[54] The self-consciousness of the narrator, and his distance from his own narrative, have made the book seem an anti-novel *par excellence*; it has been asserted that Diderot's intention was 'to denounce the novel, think about the novel, unmask the novel', he was engaged on 'an enterprise of literary demystification', i.e. an early deconstructionist.[55] Others have seen the book as reflecting his final position on the thorny problem of determinism and free will. For my part, I think that in this book Diderot took a holiday from himself. The sense of release, of good humour, of simple pleasure with which he treats what were undoubtedly serious preoccupations, prevents the reader also from taking any single theme or aspect of the book too seriously. No subject is now insistent, not even that of fatalism; we are at a distance from them all. Like a good holiday the book takes its own unplanned course, it celebrates the unpredictable, it is the apotheosis of Diderot's penchant for disorder. And like most holidays it has its tedious moments. But despite bad weather now and then, the sun shines. Like *Tristram Shandy* it exists in a 'clear climate of fantasy and perspiration, where every idea, sensible and insensible, gets vent' and nothing occurs 'coolly, critically and canonically . . . in straight lines . . . without ever and anon straddling out, or sidling into some bastardly digression'.[56] God knows, Diderot worked hard enough; he deserved a break.

8

Painting

Diderot's writing on painting has a fascination which his writing on theatre, important though it is, never achieves. The reasons for this contrast are revealing. The latter took a public form, addressed openly to the contemporary audience, and made a call to reform. Diderot spoke authoritatively about a subject he believed he understood well; he wrote within a tradition that had been clearly defined since the Renaissance; he dealt with generalities. When he wrote about painting, on the other hand, he wrote for a very restricted, private audience, about a subject on which he was conscious of his ignorance. He wrote before art criticism had developed as a particular form, and he dealt for the most part with individual paintings. His main preoccupation was not how his imaginative demands could be related to an established framework of fixed intellectual categories, but rather with exploring what his own imaginative responses were. The result was some of his most idiosyncratic, perceptive and attractive work.

Throughout the second half of the eighteenth century the Académie royale de Peinture et Sculpture gave an exhibition of members' work in the Louvre every other year. Between 200 and 400 items were on show. Entry to the exhibition was free and large numbers of people came. As a major cultural event it also attracted comment and Grimm asked Diderot to write a report for the exclusive audience who formed the readership of the *Correspondance littéraire.* Since these readers did not see the paintings a first requirement of Diderot's work was to give a description of the items on display. This was a case of fortunate necessity, since writing such descriptions was to him 'the part which amused me and stretched my imagination'.[1] The fact that none of the artists involved would read what he wrote was also fortunate: 'I do not wish to upset anyone . . . and artists are easily made angry';[2] he could speak his mind with ease and freedom. 'I write for my friend [Grimm] and not for the public.'[3]

The task was not one that he was immediately at ease with; the first two *Salons* of 1759 and 1761 are fairly short and show no particular flair. But with the *Salon de 1763* Diderot became interested. He had become aware of the immense amount of work that painting involved: 'there are so many things relating to technique which it is impossible to judge unless you have spent some time with your thumb in the palette!'[4] He discussed these matters with artists, notably Chardin, Maurice de la Tour and Falconet. At the beginning of the next *Salon*, that of 1765, he could write:

> I have questioned the artist and I have understood what *finesse* of design and being true to nature mean. I have grasped the magic of light and shade. I have seen colour; I have acquired the feeling for flesh tones. On my own I have thought about what I have seen and understood, and these terms of art—unity, variety, contrast, order, composition, character, expression—so frequent on my lips, so vague in my mind, have become circumscribed and fixed.[5]

Closer acquaintance with the problems brought new appreciation of the achievements: 'Paris is the only town in the world where a spectacle like this can be enjoyed every two years.'[6] His comments became fuller, his account more extensive. 'I may be a bit long,' he explained to Grimm, 'but if you only knew how much I am enjoying myself.'[7] At the end of this *Salon* he declared that he would produce 'a short treatise on painting'[8] and the following year he did so, writing his *Essais sur la peinture*. These dealt in a brief and general fashion with design, colour, *chiaroscuro*, expression, composition, and architecture. A year later, in the *Salon de 1767* he complained to Grimm: 'Do not expect me to be as rich, varied, wise, mad and resourceful this time as I have been able to be in the preceding *Salons*.'[9] However, he had hardly written a dozen pages before he was seized by a sense of his own potential: 'Who knows what I am capable of? I do not feel I have yet used half my strength. Up to now I have only been ambling about.'[10] His invention and responsiveness were nothing less than phenomenal. The *Salon de*

1765 was over three times as long as that of 1763, the *Salon de 1767* was over five times as long. With the labour of editing the *Encyclopédie* over Diderot experienced an invigorating sense of release and in these two *Salons*, more than any other of his works, we see him eagerly breaking out of the confines within which his principal energies had been channelled. They are rich with the ideas which later developed into his mature masterpieces.

The very looseness and informality of his accounts allowed him the flexibility and, in a sense, the irresponsibility he needed. He was not having to produce a polished piece of writing; on more than one occasion he tells Grimm to alter his text as he thinks fit.[11] He allowed his immediate response to prevail over general con-siderations: 'I praise and blame according to my particular feeling, which does not make a law.'[12] A critic must above all be versatile, and at times he despaired of being versatile enough,[13] but in fact his own temperament was ideally suited to this requirement. He could indulge to the full his inclination to go off in any direction he fancied – 'digression relaxes me'[14] – and treat the written word as the closest possible equivalent to the spoken word. He was himself conscious of his success. He wrote to Sophie Volland about his *Salon de 1765*:

> It is certainly the best thing I have done since I took up writing, in whatever way it is considered, whether for the diversity of style, the variety of subjects, or the abundance of ideas which, I imagine, have never passed through any head except mine. It is a hoard of bright ideas (*plaisanteries*), some light, some strong. Sometimes it is conversation exactly as it is carried on at the fireside. At other times it is as eloquent and as profound as you could imagine.[15]

'If it happens,' he wrote in the *Salon de 1767*, 'that from one moment to another I contradict myself, that is because from one moment to another I have been differently affected.'[16] Contra-dictions existed; what mattered was not reconciling them into some conceptual harmony, but allowing them to exist, being true to the moment.

The paintings which filled these exhibitions covered a wide range of styles and genres. There were the large late rococo canvases of painters like Boucher, elegant compositions of highly artificial subjects. Diderot admired Boucher's technical skill but deplored the subjects on which it was used: 'This man has everything, except the truth.'[17] He disliked the frivolity, the artificiality and also a certain coarseness which he felt Boucher displayed. Then there were the painters who depicted domestic scenes, notably Greuze and Chardin, painters whom Diderot greatly admired and with whom he felt a close affinity. And then there were those who were developing a new kind of landscape painting, in particular Vernet and Hubert Robert, which was much more dramatic and arresting than previous landscapes, more concerned to reflect or arouse human emotions. These also won Diderot's approval.

These paintings were listed in the catalogues, and officially graded, according to a certain hierarchy. At the top were historical subjects, which could be religious, mythological or based on classical history; next came landscapes, then portraits, and lowest of all were still lifes. There had also been, from the late seventeenth century, what could be called an official tradition of aesthetic excellence, in which the admired models were the statues of classical antiquity and the paintings of Raphael and Poussin. Diderot accepted this hierarchy and he went along with this tradition, just as he accepted the classical doctrine that art was essentially the imitation of nature. However, in the course of the *Salons* all these aspects were subject to conscious or unconscious criticism, alteration and modification.

The historical paintings which were accorded the most serious attention often clashed with Diderot's desire for a realistic treatment of subjects to which he could easily relate. His reaction to this aspect of the exhibitions was very similar to his ideas about *le drame*. Painters who threw themselves into mythological subjects lost all sense of what is natural, he wrote; 'only extravagant, idealized, stupid or indecent pictures come from their brushes'.[18] It would be far better if they took a subject from French history, an event like the death of Turenne, for instance.[19] Diderot valued serious historical paintings because they had an evident moral purpose, and paintings based on classical history could have particular force: they could accord with the 'severity of art',[20] like the 'simple and noble figures'[21] made by the sculptor Falconet (these remarks occur in the *Salon de 1761*), and they brought to mind a better time – 'we are dissatisfied with the present, and this return to ancient times pleases us'[22] (this comment was made in the *Essais* of 1766).

In the 1770s there was a development in French painting along these lines. The excavations at Herculaneum and Pompeii, and the writings of Winckelmann, had stimulated a new interest in the history, rather than the mythology, of classical antiquity. The Marquis de Marigny, Madame de Pompadour's brother, had been sent to Italy to see the new discoveries and on his return he sponsored paintings which treated historical subjects with appropriate moral seriousness. Although Diderot wrote accounts of the Salons in 1771 and 1775 they were disappointingly perfunctory. In the *Salon de 1781*, however, despite its brevity and inadequacy (compared with the earlier *Salons*), he recognized the new spirit. The great success of the Salon was Menageot's painting of Leonardo da Vinci dying in the arms of François I. 'We love to see the heroes of our nation,'[23] wrote a contemporary. The other striking newcomer was David. 'This young man shows the grand manner in the way he does his work; he has soul, his heads have expression without affectation; his postures are natural and noble.'[24] His picture of the funeral of Patroclus was a 'superb sketch, beautiful effect, full of feeling'.[25] In an uneven work of the mid-1770s, his *Pensées détachées sur la peinture*, Diderot had written: 'Paint as people used to speak in Sparta.'[26] This remark had no more effect on the development of the neoclassical style than any other comments by Diderot, since the *Pensées détachées* were not published till 1798. But the affinity that existed between the writer and the painters is evident. Diderot was critical of excessive admiration of antiquity and took issue with Winckelmann over this.[27] Nor did he want a re-creation of an idealized antiquity, the classical calm of Poussin. His desire was for a combination of the strength, seriousness and simplicity of classical models with a new kind of energy and intensity. David's later canvases would have delighted him.

The desire for a greater degree of realism is a constant theme of these writings. 'Ah! if a sacrifice, a battle, a triumph, a public scene could be conveyed with the same truth in all its details as a domestic scene by Greuze or Chardin!'[28] These two painters won Diderot's continual admiration. They worked in a genre that did not have the same status and esteem as historical painting, but Greuze's canvases showed that 'this genre can provide compositions capable of doing honour to the talents and feelings of artists'.[29] Greuze's mixture of moralism and sensuality produced some of Diderot's most delighted commentaries; they provoked a response very similar to that generated by reading Richardson's novels. He showed unequivocal pleasure in the serious (if, to our eyes, somewhat melodramatic) honesty of *L'Accordée de village*,[30] or *Le Mauvais Fils puni*,[31] or in the enticing ambiguity of *La Jeune Fille qui pleure son oiseau mort*[32] (all of which are now in the Louvre). He showed comparable pleasure in the lucid poised work of Chardin: 'It is always nature and truth';[33] 'it is the very substance of things';[34] 'it is nature itself'.[35] These were terms of the highest praise in Diderot's vocabulary.

Diderot's enthusiasm for these painters is not surprising, given the predilections he showed in other areas of criticism. What is remarkable in the *Salons* is how he shows equal enthusiasm for very different qualities. A thread that runs through the *Salons* is a delight in 'horror', the 'terrible', the 'sublime'; there are references to all three from the *Salon de 1761* onwards.[36] The imitative arts, he wrote in his *Essais* of 1766, need something 'wild, raw, striking, tremendous . . . Move me, astonish me, tear me apart; make me shudder, weep, tremble.'[37] In the *Salon de 1767* he drew heavily on Burke's *On the Sublime and Beautiful* to describe these reactions,[38] but this was less borrowing Burke's ideas than using his words to articulate ideas which Diderot himself had previously expressed elsewhere. Another thread evident from the *Salon de 1761* onwards was pleasure in paintings of ruins, with a few figures who would 'most often incline you to reverie and melancholy'.[39] 'There is more poetry . . . in a single tree which has suffered the effect of years and seasons than in the façade of a whole palace. A palace must be ruined to become an object of interest.'[40] 'O beautiful sublime ruins!' he exclaims in front of a canvas by Hubert Robert; 'I cannot prevent myself from going to dream under this vault, sit down among these columns . . . The ideas which ruins arouse in me are great. Everything is destroyed, all perish, everything passes away. Only the world remains; only time lasts.'[41] Likewise, in his detailed specification of what a landscape should provide, he wanted 'a certain poetry' which would speak to his soul.[42]

These comments reveal a completely different aesthetic dimension. The landscapes and ruins in question were valued not like the works of Greuze and Chardin for their accurate portrayal of what Diderot regarded as his world,[43] but rather for their emotional effect, for the ideas, feelings and associations they stimulated. The criterion is not accuracy but evocation, what Diderot called the '*idées accessoires*'.[44] 'Painting is the art of reaching the soul by the mediation of the eyes. If the effect stops at the eyes the painter has only covered the least part of the route.'[45]*

This regard for what an artist could suggest in preference to what he stated led Diderot sometimes to value a sketch more highly than a painting.

> Sketches generally have a fire that a painting does not have. It is the moment of the artist's warmth, inspiration, with no element of the finish that reflection brings to everything; it is the painter's soul spread freely on the canvas . . . The more vague the expression is, the more at ease is the imagination. In vocal music you must hear what [that music] expresses. In a well-made symphony I can hear virtually what I please.[47] . . . The sketch affects us so strongly perhaps only because being indeterminate it leaves more freedom to our imagination, which sees in it everything it pleases.[48]

Looking at a sketch the viewer is 'inspired by the divine breath of the artist'.[49] We are here on the high road to romanticism.

Another theme that runs through the *Salons*, and pointed in the same direction, was Diderot's admiration for what the artist achieved. The painter he examined in greatest detail, Chardin, continually baffled him: 'we understand nothing about this magic . . . Go close and everything is confused, flattened, shapeless; step back and it all takes shapes again and reappears.'[50] Chardin was

> a great magician . . . If it is true, as philosophers say, that there is nothing real except our sensations; that neither the void of space or even perhaps the solidity of bodies can perhaps have anything in themselves of what we experience, then let these philosophers teach me what difference there is for them, at four feet from your paintings, between the Creator and you.[51] . . . Chardin is between nature and art; he consigns the other imitators to the third level [of imitation]. There is nothing in him which indicates the palette. He produces a harmony which one does not dream of being surpassed; it winds imperceptibly through his composition, complete in every corner of the canvas; it is, as the theologians say of the spirit, palpable in the whole and secret in every detail.[52]

---

* In this respect the value of painting for Diderot was exactly like the value of music for Rousseau.[46]

Chardin performed a kind of magic. So did all accomplished artists. (Diderot used the term about Boucher as well as Vernet and Chardin.) Their art did not so much copy nature as re-create it. Every artist had first of all his own way of selecting subjects and colours, but

> even after this choice, however well done it may be, the best and most harmonious painting is only a tissue of falsities which mask one another. Some objects get more attention, others less, and the great magic consists in coming very close to nature and ensuring that the emphasis is in proportion. But then it is no longer the real scene that we see; it is only, so to speak, the translation of it.[53]

The combined effect of these considerations about technique and the interest in paintings less for what they portray than for the feelings they arouse, led Diderot to rethink the function of the artist. According to the classical tradition, which was the orthodox view till the last years of the eighteenth century, the artist imitated nature. He could do this in a number of ways: he could make a direct (we would now say photographic) copy of the natural world, or he could choose the most beautiful aspects of nature and assemble them in his work, or he could model himself on the most beautiful art-works of the past (themselves copies of nature) and hope, with their help, to do still better. In the opening pages of the *Salon de 1767* Diderot took issue with all these ways of proceeding. First of all he showed how every natural phenomenon is subject to constant change, wear and tear, and as a result 'there is neither a complete animal that exists, nor any part of one either, that you could strictly take as a first model'. The model an artist has therefore 'is purely ideal and is not directly derived from any individual image in nature'. 'You will agree then,' he says to the imaginary artist with whom he is discussing the matter, 'that when you make beauty you do not make anything that exists or even anything which can exist [in nature].'[54]

The artist replies that he nevertheless does have an external criterion of beauty, the extent to which individual features of different people conform to the classical models which he has closely studied. But, says Diderot, how did the classical sculptors themselves proceed, without any such models? They were surrounded by a no less motley and heterogeneous collection of human specimens than we are, all of which were 'more and more distant from the truth, the first model, the intellectual image'.[55]

[Your predecessors,] by . . . observation, by profound experience, by comparing organs with their natural functions, by a remarkable flair (*tact exquis*), a taste, an instinct, a kind of inspiration given to a few rare geniuses, perhaps by a plan, natural to those who worship idols, to raise man up above his condition and imprint on him a divine form – a character that excluded all the constraints of our poor, mean, pitiful, miserable life – began to become aware of the great changes, the gross deformities, the worst sufferings [that the human figure has undergone]. This was the first step which effectively reformed only the general body of the animal system or some of its main aspects. In time, by a slow hesitant progress, by a long and painful process of trial and error, by a secret, unexpressed idea of analogy, the result of a multitude of successive observations the memory of which vanishes but the effect remains, the reform was extended to the lesser aspects, from them to those still smaller, and from these to the very smallest, to the nail, the eyelids, the eyebrows, the hairs, implacably and with astonishing care effacing the changes and deformities of nature – which had been spoilt, either initially or by the necessities of life – moving even further away from the portrait, the false line, to aspire to the true ideal model of beauty, the true line. This true line, ideal model of beauty, existed nowhere except in the head of the Agasias, Raphaels, Poussins, Pugets, Pigalles, Falconets . . . An ideal model of beauty which over the course of time forms the spirit, character and taste of the works of art of a people, a century, a school; an ideal model of beauty, true line, of which the man of genius will have an idea which will be more or less exact according to the climate, government, laws and circumstances which have attended his birth; an ideal model of beauty, true line, which is corrupted, is lost and would perhaps only be found again completely among a people by a return to a state of barbarism, for that is the only condition in which men, convinced of their ignorance, can apply themselves to the slow process of trial and error; the others remain mediocre precisely because they are born, so to speak, educated. Slavish and almost stupid imitators of those who have preceded them, they study nature as perfect and not perfectible.[56]

In the passage that follows Diderot dismisses as absurd and impossible the idea that artists formed their model from 'the most beautiful aspects oı ᴄn infinite number of individuals from which they then composed a whole'.[57] For how would they have recognized which aspects were beautiful in the first place unless they already possessed the perception, the flair, the imagination? 'I tell you that it is not with the help of an infinite number of isolated little portraits that one aspires to the original and first model either of the part or the whole; they followed another way, and that way, which I have just described, is that of the human mind in all its researches.'[58] The process, in other words, is like that conducted by the scientist, outlined in the *Pensées sur l'interprétation de la nature*, or by the philosopher Ariste at the conclusion of the *Discours sur la poésie dramatique*.

In these pages Diderot took a decisive step away from the concept of art as imitation. It was not a complete break, nor was it final. It was not complete because there lingered in his mind the idea that although the work of art was created by the artist nevertheless the criterion of its efficacy was its truth to 'original' or 'unspoilt' nature; the artist did not so much create an imaginary world as glimpse the hidden order of the existing world. In this respect he was exactly like the great scientist: 'you could say of Monsieur de Chardin and of Monsieur de Buffon that nature has taken them into her confidence'.[59] It was not a final break because although the idea of the ideal model occurs again in the *Salon de 1767*[60] and in several later writings,[61] we find the earlier concepts in use in the *Pensées détachées sur la peinture* as if there had been no development away from them.[62] And Diderot continued to believe that the study of classical models was vital.[63] As so often, new ideas break out almost unawares. But they were no less significant for that.

The *Salons* contain many reflections on many subjects, including the relation of poetry to painting,[64] and the relation of the arts to luxury.[65] The actual discussion of the paintings is extremely uneven. A mediocre painting can provoke Diderot's imagination as much as a good one; while the latter may arouse his admiration and enthusiasm the former may stimulate him to reconstruct the painting as he thinks it ought to be done, or castigate the artist for what he has failed to do. One result of this unpredictability is that selected extracts, without illustrations, tend to be quite inadequate to convey the flavour of the writing. However, there is one notably sustained passage in the *Salon de 1767*, the *Promenade de Vernet*. Diderot himself gave this title[66] to his discussion of some of Vernet's canvases in which he imagines the paintings to be real landscapes and seascapes that he visits. The surroundings lead him to reflect on his central preoccupations, like the relationship of the true, the good and the beautiful, or the nature of language. They also on occasion arouse in him feelings that were strikingly similar to those expressed by Rousseau in his *Rêveries d'un promeneur solitaire*. Although Diderot did not experience the same discomfort in cities that Rousseau often felt he did find sometimes the same beneficial effect of being in the country.[67] This effect could also be produced by art. Indeed, the very way we look at the world is affected by what artists show us. In these pages we are crossing the threshold that leads from the tradition that had dominated European thought for over two thousand years into a world which we now call modern, a world that can only be perceived, understood and valued in specifically human terms.

Salon de 1767

VERNET

I had written the name of this artist at the top of my page, and I was going to talk to you about this work, when I left to visit the country near the sea [at a place] famous for the beauty of its setting. There, while [the others played cards or discussed philosophy] I went out with my stick and my notebooks, accompanied by the children's tutor, an Abbé, to visit the most beautiful site in the world . . .

[He describes the first of these sites, in the background of which is a mountain and in the foreground a rocky causeway leading to a village.]

'Which of your artists,' said my guide, 'could have imagined breaking the continuity of that rocky causeway with a clump of trees?'

'Vernet, perhaps.'

'Very well. But would your Vernet have imagined the elegance and charm of it? Would he have been able to convey the warm and striking effect of that light playing between the trunks and the branches?'

'Why not?'

'Convey the immense sense of space which your eyes see beyond?'

'That is what he has done on occasion. You do not know the man; how acquainted he is with the phenomena of nature . . .'

'It is in vain that [you repeat his name]. I will not leave nature to   101
run after his image. However sublime a man may be, he is not God.'

'I agree. But if you had spent more time in the artist's company he might have taught you to see things in nature which you do not see. How many things you would find to pick out. How many things which art would omit, so as not to spoil the ensemble and harm the effect; how many it would bring together to double our delight!'

'What! You seriously think that Vernet could have done better than make an exact copy of this scene?'

'Yes, I think so.'

'Then tell me how he should treat it to make it [more] beautiful.'

'I do not know; if I did I would be a greater poet and greater painter than he is. But if Vernet may have taught you to see nature better, nature, for her part, may have taught you to see Vernet better.'

'But Vernet will always only be Vernet, a man.'

'And for that very reason, how much more astonishing he is, and how much more worthy of admiration is his work. This universe is undoubtedly a great thing; but when I compare it with the energy of the productive cause, if there is something which makes me marvel it is that the achievement [of this cause] is not more beautiful and   102
perfect. It is quite the opposite when I think of the weakness of man, his meagre means, the obstacles and the short duration of his life, and of certain things which he has undertaken and carried out . . .'

[The Abbé is amazed that Diderot should find the work of man more admirable than the work of God, but Diderot denies that the order of the universe is beautiful; it merely is as it must be. We have no other order to compare it with, and we have no choice except to coexist with it. They then walk among the mountains and come to a scene where a waterfall falls off the mountainside, where there was a dark cave among the rocks, and some people were grouped around the shores of a lake.]

I was motionless, my mouth half-open; my arms fell to my sides.   106
My gaze wandered without coming to rest on any object . . . I

cannot tell you how long my enchantment lasted. The immobility of the creatures, the solitude of the place, its profound silence, held time in suspense; it no longer existed. Nothing measured it; man became as it were eternal . . .

[After a while the men resume their conversation and then return to where they are staying.]

I was tired, but I had seen beautiful things, breathed the purest   112
air, and taken the healthiest exercise. I ate well and had the most calm and peaceful night. Next morning, when I awoke, I said: 'This is the true life, the true place for man. All the glamour of society will never be able to eradicate the taste for it. Kept within the narrow confines of towns by boring jobs and dull duties, if we cannot return to the forest, our first refuge, we give up some of our wealth to bring the forest around our houses. But there they have lost, under the symmetrical hand of art, their silence, innocence, liberty, majesty, repose. There we go to perform for a short while the part of the savage; slaves of customs and passions, playing the pantomime of the natural man. In the impossibility of surrendering to the occupations and pleasures of country life, of wandering in a field, following a herd of cattle, living in a cottage, we invite, at a price, the brush of Wouwermans, Berghem or Vernet, to relate for us the life and history of our forebears. And the walls of our sumptuous and gloomy dwellings are covered with the images of a happiness we miss . . . and we are devoured by the thirst for honour and wealth in the midst of scenes of innocence and poverty – if the person who has everything can ever be called poor. We are unhappy people around whom happiness is depicted in a thousand different ways. *O rus! quando te aspiciam*? said the poet;* and that is a desire which arises up from the depths of our heart a hundred times.'

I lay there in my reverie, casually stretched out on a sofa, letting   113
my mind wander where it wanted, a delicious state in which the soul is upright without reflection, the mind accurate and perceptive without effort; when the idea, the feeling seems to be born in us of its own accord, as if from fertile soil. My eyes were fixed on an admirable landscape and I said: 'The Abbé is right; artists understand nothing about that, for their most beautiful works have never made me experience the enthusiasm which I feel, the pleasure of being myself, the pleasure of knowing myself to be as good as I am,

* 'O countryside! When will I see you?' A quotation from Horace.[68]

the pleasure of seeing myself and taking delight in myself, the even
sweeter pleasure of forgetting myself. Where am I at this moment?
I do not know, I have no idea. What do I lack? Nothing. What shall
I say? Nothing. If there was a God, this is how he would be. He
would take pleasure in himself.' A distant noise, the sound of the
activity of a washer-woman, suddenly struck my ear, and farewell
to my divine existence. But if it is pleasant to exist as God does, it is
also sometimes quite pleasant to exist as men do . . .

[Diderot reflects on the landscape in front of him until the Abbé
arrives and the two men go out for a walk in the morning air. They
discuss what beauty consists of, how different qualities evoke the
same epithet.]

'It is quite simple,' [says Diderot]. 'Your general term of praise   116
comes, dear Abbé, from some common ideas or sensations aroused
in your soul by physical qualities which are utterly different.'

'I understand. Like admiration.'

'And pleasure, as well. If you examine the matter closely you will
discover that the objects which cause astonishment or admiration,
without producing pleasure, are not beautiful, and those which
produce pleasure, without causing surprise or admiration, are not
beautiful either . . . Take away from a sound all moral and mental
association, and you will take away its beauty. Stop an image at the
surface of the eye, so that it reaches neither the mind nor the heart;
and it will not possess any more beauty. There is yet another
distinction: it is the object in nature, and the same object in art or
imitation . . . [From a real fire you turn away in horror, but] let
someone show you the details of such a disaster on a canvas, and
your eyes will look on it with pleasure . . .

[After further discussion on this point, and then about language,
their walk brings them to the sea. The sight of how the various boats
were all in different situations, although being blown by the same
wind, leads Diderot to reflect on how laws, language and morality
can all assume different forms, according to circumstances.]

[Returning home] I thought that if there was a morality appro-   124
priate to each species, perhaps in the same species there is a
morality appropriate to different individuals, or at least to different
conditions or groups of similar individuals; and, so as not to scan-
dalize you by too serious an example, perhaps there is a morality
appropriate to artists or to art, and that that morality could well be
the opposite of the usual morality. Yes, my friend, I am very much
afraid that the path which leads the imitator of nature to the

sublime would lead another man straight to misfortune. The rule
for the poet is to throw himself to the extremes. The rule for
happiness is to keep a just measure in everything. You should not   125
make poetry of your life . . . It is a common experience that the
man to whom nature has granted genius and the woman whom she
has endowed with beauty are condemned to unhappiness; it is
because they are poetic creatures. I called to mind the number of
great men and beautiful women who had been made unhappy by the
very quality which distinguished them from their species. I sang to
myself the praise of ordinariness which gives protection from both
blame and envy; and I wondered why, nevertheless, no one wanted
to lose his *sensibilité* and become ordinary. O vanity of men!

[The following day Diderot and the Abbé go for another walk,
to another site] and, continually distracted by the beauties of
nature, we did not so much carry on a conversation as throw out
disconnected remarks.   130

'Why are so few men affected by the attractions of nature?'

'It is because society has produced an artificial taste and sense of
beauty in them.'

'It seems to me that the progress of the logic of reason has been
quite different to that of the logic of taste.'

'And the latter is so fine, subtle and sensitive that it presupposes
a knowledge of the human mind and heart, its passions, prejudices,
errors, fears and inclinations, which must be so profound that few
are in a state to understand it, and even fewer in a state to find it. It
is very much easier to sort out the mistake in a piece of reasoning
than the reason for something beautiful. Besides, one is much older
than the other. Reason is concerned with things, taste with their
manner of being . . . Nature demands whatever is necessary . . .
Taste demands in addition the qualities which make whatever is
necessary agreeable . . .'

'[Then] the imagination and the judgement are two qualities   131
common to all but almost the opposite of one another. The imagination does not create anything, it imitates, composes, combines,
exaggerates, enlarges, diminishes. It is continually concerned with
resemblances. Judgement observes, compares, and only looks for
differences. Judgement is the dominant quality in the philosopher,
imagination the dominant quality in the poet.'

'Is the philosophical spirit favourable or unfavourable to poetry?
A great question which these few words have virtually settled
already.'

'It is true. Barbaric people have more vigour than civilized people . . . Everywhere vigour and poetry decline as the philosophical spirit has made progress . . . [The latter] wants more strict, exact and rigorous comparisons: its cautious progress is the enemy of the fluent and the figurative. As the reign of things grows that of images passes away. With reason there is introduced an exactness, precision, method, and, if you will excuse the word, a kind of pedantry which kills everything. All civil and religious prejudices are dispelled and it is incredible how disbelief dries up the well-spring of poetry . . . [After further discussion he adds:]   136 There is always an element of untruth in poetry. The philosophical spirit makes us used to noticing that, and farewell illusion and effect . . .'

[Diderot now reveals that the landscapes have been those painted by Vernet, and he talks about the artist.]

What is astonishing is that the artist recalls the effects [we see on   140 his canvas] at two hundred leagues from nature; the only model present is the one in his imagination. And he paints with incredible speed. He says: Let there be light, and there is light; let night follow day and day follow darkness, and he makes night and day. His imagination, as precise as it is fertile, provides him with these truths; and they are such that the person who beside the sea was a cold and unmoved spectator, marvels when he sees them on the canvas. In effect these compositions preach the power, greatness and majesty of nature more strongly than does nature itself. It is written: The heavens proclaim the glory of the Lord. But these are Vernet's heavens, and it is his glory.

[Diderot concludes with some reflections on the sublime, often adopting virtually the same words as Burke.]

Everything that astonishes the soul, everything that gives it a   146 feeling of terror, leads to the sublime. A vast plain does not astonish as the ocean does, nor a calm sea as a stormy sea. Darkness adds to terror . . . Night hides shapes, makes sounds fearful; it can arouse the imagination by the sound of a single leaf, falling in a   147 forest. Our imagination makes our insides tremble, everything is exaggerated. The cautious man enters warily; the cowardly man stops, shudders, or runs away; the brave man puts his hand on the hilt of his sword.

Temples are dark places. Tyrants keep themselves hidden; they are never on view and because of their atrocities they are assumed to be larger than life . . . Light is good if you want to convince someone, it is worthless if you want to move him. Light, however it is understood, harms enthusiasm. Poets always speak of eternity, infinity, immensity, of time, space, the divinity, tombs, spirits, hell, of overcast skies, deep seas, dark forests, thunder, lightning breaking through the clouds. Be mysterious. Great noises heard from a distance, waterfalls heard without being seen, silence, solitude, desert, ruins, caves, the sound of muffled drums, their beats separated by silences, the tolling of bells . . . there is in all these things something inexplicably terrible, great and mysterious . . .

Ideas of power are also sublime, but more so with power which   148
threatens than power which protects. The bull is more beautiful than the ox; the horned bull bellowing is more beautiful than the bull walking about and feeding; the horse that is free, its mane flying in the wind, rather than the horse under its rider; . . . the tyrant, rather than the king; crime, perhaps, rather than virtue; cruel gods rather than good gods; and the sacred lawgivers knew that well.

The season of spring does not suit a sombre occasion. Magnificence is only beautiful in disorder.

9

Rameau's Nephew

In 1805 there was published in Leipzig a book entitled *Rameaus Neffe*; on the title-page were the names of Diderot, as author, and Goethe, as translator. The dialogue made an immediate and lasting impression. Along with the first version of Goethe's *Faust* it was the only modern work referred to in Hegel's *Phenomenology of the Spirit* when that epoch-making masterpiece appeared two years later. Yet although it read like Diderot and was about Diderot, and Goethe assured his readers that Diderot was the author, there was no direct evidence of his authorship. Such a work had not been mentioned by him, nor referred to by any of his contemporaries; the first proper edition of his *Oeuvres*, edited by his friend and disciple Naigeon in 1798, had not included it nor spoken of it; and the manuscript Goethe had used disappeared.

In 1821 the publishers of a new edition of the *Oeuvres* printed Naigeon's *Mémoires* on Diderot's life and works, (Naigeon himself had died in 1810), and there was one brief tantalizing reference to 'an excellent satire under the name of *Le Neveu de Rameau*, as original as the person named in its title';[1] according to Naigeon the manuscript of this work was as old as that of *La Religieuse*. This edition of the *Oeuvres* did include a French verson of the text which the editor, Brière, had obtained from Diderot's daughter, Madame de Vandeul, but the manuscript was only lent to him for a short while; so although the work was available from 1823 in a form which presumably was authentic it was not possible to verify this. Astonishingly, the same thing happened with the next edition, by Assézat in 1875; a different manuscript was used, of uncertain provenance, which was also only on loan and immediately disappeared from sight. Only in 1884, when Tourneux discovered a manuscript in the collection at St Petersburg, was a verifiable attribution possible. Then in 1890 the librarian of the Comédie-Française, browsing in the bookstalls on the banks of the Seine, came across a collection of eighteenth-century texts; bound in among them was an autograph manuscript by Diderot himself of *Le Neveu*. A fully authentic version of the dialogue did indeed exist and was at last available.

This strange story of the text of *Le Neveu* is only one of the work's mysteries. Although it is now generally recognized as Diderot's masterpiece there is no reference to it in any other work by him, nor in any of his letters. In one place[2] he mentions 'Rameau the mad' quoting the Latin tag *Quisque suos patimur manes* which comes at the end of the work; otherwise, silence. We therefore have to date the composition of the piece from the internal evidence of the dialogue itself. Fortunately it is so dense with particular references that this is not too difficult. The immediate causes of the Nephew's distress can be dated: his expulsion from the household of the financier Bertin and his actress mistress Mademoiselle Hus must have happened before September 1761 since these two then broke up. It is also known that the wife of Jean-François Rameau (the Nephew) died in the summer of 1761. In the dialogue Diderot mentions his daughter as being eight years old, and Angélique's eighth birthday occurred in September 1761. There are also parallels to some sentences of the work in Diderot's correspondence between 1760 and 1762, and the success of Palissot's play *Les Philosophes*, which had ridiculed Diderot and the bitter memory of which provides one of the driving forces of the work, had taken place in May 1760. It is therefore assumed that the first draft was written in 1761 and/or 1762.

But it is also clear that Diderot revised the work over the years. There are many parallel remarks in the *Salons* of 1765 and 1767, and references in *Le Neveu* itself to events that happened after 1762: the death of Jean-Philippe Rameau (the uncle and composer) (1764), the rehabilitation of Calas (1765), Diderot's conversations with Bemetzrieder whom he employed to teach Angélique (after 1769), Voltaire's praise of Maupeou (1771), Sabatière's *Trois Siècles de la littérature* (1772), and the episode of the Dutch Jew, which is recorded in the *Voyage en Hollande* (1773/4). The version we read now is evidently the result of prolonged attention.

Diderot presumably gave the dialogue this attention because he cared greatly about it, but what was the purpose of the work? We do not know. What we are confronted with is 'something tremendous, barbaric and wild' (see p. 146). On the basis of a meeting (or several meetings) with the eccentric and strangely gifted Nephew – a character whose historical existence is confirmed by several contemporary accounts describing him in similar terms[3] – Diderot has constructed a work of explosive power but bewildering effect. The dialogue flows like the torrent of his own conversation.[4] Topics succeed one another helter-skelter, profound insight and personal abuse go hand in hand; the mood, focus and subject-matter shift subtly or alter abruptly. The two main contemporary issues – the battle over the *Encyclopédie* and the *Querelle des Bouffons*, the battle over Italian versus French opera – do not divide the two speakers in the expected way. To be for the *Encyclopédie* was also usually to be for the Italian *opera buffa*, but the Nephew identifies himself with all those against the *Encyclopédie* yet is a passionate devotee of the Italian composers. And what is the outcome of this conversation? It is difficult to say.

Various interpretations have been put forward. It has been seen as 'a literary confrontation between the folly of the age and the spirit of Greek philosophy', the central preoccupation of which is 'the opposition of enlightenment to enthusiasm'.[5] Or, the conflict is 'between the conviction that humanism is possible and the affirmation that the world is without hope', a conflict in which the humanist values upheld by the character of Diderot have a 'revolutionary value'.[6] In this reading the central concern of the work is education, since there 'is posed, in all its sharpness, the conflict of the ideal and reality'.[7] Alternatively, the Diderot character *Moi* is seen as being defeated on all the points at issue[8] and it is the Nephew *Lui* who by the end 'has come in a way to represent humanity'.[9]

Diderot's own title for the work, in the autograph manuscript, is *Satire seconde*. He wrote another, much shorter work, which he entitled *Satire première*.[10] The word 'satire' was used in the general sense which it has today, to mean a mocking attack on an individual or a group of people; Palissot's play *Les Philosophes* was described as a 'satire' at the time,[11] and the word occurs in this sense in *Le Neveu* itself.[12] But the word could also have a more specific sense, as a particular literary genre. In this meaning, which Diderot himself used in his *Entretiens sur le Fils naturel*,[13] a satire is a portrait of an extraordinary individual or a particular vice and is written in a loose, almost improvised form. The fact that Diderot's title – and that of the *Satire première* – is immediately followed by an epigraph from one of Horace's *Satires* suggests that he did have this specific sense of satire in mind. The parallels between *Le Neveu* and the Horatian *Satire* in question (Bk II.7) are also suggestive, for the latter is set at the time of the Saturnalia, when servants could speak their minds to their masters with impunity, and it has the theme that the philosopher alone is free. Yet this connection does not take us far in understanding why *Le Neveu* has such extraordinary impact.

One of the aspects of the work that makes an immediate impression is the amount of personal feeling involved. Not only has Diderot put himself into the dialogue, he also discusses personal issues. These take several forms. There is, first of all, the battle of the *Encyclopédie*. The name Palissot occurs twenty-three times in the dialogue, and he and other critics of the *Encyclopédie* are described in bitter terms, in ludicrous situations, and with unqualified disgust. The success of Palissot's *Les Philosophes* may only have been one of the sparks that set Diderot's imagination alight, but it left a permanent mark.* Then there is the fact that the following year had seen the failure of Diderot's own play *Le Père de famille* and the immense success of Rousseau's *La Nouvelle Héloïse*. 'I am moving into the final period [of my life],' he wrote in his *Éloge de Richardson* (1761), 'without having attempted anything that could recommend me to the times to come.'[14] These feelings seem to have contributed to the terrible sense of failure which the Nephew experiences, his sense of being 'mediocre', of not being able to write anything worth while.[15] Another matter which preoccupies the Nephew, and which worried Diderot as the end of his work on the *Encyclopédie* came in sight, was money. The detached Diderot in the dialogue may distance himself from the Nephew's continual emphasis on the need for money, but the historical Diderot knew the feeling very well; it is difficult not to be aware of Diderot's own anxiety over financial security in the passages where the Nephew expresses similar anxiety. There may also be a hint of nostalgia for the kind of life which Diderot had himself

* Palissot's play enjoyed a long run at the Comédie-Française at a time when the production of the *Encyclopédie* had been officially halted and the confidence of the early 1750s severely shaken. It was not the only work in which Palissot attacked Diderot in particular; his *Petites lettres sur les grands philosophes* (1757) had been very critical of his theory of *le drame*.

lived in his early years in Paris. All these personal elements can be
sensed, even when not visible on the surface of the work.

But there is no clear division between the 'personal' feelings and
the 'intellectual' discussion, the actual subject-matter of the dialogue. Because the intellectual issues were also, for Diderot, very
personal. Indeed, one of the reasons for the work's impact lies in
the fact that the ideas which the Nephew puts forward are diametrically opposed to those which Diderot in the dialogue (or
elsewhere in other writings) upholds; they therefore present a
serious threat to him. Instead of maintaining that moral values are
universal and desirable, the Nephew declares that such morality is
useless, inadequate and harmful, because it distorts a person's
natural inclinations. Instead of believing that our moral and
aesthetic faculties are essentially related, the Nephew demonstrates that there is a refined aesthetic pleasure to be derived from
what is morally repulsive. Instead of agreeing that the truth benefits society and that greed, flattery and self-promotion are harmful,
the Nephew insists that the truth causes more trouble than benefit,
that self-interest is the only general good, and that society is a state
of continual war and mutual deceit which yet has its own logic and
brings about its own sort of justice. It is no accident that he is
associated with the critics of the *Encyclopédie*, he regards the ideas
of the *philosophes* as facile, or pernicious, rubbish: 'Imagine the
universe wise and philosophical; you must admit it would be
unbearably dull.' When he describes the Bertin-Hus household as
'a school for humanity' he is uttering both a grotesque parody and
what he regards as a true comment.

These ideas are conveyed in a language of remarkable fluency,
idiosyncrasy and vigour. The Nephew describes his own speech as
'a bloody ludicrous patchwork, half market-place, half sophisti-
cated and literary'.[16] There is a vivid particularity to his conversation, endless references to individual people, places and episodes,
and also an intense physicality, ranging from the scatological and
obscene, through the sensual and sexual, to his characterization of
the Bertin-Hus household as a 'menagerie' and his continual stress
of the purely animal aspects of existence, getting (and enjoying)
food, and the simple (or not so simple) business of surviving. The
Nephew possesses, to an unusual degree, an astonishing capacity
for *living*. It is not enough for him to tell a story, he also wants to
perform it. He has the gift that talented actors have, of transforming the commonplace into something special;[17] but he also, like

some actors, does this not from any desire to impress, but from a deep emotional need to experience the moment more fully.

The Nephew can in fact be seen as one aspect of Diderot himself pushed to its extreme limit. The work's epigraph, from Horace, is *Vertumnis quotquot sunt natus iniquis*,[18] 'Born under the influence of Vertumnus in all his many shapes'. Vertumnus was the Roman god who presided over the changes of the seasons, and became in the effect the god of change. Horace's line refers to a character who was cursed with having no stability, no fixed point. Such change-ableness was as much a characteristic of Diderot, what he called his *héracliterie* (see p. 13), as it was of the Nephew. And the intel-lectual positions that derived from that, the emphasis on the individual and empirical, the relativity of all knowledge, also haunted Diderot. He, like the Nephew, believed that heredity played a large, perhaps decisive, part in forming a person's character, and at times wondered how any universal moral values could be upheld. He shared some of the Nephew's admiration for the amoral – 'I cannot prevent myself from admiring human nature, even sometimes when it is atrocious . . . If wicked men did not have that energy in crime, the good would not have the same energy for virtue'[19] – and for the rascal: 'All my life I have had and will have a weakness for rogues.'[20] He too was fascinated by the nature of genius and by the way what was morally undesirable could be creatively fruitful. He too at times saw no hope in social change.

In the character of Jean-François Rameau Diderot confronted his *alter ego*, uncertain but open-minded, and therefore at variance with his own fixed, well-meaning, but inadequate intellectual cate-gories. *Le Neveu* epitomizes Diderot's own predicament, caught between acute instincts and brilliant insights, and a somewhat ponderous conceptual apparatus which lacked the range or flexi-bility to cope with them. To be aware of this fact is to end some of the mystery about the work's purpose. If Diderot had consciously formulated such a purpose he would not have been able to realize it. (The contrast with his plays is obvious.) 'The madness of this man,' he writes of the Nephew, 'the stories of the Abbé Galiani, and the extravagances of Rabelais, have sometimes made me think profoundly.' They all cast a new light on what is around us, they all make us aware of our 'natural individuality'. In writing *Le Neveu de Rameau* Diderot himself joined this company. He created a work that could be compared with those of Rabelais or Sterne – 'the

English Rabelais'[21] – and reading *Le Neveu* now is for us like meeting the Nephew was for Diderot: it makes us aware of our own limitations, it makes us feel more alive.

Le Neveu de Rameau*

In good weather or bad it's my habit to go for a walk, at five   3
o'clock in the evening, to the Palais-Royal. It's me you see there sitting on a bench, always alone, wrapt in thought. I am discussing with myself politics, love, art, philosophy. I'm indulging my mind in whatever it fancies, letting it follow the first thought, daft or wise, that it comes across – like our young rakes following a courtesan with a carefree look, a welcoming face and a lively eye, then leaving her for another – trying them all, staying with none. My thoughts are my whores.

If it's too wet or cold I take refuge in the Café de la Régence and amuse myself watching the chess. Paris is the place in the world, and the Café de la Régence the place in Paris, where the best chess is played. One afternoon I was sitting there, my eyes open, my   4
mouth shut, my ears as closed as I could make them, when I was accosted by one of the most extraordinary characters this country possesses – and God knows we're not short of them! He's a mixture of the noble and the base, intelligence and madness. His ideas of right and wrong must be all jumbled up in his head, for he shows his good qualities without ostentation and his bad qualities without shame. He has a strong constitution, a strange vivid imagination, and the most unusually powerful set of lungs. God, what terrible lungs! Nothing is more unlike him than himself. Sometimes he is thin and pale, like a consumptive in the last stages of his illness, and you can count his teeth through his cheeks; you'd say he'd spent several days without food or he'd just come out of a Trappist monastery. The next month he is fat and full, as if he'd not been away from a rich man's dining-table or he'd been kept locked up in a Benedictine monastery. He lives from day to day, happy or depressed, according to circumstances. His first concern in the   5

---

* The text given here has been abridged and condensed for the sake of fluency. Omissions are so frequent (and often so slight) that they are not indicated in the manner used elsewhere in this book, but the page numbers in the margin provide reference to the French text.

morning when he gets up is to know where he will lunch; after lunch he thinks about where he will have supper. Night-time brings another anxiety; whether he will walk back to the tiny attic he occupies – if the landlady, fed up with waiting for his rent, has not asked for the key back – or whether he'll make do with a local tavern, where he'll wait for the day with a piece of bread and a pot of beer beside him. When he does not have any money in his pocket he falls back on the coachman of some friend or great lord who will give him a bed on the straw, next to the horses.

I don't care for oddities like him. Others get to know them, even become friends, but once a year is enough for me. They are interesting, their personality clashes with other people. They break that tiresome uniformity which has come about through our education, our social conventions, our accepted patterns of behaviour. Someone like him is a grain of yeast which causes fermentation, restoring to those around him some of their natural individuality, stirring them up, making them love or hate. He provokes the truth, revealing the good, exposing the bad. That's when a sensible man pays attention and sorts out those around him.

I had known this particular oddity for a long time. You will be wondering what his name is. He is the nephew of that famous Rameau who freed us from the plainsong of Lully. Having buried that Florentine composer he in turn is going to be buried by the new Italian virtuosi, something which he suspects and which makes him gloomy and bad-tempered. For no one is as moody as a writer whose reputation is threatened, not even a pretty woman who wakes up with a spot on her nose.   6

HE   Ah! There you are, Mister Philosopher! What are you   7
doing among this bunch of layabouts? You too wasting your time pushing the wood around?

(That's the scornful way people talk of playing at chess or draughts.)

I   I enjoy watching the game for a while, when I've nothing better to do.

HE   Well you can't get much enjoyment here. Most of them know no more than anyone could learn.

I   You're very particular. I suppose you only care for the brilliant players?

HE   I do. In chess, poetry, eloquence, music and other trifles like that, what's the good of being average?

I   Not much, I agree. But you need a large number of people involved to produce a man of genius. He's one in a million. But let's not go into that. It's ages since I saw you. I scarcely think of you when I don't see you, but I'm always pleased to see you again. Are things going well?

HE   On the whole. Though not so well today.   8

I   How come? Your stomach looks cheerful enough.

HE   But not my face. The bad mood which is shrivelling up my dear uncle seems to be fattening up his nephew.

I   Talking of your uncle, do you see much of him?

HE   Passing by in the street.

I   Hasn't he been good to you?

HE   If he's good to anyone it's through absent-mindedness. He's a typical philosopher. Thinks only of himself. The rest of the world is just a bubble of air. His wife and daughter can die when they like, so long as when the church bells ring they do so in thirds   9 and fifths. That is his good fortune, and that's what I admire about men of genius. They're only good for one thing. Apart from that, nothing. They've no sense of being citizens, fathers, mothers, friends. Between you and me, we might want to be just like them but we shouldn't want the breed to be too fruitful. We need men, but not men of genius. No, God help us, not them. They always change the way things are. And as stupidity is everywhere in command nothing is ever changed, not the slightest thing, without trouble. So part of what they had in mind comes about and the rest stays as it was. Result? Two gospels; a Harlequin's coat.

No. If you want a quiet life stick to the teaching of Rabelais' monk. That's real wisdom – do your duty, more or less; always speak well of the abbot; and let the world carry on as it will. It must carry on all right, because most people put up with it. If I knew any history I'd show you how evil has always come about through some man of genius. But I don't know any history because I don't know anything. To hell with it, if I've ever learnt anything; and if I've ever been worse off for not having learnt anything. But I was eating one day with one of the king's ministers. He's as bright as they come. And he demonstrated to us, as clearly as one and one make two, that nothing benefits people more than a lie, and nothing does more harm than the truth. I don't remember exactly how he did it, but it obviously followed from that that men of genius are a menace. And if a child at birth had on its forehead the mark of this dangerous gift of nature, that child should be smothered or drowned.

I   But these people so opposed to genius always claim to have   10
some.

HE   They might think that to themselves. They don't dare
admit it.

I   That's modesty. So you have developed a violent dislike of
genius?

HE   Which will never diminish.

I   But I have seen you in despair at being only an ordinary man.
You will never be happy if you are pulled in two opposite directions. I agree with you that men of genius are generally peculiar – as
the proverb says: there's no great mind without a streak of madness
– but that doesn't alter my opinion. We despise the centuries that
did not produce any. They honour the people they lived among.
Sooner or later statues are put up to them and they are seen as
benefactors of the human race. A lie may be useful for a moment,
but in the long run it must be harmful; the truth may hurt for a
moment, but in the long run it must be useful. That is why I am led
to think that the man of genius who exposes a widespread error, or
who establishes a great truth, must always deserve our deepest
respect. He may fall foul of prejudice or the law, but there are two
kinds of law – that which has a universal and absolute value, and
that which owes its force to short-sightedness or local circumstances. The person who is guilty of infringing the latter suffers only
a brief disgrace. Time turns that disgrace back onto the judges and   11
people, and that lasts for ever. Whom do we revile today – Socrates?
or the court which made him drink the hemlock?

HE   And a fat lot of good that is to him! Was he any the less
convicted, any the less put to death? Was he any the less troublesome? Did his contempt for a bad law encourage idiots to have any
the less contempt for good laws? Was he any the less a provocative
and pokey-nosed individual? You almost admitted as much,
just now.

I   I did not say that genius and wickedness necessarily went
together. A stupid person will more often do wrong than an intelligent man. But what if a man of genius *is* difficult, prickly,
impossible to live with, yes and maybe wicked as well, so what?

HE   Then he should be drowned.

I   Steady on. Let's take an example. I won't take your uncle.
He's a hard man, a bad father, and so on; and it's not yet certain
that he is a genius. But let's take Racine. He certainly had genius
and was not thought to be a good man. Or Voltaire?

HE   Don't rush me. I am consistent.

I   Which would you prefer? For him to be straightforward, reli-   12
able, honest, but nothing more? Or arrogant, deceitful and dishonest, and the author of *Andromaque, Britannicus, Phèdre*?

HE   Of those two, I think it would have been better if he'd been
the first.

I   Why?

HE   All those beautiful works Racine wrote, did they bring him
in twenty thousand francs? But if he'd been in the silk business in
the Rue St-Denis he'd have made a fortune. And then he'd have
had every pleasure that's on offer. Occasionally he'd have given a
few coins to a down-and-out clown like me, to make him laugh, or
to get him a girl. And what meals we'd have eaten! What wines,
liqueurs, what parties in the country! You see, I know what I'm
talking about. You laugh. But let me tell you: it would certainly
have been better for those around him. While as it was Racine was   13
only good for people he never knew, for a time when he was six foot
under.

I   But a thousand years from now he will still fill people with
feelings of humanity, pity and love. They will wonder who he was
and where he came from, and they will envy France because of him.
A great man is a tree which stunts the trees around it, and stifles the
plants beneath it, but its top reaches up into the clouds and its
branches spread out into the distance. Those who pass by take rest
around its mighty trunk. Its fruit which they enjoy has an exquisite
flavour and is always fresh.

HE   But if nature was as powerful as she is wise why didn't she   14
make them as good as she made them great?

I   But don't you see? If everything was excellent, nothing would
be excellent.

HE   That's true. The important thing is that you and I exist, and
we are who we are. The best arrangement, in my opinion, is that
which includes me. To hell with the most perfect of worlds if I'm
not in it. I prefer to be, even if I am insolent and quarrelsome, than
not to be.

I   Right. So let us accept things as they are. Let us see what they   15
demand of us and how they relate to us, and let us leave aside the
whole which we do not know enough about either to praise or to
blame. And which perhaps is neither good nor bad if, as many good
people think, it is necessary.

HE   I don't understand all that but what I do know is that I

would certainly like to be someone else, on the chance of being a
genius or a great man. Yes, that's something which I must admit. I
have never heard a genius being praised without being secretly
infuriated. I am jealous. I love to hear about some aspect of their
private life which is degrading; that makes us closer. I can bear my
ordinariness more easily. I am angry that I am mediocre. Yes, I am
mediocre and I'm angry. I can never hear the overture to *Les Indes
galantes** played without saying to myself sadly: that is something
you will never do. (Then he started humming the overture, and   16
added:) The something which is inside me speaks to me, and says:
Rameau, if you had really wanted to compose a piece like that you
would have done it, then another, and when you had done a certain
number you would be sung and played everywhere. People would
point you out and say: he was the person who wrote those pretty
tunes (and he sang the tunes). You would have a good house (and
he demonstrated how large), a good bed (and he lay down non-
chalantly), good wines (which he tasted by clicking his tongue
against his palate), a good coach (and he lifted his foot to climb into
it), beautiful women (whom he was already caressing and looking
at suggestively), a hundred rascals coming to flatter me every day
(and he imagined he saw them around him – Palissot, Poincinet,
Frèron father and son†); in the morning you'd be told you are a
great man, in the *Trois Siècles* you'd read you are a great man, and   17
in the evening you'd be convinced you were a great man. And the
great man, Rameau the nephew, would go to sleep to the sweet
sound of the praise ringing in his ear. Even in sleep he would look
satisfied: his chest would swell, rise and fall with assurance. He
would snore like a great man. (And so saying he stretched himself
out languidly on a bench, closed his eyes and imitated the happy
sleep which he imagined. After a few moments' enjoyment of this
delightful rest he woke up, yawned, rubbed his eyes, and looked
around him for his empty-headed flatterers.)

I   So you think a happy man has a particular way of sleeping?

HE   You bet I do! Not like me, poor wretch. But what bothers
me today is not snoring or sleeping like a pauper. What's happened
to me is much worse.

I   What's that?

* An opera by Jean-Philippe Rameau.
† All critics of the *Encyclopédie*.

HE   You've always taken some interest in me because, although I'm a poor devil whom really you despise, I amuse you.

I   That's correct.

HE   Well, I'll tell you. (Before beginning he let out a deep sigh and put his hands to his head. Then he became calm again and said:) You know me – a lazy, insolent blockhead, a lying, greedy, cretinous oaf.   18

I   What praise!

HE   It's all true, every word. No one knows me better than I do. And I haven't said it all.

I   I'm not denying it.

HE   Well then. I've been living with some people who'd taken a liking to me precisely because I was gifted, to a rare degree, with all those qualities . . . I was as cosy as a cucumber. They made such a fuss of me. I was their little Rameau, their pretty Rameau, their Rameau the blockhead, the insolent, the great big greedy brute! Every one of those friendly phrases brought me a smile, a hug, a box on the ear, a tasty mouthful at table. Great idiot that I am! I've   19 lost it all. Lost it, because once, the only time in my life, I showed a bit of common sense. Agh!

I   How come?

HE   Stupidity. Sheer stupidity.

I   Yes but how?

HE   The stupidity of showing a bit of intelligence. Ah Rameau, that'll teach you to stay the way God made you, the way your protectors wanted you. They grabbed you by the shoulders and led you to the door. 'Out!' they said. 'Out, you bum! And don't come back! You want to be intelligent, do you? We're the intelligent ones round here. Out!' So out I went, biting my fingernails; I should have bitten off my wretched tongue beforehand. So here I am, homeless, and the prospect of a night in a stable. Miserable idiot, whatever got into you?

I   But isn't there any way of being reconciled? Surely they'd take   20 you back. If I was you I'd at least go and see them. Yes, just as you are, looking as pitiful as you do. I'd throw myself at Madame's feet and say, in a tearful voice: 'Forgive me, Madame. I am worthless, unspeakable. It just slipped out. You know I'm not liable to suffer from common sense and I promise, I won't do it again.' (What was amusing was that while I was suggesting this speech he acted it out. He got down on his knees, glued his face to the ground, and said crying and sobbing: 'Yes, my little queen; yes, I promise; I will

never do it again, never, never, never.' Then, standing up   21
abruptly, he said in a serious and thoughtful voice:)

HE   Yes you're right . . . But even so, to beg forgiveness from
that bitch, a miserable little actress who's whistled off the stage
every time she appears. I, Rameau, son of Rameau the Dijon
chemist who's never bent his knee to anyone! I, Rameau, the
nephew of the man called the great Rameau! I, who have myself
composed some keyboard pieces which nobody plays but which –
who knows? – in time may be the only ones people will play. I! That
I should go . . . No, Sir; not me. (And putting his right hand on his
heart he added:) I can feel something inside me which rises up and
says: 'Rameau, you'll do no such thing.' To be human means to
have a certain dignity, which nothing can suppress. It is aroused by
a trifle. Yes, by a trifle. On another day I could be as servile as they
come. Another day I'd kiss her arse for a farthing.

I   Well there you are. She's young, pretty, well endowed.
Someone more fastidious than you would, if need be, perform such
an act.

HE   Now listen: there is arse-kissing literal and arse-kissing
metaphorical. Ask that fat Bergier who kisses Madame de la
Marck's arse both literally and metaphorically. And dear God, I'd
object to both kinds there.

I   If you don't like the method I suggest you'll have to put up   22
with being poor.

HE   It's hard being poor when there are so many wealthy fools
you can sponge off. And then the self-loathing. It's tough.

I   What do you know about that?

HE   I know all right. How many times have I thought: All those
places laid, at all the thousands of tables in Paris, and not one of
them for you, Rameau. All the swollen purses being emptied left
and right, and not a coin comes to you. A thousand dim-witted
plain-faced schemers, all well dressed, and you go about stark
naked. Are you mentally retarded? Can't you lie, promise, keep
your word or break your word as well as the next man? Can't you
crawl on all fours? Carry on an affair for Madame, take messages
for Monsieur? Or make this little middle-class daughter realize she
looks dreadful, but with some ear-rings and make-up and lace she'd
be stunning. That her little feet are not made to walk in the street.
And there's this handsome young wealthy Monsieur, with a magnificent coach and six footmen in attendance, who has seen her and
hasn't been able to eat or drink or sleep since that moment. 'But my

father.' Yes yes, he may be a little angry, at first. 'But mummy said   23
I should be a good girl, and that's what's most important.' They all
say that, doesn't mean a thing. 'But my father-confessor?' Don't
see him. Or if you must, take him some coffee. 'He's very strict.'
That's because you haven't given him anything. Wait till he sees
you in lace. 'I'll have a lace dress?' Of course; and some beautiful
diamond ear-rings. 'Diamond!' Yes. 'Like the Marquise who
comes to buy gloves in our shop?' That's right. And you'll go in a
beautiful coach, with dappled greys, two tall footmen, a little negro
boy, an outrider in front, with make-up and beauty-spots on your
face, and your train carried behind you. 'To the ball?' To the ball,
and the theatre and the opera. Her heart is pounding with
excitement. You fiddle with a piece of paper. 'What's that?'
Nothing. 'It is.' Just a message. 'Who for?' For you, if you're
interested. 'Let me see it.' She reads it. 'A meeting? Not possible.'
On the way to Mass. 'Mummy's always with me. But if he comes
here, early one morning. I'm first up and into the shop.' He comes,
he pleases. One fine day, at dusk, the girl disappears and I get my
two hundred crowns. And with a talent like that I go hungry! . . .
So you see: I do know what self-loathing is, and the pain that comes
from the neglect of the gifts we've been given. That's the worst of   24
all. Almost better not to have been born.

(I listened to him, and as he enacted the scene of the pimp and the
girl he was seducing my soul was pulled in two contrary directions. I
was not sure whether to roar with laughter or shout out in
indignation. It hurt. Twenty times a burst of laughter prevented a
roar of anger: twenty times the anger rising up inside me came out
as a roar of laughter. I was bewildered by so much perception and
so much deceit, so many truths and so much dishonesty, such a
complete distortion of feelings, such utter depravity and such
extraordinary frankness. He saw the trouble I was experiencing.)

HE   What's up?

I   Nothing.   25

HE   You look bothered.

I   Yes, I am.

HE   You don't care about me. And I didn't tell you this to upset
you. I saved a bit from what those people gave me. It should be
worth a bit more by now.

I   You mean, less.

HE   No, more. Every minute we get richer. One day less to live
is the same as one crown more. The important thing is to empty

your bowels every evening – easily, enjoyably and abundantly. O blessed excrement! That is all that life amounts to, whoever you are. When our time's up we're all as rich as one another. Both Samuel Bernard who through theft, plunder and bankruptcies leaves twenty-seven millions in gold, and Rameau who will be wrapped in a shroud provided by charity. The dead don't hear the churchbells. Or the difference between a hundred priests or none. Whether you rot beneath marble or plain earth, you still rot. Whether you have choirboys in red and choirboys in blue around your coffin, or no one, so what? And then, take a look at this wrist.   26 Fingers like sticks, tendons like dried-up gut-strings. But I've stretched and twisted and beaten them. You won't go? By God you bloody well will go. Come on! (And so saying he grabbed the fingers of his left hand in his right hand and bent them forwards and backwards till the tips of the fingers touched his arm, the joints cracked, and I was afraid the bones would be dislocated.)

I   Take care. You'll do yourself an injury.

HE   Don't worry, they're used to it. The buggers have got to work, haven't they? Hit the keys, move up and down the violin strings. They still function. Oh yes. (As he spoke he took up the position of a violin-player and began humming an allegro by Locatelli . . .) Well. How was that?   27

I   Fine.

HE   Yes, they seem to be in working order. [Now for the keyboard.]

I   Please.

HE   No. You must see for yourself. Then you might get me a pupil or two.

I   But it's not worth it. I don't know many people. (But he sat down as if at a keyboard and performed a piece by Alberti or Galuppi, I was not sure which. His voice was like the wind and his fingers flew over the notes; sometimes leaving the treble to play the   28 bass, sometimes leaving the accompaniment to play the treble again. On his face one emotion followed another; you could see gentleness, anger, delight, grief. But what was extraordinary was that from time to time he lost his way, groped around and then repeated the passage, as if he had made a mistake and was annoyed with himself for being out of practice. Then he stood up and wiped away the drops of sweat running down his cheek.)

HE   So you see, we can still manage a tritone or an augmented fifth. Those enharmonic progressions which my dear uncle makes so much of, they aren't such a big deal, we can cope with them.

I   You didn't have to demonstrate your talent. I would have taken your word for it.

HE   Talent? Not me. I know enough for my job, and that's more than I need. For in this country who has to know what he teaches?

I   No more than you have to know what you learn.

HE   Right, yes, very good. Now, Mister Philosopher, your hand on your heart, tell me straight. Wasn't there a time when you weren't so well off?

I   I'm still not that well off.

HE   But you no longer go to the Luxembourg Gardens in the summer, you remember . . .

I   That's enough. I remember.   29

HE   In a rough grey overcoat.

I   Yes, yes.

HE   Worn out on one side, the sleeve torn; and black woollen stockings, the heels stitched up with white thread.

I   Yes, yes; just as you wish.

HE   You gave lessons in maths.

I   Without knowing a word. Isn't that what you are going to say?

HE   Exactly.

I   I learnt as I was teaching, and I made some good pupils.

HE   Now today, when you've come up in the world . . .

I   Not much.

HE   You employ teachers for your daughter.

I   Not yet. It's her mother who's looking after her education. You've got to have peace at home.

HE   Peace? You only get that by being servant or master. And you ought to be the master. I had a wife, God bless her, but when she ever answered back I'd exercise my lungs. I used to say, like God, Let there be light. And there was light. In four years we didn't have a dozen cross words. How old's your daughter?   30

I   It's beside the point.

HE   How old is your daughter?

I   For Christ's sake let's forget my daughter, and her age.

HE   Oh dear, oh dear, there's never anyone so touchy as a philosopher. I beseech you very humbly, Your Most Gracious Wisdom, for the vaguely approximate age of your esteemed off-spring.

I   Let us suppose she's . . . eight.

HE   Eight! She should have been doing her scales four

years ago!

I   Perhaps I'm not concerned that she should study a subject that takes up so much time and is of so little use.

HE   Then what will you teach her?

I   To be able to think properly, if possible.

HE   Let her think as little as she likes, provided she's attractive, amusing, and well dressed. No dancing lessons, singing lessons? No music at all?   31

I   A bit of theory, maybe for a year or two.

HE   And in place of these essential subjects, which you forbid . . .

I   She will learn grammar, history, geography, a little drawing and a lot of ethics.

HE   How easy it would be to show you the uselessness of that sort of learning, in a world like ours. Not just the uselessness, maybe the danger as well. And who will teach these subjects?

I   Some tutors, obviously.

HE   And you think they'll know their subjects?

I   Why not?

HE   Not possible. In order to know about them, in order to teach them, they'd have to spend their whole life learning them. It was only after thirty or forty years' application that my uncle glimpsed the first signs of his musical theory.

I   You madman, lunatic! What kind of brain have you got, so   32
many good ideas mixed up with crazy ones?

HE   Who knows? It's all a matter of chance.

I   You've taught, haven't you? Accompaniment and com-position.

HE   That's right.

I   There you are then. I presume you knew something about them.

HE   Certainly not. And as my pupils learnt nothing from me, they also had nothing to unlearn.

I   How did you do it?

HE   How everyone does it. I arrive, I collapse in a chair, 'What   33
terrible awful weather! What a state the pavement's in!' I chat about this and that. 'Mademoiselle Lemière was going to play a vestal virgin in the new opera but she's pregnant again. No one knows who'll take over from her . . . Come along, Mademoiselle, get your book.' While Mademoiselle, who is in no hurry, looks for her book, which she's mislaid, and the servant girl is called and a fuss is made, I carry on: 'Clairon really is impossible to understand.

People are talking of some absurd marriage . . . Rumour has it that
Voltaire is dead. So much the better – Why so much the better? –
Because he must be about to give us some firework. It's his habit to
die a fortnight beforehand.' I play the fool. They listen, they laugh,
they exclaim 'He's always such a delight!' Finally Mademoiselle's   34
book is discovered under the sofa, where it had been dragged torn
and chewed up by some kitten or a doggy-wog. She sits down at the
keyboard and hammers away by herself. Then I approach, having
made a sign of approval to the mother. The mother: 'That's not
bad. If one only wanted to, but one does not. One prefers to waste
one's time chattering and trifling and running about. As soon as
you've gone the book is shut, it's only opened when you next
appear. And you never criticize her.' But I must do something, so I
take her hands and alter their position. I get annoyed and shout
out: 'G, G, G; that's G, Mademoiselle.' The mother:
'Mademoiselle, haven't you got any ears? Even I, sitting over here
with no book in front of me, even I can hear that that must be G.
What trouble you give Monsieur. I can't understand why he's so
patient. You don't remember a thing he tells you; you don't make
any progress.' Then I let up the pressure and shake my head. 'I'm
sorry, Madame. It could be much better, if Mademoiselle wished,
if she practised a bit. But it's not bad.' The mother: 'If I was you I'd
keep her on the same piece for a year.' 'She'll only move on when
she's mastered all the problems; but that will not be as long as
Madame thinks.' The mother: 'Monsieur Rameau, you flatter her.
You're too kind. That is the only thing she'll remember from her
lesson, and she'll repeat it to me whenever she wants.' The hour
passes. My pupil presents me with my fee with the elegance and
grace she has learnt from the dancing-master. The mother: 'Very   35
good, Mademoiselle. If Javillier was here he would have been
delighted.' I chatter for a moment more, for politeness' sake, and
then disappear. And that is what was once called a music lesson.

I　　And today it's something else?

HE　　Dear God, I'll say so. I arrive. I am serious. I take off my
gloves at once, open the instrument, try out the keys. I am always in
a hurry. If I'm kept waiting a moment I shout out as if I'd been
robbed of a crown. In an hour from now I must be there; in two
hours, at Madame la Duchesse of so-and-so; I am expected for
dinner at the house of a beautiful Marquise, and after that it's a
concert at Monsieur le Baron de Bacq.

I　　And yet you aren't expected anywhere?

HE   Exactly.

I   And why do you use all these nasty little tricks?

HE   Why are they nasty? I'm doing what everyone does. I didn't invent them. And I'd be a fool if I didn't behave like the rest. If you start applying some general rules of some morality or other – which everyone preaches and no one practises – you'll end up making black white and white black. There is a universal morality, like there is a universal grammar. And just as there are exceptions in every language, which are called . . . er . . . what do you call them?

I   Idioms.   36

HE   Right. So then: every profession has its exceptions to the universal morality, which could be called that profession's idioms. The minister, magistrate, soldier, lawyer, singing-teacher, they're all quite honest people even though their behaviour deviates in some way from the universal morality; it's merely full of moral idioms. The older the profession, the more the idioms; the harder things are, the more the idioms increase.

I   And the end result is that there are few jobs done honestly, or few honest people in their jobs.

HE   Correct. There are none. But on the other hand, there are only a few who are dishonest outside their work. In fact all would be well if there weren't a handful of earnest, disciplined, hard-working people who're at work morning and night and never do anything else. They're the only ones who become rich.

I   By using the idioms.

HE   Exactly. As for me, when I'm actually giving the lesson,   37
I do it well. That's in accordance with the universal rule. When I make people think I have more lessons to give than there are hours in the day, that is the idiom. There was a time, I admit, when I virtually stole the money from my pupils. But today I earn it; at least, I earn it as much as anyone else.

I   And when you did steal it, did you not feel any guilt?

HE   None at all. When one thief steals from another the devil laughs. The parents were rolling in money, God knows where they got it. They were court people, financiers, big merchants, bankers, businessmen. I helped them pay it back. I and a bunch of others employed like me. In nature all the species devour one another, in society all the ranks do the same. We deal out justice to each other without the law having anything to do with it. So these moral   38
idioms, which so much fuss is made about, they don't matter. The only thing that does is to have your eyes open.

I   As I see yours are.

HE   And then there's poverty. The voice of morality doesn't speak very loud when your guts are crying out. Anyhow, if I ever do become rich I'll certainly do my bit to pay it back, every possible way – eating, drinking, gambling, women.

I   I'm afraid I don't think you'll ever be rich.

HE   I'll be the most outrageous scoundrel that's ever been seen. I'll remember all they've made me suffer. I'll return all the insults they've thrown at me. I love to command and I shall command. I love to be praised and I shall be praised. I'll have a whole gang of toadies in my pay and I'll say to them, as was said to me: 'Come on, scum, amuse me.' And I shall be amused. We'll have girls and we'll get pissed and we'll enjoy every vice that's known. Wonderful!   39 Then we'll prove that Voltaire has no talent, that Buffon's only a puffed-up windbag, Montesquieu only a trifling wit, and we'll really take it out of all those self-righteous little squirts like you, whose envy makes you despise us, whose modesty is just a disguise for their conceit, and who are sober only because they can't afford otherwise. And as for music? Then we'll have some music!

I   In view of the excellent use you would make of being rich it's really a great pity you're so poor. Your way of life would be so useful to your fellow-citizens, would bring such renown to humanity, such credit to yourself.

HE   You can laugh if you like; but you don't know who you're dealing with. What I think is what the most important part of the court and the town think. They might not admit it, but the life I'd lead if I had the money is exactly the life they do lead. So that's where you stand. You think the same happiness should suit everyone. How absurd! Your kind of happiness presupposes a certain fanciful frame of mind, a bizarre sort of temperament. You embellish that odd condition with the name of 'virtue', you call it 'philosophy'. But are virtue and philosophy made for everyone?   40 Only for him who can achieve it, he who can stick to it. Imagine the world wise and philosophical; you must admit, it would be unbearably dull. The philosophy to follow is the wisdom of Solomon – drink good wine, stuff yourself with delicious food, take your exercise on pretty women, and take your rest on a nice soft bed. Apart from that, it's all vanity . . .

I   You know, I don't despise the pleasures of the senses. I too   42 have a palate, and enjoy good food and wine. I have a heart and two eyes. I like to see a pretty woman, to feel the curve of her breast, press her lips to mine, die of pleasure in her arms. But I won't deny that it is infinitely more satisfying to have helped some unfortunate person, to have sorted out some difficult business, to have gone for a walk with a close friend, spent a few hours teaching my children, written a good page, carried out my duty. I know what deed I would have given everything to have done. Voltaire's play *Mahomet* is a magnificent work, but I would have preferred to have rehabilitated Calas.*

HE   You're a strange lot!   43

I   And you're a sad lot, if you don't realize that by deeds like that one is raised up above one's fate, one overcomes unhappiness.

HE   It's a kind of satisfaction I'll have some difficulty getting to know, for it's certainly not common. But do you really think that people should be honest?

I   If they want to be happy, certainly.

HE   Then how come there are all these honest people who aren't happy, and happy people who aren't honest?

I   That's only how it appears to you.

HE   Wasn't it because I had a bit of common sense and was honest about it for once that I don't know where I'll be eating this evening?

I   No, it's because you have not been honest all the time. It's for not having realized sooner that your first priority was to free your-   44
self from dependence.

HE   Free or not the course I took was at least the most comfortable.

I   And the most uncertain, and the least honest.

HE   But the best suited to my character, as an idle, stupid bum.

I   That may be.

HE   Well, then, if I can make myself happy with the faults which I naturally have, which are no trouble to stick to, which fit in with everyone else and are to the liking of those who look after me, why should I start tormenting myself to make myself different? My benefactors don't want me criticizing them from morning to night. People praise virtue, but they hate it, they run away from it. It's ice-cold and in this world you need to keep your feet warm. And

---

* Jean Calas was a Protestant merchant in Toulouse who was wrongfully executed in 1762 for the murder of his son, a crime he had committed – it was alleged – to prevent his son's conversion to Catholicism. Voltaire campaigned vigorously to clear his name and in 1765 succeeded in achieving this.

then it always puts me in a bad mood. Why do we so often see
devout people who are so hard, angry and unsociable? It's because
they have imposed on themselves a task which is unnatural. They
are suffering, and when you suffer you make others suffer. That's
not for me, nor for my protectors; I must be bright, cheerful,
funny, amusing. Virtue must be admired and admiration is boring.   45
I deal with people who are bored, and I must make them laugh. It's
ridicule and madness which cause laughter, so I must be ridiculous
and mad. If one day friend Rameau started despising wealth,
women, good food, and began to moralize, he'd be a hypocrite.   46
That wouldn't do! Rameau must be what he is – a happy scoundrel
among rich scoundrels.

   I   In that case the only advice I can give you is to go back as fast
as you can to where you were so careless as to get yourself
thrown out.

   HE   And to do what you don't disapprove of literally but which
you're a bit averse to metaphorically?

   I   That is my advice.

   HE   Well another time I might not mind, but at the moment . . .
I don't like it.

   I   What a peculiar fellow you are.

   HE   What's peculiar about it? I'm happy to crawl, but I want it   47
to be of my own free will. Worms crawl and so do I. But if someone
treads on our tail we rear up. And that's what I do now. Oh, and
you can't imagine what a madhouse it is. That sour-faced misery
Bertin, wrapped up in his dressing-gowns, fed up with everyone
except himself, making me perform like a lunatic to try to get the
merest hint of a smile . . . Gloomy, abrupt and mysterious, like
fate, that's our boss. And that stuck-up strait-laced Mademoiselle   48
Hus. Ten times a day we must bend the knee, stretch out our arms   49
to the goddess, search in her eyes, hang on her every word, to know
what she desires and fulfil it in a flash. And you have to ring the
changes. If your compliments were all the same they'd become
boring, ineffective; they'd seem insincere. You must be skilful and   50
inventive to avoid that. There is an art in performing compliments,
whether it's the Praise Sudden and Extravagant, or the Praise
Subtle and Prepared. You should see my repertoire of approving
looks, how I can twist the spine, incline the head, lower the eyelids
and appear altogether overwhelmed, as if I had heard an angelic
voice come down from heaven. I didn't invent that, but no one has
ever done it better. Watch me.

I   That's amusing.

HE   Could any woman with an ounce of vanity resist it?

I   No.

HE   They can do what they like, any of them, they'll never rival   51
me in that. The best of them, Palissot, will never be more than a
novice . . . [He tells a story about Bouret, a man whom he regards
as a genius among flatterers.]

I   You should write these things down. It's a pity they should be   53
lost.

HE   True. But I don't care for rules and examples. Anyone who
needs instruction won't go far. Geniuses read little, practise a lot,
and go their own way. Who gave lessons to Bouret? No one. It is
nature who forms rare men like him . . .

I   In spite of the awful servile things you do I think that under-   56
neath it all you have a sensitive soul.

HE   Me? Certainly not. God help me if I know what I am
underneath. My mind, I would say, is as round as a ball and my
character as supple as a willow; never false, if it's in my interest to
be true, never true if it's in my interest to be false. I say things as
they come to me. Since nothing is premeditated, no one is offended.

I   But look what's happened as a result, with the people you
lived with.

HE   What do you expect? It's a bit of bad luck; no happiness   57
lasts. What company we had! It was a school of humanity, the
renewal of ancient hospitality. All the failed poets, unread authors,
out-of-work actors; a mob of poor, ugly parasites, with me at the
head of them, bold leader of a craven bunch. It's me who
encourages them to eat, the first time they arrive, or calls for a
drink for them. They take up so little room! We seem cheerful but
deep down we're all bad-tempered and ravenous. We eat like
wolves when the earth has been long under snow. We tear apart
like tigers anyone who is a success. Then there's a fine noise in the
menagerie. You've never seen so many bitter, malicious and angry
animals together. The only names you hear are Buffon, Duclos,
Montesquieu, Rousseau, Voltaire, D'Alembert, Diderot and God
knows what things they're called. No one is allowed any
intelligence unless he's as stupid as we are. That's where the idea
for the play *Les Philosophes* was thought up. You weren't spared
any more than anyone else.

I   So much the better. You may have paid me more of a compli-   58
ment than I deserve.

HE   After we've sacrificed the big animals we bury the others.

I   To live by insulting science and virtue is a high price to pay.

HE   You can benefit from bad company as you can from   59
debauchery. You are compensated for the loss of your innocence
by the loss of your prejudices. Among wicked people vice is on
display with its mask raised, you learn to recognize it. And then
I've read a bit.

I   What have you read?

HE   Theophrastus, La Bruyère, Molière.

I   Excellent books.

HE   Much better than people think. But who knows how to read   60
them?

I   Everyone, according to his ability.

HE   Almost no one. Could you tell me what people look for in
them?

I   Entertainment and instruction.

HE   But what kind of instruction? That's the thing.

I   The knowledge of one's duties, the love of virtue, the hatred
of vice.

HE   For my part, I pick up everything to do, and everything not
to say. So, when I read *L'Avare* I say to myself: be miserly, if you
want, but take care not to talk like a miser. When I read *Tartuffe* I
say to myself: be a hypocrite, if you want, but don't speak like one.
Keep the vices that are of use to you, but avoid the behaviour that
would give you away. To be sure about that behaviour you must
know what it looks like. Now, these writers have made excellent
portraits of that. I am myself and I remain who I am; but I act and
speak as it is appropriate. I'm not one of those people who despise
moralists. They have a lot to teach, especially those who have
shown morality in action . . . Mind you, for every occasion when   61
you must avoid ridicule there are, fortunately, a hundred others
when you should surrender to it. There's no better role to play
among the rich, than the fool. For a long time the royal fool was an
official post; and there was no royal philosopher. I am that fool for
Bertin, and for lots of others, perhaps, at this moment, for you. Or
perhaps you are the fool for me. He who would be wise would not
have a fool; ergo, he who has a fool is not wise. And if he is not wise
he must be a fool. And maybe, were he the king, he would be the
fool's fool. Anyway, bear in mind that in a subject as variable as
behaviour there is no absolute, essential or universal true or false,
good or bad, wise or foolish, decent or ridiculous, honest or

corrupt – unless it must be what self-interest wants. If by chance
virtue had proved lucky for me, either I would have been virtuous,
or I would have simulated virtue like anyone else. I was required to
be ridiculous. So I made myself ridiculous . . . [His thoughts return
to his expulsion from the Bertin household, which came about
because Bertin took offence at an obscene witty insult he made to
one of the guests.]

I   But now, to replace the fool who's gone, they will find another   65
hundred.

HE   A hundred fools like me? Oh no, they're not so common.
Dull fools, perhaps. I am rare among my kind, very rare. Now that
I've gone what will they be up to? They'll be as bored as cabbages. I
am a bottomless pit of insolence, knockabout, amusement; I was a
complete one-man circus.

I   And in return you were warm, well dressed and fed.

HE   All right, that's the good side. But you forget the drawbacks. [He describes other tasks he has to perform, errands he has
to run, for Bertin and his mistress, Mademoiselle Hus.] Anyhow,   67
she's putting on rather a lot of weight at the moment. You should
hear the stories being told about that!

I   Not by you, though.

HE   Why not?   68

I   It's a bit improper, isn't it, to ridicule your benefactors?

HE   Is it my fault they keep bad company? Is it my fault that
when they do so they are deceived and cheated? If you decide to
live among creatures like us that's what you must expect. When
we're taken on aren't we known for what we are – greedy, corrupt
and dishonest? If they realize that, all is well. There is an unspoken
agreement: they will do us good and sooner or later we will return
their goodness by doing them harm. Isn't that the agreement that
exists between a man and his monkey, or a man and his parrot? If   69
you take someone up from the country to the zoo at Versailles and
he stupidly puts his arm through the bars of the tiger's cage and his
hand ends up in the tiger's mouth – whose fault is that? It's all part
of the unspoken agreement. Tough luck on him who forgets it or
who's never learnt it. From time immemorial providence meant us
to do justice to the Bertins of today; and it will be those like us   70
among our descendants whom she has destined to do justice to the
Bertins to come. But while we carry out her just measures against
stupidity, you – depicting us as we are – you carry out her just
measures against us. What would you think of us if with our

shameful ways we presumed to merit public approval? That we were crazy. Everyone has his just deserts in this world. There are two public prosecutors: the one at the door who punishes crimes against society, and the other is nature who sees all the faults that escape the law. Overdo it with women, you will get dropsy; overdo it with drink, you will get consumption. Open your door to rascals, you will be deceived, despised and jeered at. Anyhow, I don't make up any of these stories: I merely restrict myself to passing them on.   71

I   Let's talk of something else. Ever since I saw you today there's something I've been wanting to ask you.

HE   Why have you waited so long?

I   I was afraid of being indiscreet.

HE   After all I've told you about myself?

I   You are aware of what I think of you?

HE   Entirely. To you I am utterly worthless and despicable. I'm sometimes that to myself, but more often than not I'm pleased with my faults.   72

I   But listen: why do you display all your worthlessness?

HE   As you know so much, why should I hide the rest? And then, in telling you the rest I gain more than I lose.

I   How so?

HE   If there's one activity in which you should be sublime it is in evil. A petty criminal is someone we spit on, but a great criminal wins a kind of respect. His courage astounds us; his cruelty makes us shudder. We admire, above all, his integrity, the way he's all of a piece.

I   But that isn't something you have. You fluctuate in your behaviour. I can't make out if your wickedness is natural or acquired; or even if you've gone as far as you might.

HE   I agree. But haven't I been modest enough to recognize that others are superior? Haven't I spoken of Bouret with the deepest admiration? Bouret is the very tops by my reckoning.

I   But immediately after Bouret, it's you.

HE   No.

I   Is it Palissot, then?

HE   Yes, but not on his own.

I   Who could be worthy of sharing second place with him?

HE   The renegade of Avignon.

I   I've never heard of him.

HE   A remarkable man.   73

I   [Tell me about him.] I always like stories about great men.

HE   He lived in the house of an honest and upright Jew. The renegade won this man's pity, then his goodwill, and in time his complete trust. Then the Jew confided in him the fact that his conscience did not allow him to eat pork. You will see what a fertile mind could make of that admission. In the following months the renegade was even more solicitous; he showed such kindness that the Jew was convinced he had no better friend in all the tribes of Israel. You have to admire this man's coolness. No hurry. He let the pear ripen before he shook the branch. If he'd been too eager he'd have ruined his plan. This is often the case, the greatness of men like him comes from the natural balance of several opposed qualities.

I   Forget the reflections; get on with the story.

HE   It's not as easy as that. Some days I just have to reflect. It's   74
like an allergy. Where was I?

I   The Jew and the renegade had become close friends.

HE   So the pear was ripe. One evening the renegade comes back to the house trembling all over, his face as pale as death. 'What's up?' 'We are lost.' 'Lost? How?' 'Lost, I tell you, lost without hope.' 'Explain yourself.' 'Just a moment . . .' 'Here, take it easy,' said the Jew, instead of saying: 'You bastard, pretending to be terrified like that.'

I   Why should he have said that?

HE   Because it wasn't true and he'd gone too far. It's obvious. Now don't interrupt. 'We are lost, lost without hope.' Can't you hear the exaggeration in that repetition of 'lost'? 'Some traitor has informed on us to the Holy Inquisition, you as a Jew, me as a renegade.' The Jew panics: he sees the military at his door, the   75
flames of an *auto-da-fé* rising up before him. 'My friend, my dear friend, my only friend, what can we do?' 'What we must do is carry on as before, seem as confident as we can. The tribunal sits in secret but it takes time. We must use that delay to sell up. I will hire a boat, through a third party; we'll put your fortune in it, because that's what they're after, and then the two of us, you and I, will go and seek elsewhere a place where we can serve God and our conscience. The vital thing is to do nothing rash.' No sooner said than done. The boat is hired, stocked with crew and provisions; the Jew's fortune is put on board. Tomorrow at daybreak they sail. They can eat happily and sleep soundly. Tomorrow they escape their persecutors. In the middle of the night the renegade gets up,

steals the Jew's wallet, purse and jewels, runs to the boat and sets
sail. And you think that's all? Can't you guess? No; just as well
you're honest, you'd only make a petty criminal. That's all the
renegade was up to this point. A despicable rascal whom nobody
would want to emulate. The sublime thing about his wickedness
was that he himself was the informer, the traitor who denounced
his good friend to the Holy Inquisition. They seized him next
morning when he woke up, and made a lovely bonfire for him a few
days later. And that was how the renegade became the undisturbed
owner of the wealth of one of those people whose ancestors cruci-
fied Our Lord.

I   I don't know which appals me more: the villainy of your rene-   76
gade or the tone in which you describe it.

HE   That's what I said. The cruelty of the deed is beyond simple
contempt, and that is what explains my frankness. I wanted to show
you how I excelled in my art, to make you admit that I was at least
original in my depravity, so that you'll think of me as one of the
great scoundrels and cry out 'Vivat Mascarillus, Emperor of
scoundrels.' Come on, Mister Philosopher, all together now:
'Vivat Mascarillus, Emperor of scoundrels.' (Thereupon he began
to sing an extraordinary fugue. Sometimes the melody was serious,
full of majesty; sometimes it was light and playful. One moment he
sang the bass, next one of the upper parts, and he ended with a song
of triumph, composed by himself, which made it clear that he knew
much more about music than he did about morals. For my part, I
did not know whether to stay or go, to laugh or be outraged. I
stayed, with the intention of leading the conversation on to some
subject which would drive away the disgust I was feeling. I began to
find it hard to tolerate a man who spoke of such terrible crimes like
a connoisseur of fine art examining the beauties of a painting, or a
moralist celebrating the details of some heroic achievement. I felt
depressed.)

HE   What's up? You feeling ill?

I   A bit. It'll pass.

(After a moment's silence, during which he walked about, whistling   77
and singing, I said:) What are you doing then nowadays?

HE   Nothing.

I   That must be tiring.

HE   I've been listening to this music of Duni and the other
young composers. I was a bit daft before, but they've made me go
right off my head.

I   You rate this new style highly?

HE   I'll say. Such beautiful melodies, and the way they're performed. So truthful, so expressive.

I   If that's the case you must find the music of Lully and your   79
dear uncle a bit dull.

HE   (Speaking softly into my ear he replied:) I don't want to be
overheard, because there are people here who know me, but it is
just as you say . . . Now that we've got used to melody and singing   81
that is so close to the accents of passion or the phenomena of nature
how can we care for all those triumphs and victories? And once
they've experienced the grace and flexibility which the Italian
language brings to music, how can they not be aware of how stiff
and heavy and monotonous their music sounds. How can they not
be bored by their insipid mythology? But the time will come.
Truth, beauty and goodness have their rights. We may dispute
them but we end up admiring them. In the end people give in. So
give in, gentlemen, at your leisure! The gates of hell will never
prevail   against   the   rule   of   nature   and   my   trinity   –   82
truth the Father, who begets goodness the Son, from whom pro-
ceedeth beauty the Holy Ghost.

[He then started to sing passages from French and Italian composers, mixing comic and tragic and all different kinds.]

(He is calm, he is grief-stricken, he complains, he laughs; never   83
out of style or mood or the rhythm or the meaning of the piece. All
the chess players left their boards to watch and passers-by blocked
the window outside. Shouts of laughter shook the ceiling. He saw
nothing. He continued, carried away by an alienation of mind, an
enthusiasm so close to madness that it seemed possible that he
might never come back to his senses. We might have to put him in a
carriage and take him straight to the madhouse. When he sang a
fragment of Jomelli's *Lamentations* he performed the loveliest bits
so exactly, so truly, and with such incredible warmth of feeling that
he wept copiously and made everyone else weep. Everything was   84
there – the delicacy of the tune, the force of the expression, the
grief. Did I admire him? Yes. I did. Did I feel pity? Yes, I did. But a
hint of ridicule was mixed with these feelings and spoilt them.
[Then he imitated the different instruments, and finally] the whole
opera-house, dancers, singers, musicians, playing twenty different
parts, charging about like a man possessed, a wild look in his eye.
What did I not see him do? He wept, he laughed, he sighed; he
appeared in love, or calm or angry; he was a woman overcome with

grief, an unhappy man expressing his despair, a temple rising, birds falling silent at nightfall, the murmur of water in a cool stream, the thunder of water falling off a mountainside, a storm, a gale, the cries of the dying mixed up with the howl of the wind, the roar of the thunder, night with its darkness, shadows, silence. For even silence can be depicted in sound. He had lost his head.   85

Then, overcome with exhaustion, he stopped. He looked stupid, surprised, like someone emerging from a deep sleep or a long daydream. He looked around him like a person who is lost and is trying to recognize the place where he finds himself. He waited for his strength and his wits to return. Mechanically, he wiped his face . . .)

[Even that is not the end. He admits there are some good bits in Lully, and sings at the top of his voice a passage from his uncle's *Castor and Pollux*. This leads him once more to the merits of the new music.]

HE   The emotions must be passionate. The feelings of the   87
musician or poet must be extreme. The aria is almost always the climax of the scene. We should have exclamations, interjections, interruptions, affirmations. Our pleas, cries, groans, tears, prayers and laughter should be openly expressed. And don't suppose the way our actors perform can provide an example. Perish the thought. We need something much truer, less affected, more energetic. The more monotonous and less accented a language is the more we need simple speeches, feelings as they are commonly expressed. The voice of nature or of man in a passion will provide that.

[The crowd, uninterested in this discussion, disperses. Diderot orders some beer and lemonade and the Nephew refreshes himself.]

I   Tell me: how is it that you have such acute sensitivity for the   89
beauties of music and yet are so blind to moral beauty, to the attractions of virtue?

HE   Some people, it seems, have a sense which I lack, a nerve I wasn't given. Or perhaps it's because I've lived with good musicians and bad company; my ear is keen but my heart is deaf. And then   90
there's the question of heredity. I and my father and my uncle, we have the same blood. The paternal molecule was tough and hard, and this wretched initial molecule has moulded all the rest.

I   Do you love your son?

HE   I'll say I do. I'm mad about him, the little savage.

I   Aren't you anxious to prevent his being affected by this paternal molecule?

HE   If I was it would be wasted effort. If he's destined to be good I wouldn't do him any harm. But if the molecule wanted him to be a layabout like his dad then any attempts to make him honest would be very damaging. He'd be pulled in opposite directions and would go skew-whiff down the road of life. He'd be just average, what could be worse than that? A great rogue is a great rogue, he is not run of the mill. For the moment I'm doing nothing; just watching him develop. He's already a greedy, lazy, lying cheat, so he may not have escaped the influence.

I   And will you make him a musician, to complete the picture?

HE   A musician?! I look at him sometimes and say: 'If you ever learn a note of music I'll wring your neck.'   91

I   Why?

HE   It doesn't lead anywhere.

I   Of course it does.

HE   Yes, when you're brilliant. But who can know if his child will be brilliant? Ten thousand to one he'll just be a hack like me.

I   [So what will you teach him?]

HE   About money. Money is everything, the rest without money is nothing. Whenever I've got a coin I show it to him with pride. I kiss it, I speak of it in a trembling voice. I point out a fine coat or hat or a sweet which I can get with it. Then I put it back in my pocket and strut about with confidence and make him realize that that confidence comes from the coin. I want my son to be happy or, what comes to the same thing, rich and powerful. I have some knowledge of the easiest ways to achieve that, and I'll soon teach him those. If you and your wise lot criticize me, most other people, and my success, will acquit me. He will have money, that I can assure you; and if he has plenty then he won't lack a thing, not even your respect and admiration.   92   93

(In what he said there was a great deal about how to behave which people think to themselves but do not admit. In fact this is the most striking thing about this man. The faults which others have he admitted; he was not a hypocrite. He was no more or less reprehensible than them, merely more open and consistent. Sometimes, in his depravity, he was profound.)

I   There are people, you know, odd people like myself, who do not consider wealth the most valuable thing in the world.   95

HE   You aren't born with that temperament; it's not natural.

I   Not to man?

HE   No. Everything that lives, including man, seeks its well-being at the expense of whoever's got hold of it. If I let the little savage grow up without saying anything to him I am sure that he will want to be smartly dressed, sumptuously fed, and surrounded by all the good things life offers.

I   If the little savage was left to himself, and combined the small brain of a child in the cradle with the violent passions of a man of thirty, he would strangle his father and sleep with his mother.

HE   Which only goes to show the importance of a good education! And what is a good education if not one which leads to every kind of pleasure, without danger or difficulty?   96

I   Let's not go into that. What I think about that is not something I will be able to teach you, and you have more to tell me about things I don't know – about music. Dear Rameau, let us talk about music. How is it that with all your aptitude and ability, and your enthusiasm for the great composers, you've never achieved anything worth while?

HE   The stars! The stars! When nature made Pergolesi or Duni, she smiled. When she made me . . . Bah!

I   But even so, haven't you ever tried to write some good music?   97

HE   (He began to walk about, his head down, looking thoughtful and depressed. Then he raised his eyes and knocked hard on his head with his fist.) I think there's something there. Yes, I can feel it, I can feel it. (He imitated a man getting annoyed, becoming   98 tender, then commanding.) I think it's there. It's on its way. I take up my pen, prepare to write. I bite my nails, rub my brow. No, Sir. Good night. The god is absent. I was convinced I had genius but all I see on the page is that I'm an idiot. An idiot. And then, how can I feel or think or realize my potential when I'm among the people I depend on, all that gossip and trivia. Does that inspire great things? I tell you: poverty is a terrible thing. I don't know   100 if it restricts the mind of a philosopher, it bloody well freezes the brain of a poet. [He recalls a time when he was better off, working for a Jew in Holland.] But nothing lasts in this world.   103 Wretched bleeding circumstances see to that.

I   Whatever a man ends up doing, that's what nature intended.

HE   She makes some strange mistakes. What godforsaken system is it that has some wallowing in plenty and others, who've got a stomach that is no less demanding, have nothing? They have to walk about all cramped up. Hungry men don't walk like others;   104 they go in fits and starts, grovelling, then jumping up, spending their life adopting positions.

I   What do you mean, positions?

HE   Ask Noverre, everyone has positions he performs, a panto- 105
mime he enacts. [He demonstrated the many positions people
adopt.] This is mine, the same as that performed by courtiers,
toadies, servants and beggars.

(The madness of this man, like the stories of the Abbé Galiani
and the extravagances of Rabelais, have sometimes made me think
deeply. They are three shops which have provided ridiculous masks
which I can put on the most serious people, seeing a prior as a
Pantaloon, a judge as a satyr, a minister as an ostrich, his clerk as a
goose.)

I   But according to you there are so many beggars in the world
that there can't be anyone who doesn't know some of these dance-
steps.

HE   You're right. In the whole kingdom the only person who
walks upright is the king.

I   No, even he is no exception. Don't you think that now and
then he comes across a little foot or a pretty nose which makes him
enact the pantomime? Anyone who needs someone else will adopt
a position. The king does so in front of his mistress, and in front of
God. The minister does so in front of the king. The ambitious man
does so in front of the minister. In fact this beggar's pantomime is
the way the world turns. Everyone has his Bertin and his
Mademoiselle Hus.

HE   That consoles me.

I   There is one person, though, who is exempt. That is the 106
philosopher who has nothing and asks for nothing.

HE   And where does that species hang out? If he has nothing
he'll be suffering. If he's asking for nothing he won't get anything
and he'll never stop suffering.

I   That's not so. Diogenes laughed at his needs.

HE   He still needed clothes.

I   No, he went stark naked.

HE   It must have turned cold sometimes in Athens.

I   Less so than here.

HE   What did he eat?

I   Whatever nature provided.

HE   Not very exciting.

I   Plenty of it.

HE   But very poorly served. [What about women?]   107

I   Lais gave herself to him free, for pleasure.

HE   What if she was busy elsewhere, or he was in a hurry?

I   He went back to his barrel and took the matter into his own hands.

HE   And you're advising me to copy him?

I   Surely you'll agree that that's better than having to cringe and crawl and prostitute your talent.

HE   But I need a soft bed, a tasty meal, warm clothes in winter, cool clothes in summer, leisure-time, money. And I prefer to get them through others' goodwill than work myself.

I   You're worthless; your soul is made of mud.

HE   Have I claimed otherwise?

I   Everything in life has its price. You seem to forget the price you pay, dancing your pantomime.

HE   True, but it hasn't cost me that much. And I'd do worse taking another course of action, which would only make me suffer   108 and I'd find hard to stick at. But from what you've said I realize now my wife was a sort of philosopher. She never complained when we were hard up. [He remembers his wife, how resourceful she was, and how desirable; he imitates the enticing way she walked.]

But alas, I have lost her, and all my hopes of fortune have gone   109 with her. I only took her for that, and told her my plans, and she had too much intelligence not to see that they'd succeed, and too much sense not to agree. (Then he sobbed and wept.) No, I will never be consoled. Since she went I've taken minor orders.

I   From grief?

HE   If you like. Really though it was to get a haircut. Hey, look at the time. I must be at the opera.

I   What's on?

HE   The Dauvergne. Some good things in his music. Pity he wasn't the first to use them. But then there's always someone among the dead to trouble the living. Adieu Mister Philosopher. Isn't it true I am always the same?

I   Unhappily I have to say that it is.

HE   Let's hope the unhappiness lasts another forty years. He who laughs last, laughs best.

10

D'Alembert's Dream

I

At the end of the *Pensées sur l'interprétation de la nature* Diderot posed the following problem:

> If you cast your eyes over the animals and the inert earth which they trample underfoot; over the organic molecules and the fluid in which they move; over the microscopic insects and the matter which produces them and surrounds them, it is evident that matter in general is divided into dead matter and living matter. But how does it happen that matter is not one, either all living or all dead? Is living matter always living? And is dead matter always and entirely dead? Does living matter not die? Does dead matter never begin to live?[1]

Diderot did not find a satisfactory answer to these and related questions for many years. There were answers on offer: the previous hundred years had seen much materialist writing, either explicit or implicit, by Descartes, Hobbes, Meslier, and in such anonymous works as the *Theophrastus Redivivus, Jordanus Brunus Redivivus*, the *Dissertation sur la formation du monde*, or the *Lettre de Thrasybule à Leucippe*. There had been several translations of Lucretius as well. But these works were essentially speculative; they were not based on factual evidence. For this reason Trembley's discovery of the self-generating powers of the freshwater polyp and Needham's revival of the ancient idea of spontaneous generation – the idea that living organisms could develop from non-living matter – as the result of his experiments on grain, were both of great significance. A new theory of generation was advanced by Maupertius, called epigenesis, which explained the emergence of life as a process of development through a series of steps in which successive accretions occurred. The organism was not made initially in the form in which we see it, as a previous theory – that of preformation – suggested; it develops into that form. These ideas of a self-generating, changing and developing nature, put forward by La Mettrie and Buffon as well as Maupertius, were taken up by Diderot in his *Lettre sur les aveugles* and the *Pensées sur l'interprétation de la nature*. But much was still unexplained.

The answers, he was sure, could be found in natural history, biology, physiology and chemistry. He attended the courses on chemistry given by Rouelle between 1754 and 1757. 'There is no science which offers the mind more penetrating conjectures or which fills it with more subtle analogies, than chemistry,' he wrote in his article 'Théosophes'.[2] It is clear from the obituary notice he later wrote that Rouelle made a strong impression on him;[3] but he did not provide him with the answers, as his *Réflexions* on Helvétius *De l'esprit* in 1758[4] and some remarks in a letter to Sophie Volland in 1759[5] indicate. Or rather, Rouelle and others may have helped prepare the mind but Diderot was not yet convinced.

The decisive evidence seems to have been that put forward by the Montpellier-trained doctors Bordeu, Ménuret de Chambaud and Fouquet, all of whom contributed to the *Encyclopédie*. 'There are no books I read more willingly than those by doctors, no men whose conversation I find more interesting than doctors.'[6] Bordeu, in his work on glands (1751) and the pulse (1754), maintained that every organ had its own *sensibilité* which arose out of its structure, and that a body was like a swarm of bees in which each part contributed to the life of the whole. Ménuret de Chambaud and Fouquet asserted that *sensibilité* was inherent in matter: the latter wrote the article 'Sensibilité' for Volume Fifteen of the *Encyclopédie* and the former the article 'Œconomie animale' in Volume Eleven. While in 1758 in his *Réflexions* on Helvétius Diderot had been non-committal about the idea of matter having *sensibilité*, in 1765 he wrote confidently: '*Sensibilité* is a universal property of matter, inert in raw (*bruts*) bodies . . . [then] made active in the same bodies by their assimilation with a living animal substance. It is something demonstrated all the time by the phenomenon of nutrition.'[7]

He now had an explanation for the emergence of life, but why should matter take one form rather than another, and how does thought arise from the physical body? Several important works appeared during the 1760s which dealt with these issues; Robinet's *De la nature* (1761–6), Bonnet's *Contemplation de la nature* (1764), and the *Elementa physiologiae corporis humanae* (1757–66) by the Swiss biologist, scholar and poet Albrecht von Haller. Diderot paid particular attention to the last of these, using it from the mid-1760s as both a source of information and a springboard for his own ideas, all of which he later collected in his own *Éléments de physiologie*. In the *Salon de 1767* we find the first suggestion of a solution to the unanswered questions. A discussion of dreams leads Diderot to the following remarks: 'The soft cheese that fills the space of your brain and mine . . . is the body of a spider whose feet and whose web are all the nervous threads. Each sense has its language. [The spider] has no particular idiom; he does not see, hear or even feel; but he is an excellent medium. I would make this system clearer and more plausible if I had time.'[8] In the summer of 1769 that time came. At the end of August that year he wrote to Sophie Volland:

I have written a dialogue between D'Alembert and myself. In it we converse quite good-humouredly and even quite clearly, in spite of the dryness and obscurity of the subject-matter. A second dialogue follows, much more extended, which provides clarification of the first; it is called *Le Rêve de d'Alembert*. The speakers are D'Alembert dreaming, Mademoiselle de l'Espinasse, the friend of D'Alembert, and Doctor Bordeu. If I had been willing to sacrifice the richness of the material for the sake of a noble style I would have had Democritus, Hippocrates and Leucippe* as my characters. But [the demands of] plausibility would then have confined me to classical philosophy and I would have lost too much by that. This dialogue is at one and the same time the wildest extravagance and the profoundest philosophy. It was a clever idea to put my ideas into the mouth of a man who is dreaming. Wisdom must often be given the appearance of madness in order to gain admittance. I prefer it that people say: 'But that is not as crazy as you might think', rather than say: 'Listen to me, here are some very wise things.'[10]

---

* This character, according to Diderot, was the 'mistress of Democritus'.[9]

Two weeks later he wrote that he had written in addition 'five or six pages which could make my sweetheart's hair stand on end; but she will never see them'.[11] This was a reference to the short third dialogue. The three dialogues together, the Conversation, the Dream and the Sequel, are generally referred to as a single work under the title *Le Rêve de d'Alembert*.

The first section of the work is a straightforward discussion of how *sensibilité* could replace the idea of God, as an explanation of life, and how consciousness could also be explained physically. Diderot's concern is to deny any dualism, to provide a completely materialistic account of our existence. The conversation ends inconclusively and D'Alembert goes home. The next section takes place in D'Alembert's lodgings some hours later. On his return home D'Alembert had gone to sleep but in such an agitated restless way that his mistress Mlle de l'Espinasse had called a doctor. At this point the dialogue begins. The two of them go over what D'Alembert has been saying in his sleep, ideas provoked by the earlier conversation with Diderot; Bordeu elaborates on these ideas, D'Alembert dreams and speaks again, and then wakes up. After a short conversation between the three of them Bordeu has to leave to see another patient. He returns later that day and the final section is a brief discussion between him and Mlle de l'Espinasse.*

On this simple framework Diderot constructed a work of remarkable imaginative power and speculative brilliance. His extensive reading and prolonged thought about the issues involved are here distilled and concentrated; we can feel the pressure of ideas demanding to be heard and emerging now with authoritative conviction. The dialogue in the middle section is not, like a number of other dialogues by Diderot, occasioned by disagreement or irreconcilable points of view. It is homophonic, not contrapuntal; there are several voices but the sound is that of one voice. It moves fluently from ideas of physical continuity to those of evolution, eternal flux, decay and renewal, from ideas of individual identity to the relation of the brain to sensations, sleep and dreams, freedom and determinism, imagination and language.

* This final discussion, written in a frank relaxed style, deals briefly with masturbation, which Diderot regarded as better than abstinence, with cross-breeding, and what it might reveal, and with homosexuality, one of the causes of which was in his view physiological. As these issues are only incidental to the main body of the work no extracts from this section are given below.

In his remarks about language Bordeu says that abstract ideas do not exist: 'an abstraction is merely a sign emptied of its idea'. Ideas for Diderot need to retain a physical dimension. Nothing illustrates this better than *Le Rêve de d'Alembert*. The success of the work derives not merely from the cogency of the ideas, but from the fact that Diderot had found a way of expressing those ideas. Indeed, it is inconceivable that the ideas would be so forceful without the immediacy of the setting, the reality of the people who are the characters, and the physicality of the action. The subject-matter of the opening conversation is not merely developed speculatively, it is transformed emotionally. Ideas of potential, energy and renewal are realized; we feel a sense of energy; and D'Alembert, dreaming, ejaculates. Sexuality is a manifestation of nature's creative power.

When D'Alembert eventually gets up the conversation moves to discuss consciousness. The meaning of *sensibilité* in this section alters somewhat, referring less to an element in our physical make-up and more to an emotional disposition, a readiness to be moved and affected by external events. The two meanings are, of course, related; we should talk of different emphases rather than of different meanings. Because the *sensibilité* generally present in matter is not exclusively a physical property: 'there is no point in nature which does not suffer and enjoy'. Diderot's emphasis shifts almost imperceptibly, like the transitions in nature itself. This is very characteristic. For the matters he was discussing were reflections of his personal experience; he felt in himself a continuity between the physical, emotional and intellectual as he felt part of the dynamic pulse that exists in all nature. And some of the impact of *Le Rêve de d'Alembert* stems from this quality, scientific speculation as self-portrait.

The use of the dream is also of crucial importance. *Le Rêve* illustrates, in a similar way to Saunderson in the *Lettre sur les aveugles* but much more completely, the kind of intuitive conjecture which Diderot had described in his *Pensées sur l'interprétation de la nature*. We find the same terms employed – *analogie*,[12] *délire*,[13] *déraison*.[14] 'There is a great affinity,' he wrote in the *Éléments de physiologie*, 'between *le rêve, le délire*, and *la folie*.'[15] Not only does D'Alembert dream, but Bordeu has, according to Mlle de l'Espinasse, an 'inclination towards *la folie*'.[16] The freedom and boldness which these mental states permit make it possible to go beyond the present limits of empirical evidence. By analogy we can fill in the gaps in our current information. What is put forward may be 'only theoretical at the moment, yet I believe that the more progress is made in human knowledge, the more its truth will be confirmed'. A brave claim, but one which subsequent discoveries have done much to vindicate.

Le Rêve de d'Alembert

CONVERSATION BETWEEN
D'ALEMBERT AND DIDEROT

D'ALEMBERT   I agree that a being who exists somewhere and   257
yet corresponds to no point in space, a being who lacks extension, yet occupies space; who is present in his entirety in every part of that space, who is essentially different from matter and yet is one with matter; who follows its motion, and moves it, without himself being in motion; who acts on matter and yet is subject to all its vicissitudes; a being about whom I can form no idea; I agree that a being of so contradictory a nature is an hypothesis difficult to accept. But other problems arise if we reject it; for if this *sensibilité*, which you propose as substitute, is a general and essential quality   258
of matter, then stone must be sensitive.

DIDEROT   Why not?

D'ALEMBERT   It's hard to believe.

DIDEROT   Yes, for him who cuts, chisels and crushes it, and does not hear it cry out.

D'ALEMBERT   I'd like you to tell me what difference there is,   259
according to you, between a man and a statue, between marble and flesh.

DIDEROT   Not much. Flesh can be made from marble, and marble from flesh.

D'ALEMBERT   But one is not the other.

DIDEROT   In the same way that what you call animate force is not the same as inanimate force.

D'ALEMBERT   I don't follow you.

DIDEROT   I'll explain. The transference of a body from one place to another is not itself motion, it is the consequence of motion. Motion exists equally in the body displaced and in the body that remains stationary.

D'ALEMBERT   That's a new way of looking at things.   260

DIDEROT   True none the less. Take away the obstacle that

prevents the displacement of a stationary body, and it will be transferred. Suddenly rarefy the air that surrounds the trunk of this huge oak, and the water contained in it, suddenly expanding, will burst it into a hundred thousand fragments. I say the same of your own body.

D'ALEMBERT   That may be so. But what relation is there between motion and *sensibilité*? Do you, by any chance, distinguish between an active and an inactive *sensibilité*, as between animate and inanimate force? An animate force which is revealed by displacement, an inanimate force which manifests itself by pressure; an active *sensibilité* which would be characterized by a certain recognizable behaviour in the animal and perhaps in the plant, while your inactive *sensibilité* only makes itself known when it changes over to the active state?

DIDEROT   Precisely; just as you say.

D'ALEMBERT   So, then, the statue merely has inactive *sensibilité*; and man, animals, perhaps even plants, are endowed with active *sensibilité*.

DIDEROT   There is undoubtedly that difference between the marble block and living tissue; but you can well imagine that's not the only one.

D'ALEMBERT   Of course. Whatever likeness there may be in   261
outward form between a man and a statue, there is no similarity in their internal organization. The chisel of the cleverest sculptor cannot make even an epidermis. But there is a very simple way of transforming an inanimate force into an animate one – the experiment is repeated a hundred times a day before our eyes; whereas I don't quite see how a body can be made to pass from the state of inactive to that of active *sensibilité*.

DIDEROT   Because you don't want to see it. It is just as common a phenomenon.

D'ALEMBERT   And what is this common phenomenon, if you please?

DIDEROT   I'll tell you, since you want to be put to shame; it occurs every time you eat.

D'ALEMBERT   Every time I eat!

DIDEROT   Yes, for what do you do when you eat? You remove obstacles that prevented the food from possessing active *sensibilité*. You assimilate it, you turn it into flesh, you make it animal, you give it the faculty of sensation; and, what you do to this foodstuff, I   262
can do, when I please, to marble.

D'ALEMBERT   And how?

DIDEROT   How? I shall make it edible.

D'ALEMBERT   Make marble edible? That doesn't seem easy to me . . .

DIDEROT   [I will show you. I break down the statue.] When the   263
block of marble is reduced to impalpable powder, I mix it with
humus of leaf-mould; I knead them well together; I water the
mixture, I let it decompose for one year, two years, a century; time
doesn't matter to me. When the whole has turned into a more or
less homogeneous substance, into humus, do you know what I do?

D'ALEMBERT   I'm sure you don't eat humus.

DIDEROT   No; but there is a means of union, of assimilation,
between the humus and myself, a *latus* as the chemist would say.

D'ALEMBERT   And that is plant life?

DIDEROT   Quite right. I sow peas, beans, cabbages and other
vegetables; these plants feed on the soil and I feed on the plants.

D'ALEMBERT   Whether it's true or false, I like this passage from
marble into humus, from humus to the vegetable kingdom, from   264
the vegetable to the animal kingdom, to flesh.

DIDEROT   So, then, I make flesh, or soul as my daughter said,
an actively sensitive substance; and if I do not thus solve the
problem you set me, at any rate I get pretty near solving it; for you
will admit that a piece of marble is much further removed from a
being that can feel, than a being that can feel is from a being that
can think.

D'ALEMBERT   I agree. But nevertheless the feeling being is not
yet the thinking being.

DIDEROT   Before going one step further let me tell you the
history of one of the greatest geometricians in Europe. What was   265
this wonderful creature to begin with? Nothing.

D'ALEMBERT   What, nothing? Nothing comes from nothing.

DIDEROT   You take my words too literally. I mean to say that,
before his mother, the beautiful and wicked Madame de Tencin,
had reached the age of puberty, and before the adolescence of the
soldier La Touche, the molecules which were to form the first
rudiments of our geometrician were scattered throughout the frail
young bodies of these two, filtering through with the lymph,
circulating with the blood, till at last they reach the vessels whence
they were destined to unite, the germ cells of his father and mother.
The precious germ, then, is formed. Now according to the common
belief, it is brought through the Fallopian tubes to the womb, it is

attached to the womb by a long cord; it grows gradually and
develops into a foetus; now comes the moment for it to leave the
dark prison; it is born, abandoned on the steps of Saint-Jean-le-
Rond Church, whence it receives its name; now, taken from the
foundlings' home, it is put to the breast of good Madame Rousseau,
the glazier's wife; it is given suck, it grows in body and mind,
becomes a man of letters, an expert on mechanics, a geometrician.
How was all this done? Just through eating and other purely
mechanical operations. Here, in four words you have the general
formula: Eat, digest, distil *in vasi licito, et fiat homo secundum
artem.** And to expound before the Academy the process of the   266
formation of a man or an animal, one need employ only material
agents, the successive results of which would be an inert being, a
feeling being, a thinking being, a being solving the problem of the
procession of the equinoxes,† a sublime being, a marvellous being,
a being growing old, fading away, dying, dissolved and given back
to the soil . . .

D'ALEMBERT   But how can we account for the first generation   267
of animals?

DIDEROT   If you're worried by the question 'which came first,
the chicken or the egg', it's because you suppose that animals were
originally the same as they are now. What madness! We can no
more tell what they were originally than what they will become.   268
The tiny worm, wriggling in the mud, may be in process of developing into a large animal; the huge animal, that terrifies us by its size,
is perhaps on the way to becoming a worm, is perhaps a particular
and transient production of this planet.

D'ALEMBERT   What's that you are saying?

DIDEROT   I was saying to you . . . But it'll take us away from
our original discussion.

D'ALEMBERT   What does that matter? We can get back to it or
not, as we please.

DIDEROT   Will you allow me to skip ahead a few thousand
years in time?

D'ALEMBERT   Why not? Time is nothing for nature.

DIDEROT   Will you consent to my extinguishing our sun?

D'ALEMBERT   All the more willingly since it will not be the first
to have gone out.

---

* 'In the prescribed vessel, and man can be made according to instruction.'
† An astronomical problem which D'Alembert had solved.

DIDEROT   Once the sun has been extinguished what will be the result? Plants will perish, animals will perish, the earth will become desolate and silent. Light up that star once more, and you immediately restore the necessary cause whereby an infinite number of new species will be generated, among which I cannot swear whether, in the course of centuries, the plants and animals we know today will or will not be reproduced.

D'ALEMBERT   And why should the same scattered elements   269
coming together again not give the same results?

DIDEROT   Because everything is connected in nature, and if you imagine a new phenomenon or bring back a moment of the past, you are creating a new world.

D'ALEMBERT   Anyone who thinks deeply cannot deny that. But to come back to man, since the general order of things has given him existence; remember, you left me where the feeling being is about to become the thinking being.

DIDEROT   I remember.

D'ALEMBERT   Frankly, I'd be very grateful if you would get me over that transition; I'm eager to begin thinking.

DIDEROT   Even if I should not accomplish it, what effect would that have against a sequence of incontrovertible facts?

D'ALEMBERT   None, unless we stopped short there.

DIDEROT   And in order to go further, would it be permissible for us to invent an agent whose attributes would be self-contradictory, a meaningless and unintelligible word?

D'ALEMBERT   No.   270

DIDEROT   Can you tell me what constitutes the existence of a feeling being, in relation to itself?

D'ALEMBERT   The consciousness of having been itself from the first moment of reflection to the present.

DIDEROT   And on what is this consciousness based?

D'ALEMBERT   On the memory of its actions.

DIDEROT   And without this memory?

D'ALEMBERT   Without this memory it would have no identity, since, realizing its existence only at the instant of receiving an impression, it would have no life-story. Its life would be an inter-   271
rupted series of sensations with nothing to connect them.

DIDEROT   Very good. And what is this memory? Where does it come from?

D'ALEMBERT   From a certain organization, which develops, grows weaker, and is sometimes lost entirely.

DIDEROT   If, then, a being that can feel, and that possesses this organization that gives rise to memory, connects up the impressions it receives, forms through this connection a story which is that of its life, and so acquires consciousness of itself, it can then deny, affirm, conclude and think.

D'ALEMBERT   So it appears to me; there is only one more difficulty.

DIDEROT   You are wrong; there are many more.

D'ALEMBERT   But one chief one; that is, it seems to me that we can only think of one thing at a time, and that to form even a simple proposition, let alone those vast chains of reasoning that embrace in their course thousands of ideas, one would need to have at least two things present – the object, which seems to remain in the mind's eye, and the mind considering which quality it is to attribute or to deny [to that object].

DIDEROT   I think that is so; that has made me sometimes compare the fibres of our organs to sensitive vibrating strings which vibrate and resound long after they have been plucked. It is this vibration, this kind of necessary resonance, which holds the object present, while the mind considers whatever quality it chooses. But vibrating strings have yet another property, that of making other strings vibrate; and that is how the first idea recalls a second, the two of them a third, these three a fourth and so on, so that there is no limit to the ideas awakened and interconnected in the mind of the philosopher, as he meditates and listens to himself in silence and darkness. This instrument makes surprising leaps, and an idea once aroused may sometimes set vibrating an harmonic at an inconceivable distance. If this phenomenon may be observed between resonant strings that are lifeless and separate, why should it not occur between points that are alive and connected, between fibres that are continuous and sensitive?

272

D'ALEMBERT   Even if it's not true, that is at least very ingenious. But I am inclined to think that you are, without realizing it, slipping into a difficulty that you wished to avoid.

DIDEROT   What is that? '

D'ALEMBERT   You are opposed to making a distinction between the two substances.

DIDEROT   I don't deny it.

273

D'ALEMBERT   And if you look closer, you'll see that you are making of the philosopher's mind a being distinct from the instrument, a musician, as it were, who listens to the vibrating strings and decides about their harmony or dissonance.

DIDEROT   I may have laid myself open to this objection, but you might not have made it if you had considered the difference between the philosopher instrument and the harpsichord instrument. The philosopher is an instrument that has the faculty of sensation; he is, at the same time, both the musician and the instrument. As he can feel, he is immediately conscious of the sound he gives forth; as he is an animal, he retains the memory of it. This faculty of the organism, connecting up the sounds within him,   274
produces and preserves the melody there. Just suppose that your harpsichord has *sensibilité* and memory and tell me if it will not know and repeat of its own accord the airs that you have played on its keys. We are instruments endowed with *sensibilité* and memory; our senses are so many keys that are struck by surrounding nature, and that often strike themselves. This is all, in my opinion, that happens in a harpsichord which is organized like you or me. . .

D'ALEMBERT   And how is the convention of sounds established   278
between your two harpsichords?

DIDEROT   Since an animal is a sensitive instrument, resembling any other in all respects, having the same structure, being strung with the same chords, stimulated in the same way by joy, pain, hunger, thirst, colic, wonder, terror, it is impossible that at the Pole and at the Equator it should utter different sounds. And so you will find that interjections are about the same in all languages, living and dead. The origin of conventional sounds must be ascribed to need and to proximity. The instrument endowed with the faculty of   279
sensation, or the animal, has discovered by experience that when it uttered a certain sound a certain result followed outside it, feeling instruments like itself or other animals drew nearer, went away, asked or offered things, hurt or caressed it. All these consequences became connected in its memory and in that of others with the utterance of these sounds; and note that human intercourse consists only of sounds and actions . . .

D'ALEMBERT   There's a lot to be said on all that.

DIDEROT   True.

D'ALEMBERT   For instance, your system doesn't make it clear how we form syllogisms or draw inferences.

DIDEROT   We don't draw them; they are all drawn by nature. We only state the existence of connected phenomena, known to us by experience, the connection between which may be either necessary or contingent; necessary in the case of mathematics, physics, and other exact sciences; contingent in ethics, politics and other conjectural sciences.

D'ALEMBERT   Is the connection between phenomena less   280
necessary in one case than in another?

DIDEROT   No, but the cause undergoes too many particular vicissitudes, which escape our observation, for us to be able to count with certainty upon the result that will ensue. Our certainty that a violent-tempered man will grow angry at an insult is not the same as our certainty that one body striking a smaller body will set it in motion.

D'ALEMBERT   What about analogy?

DIDEROT   Analogy, in the most complex cases, is only a rule of three working itself out in the sensitive instrument. If a familiar natural phenomenon is followed by another familiar natural phenomenon, what will be the fourth phenomenon that will follow a third, either provided by nature or imagined in imitation of nature? If the lance of an ordinary warrior is ten feet long, how long will the lance of Ajax be? If I can throw a stone weighing four pounds, Diomedes must be able to shift a large block of rock. The strides of gods and the leaps of their horses will correspond to the imagined proportion between gods and men. You have here a fourth note in harmony with and proportional to three others; and the animal awaits its resonance, which always occurs within itself, though not always in nature. The poet doesn't mind about that, it doesn't affect his kind of truth. But it is otherwise with the philosopher; he   281
must proceed to examine nature, which often shows him a phenomenon quite different from what he had supposed, and then he perceives that he had been seduced by an analogy.

D'ALEMBERT   Farewell, my friend, good evening and good night to you.

DIDEROT   You're joking: but you will dream on your pillow about this conversation, and if it doesn't take on substance there, so much the worse for you; for you will be obliged to adopt far more absurd hypotheses.

D'ALEMBERT   You're wrong there; I shall go to bed a sceptic, and a sceptic I shall arise.

DIDEROT   Sceptic! Is there such a thing as a sceptic?

D'ALEMBERT   That's a good one! Are you going to tell me, now, that I'm no sceptic? Who should know about that better than I? . . .

[Diderot argues that the scales are never evenly balanced

between a *for* and an *against*.]

DIDEROT   Come, my friend, if you think over it well, you will   283
find that, in everything, our true feeling is not that about which we
have never vacillated, but that to which we have most constantly
returned.

D'ALEMBERT   I believe you're right.

DIDEROT   And so do I. Good night, my friend, and remember
that 'dust thou art, to dust thou shalt return'.

D'ALEMBERT   That is sad.

DIDEROT   And yet necessary. Grant man, I don't say immortality, but merely a double span of life, and you'll see what will
happen.   284

D'ALEMBERT   And what do you expect to happen? . . . But
what do I care? Let happen what may. I want to sleep, so good
night to you.

D'ALEMBERT'S DREAM

(Speakers: D'Alembert, Mademoiselle de l'Espinasse and Doctor
Bordeu)

BORDEU   Well! What's been happening now? Is he ill?   285

MLLE DE L'ESPINASSE   I'm afraid so; he had the most restless
night.

BORDEU   Is he awake?

MLLE DE L'ESPINASSE   Not yet.

BORDEU   (After going up to D'Alembert's bed and feeling his
pulse and his skin:) It'll be nothing.

MLLE DE L'ESPINASSE   You think so?

BORDEU   I'm sure of it. His pulse is good . . . somewhat weak
. . . his skin moist . . . his breathing easy.

MLLE DE L'ESPINASSE   Is there anything to be done for him?   286

BORDEU   Nothing.

MLLE DE L'ESPINASSE   So much the better, for he hates medi-
cines.

BORDEU   And so do I. What did he eat for supper?

MLLE DE L'ESPINASSE   He wouldn't take anything. I don't
know where he had been spending the evening, but he seemed
worried when he came back.

BORDEU   Just a slight touch of fever that won't have any ill
effects.

MLLE DE L'ESPINASSE   When he got home, he put on his

dressing-gown and nightcap and flung himself into his armchair, where he dozed.

BORDEU   Sleep is good anywhere, but he would have been better in bed.

MLLE DE L'ESPINASSE   He was angry with Antoine for telling him so; he had to be pestered for half an hour to get him to bed.

BORDEU   That happens to me every day, although I'm in good health.

MLLE DE L'ESPINASSE   When he was in bed, instead of resting   287 as usual, for he sleeps like a child, he began to toss and turn, to stretch out his arms, throw off his covers and talk aloud.

BORDEU   And what was he talking about? Geometry?

MLLE DE L'ESPINASSE   No; it sounded like delirium. To begin with, a lot of nonsense about vibrating strings and sensitive fibres. It seemed so crazy to me that I resolved not to leave him alone all night, and not knowing what else to do I drew up a little table to the foot of his bed, and began to write down all I could make out of his ramblings.

BORDEU   A good idea, and typical of you. Can I have a look at it?

MLLE DE L'ESPINASSE   Surely; but I'll stake my life you won't understand a thing.

BORDEU   Perhaps I may.

MLLE DE L'ESPINASSE   Are to ready, Doctor?

BORDEU   Yes.

MLLE DE L'ESPINASSE   Listen. 'A living point . . . No, I'm wrong. First nothing, then a living point . . . To this living point is   288 applied another, and yet another; and the result of these successive increments is a being that has unity, for I cannot doubt my own unity . . . ' As he said this, he felt himself all over. 'But how did this unity come to be?' Oh, my friend, I said to him, what does that matter to you? Go to sleep . . . He was silent for a moment, but began again as if speaking to someone: 'I tell you, philosopher, I can understand an aggregate or tissue of tiny sensitive beings, but not an animal! . . . a whole! a system, an individual, having con-sciousness of its unity! I can't accept that, no, I can't accept it . . . '   289 Doctor, can you make anything of it?

BORDEU   A great deal.

MLLE DE L'ESPINASSE   Well, you're lucky . . . 'Perhaps my difficulty comes from a mistaken idea.'

BORDEU   Are you speaking yourself?

MLLE DE L'ESPINASSE   No, that's the dreamer. I'll go on . . .
He added, addressing himself: 'Take care, friend D'Alembert, you
are assuming only contiguity where there exists continuity . . . yes,
he's clever enough to tell me that . . . And how is this continuity
formed? That won't offer any difficulty to him . . . As one drop of
mercury coalesces with another drop of mercury, so one living and
sensitive molecule coalesces with another living and sensitive molecule . . . First there were two drops, after the contact there is only
one . . . Before assimilation there were two molecules, afterwards
there was only one . . . *sensibilité* becomes a common property of
the common mass . . . And indeed why not? I may imagine the   290
animal fibre divided up into as many sections as I please, but that
fibre will be continuous, will be a whole, yes, a whole . . . Continuity arises from the contact of two perfectly homogeneous molecules; and this constitutes the most complete union, cohesion,
combination, identity that can be imagined . . . Yes, philosopher,
if these molecules are elementary and simple; but what if they are
aggregates, what if they are compound? . . . They will combine
none the less, and in consequence will have identity and continuity.
. . . And then there is continual action and reaction . . . It is certain
that contact between two living molecules is quite different from
contiguity between two inert masses . . . Let that pass; it might be
possible to start a quarrel with you on that point; but I don't care to
do so, I don't like carping . . . Let's go back to where we were. A
thread of purest gold, I remember, was one comparison he used; a
homogeneous network, between the molecules of which others
thrust themselves and form, it may be, another unified network, a
tissue of sensitive matter; contact involving assimilation; *sensibilité*,
active in one case, inert in another, which is communicated like
motion, not to mention that, as he very well put it, there must be a
difference between the contact of two sensitive molecules and the
contact of two that are not sensitive; and wherein can that difference lie? . . . a habitual action and reaction . . . and this action
and reaction having a particular character . . . Everything then,
concurs to produce a sort of unity which exists only in the animal
. . . Well! if that's not truth it's very like it . . . ' Doctor, you're
laughing; can you see any sense in this?

BORDEU   A great deal.

MLLE DE L'ESPINASSE   Then he's not mad?

BORDEU   By no means.   291

MLLE DE L'ESPINASSE   After this preamble he began to cry:

'Mademoiselle de l'Espinasse! Mademoiselle de l'Espinasse!' 'What do you want?' 'Have you sometimes seen a swarm of bees escaping from their hive? . . . The world, or the general mass of matter, is the great hive . . . Have you seen them go and form, at the end of the branch of a tree, a long cluster of little winged animals, all clinging to one another by their feet? . . . This cluster is a being, an individual, an animal of sorts . . . But such clusters should all be alike. Yes, if he accepted only a single homogeneous matter . . . Have you seen them?' 'Yes, I've seen them.' 'You've seen them?' 'Yes, my friend, I tell you, yes.' 'If one of these bees should take a fancy to pinch, in some way, the next bee it's attached to, what do you think will happen? Tell me.' 'I don't know.' 'Go on, tell me . . . You don't know then, but the philosopher knows well enough. If you ever see him – and you may or may not see him, for he promised you would – he will tell you that this bee will pinch the next; that, throughout the cluster, there will be aroused as many sensations as there are little animals; that the whole will be disturbed, will stir, will change its position and its shape; that a noise will arise, little cries, and that anyone who had never seen a similar cluster in formation would be inclined to take it for an animal with five or six hundred heads and a thousand or twelve hundred wings . . . ' Well, Doctor?

BORDEU   Well, do you know, that's a very fine dream, and you   292
were quite right to take it down.

MLLE DE L'ESPINASSE   Are you dreaming too?

BORDEU   So far from it, that I'd almost undertake to tell you how it goes on.

MLLE DE L'ESPINASSE   I defy you to.

BORDEU   You defy me?

MLLE DE L'ESPINASSE   Yes.

BORDEU   And if I get it right?

MLLE DE L'ESPINASSE   If you get it right I promise . . . I promise . . . to take you for the greatest madman on earth.

BORDEU   Look at your paper and listen to me. 'A man who   293
took this cluster to be an animal would be wrong.' But, Mademoiselle, I presume he went on addressing you. 'Would you like him to judge more sanely? Would you like to transform the cluster of bees into one single animal? Modify a little the feet by which they cling together; make them continuous instead of contiguous. Between this new condition of the cluster and the previous condition there is certainly a marked difference; and what can that

difference be, if not that now it is a whole, a single animal, whereas before it was a collection of animals? . . . All our organs . . . '

MLLE DE L'ESPINASSE   All our organs!

BORDEU   'To one who has practised medicine and made a few observations . . .'

MLLE DE L'ESPINASSE   Next?

BORDEU   Next? 'Are just separate animals held together by the law of continuity in a general sympathy, unity and identity.'

MLLE DE L'ESPINASSE   I'm dumbfounded! You've got it almost word for word. Now I can proclaim to all the world that there's no difference between a waking doctor and a dreaming philosopher.

BORDEU   That was already suspected. Is that the whole of it?   294

MLLE DE L'ESPINASSE   Oh no, not nearly. After your, or his, ravings, he said: 'Mademoiselle?' 'Yes, my friend?' 'Come here . . . nearer, nearer . . . I want you to do something.' 'What is it?' 'Take this cluster, here it is, you're sure it's there? Now, let's make an experiment.' 'What experiment?' 'Take your scissors: do they cut well?' 'Perfectly.' 'Go up gently, very gently, and separate these bees, but be careful not to divide them through the middle of the body; cut just where they're joined on to one another by the feet. Don't be afraid. You may hurt them a little, but you won't kill them . . . Very good, you're as skilful as a fairy . . . Do you see how they fly apart on every side? They fly one by one, in twos, in threes. What a lot of them there are! If you've understood me . . . you're sure you've understood me?' 'Quite sure.' 'Now suppose . . . suppose . . . ' Oh my word, Doctor, I understood so little of what I was writing, he was speaking so softly, this part of my paper is so much scribbled over, that I can't read it.

BORDEU   I'll fill in the gaps, if you like.

MLLE DE L'ESPINASSE   If you can.

BORDEU   Nothing easier. 'Suppose these bees to be so tiny, that their organisms always escaped the coarse blade of your scissors: you could go on dividing as much as you pleased, without killing one of them, and this whole, composed of imperceptible bees, would really be a polyp that you could destroy only by crushing. The difference between the cluster of continuous bees   295 and the cluster of contiguous bees is precisely that existing between ordinary animals like ourselves or the fishes on the one hand and worms, serpents and polypous animals; moreover the whole of this theory undergoes further modifications' . . . (Here Mlle de l'Espinasse gets up suddenly and pulls the bell-cord.) Gently,

gently Mademoiselle, you will wake him, and he needs rest.

MLLE DE L'ESPINASSE   I'm so bewildered I never thought of that. (To the servant who enters:) Which of you went to the doctor's?

SERVANT   I did, Mademoiselle.

MLLE DE L'ESPINASSE   How long ago?

SERVANT   I've not been back an hour.

MLLE DE L'ESPINASSE   Did you take anything there?

SERVANT   Nothing.

MLLE DE L'ESPINASSE   No paper?

SERVANT   None.   296

MLLE DE L'ESPINASSE   All right, you may go . . . I can't get over it! You see, Doctor, I suspected one of them of showing you my scribble.

BORDEU   I assure you that's not so.

MLLE DE L'ESPINASSE   Now that I've discovered your gift, you'll be a great help to me socially. His rambling didn't end there.

BORDEU   All the better.

MLLE DE L'ESPINASSE   You see nothing to worry about in that?

BORDEU   Nothing at all.

MLLE DE L'ESPINASSE   He went on . . . 'Well, then, philosopher, do you imagine polyps of every sort, even human polyps? . . . But nature shows us none.'

BORDEU   He did not know of the two girls who were joined together by their heads, shoulders, backs, buttocks and thighs, who lived joined together like that until the age of twenty-two, and died within a few minutes of each other. Then what did he say? . . .

MLLE DE L'ESPINASSE   The sort of things you hear only in a   297
madhouse. He said: 'It has happened or else it will happen. And who knows the state of things on other planets?'

BORDEU   Perhaps there's no need to go so far.

MLLE DE L'ESPINASSE   'On Jupiter or on Saturn, human polyps! Males splitting up into males, females into females, it's an amusing notion . . . ' Thereupon he burst into fits of laughter that were quite terrifying. 'Man splitting up into an infinite number of atom-sized men, that can be wrapped between sheets of paper like insects' eggs, that spin their cocoons, remain as chrysalides for a certain time, then break through their cocoons and escape like butterflies, a society of men formed and a whole province peopled out of the fragments of a single man, it's quite delightful to imagine . . . ' And then he burst out laughing again. 'If, somewhere or other, man splits up into an infinite number of human animalcules, there must be less to fear about death; the loss of a man is so easily repaired that it ought to cause very little grief.'

BORDEU   This extravagant hypothesis is almost the true story   298
of all the species of animals which exist now and which are to come. If man does not split up into an infinite number of men, at any rate he splits up into an infinite number of animalcules, whose metamorphoses and whose future and final organization cannot be foreseen. Who knows if this is not the nursery of a second generation of beings, separated from this generation by an inconceivable interval of centuries and successive developments?

MLLE DE L'ESPINASSE   What are you muttering away there, Doctor?

BORDEU   Nothing, nothing, I was just dreaming on my own account. Go on reading, Mademoiselle.

MLLE DE L'ESPINASSE   'Everything considered, however, I prefer our way of renewing the population,' he added . . . 'Philosopher, you who know what happens here, there and everywhere, tell me, doesn't the dissolution of different parts produce men of different characters? The brain, the heart, the chest, the feet, the hands, the testicles . . . Oh! how this simplifies morality! . . . A man born, a woman brought forth' . . . Doctor, you'll allow me to pass over this . . . 'A warm chamber, lined with little packets, on each packet a label: warriors, magistrates, philosophers, poets, packet of courtiers, packet of whores, packet of kings.'

BORDEU   This is very funny and very mad. This is a dream indeed, and a vision that calls up certain strange phenomena to my mind.

MLLE DE L'ESPINASSE   Then he began to mutter something or other about grains, strips of flesh put to soak in water, different and successive races of creatures that he beheld being born and passing   299
away. With his right hand he had imitated the tube of a microscope, and with his left, I think, the mouth of a vessel. He was looking into this vessel through the tube and saying: 'Voltaire can make fun of it as much as he likes, but the "Eel-man"* is right; I believe my eyes; I can see them; what a lot there are! how they come and go, how they wriggle!' The vessel in which he perceived so many short-lived generations, he compared to the Universe: he saw the history of the

---

* This was Voltaire's nickname for the English biologist John Needham, who believed he had seen the spontaneous generation of tiny eels in fermenting flour.

world in a drop of water. This idea seemed a tremendous one to him; it appeared to fit in perfectly with sound philosophy, which studies great bodies in little ones. He said: 'In Needham's drop of water, everything occurs and passes away in the twinkling of an eye. In the world, the same phenomenon lasts a little longer; but what is our duration compared with the eternity of time? Less than the drop I have taken up on the point of a needle compared with the limitless space that surrounds me. An unlimited succession of animalcules in the fermenting atom, the same unlimited succession of animalcules in this other atom that is called the Earth. Who knows what races of animals have preceded us? Who knows what races of animals will come after ours? Everything changes and everything passes away, only the whole endures. The world is for ever beginning and ending; each instant is its first and its last; it never has had, it never will have, any other beginning or end. In this vast ocean of matter, not one molecule is like another, no molecule is for one moment like itself. *Rerum novus nascitur ordo,** that is what is eternally inscribed upon it' . . . Then he added with a sigh: 'O the vanity of our thoughts! O the poverty of fame and of all our labours! O wretchedness! O the brief scope of our understanding! Nothing is solid save drinking, eating, living, loving and sleeping . . . Mademoiselle de l'Espinasse, where are you?' 'Here I am . . . ' Then his face flushed. I wanted to feel his pulse, but I did not know where he had hidden his hand. He appeared to undergo a convulsive movement. His mouth was half-open, his breathing hurried: he heaved a deep sigh, then a weaker and still deeper sigh; he turned his head over on his pillow and fell asleep. I looked at him attentively, and was much moved without knowing why; my heart was throbbing, and it wasn't from fear. After a few minutes, I saw a slight smile flit across his lips; he whispered: 'On a planet where men multiplied after the fashion of fishes, where the spawn of a man in contact with a woman's spawn . . . then I'd regret it less . . . Nothing should be lost that might be useful. Mademoiselle, if it could be collected, sealed in a flask and sent very early to Needham' . . . Doctor don't you call this madness?

    BORDEU   When he was near you, assuredly!

    MLLE DE L'ESPINASSE   Near me, away from me, it's all the same; you don't know what you're talking about. I had hoped that the rest of the night would be quiet.

300

301

---

* A new order of things comes into being.

BORDEU　Such is usually the result.

MLLE DE L'ESPINASSE　Not at all; about two in the morning he harked back to his drop of water, calling it a mi . . . cro . . .

BORDEU　A microcosm.

MLLE DE L'ESPINASSE　That was the word he used. He was admiring the wisdom of the ancient philosophers. He was saying, or making his philosopher say, I don't know which: 'If when Epicurus maintained that the earth contained the germs of every-thing, and that the animal species was a product of fermentation, he had proposed to show an illustration on a small scale of what happened on a large scale at the beginning of all time, what would have been the answer? . . . And you have such an illustration before your eyes, and it teaches you nothing . . . who knows whether fermentation and its products are exhausted? Who knows what point we have reached in the succession of these generations of animals? Who knows whether that deformed biped, a mere four feet high, who is still called a man in the region of the Pole and who would quickly lose the name by growing a little more deformed, does not represent a disappearing species? Who knows if this is not the case with all species of animals? . . . What was the elephant originally? Maybe the same huge animal that we know today, maybe an atom – both are equally possible; you need assume only motion and the varied properties of matter. The elephant, that huge organized mass, a sudden product of fermentation! Why not? There is less difference between that great quadruped and the womb it came from than between the tiny worm and the molecule of flour whence it sprang; but the worm is only a worm . . . that is, its smallness, by concealing its organization from you, takes away the element of wonder . . . Life, *sensibilité*, therein lies the miracle; and that miracle is one no longer . . . When once I have seen inert matter attain the state of feeling there is nothing left that can astonish me . . . You have two great phenomena, the transition from the state of inertia to the state of *sensibilité*, and spontaneous generation; let these suffice; draw correct conclusions from them, and in an order of things which allows no absolute degree of greatness or smallness, permanence or transience, avoid the fallacy of the ephemeral' . . . Doctor, what is this fallacy of the ephemeral?

BORDEU　That of a transient being who believes in the immor-tality of things.

MLLE DE L'ESPINASSE　Fontenelle's rose, saying that within the

302

303

304

memory of a rose no gardener had been known to die?

BORDEU   Precisely; that is graceful and profound . . .

[Mlle de l'Espinasse complains about the confusion of D'Alembert's and Bordeu's remarks; important matters can be decided more simply.]

BORDEU   May I ask you which are those problems which you   306
find so plain that examination of them appears to you superfluous?

MLLE DE L'ESPINASSE   The question of my unity, of my individual identity, for instance. Heavens, it seems to me there's no need of so much talk to tell me that I am myself, that I have always been myself and shall never be anybody else . . . Let me explain myself by means of a comparison, since comparisons make up   307
almost the whole argument for women and poets. Imagine a spider . . .

D'ALEMBERT   Who's there? . . . Is it you Mademoiselle de l'Espinasse?

MLLE DE L'ESPINASSE   Hush, hush . . . (Mlle de l'Espinasse   308
and the doctor are silent for some time, then Mlle de l'Espinasse says softly:) I think he's gone to sleep again.

BORDEU   No, I fancy I hear something.

MLLE DE L'ESPINASSE   You're right; is he beginning to dream again?

BORDEU   Let's listen.

D'ALEMBERT   Why am I what I am? Because it was inevitable I should be. Here, yes, but elsewhere? at the Pole, below the Equator, or Saturn? If a distance of a few thousand leagues can alter my species, what will be the effect of an interval of many thousand times the world's diameter? And if all is in perpetual flux, as the spectacle of the Universe everywhere shows me, what may not be produced here and elsewhere by the duration and vicissitudes of several million centuries? Who knows what the thinking and feeling creature may be on Saturn? . . . Perhaps the feeling and thinking creature on Saturn has more senses than I have? If that is so, ah, how wretched is the Saturnian! . . . The more senses, the more needs.

BORDEU   He is right: organs produce needs, and reciprocally, needs produce organs.

MLLE DE L'ESPINASSE   Doctor, are you raving too?   309

BORDEU   Why not? I have seen two stumps end up by becoming two arms.

MLLE DE L'ESPINASSE   That's a lie.

BORDEU   True; but, where the two arms were lacking, I have seen the shoulder-blades grow long, move together like pincers,   310
and become two stumps.

MLLE DE L'ESPINASSE   That's nonsense.

BORDEU   It's a fact. Assume a long succession of armless generations, assume continual efforts, and you will see the two ends of this pincer stretch out, stretch further and further, cross at the back, come round in front, perhaps develop fingers at their ends, and make arms and hands once more. The original conformation changes or is improved by necessity and by habitual functions. We walk so little, we work so little and we think so much, that I don't despair that man may end by being only a head.

MLLE DE L'ESPINASSE   A head! a head! that's not very much: I hope that excessive love-making won't . . . But you're suggesting some very ridiculous ideas to me . . .

BORDEU   Hush!

D'ALEMBERT   So I am what I am, because I had to be so. Change the whole, and you will necessarily change me; but the whole is constantly changing . . . man is merely a common product, the monster an uncommon product; both equally natural, equally   311
necessary, equally part of the universal and general order of things . . . And what is astonishing about that? . . . All creatures intermingle with each other, consequently all species . . . everything is in perpetual flux . . . Every animal is more or less man; every mineral is more or less plant; every plant more or less animal. There is nothing precise in nature . . .

And you talk of individuals, poor philosophers! Stop thinking of   312
individuals. Answer me. Is there in nature one atom that strictly resembles another atom? . . . No . . . Don't you agree that everything is connected in nature, and that it is impossible that there should be a missing link in the chain? Then what do you mean by your individuals? There aren't any, no, there aren't any . . . There is only one great individual, that is the whole. In that whole, as in a machine or some animal, you may give a certain name to a certain part, but if you call this part of the whole an individual you are making as great a mistake as if you called the wing of a bird, or a feather on that wing, an individual . . . And you talk of essences, poor philosophers! Leave your essences out of it. Consider the general mass, or if your imagination is too feeble to embrace that, consider your first origin and your latter end . . . What is a being? The sum of a certain number of tendencies . . . Can I be anything

other than a tendency? . . . No, I am moving towards some limit. And species? Species are only tendencies towards a common limit which is peculiar to them . . . And life? . . . Life, a sequence of actions and reactions . . . Living, I act and react as a mass . . . dead, I act and react in the form of molecules . . . Then I do not die? . . . No, without doubt, I don't die in that sense, neither I myself nor anything else . . . Birth, life, decay, are merely changes of form . . . And what does the form matter? Each form has the happiness and misfortune which pertain to it . . . From the elephant to the flea, from the flea to the living and sensitive molecule, the origin of all, there is no point in nature which does not suffer and enjoy.

MLLE DE L'ESPINASSE   He says nothing more.

BORDEU   No. That was a fine flight he made; that was very lofty philosophy: only theoretical at the moment, yet I believe that the more progress is made in human knowledge, the more its truth will be confirmed.

MLLE DE L'ESPINASSE   And where had we got to meanwhile?

BORDEU   Really, I don't remember; he suggested so many phenomena to my mind while I was listening to him!

MLLE DE L'ESPINASSE   Wait, wait . . . I'd got as far as my spider.

BORDEU   Yes, yes.

MLLE DE L'ESPINASSE   Come here, Doctor. Imagine a spider in the centre of its web. Shake one thread, and you will see the attentive creature run up. Well! How if the threads that the insect draws out of its intestines, and draws back in when it pleases, were a sensitive part of itself?

BORDEU   I understand you. You imagine inside yourself, somewhere, in some corner of your head, in that part for instance that is called the meninges, one or several points to which are referred back all the sensations aroused along the threads.

MLLE DE L'ESPINASSE   Exactly.

BORDEU   Your idea is perfectly correct; but don't you see that it comes to much the same thing as a certain cluster of bees?

MLLE DE L'ESPINASSE   Why, so it does; I've been speaking prose without knowing it.

BORDEU   And very good prose too, as you will see. Anyone who knows man only in the form he appears in at birth, has not the slightest idea what he is really like. His head, his feet, his hands, all his limbs, all his viscera, all his organs, his nose, his eyes, his ears, his heart, his lungs, his intestines, his muscles, his bones, his nerves, his membranes, are, properly speaking, only the gross developments of a network that forms itself, increases, extends, throws out a multitude of imperceptible threads.

MLLE DE L'ESPINASSE   That's my web; and the point whence all these threads originate is my spider.

BORDEU   Perfect.

MLLE DE L'ESPINASSE   Where are the threads? Where is the spider placed?

BORDEU   The threads are everywhere; there is no point on the surface of your body which their ends do not reach; and the spider has its seat in the part of your head that I have mentioned, the meninges, the slightest touch on which would make the whole organism fall into torpor.

MLLE DE L'ESPINASSE   But if an atom sets one of the threads of the web quivering, the spider is alarmed and disturbed, runs away or comes hurrying up. At the centre it learns all that is happening in any part of the huge chamber over which it has spun its web. Why can I not know what is happening [everywhere] in my chamber, the world, since I am a group of sensitive points, pressing on everything and subject to impressions from everything?

BORDEU   Because the impressions grow weaker in proportion to the distance whence they come . . .

[If there were a creature who was aware of everything, that creature would not be God since it would, like us, be material and subject to change. At this point D'Alembert wakes up.]

D'ALEMBERT   Mademoiselle, you are with someone; who is that talking to you?

MLLE DE L'ESPINASSE   It's the doctor.

D'ALEMBERT   Good morning, Doctor; what are you doing here so early?

BORDEU   You shall hear later: go to sleep now.

D'ALEMBERT   I certainly need to. I do not think I ever passed a more restless night than this one. Don't go away before I am up.

BORDEU   No. I'll wager, Mademoiselle, that you have assumed that you were at twelve years old a woman half your present size, at four years a woman half as small again, as a foetus a tiny woman, in your mother's ovaries a very tiny woman, and that you have always been a woman in the same shape as today, so that only your successive increases in size have made all the difference between yourself at your origin and yourself as you are today.

319

MLLE DE L'ESPINASSE   I admit it.

BORDEU   And yet nothing is further from the truth than this idea. At first you were nothing at all. You began as an imperceptible speck, formed from still smaller molecules scattered through the blood and lymph of your father and mother; that speck became a fine thread, then a bundle of threads. Up till then, not the slightest trace of your own agreeable form; your eyes, those beautiful eyes, were no more like eyes than the tip of an anemone's feeler is like an anemone. Each of the fibres in the bundle of threads was transformed solely by nutrition and according to its conformation, into a particular organ; exception being made of those organs in which the fibres of the bundle are metamorphosed, and to which they give birth. The bundle is a purely sensitive system; if it continued under that form, it would be susceptible to all those impressions that affect simple *sensibilité*, such as cold and heat, softness and harshness. These impressions, experienced successively, varied amongst themselves and each varying in intensity, might perhaps produce memory, self-consciousness, a very limited form of reason. But this pure and simple *sensibilité*, this sense of touch, is differentiated through the organs that arise from each separate fibre; one fibre, forming an ear, gives rise to a kind of touch that we call noise or sound; another forming the palate, gives rise to a second kind of touch that we call taste; a third, forming   the nose and its inner lining, gives rise to a third kind of touch that we call smell; a fourth, forming an eye, gives rise to a fourth kind of touch that we call colour.

MLLE DE L'ESPINASSE   But, if I've understood you right, those who deny the possibility of a sixth sense, [producing] a real hermaphrodite, are very stupid. Who has told them that nature could not form a bundle with a peculiar fibre which would give rise to an organ unknown to us?

BORDEU   Or with the two fibres that characterize the two sexes? You are right; it's a pleasure to talk with you; not only do you follow what is said to you, but you draw from it conclusions that astonish me by their soundness.

MLLE DE L'ESPINASSE   Doctor, you're saying that to encourage me.

BORDEU   No, on my word, I'm saying what I really think.

MLLE DE L'ESPINASSE   I can quite well see the purpose of some of the fibres in the bundle; but what becomes of the others?

BORDEU   And do you think any other woman but yourself

would have thought of that question?

MLLE DE L'ESPINASSE   Certainly.

BORDEU   You're not vain. The rest of the fibres go to form as many different kinds of touch as there are different organs and parts of the body.

MLLE DE L'ESPINASSE   And what are they called? I never heard   322 anyone speak of them.

BORDEU   They have no name.

MLLE DE L'ESPINASSE   Why not?

BORDEU   Because there is less difference between the sensations aroused by them, than there is between the sensations aroused by means of the other organs.

MLLE DE L'ESPINASSE   In all seriousness, do you believe that the foot, the hand, the thighs, the belly, the stomach, the chest, the lungs, the heart, have their own particular sensations?

BORDEU   I do believe so. If I dared, I would ask you if, among those sensations that are not named . . .

MLLE DE L'ESPINASSE   I understand you. No. That one is quite unique of its kind, the more's the pity. But what reason have you for assuming this multiplicity of sensations, more painful than pleasant, which you are pleased to bestow on us?

BORDEU   The reason? That we do distinguish them to a considerable extent. If this infinite variety of touch did not exist we should know that we experienced pleasure or pain but we should not know where they arose. We should need the aid of sight. It would no longer be a question of sensation, but of experiment and observation.

MLLE DE L'ESPINASSE   Then, if I should say my finger hurt, and I were asked why I declared it was my finger that hurt, I should be obliged to say, not that I felt it hurt, but that I felt pain and that I   323 saw my finger was injured.

BORDEU   That's it. Come and let me kiss you.

MLLE DE L'ESPINASSE   With pleasure.

D'ALEMBERT   Doctor, you are kissing Mademoiselle. A good thing to do . . .

[Bordeu expands on his suggestion of bodies being formed by the amalgam of different fibres. Proof for the idea could be found if abnormal creatures were dissected. One such abnormality had recently been examined, after his death, a young man called Jean-Baptiste Macé; his internal organs had all been the wrong way round.]

BORDEU   If Jean-Baptiste Macé had married and had children . . .   327

MLLE DE L'ESPINASSE   Well, Doctor, these children? . . .

BORDEU   Would be formed in the normal way; but some of their children's children, after a hundred years or so, since these irregularities make leaps, will revert to the extraordinary conformation of his ancestor.

MLLE DE L'ESPINASSE   And what causes these leaps?

BORDEU   Who knows? It takes two to make a child, as you know. It may be that one of the agents counteracts the other's defect, and that the faulty network only reappears when the descendant of the monstrous breed is dominant and controls the   328 formation of the network. The bundle of fibres constitutes the original primary difference between all species of animals. The varieties in the form of the bundle of each species constitute the monstrous varieties within that species.

(After a long silence, Mlle de l'Espinasse emerged from her reverie and awoke the doctor from his by the following question:)

MLLE DE L'ESPINASSE   I have just had a very mad idea.

BORDEU   What's that?

MLLE DE L'ESPINASSE   Man may be merely a monstrous form of woman, or woman a monstrous form of man.

BORDEU   You would have had that idea much sooner if you had known that a woman has all a man's organs, and that the only difference between them is that between a bag hanging down outside, and an inverted bag inside; that a female foetus looks deceptively like a male foetus; that the part that causes this confusion is gradually effaced in the female foetus, as the interior bag grows bigger; that it is never obliterated to the point of losing its original form, but keeps this form on a small scale; that it is liable to the same movements, that it, too, gives rise to the voluptuous impulse; that it has its glands, its foreskin, and that on the tip of it there can be seen a point which appears to be the opening of a urinary canal that is now closed; that there is in man, from the anus to the scrotum, a space called the perineum, and from the scrotum to the tip of the penis, a scar that looks like a sewn-up vulva; that women whose clitoris is over-developed grow beards, that eunuchs are beardless, while their thighs broaden, their hips curve, their knees grow rounded, and that, by losing the characteristic organiz-   329 ation of one sex, they seem to revert to the characteristic conformation of the other. Those Arabs who have become castrated through continual horseback-riding lose their beards, develop a high voice, dress like women, ride with the women in the wagons, squat to urinate, and assume female ways and customs . . . But we have wandered far from our subject. Let us get back to our bundle of animated and living filaments . . . When we examine our sensations in general, which are all merely a differentiated sense of touch, we must neglect the successive forms assumed by the network, and consider only the network itself.

MLLE DE L'ESPINASSE   Every filament of the sensitive network can be hurt or stimulated along its whole length. Pleasure or pain is here or there, in one spot or another along the prolonged legs of my spider, for I always come back to my spider; that spider is the common origin of all the legs and their prolongations, and refers the pain or the pleasure to such and such a place without feeling it.   330

BORDEU   It is the constant and unvarying communication of all impressions to this common origin which constitutes the unity of the animal.

MLLE DE L'ESPINASSE   It is the memory of all these successive impressions which makes up, for each animal, the story of its life and of its self.

BORDEU   And it is memory, and the process of comparison which inevitably results from all these impressions, which form thought and reasoning.

MLLE DE L'ESPINASSE   And where does this process of comparison take place?

BORDEU   At the origin of the network.

MLLE DE L'ESPINASSE   And this network?

BORDEU   Has, at its origin, no sense peculiarly its own; it does not see, hear, or suffer. It is produced and nourished; it emanates from a soft, insensitive, inert substance, that serves it as a pillow,   331 seated on which it listens, judges and decides.

MLLE DE L'ESPINASSE   It feels no pain?

BORDEU   No; the slightest pressure cuts short its power to judge and the whole animal falls into a deathlike condition. Remove the pressure, and the judge resumes its functions, and the animal lives again.

MLLE DE L'ESPINASSE   And how do you know this? Has a man ever been made to die and live again at will?

BORDEU   Yes . . . [He gives an account of a man operated on because of brain damage who during his operation lost all signs of life but afterwards revived completely.]

MLLE DE L'ESPINASSE   This judge of yours is a most extra-   332 ordinary creature.

BORDEU   He, too, makes mistakes at times; he is subject to errors due to habit; one feels pain in a limb which one no longer has. You can deceive him when you wish; cross two of your fingers over each other, touch a little ball, and the judge will declare that there are two.

MLLE DE L'ESPINASSE   That's because he is like all the judges in the world, and needs experience, without which he would mistake the feeling of ice for that of fire . . .

[Bordeu gives other examples of how our senses can deceive us.]

MLLE DE L'ESPINASSE   And what is the reason for these queer   335
sensations?

BORDEU   In their natural and quiet state, the fibres that make up the bundle have a certain degree of tension; a customary tone and energy that limits the extent – real or imagined – of one's body. I say real or imagined, for this tension, this tone, this energy being variable, our body has not always the same volume.

MLLE DE L'ESPINASSE   Then, physically as well as morally, we are liable to fancy ourselves greater than we are?

BORDEU   Cold makes us shrink, heat makes us expand, and an individual may go through life thinking himself smaller or bigger than he really is. [After examples of the evidence of abnormalities Bordeu says it is time for him to leave.]

D'ALEMBERT   Doctor, one word more and then I send you to   341
your patient. Through all the changes I have undergone in the course of my existence, perhaps not having now a single one of the molecules which formed me at birth, how have I maintained my identity for others and for myself?

BORDEU   You told us yourself in your dream.

D'ALEMBERT   Have I been dreaming?

MLLE DE L'ESPINASSE   All night long, and it sounded so like delirium that I sent for the doctor this morning.

D'ALEMBERT   And all because a certain spider's legs were moving of their own accord, kept the spider on the watch, and made the animal talk. And what did the animal say?

BORDEU   That it was through memory that he maintained his identity for others and for himself; and, let me add, through the slowness of the changes. If you had passed in the twinkling of an eye from youth to decay, you would have been thrown into the world as at the first moment of birth; you would not have been yourself in your own eyes, nor in those of others; while they would not have been themselves in your eyes. All connecting links would have been destroyed; all that makes up the history of your life for me, all that makes up the history of my life for you, thrown into confusion . . . D'Alembert grown old would not have the slightest recollection of D'Alembert young.

    MLLE DE L'ESPINASSE   In the cluster of bees, not one would have had time to take on the spirit of the whole.

    D'ALEMBERT   What's that you're saying?

    MLLE DE L'ESPINASSE   I am saying that the monastic spirit is preserved, because the monastery repeoples itself gradually, and when a new monk enters it he finds a hundred old ones, who induce him to think and feel as they do. When one bee goes, its place in the cluster is taken by another that rapidly adapts itself.

    D'ALEMBERT   Come, you are crazy with your talk of monks, bees, clusters and convents.

    BORDEU   Not as crazy as you might think. Although the animal has only one consciousness, it has an infinite number of wills; each organ has its own.

    D'ALEMBERT   What do you mean by that?

    BORDEU   I mean that the stomach desires food, while the palate will have none of it; that the difference between the whole animal on one hand and the stomach and palate on the other is that the animal knows what it wants, while the stomach and palate want without knowing it; and the palate and the stomach are related like man is to the brute. The bees lose individual consciousness and retain their appetites and wills. The fibre is a simple animal, man a complex animal; but we will keep this text for another time . . . [After another digression he continues:] Disturb the origin of the bundle and you change the whole animal; sometimes it seems to dominate the branches, and sometimes to be dominated by them.

    MLLE DE L'ESPINASSE   And the animal is either under a despot's rule or under anarchy.

    BORDEU   A despot's rule is an apt description. The origin of the bundle commands and all the rest obeys . . .

    MLLE DE L'ESPINASSE   Under anarchy, when all the fibres of the network rise up against their ruler, there is no longer any supreme authority.

    BORDEU   Exactly. In strong fits of passion, in delirium, at times of imminent peril, if the master brings all his subjects' strength to bear in one direction, the weakest animal may display an incredible strength.

342
343
346

MLLE DE L'ESPINASSE   In the vapours, that variety of anarchy to which we women are peculiarly liable.

BORDEU   There you have the picture of a weak administration, in which everyone claims the supreme authority himself. I know only one way of recovering; it is difficult, but infallible; it is for the origin of the sensitive network, that part that constitutes the individual's self, to have some powerful motive for regaining its authority.   347

MLLE DE L'ESPINASSE   And what happens then?

BORDEU   It happens that it does indeed regain it, or else that the animal perishes . . .

MLLE DE L'ESPINASSE   I see. One is strong, if, through education, habit or through one's organization, the origin of the bundle dominates the fibres; weak if, on the contrary, it is dominated by them.   348

BORDEU   There are many other conclusions to be drawn from this . . . I should know more if the organization of the origin of the network were as familiar to me as that of its fibres, if I had had the same opportunity of observing it. But, if I am weak about particular phenomena, I make up for it where general phenomena are concerned.   354

MLLE DE L'ESPINASSE   Such as . . . ?

BORDEU   Reason, judgement, imagination, madness, idiocy, ferocity, instinct.

MLLE DE L'ESPINASSE   I understand. All these qualities are only consequences of the relation, original or acquired by habit, between the origin of the bundle and its branches.

BORDEU   Exactly. Where the origin or trunk is too vigorous in relation to the branches, you have poets, artists, imaginative people, cowards, fanatics, madmen. Where it is too weak you get so-called brutes and savage beasts. Where the whole system is slack and soft, without energy, you get imbeciles; where the whole system is energetic, harmonious, well disciplined, you have sound thinkers, philosophers, sages.

MLLE DE L'ESPINASSE   And according to which branch is dominant, we have the different forms of instinct in animals and the different forms of genius in man; the dog has its scent, the fish its hearing, the eagle its sight; D'Alembert is a geometrician, Vaucanson a mechanical engineer, Grétry a musician, Voltaire a poet; the varied effects of some one fibre in the bundle being stronger in them than any other, and stronger than the corresponding fibre in other beings of the same species.   355

BORDEU   And there is also the force of habit; old men go on loving women, Voltaire goes on writing tragedies.

(Here the doctor began to muse and Mlle de l'Espinasse said to him:)

MLLE DE L'ESPINASSE   Doctor, you are day-dreaming.

BORDEU   True.

MLLE DE L'ESPINASSE   What about?

BORDEU   Voltaire.

MLLE DE L'ESPINASSE   Well?

BORDEU   I was wondering what makes a great man.   356

MLLE DE L'ESPINASSE   And what is it?

BORDEU   How *sensibilité* . . .

MLLE DE L'ESPINASSE [interrupting]   *Sensibilité*?

BORDEU   Or the extreme mobility of certain fibres of the network, is the dominant quality of second-rate people.

MLLE DE L'ESPINASSE   Oh! Doctor, what blasphemy!

BORDEU   I was expecting that. But what is a creature possessed of *sensibilité*? One abandoned to the mercy of his diaphragm; should an evocative phrase strike his ear, a strange phenomenon   357
meet his eye, all of a sudden an inward tumult is set up, all the fibres of the bundle are agitated, a shudder runs through his frame, he is seized with horror, his tears flow, sighs choke him, his voice breaks, and the origin of the bundle does not know what it is doing: farewell to self-control, reason, judgement, discrimination and resourcefulness.

MLLE DE L'ESPINASSE   I recognize myself.

BORDEU   The great man, if he has been unlucky enough to receive such a disposition from nature, will ceaselessly strive to weaken it, to dominate it, to gain the mastery over his movements and to let the origin of the bundle retain all the power. Then he will have self-control in the midst of the greatest dangers, he will judge coldly, but sanely. Nothing that might further his desires, help towards his object, will escape him; he will not be easily surprised; at forty-five he will be a great king, a great minister, a great politician, a great artist, above all a great actor, a great philosopher, a great poet, a great musician, a great doctor; he will rule over himself and all around him. He will have no fear of death, that fear which, in the Stoic's sublime phrase, the strong man grasps as a handle to lead the weak man where he wishes; he will have broken that handle and will, at the same time, be delivered from every tyranny in the world. Men of *sensibilité* and madmen are on the stage, he is in the stalls, he is the wise man.

MLLE DE L'ESPINASSE   God preserve me from the society of   358
such a wise man! . . .

[D'Alembert now gets up and asks Bordeu about sleep and
dreaming.]

D'ALEMBERT   What are the will and liberty of a dreaming man?   362

BORDEU   What are they? The same as those of a waking man;
the latest impulse of desire and aversion, the last result of all that
one has been from birth to the actual moment; and I defy the
subtlest mind to perceive the least difference between them.

D'ALEMBERT   Do you think so?

BORDEU   And it's you who ask me that! You, who, absorbed in
profound speculations, have passed two-thirds of your life dreaming with your eyes open and doing involuntary actions; yes, far
more involuntary than in your dream. In your dream, you com-
manded, you gave orders, you were obeyed; you were displeased
or satisfied, you found your will opposed, you encountered
obstacles, you grew angry, you loved, hated, blamed, you came
and went. During your meditations, hardly were your eyes open in
the morning than, possessed anew by the idea that had been
occupying you the night before, you would dress, sit at your table,
ponder, draw figures, make calculations, eat your dinner, resume   363
your calculations, sometimes getting up from the table to verify
them; you would speak to other people, give orders to your
servants, eat your supper, go to bed and sleep, without having
performed one voluntary action. You have been reduced to a single
point; you have acted, but you have not exerted your will. Does
one exert will by instinct? Will is always moved by some inward or
outward stimulus, by some present impression or recollection of
the past, or by some passion or project for the future. After this I
need only say one word about freedom, that is, that the most recent
action of each one of us is the necessary result of a single cause –
oneself; a highly complex cause, but a single one.

MLLE DE L'ESPINASSE   And necessary?

BORDEU   Undoubtedly. Try to imagine any other action resulting, assuming that the creature who acts is the same.

MLLE DE L'ESPINASSE   He is right. Since I act in a certain way,   364
the person who could act differently is no longer me; and to declare
that, at the moment I am doing or saying one thing, I might be
saying or doing another, is to declare that I am myself and someone
else. But, Doctor, what about vice and virtue? Virtue, so holy a

word in all language, so sacred an idea to all nations.

BORDEU   We must change it for that of doing good, and its contrary for that of doing harm. One is born well or ill by nature; one is irresistibly carried away by the general torrent that brings one man to glory and another to disgrace.

MLLE DE L'ESPINASSE   What of self-esteem, and shame and remorse?

BORDEU   Childish reactions founded on the ignorance and vanity of a person who attributes to himself praise and blame for a moment of time that necessarily had to be.   365

MLLE DE L'ESPINASSE   And rewards and punishments?

BORDEU   Ways of correcting that person whom we call wicked, but who can be modified, and of encouraging the one we call good.

MLLE DE L'ESPINASSE   Isn't there something dangerous about this doctrine?

BORDEU   Is is true or is it false?

MLLE DE L'ESPINASSE   I believe it to be true . . .

D'ALEMBERT   Very good; now all is reduced to a question of the faculty of sensation or feeling, memory, organic movements; that suits me very well. But what about imagination? And abstract ideas?   366

BORDEU   Imagination . . . Imagination is the recollection of forms and colours. The picture of a scene or an object inevitably tunes up the sensitive instrument in a certain fashion: either it tunes itself, or it is tuned up by some outside cause. Then it vibrates within, or resounds externally; it retraces in silence the impressions it has received, or makes them public in conventional sounds.   367

D'ALEMBERT   But its recital exaggerates, omits certain circumstances and adds others, distorts the fact or embellishes it, and the sensitive instruments around it receive impressions which assuredly correspond to those of the instrument which is sounding, but not to the original thing that took place.   368

BORDEU   True, the recital may be either historical or poetical.

D'ALEMBERT   But how does this poetry or falsehood find its way into the recital?

BORDEU   Because ideas awaken one another, and they awaken one another because they have always been connected. Since you took the liberty of comparing an animal to a harpsichord, you will surely allow me to compare the poet's recital to a song.

D'ALEMBERT   That is quite fair.

BORDEU   In any song there is a scale. This scale has its intervals; each of its notes has its harmonics, and these in turn have their own harmonics. That is how modulations are introduced into the melody, and how the song is enriched and extended. The fact is a given theme that each musician feels in his own way.

MLLE DE L'ESPINASSE   But why confuse the question with this figurative style? I should say that, since every one has his own eyes, every one sees and tells a thing differently. I should say that each idea awakens others and that, according to one's turn of mind and one's character, either one keeps to those ideas that strictly represent that fact, or one introduces ideas suggested by association; I should say that there is a choice to be made among these ideas; I should say that this one subject, treated thoroughly, would furnish a whole book.

D'ALEMBERT   You are right; but that won't prevent me from asking the doctor if he is convinced that a form that was not like anything else could not be engendered in the imagination and introduced into the recital.   369

BORDEU   I think that is the case. The wildest fantasy of this faculty is nothing more than the talent of those tricksters who, from the parts of several animals, compose a strange creature that was never seen in nature.

D'ALEMBERT   And abstract ideas?

BORDEU   They don't exist; there are only habitual omissions, ellipses, that make propositions more general and language swifter and more convenient. It is the linguistic signs that have given rise to the abstract sciences. A quality common to several actions gave rise to the words 'virtue' and 'vice'. A quality common to several beings engendered the terms ugliness and beauty. We first said one man, one horse, two animals; then we said one, two, three, and the whole science of numbers was born. There is no idea that corresponds to an abstract word. It was observed that all bodies have three dimensions, length, breadth and depth; each of these was studied, and hence arose all mathematical sciences. An abstraction is merely a sign emptied of its idea. The idea has been excluded by separating the sign from the physical object, and it is only when the sign is attached once more to the physical object that science becomes a science of ideas again; hence the need, so frequently felt both in conversation and in books, of having recourse to examples. When, after a long series of signs, you ask for an example, you are only requiring the speaker to give body, shape, reality, to attach an idea to the series of sounds made by his speech, by connecting those sounds with sensations that have been experienced.

D'ALEMBERT   Is this quite clear to you, Mademoiselle?   370

MLLE DE L'ESPINASSE   Not entirely, but the doctor will explain.

BORDEU   You are good enough to say so! No doubt there is some correction and much addition to be made to what I've said; but it is half-past eleven, and at twelve I have a consultation at the Marais.

D'ALEMBERT   Language swifter and more convenient! Doctor, does one ever understand? Is one ever understood?

BORDEU   Almost all conversations are like accounts already made up . . . where has my stick got to? . . . one has no idea present in one's mind . . . and my hat? . . . And for the simple reason that no man is exactly like another, we never understand precisely, we are never precisely understood; it is always a case of more or less, in everything; our speech always falls short of experience or goes beyond it. A great difference between men's judgements can be observed, an infinitely greater difference passes unobserved, and luckily can never be observed . . . Good-bye, good-bye.

MLLE DE L'ESPINASSE   One word more, I implore you!

BORDEU   Quickly then.

MLLE DE L'ESPINASSE   Do you remember those leaps of which you spoke to me?

BORDEU   Yes.

MLLE DE L'ESPINASSE   Do you think that fools and men of   371
intelligence might have those leaps in their lineage?

BORDEU   Why not?

MLLE DE L'ESPINASSE   All the better for our great-nephews; perhaps a second Henri IV will appear.

BORDEU   Perhaps he has already appeared.*

MLLE DE L'ESPINASSE   Doctor, you must come and dine with us.

BORDEU   I'll do what I can, I don't promise: expect me when you see me.

MLLE DE L'ESPINASSE   We will wait for you till two o'clock.

BORDEU   So be it.

---

* A reference to Louis XVI.

II

Diderot continued to take an interest in, and gather notes on, the issues dealt with in *Le Rêve de d'Alembert*. He organized these notes towards the end of his life under the title *Éléments de physiologie*. This work was divided into three parts – Beings (vegeto-animal, animal, man), Elements of the human body, and Phenomena of the brain (sensation, understanding, imagination, sleep, will, etc.). It contains many interesting reflections which sometimes confirm, sometimes qualify, and sometimes contradict the assertions made in *Le Rêve*. In that work he was uncertain whether *sensibilité* was 'a general property of matter, or a product of physical structure (*organisation*)';[17] and he was also uncertain at what point life could be said to exist – 'life belongs to the assembly (*agrégat*) [of elements], *sensibilité* to the [individual] element'.[18] On both these matters further thoughts were put forward.

The *Éléments* also shed further light on the vexed question of Diderot's theory of evolution: to what extent did he have a theory, to what extent were his ideas only random suggestions?* It is sometimes suggested that his debt to Lucretius was so great that he was closer to the first century BC than to the first coherent theory of evolution, put forward by Lamarck twenty-five years after his death.[23] There is no doubt that Diderot did regard Lucretius as a kindred spirit, but the fact that he shared ideas with him does not necessarily mean that he derived those ideas from him; nor do the references to Lucretius in *Le Rêve* establish any such derivation, any more than references we find elsewhere to Horace, another kindred spirit, indicate that Horace is the source of those ideas. In this respect *Le Rêve* and the *Éléments* together mark a definite advance from the *Lettre sur les aveugles*; Diderot has moved from semi-literary speculation to scientific speculation. He knows what a scientific theory requires and he looks for the evidence to support it.

The evidence is not yet sufficient. 'How many metamorphoses escape us',[24] 'How many phenomena [are still] very uncertain, whose first cause is unknown. Who knows how movement exists in

---

* Diderot made suggestions about four components of a theory of evolution (apart from his general suppositions that all nature is continuous and in a state of constant change) – the derivation of all animals from a single species,[19] the elimination of species that cannot coexist with their environment,[20] the adaptation of organs to needs,[21] and the inheritance of acquired characteristics.[22]

the body? Who knows how attraction is situated there? Who knows how the one is communicated, and the other acts?'[25] 'What do I see? Forms, and what else? I do not know the substance of the forms. We walk among shadows, we ourselves are shadows for others, and for ourselves.'[26] In the *Réfutation d'Helvétius* he wrote:

> Ideas of matter, physical structure, movement, heat, flesh, *sensibilité* and life are still very incomplete. It must be admitted: the physical constitution or the co-ordination of inert parts does in no way lead to *sensibilité* and the general *sensibilité* of the molecules of matter is only a supposition which derives all its force from the difficulties which it overcomes. That is not sufficient for good philosophy.[27]

Diderot makes no great claims for his speculations, and he made no attempt to publish them. But they were more than second-hand Lucretius. Nothing demonstrates this better than the *Éléments*, for there we see the interest he took in what facts were then available, the effort he made to assemble the necessary evidence, the attention he gave to the problems. He felt that he was on the right lines – 'Some day someone will demonstrate that *sensibilité* or touch is a sense which all beings have in common'[28] – and in many respects he was.

Éléments de physiologie

Creatures are called contradictory if their physical constitution does not fit in with the rest of the Universe. Blind nature produces them and exterminates them. Only those which can more or less coexist with the general order does she let survive.   5

What is a plant? What is an animal? A co-ordination of infinitely active molecules, an interconnection of small forces which everything [else] tends to separate; so it is not surprising that these beings pass away so quickly.   8

Sensibilité is a quality specific to the animal, which informs it of the relations between it and all that is around it. All parts of the animal do not seem to have this quality . . . [but] I do not believe any part of the animal is completely lacking in *sensibilité*.   21–2

Without *sensibilité* and the law of continuity in the animal structure . . . the animal cannot be one.

23

There are definitely two quite distinct lives, maybe three: the life of the whole animal, the life of each of its organs, the life of the molecule.

27

Instinct guides the animal better than the man. In the animal it is pure, in man it is led astray by his reason and intelligence.

33

Each order of beings has its individual mechanism, that of the stone is not that of iron, that of iron not that of wood, that of wood not that of flesh, that of flesh not that of the animal, that of the animal not that of man, that of man not that of his organs.

38

Why should the long series of animals not be the developments of a single animal?

41

The animal is a being whose form is determined by internal and external causes, which [as they are] diverse must produce different animals. The physical constitution of each one determines its functions and its needs, and sometimes needs have an influence on the constitution . . . The influence of needs on the constitution can go so far as to produce organs, or at least to transform them.

42–3

The intermediary between man and the other animals is the monkey.

48

Reason or the instinct of man is determined by his physical constitution and by the tastes, inclinations, aptitudes, which the mother communicates to the child during the nine months that she and it were one. [Man's] perfectibility arises from the feebleness of the other senses, none of which predominates over the organ of reason.

50

The animal is a complete unity, and it is perhaps this unity which with the help of memory constitutes the soul, the self, consciousness. All thoughts arise from one another; that seems to me evident. Intellectual operations are equally interconnected: perception arises from sensation, from perception comes reflection, meditation, judgement. There is no freedom in intellectual operations.

59–60

Pleasure and suffering were the first masters of the animal. It is they who perhaps taught all the parts their functions and made them habitual and hereditary. The animal seeks its well-being by its *sensibilité*.

102–3

The diaphragm is the seat of all our pleasures and all our pains . . .
It is the difference in the diaphragm which makes strong or cowardly souls . . . The head makes wise men, the diaphragm makes
compassionate and moral men. These are the two great springs of
the human machine.   138

I would be tempted to reduce the generation of man to that of the
polyp which reproduces itself by division.   189

The Universe seems sometimes to be nothing other than a collection of monstrous creatures. What is a monster? A creature whose
continuation is incompatible with the existing order. But the
general order changes all the time. The virtues and vices of the
preceding order have brought about the order which exists and the
virtues and vices of this order will bring about that which will
follow, without our being able to say that the whole is getting better
or worse. Better and worse are terms relative to individuals of a
species and to different species among one another.   209

In the animal generally and in each of its parts – life, *sensibilité*,
irritation. Nothing similar in inert matter.   216

If you see the thing as it is in nature you are a philosopher. If you
form an object by a selection of different parts which makes the
experience of them stronger in the imitation than it had been in
nature you are a poet.   236

Analogy is the comparison of things which have been and which are
in order to deduce (*conclure*) those which will be.   236

What we know least about are the intimate senses, ourselves,
subject, impression, representation, attention. The will, the freedom, the suffering which protects man, the pleasure which destroys
him, the desire which torments him, aversion, fear, cruelty, terror,
courage, boredom, what are all these things?   240

To explain the mechanism of memory you must look on the soft
substance of the brain as a mass of sensitive and living wax, susceptible to every kind of impression, not losing any it has taken,
and continually receiving new ones which it preserves. That is the
book. But where is the reader? The reader is the book itself. For
this book feels, lives, speaks.   243

The organ of memory seems to me to be always passive; it does not
recall anything by itself. It needs a cause to make it active.   246

The imagination reawakes in man the voices, sounds, images and natural events which become so many opportunities to lead him astray. The imaginative man walks about in his head like a busybody in a palace, every moment going off in a different direction at the sight of something of interest. He goes backwards and forwards and never leaves. The imagination is the image of childhood which is attracted by everything without distinction. It is the inner eye.   250

The will is no less mechanical than the understanding . . . The will is the effect of a cause which moves it and determines it; an act of will without a cause is a fantasy. Nothing is done by leaps in nature; everything is connected. This general law applies to the animal, to man, every creature.   262

Voluntary action, involuntary action. What we call voluntary is no more so than the [involuntary], the cause of it is merely further away from the brain. In the voluntary action the brain is active, in the involuntary action the brain is passive and the rest acts. That is all the difference.   263

There is only one passion, that of being happy. It takes different names according to the objects. It is vice or virtue according to its violence, means and effects.   266

Love is more difficult to explain than hunger; for the fruit does not experience the desire to be eaten.   277

Genius always supposes some disorder in the machine.   296

Nothing is more contrary to nature than habitual meditation or the condition of the scholar. Man is born to act. His health depends on movement.   300

On the whole surface of the earth there is not a single man who is perfectly constituted, perfectly healthy. The human race is only a collection of individuals who are more or less alike, more or less ill.   307

There is only one virtue, justice; only one duty, to make oneself happy; only one corollary, not to overrate one's life and not to fear death.   308

Every phenomenon depends on the current condition of the whole.   330

III

The essential principles of Diderot's materialism were shared by a number of writers whose work had appeared earlier in the century. What distinguished his contribution was the elaboration of detail, the attention to new evidence, and a certain number of suggestions based on this evidence. During the 1760s several of these earlier writings were published at the instigation of Diderot's friends Holbach and Naigeon. One of the reasons for making them public was the disagreement that had arisen between this group of *philosophes* and Voltaire. The latter was a deist, convinced that the world did display signs of a divine intelligence and that life without the existence of a God would be insupportable. When he learnt in 1765 that materialist beliefs were, if not widespread, at least strongly held by an influential body of *philosophes* in Paris he took up his pen against them. From *Le Philosophe ignorant* (1766) onwards he argued energetically against their ideas. Holbach and Naigeon replied with various publications, culminating in 1770 with the former's *Système de la nature*, a thoroughgoing materialist treatise that caused an uproar.

Diderot was a close friend of Holbach and certainly discussed with him the problems which arose from the ideas they shared; he may even have contributed to the *Système de la nature*.[29] It is also possible that the knowledge that this work was soon to appear, and likewise Helvétius' *De l'homme*, encouraged him to articulate his own ideas in *Le Rêve de d'Alembert*. Be that as it may, he was certainly involved in this general movement of ideas, and in 1770 he made a specific contribution to it, the *Principes philosophiques de la matière et le mouvement*.

This is a short work which argues that movement is essential to matter, that matter is heterogeneous, and that 'in this universe everything is in a state of transition or *in nisu*, or in a state of transition and *in nisu* at one and the same time'.[30] By *nisus* he meant potential energy.

> The molecule, [he wrote], endowed with a quality that is specific to its nature, is by itself an active force.[31] . . . Absolute rest is an abstract concept which does not exist in nature[32] [and] the supposition that there is any being placed outside the material universe is impossible[33] . . . There exists an infinite number of

diverse elements in nature; each of these elements, by its diversity, has its innate, indestructible, eternal, unchanging, individual force; and these forces within the bodies act on what is outside them; from this arises the movement or rather the general fermentation of the universe.[34]

This essay, which draws on one of the works published two years earlier by Holbach and Naigeon, a translation of John Toland's *Letters to Serena*, adds nothing to what Diderot had written elsewhere. But it serves to remind us that his concerns, even when they remained private and unpublished, were part of a wider context, and that context laid the foundations of modern materialism.

11

Aesthetics

I

In February 1761 a short work by Diderot was published anonymously, the *Lettre sur les sourds et muets*. The letter was addressed to the Abbé Batteux, the author of a well-known work on aesthetics, *Les Beaux-arts réduits à un même principe* (1746), and there seems to have been some personal issue between the two men, for the Abbé is treated by Diderot with more sarcasm and scorn than the intellectual differences between them justified. What that issue was we do not know; it is merely one obscure aspect about a work that is full of obscurities. The *Lettre* is one of the most wayward and confusing works Diderot wrote, constantly changing direction and veering between the brilliant and the banal. He himself was aware of its uneven character, for he wrote: 'I am more concerned to make clouds than disperse them, and to suspend judgement than to judge.'[1]

The starting-point of the work is straightforward; it deals with the problem of inversions, how languages come to adopt the word-order they use. This was one element of a major intellectual issue of the time, the origin of languages. Diderot makes the suggestion that one way of discovering what is a 'natural' word-order would be to see the order in which a deaf-mute communicated his ideas (hence the *sourds et muets* of the title). This leads him to consider gestures generally, how much can be expressed by non-verbal means, and the place of mime in the theatre. He then returns to the problem of inversions and takes up the question of how thought relates to language. It is here that the originality of the *Lettre* becomes apparent, for Diderot suggests that there is no exact correspondence between how we think and how we articulate our thought: 'who knows if the mind cannot contain a certain number [of ideas] at exactly the same moment?'[2] What we experience in our minds 'does not have the sequential development of speech'.[3]

> Our soul is a moving picture which we are continually painting; we take up a lot of time conveying it accurately but it exists completely and all at once; the brush only depicts bit by bit what the eye of the painter grasps immediately . . . Ah, Monsieur! How greatly our understanding is modified by the signs [of language], and the liveliest speech is only a cold copy of what happens in our mind.[4]

This idea leads Diderot to a new evaluation of metaphorical language and the nature of poetry:

> In all speech we must distinguish between the thought and the expression. If the thought is conveyed with clarity, purity and precision, that is quite adequate for normal conversation. If you add to these qualities a choice use of words, a sense of rhythm and harmony, you will have the style that is appropriate for oratory. But you will still be a long way from poetry, especially the poetry of the descriptive passages in an ode or an epic poem. In those instances there is a spirit in the poet's speech which moves and animates every syllable. What is this spirit? I have sometimes felt its presence. But all I know about it is that by means of it things are spoken and represented at one and the same time; in the same moment that the understanding grasps them, the soul is moved by them, the imagination sees them, and the ear hears them. And then the speech is no longer merely a sequence of energetic words which display the thought forcefully and nobly, but it is a tissue of hieroglyphs piled up one on top of the other which depicts [the very thought itself]. I could say that in this sense all poetry is emblematic. But it is not given to everyone to understand the poetic emblem. It is virtually necessary to be in a condition to create it in order to experience its full force.[5]

A consideration of these 'hieroglyphs' leads Diderot to two further reflections. The first is about translating poetry:

> I used to believe, like everyone else, that one poet could trans-

late another. That is a mistake, and I have rid myself of it. The
thought can be conveyed and you will perhaps have the happiness of finding the equivalent of some expression . . . That is
something, but it is not everything. The delicate emblem, the
subtle hieroglyph which runs through a whole description, and
which depends on the distribution of long and short syllables in
unaccented languages, and on the distribution of vowels and
consonants in all languages, all that will necessarily disappear in
the best translation.[6]

Diderot's other reflection, which occupies the last section of the
Lettre, is about the relationship between the various arts: 'Every
imitative art has its particular [kind of] hieroglyphs',[7] and Diderot
demonstrates what he means by comparing the different way
poetry, painting and music treat the same subject. In one of the
Additions attached to the second edition of the *Lettre* he developed
these ideas and asked, apropos of music: 'How is it that of the three
arts which imitate nature the one with the most arbitrary and least
precise expression speaks most strongly to the soul? Would it be
the case that in showing objects less, it leaves more scope for the
imagination?'[8]

These ideas, undeveloped though they were, reveal Diderot's
remarkably acute perception in aesthetic matters. Whenever he
tackled these matters systematically, as in the article 'Beau' in
Volume Two of the *Encyclopédie*, in his public writings on the
theatre, or the *Essais* or *Pensées détachées* on painting, he based his
discussion on the general assumptions then prevailing. But whenever he allowed his mind to roam freely, as here or in the *Salons*, he
displayed great originality. To take as his starting-point the
experience of the poet, rather than that of the completed work of
art, to suggest that poetry could be closer to the truth than philosophical exposition, to wonder whether art is more important for
the feelings it arouses than for the objects it depicts, these were all
ideas of the greatest significance.

In the *Lettre sur les sourds et muets* Diderot showed that he was
conscious of feelings which he found difficult to express personally
and which called into question the possibilities of expression
generally. This latter aspect, the limitations of language, remained
a constant preoccupation throughout his life. With the other
aspect, his own articulation of the problem, we can see a gradual
development from the suggestive but confused assertions of the

Lettre. In the *Pensées sur l'interprétation de la nature*, two years later, he dealt with the way the mind worked in the process of scientific discovery. He wrote of an 'instinct', a 'spirit of divination', a 'habit of folly', and 'kinds of dreams' which revealed 'analogies'. This ability 'to imagine or perceive oppositions or analogies' was, like the poet's use of 'hieroglyphs', a way of grasping the essence of something in an immediate non-rational manner. In later writings Diderot applied this faculty to see 'analogies' to both scientists and to painters. Rouelle, the chemist, possessed it;[9] Helvétius made no allowance for it;[10] in the *Rêve de d'Alembert* Diderot explained it.[11] It is analogy which 'secretly directs the artist in his choice of associations' he wrote in the *Salon de 1765*,[12] and by means of which an ideal model is built up in the artist's mind (see p. 175).

Evidently Diderot was talking about the imagination; at this stage, however, he was either not sure of that fact or he was reluctant to use that term. There were good reasons for this. In the first place there was a strong intellectual tradition, deriving in its modern form from Descartes, Pascal and Malebranche, of distrusting the imagination. Although D'Alembert in his *Discours préliminaire* had given the imagination a much more elevated status,[13] this tradition remained forceful and Diderot himself at times went along with it, saying that imagination 'adorns the lie and obscures the truth'.[14] In the second place there was the problem which faced all empirical theories of knowledge, of how exactly the imagination worked, of how the mind could produce new forms which were something different from combinations of material previously received. Whenever Diderot considered this problem from a scientific point of view, as in *Le Rêve de d'Alembert* or the chapter devoted to the imagination in the *Éléments de physiologie*,[15] he took a low view of the imaginative faculty. Whenever he considered it from an artistic point of view he took an elevated view.

This was first apparent in the *Discours sur la poésie dramatique*: 'The imagination, that is the quality without which one is neither a poet, a *philosophe*, a man of wit, a reasoning creature, or a man. "Then what is imagination?" you will ask me . . . The imagination is the faculty of recalling images.' An image, he explains, is not abstract or general but it is a 'palpable representation [which is at] the very limit where reason ceases'.[16] He then continues:

To recall a necessary sequence of images exactly as they occur in nature is to reason after the facts. To recall a sequence of images as they would necessarily occur in nature, given some or other phenomenon, is to reason after a hypothesis, or to pretend (*feindre*). It is to be a philosopher or a poet, according to the aim one has in mind. Both the poet who pretends, and the philosopher who reasons, are equally and in the same sense consistent or inconsistent; for to be consistent, and to have experience of the necessary interconnection of phenomena, is the same thing. And this is sufficient, it seems to me, to show the analogy of truth and fiction, to characterize the poet and the philosopher, and to point out the merit of the poet, especially the epic or dramatic poet. He has received from nature, to a greater extent, the quality which distinguishes the man of genius from the ordinary man, and the latter from the stupid man: imagination, without which discourse is reduced to the mechanical habit of applying combined sounds.[17]

The poet, he had written a few pages earlier, 'is, in his sphere what the all-powerful Being is in nature. It is he who creates.'[18]

Diderot was always reluctant to say that the imagination can create (though he did do so on at least one occasion)[19] but there was a kind of person who did create, and this was the genius. In the *Pensées sur l'interprétation de la nature* he had spoken of 'creative geniuses'[20] and the 'genius who creates'.[21] In Volume Seven of the *Encyclopédie*, published in 1757, there was an article devoted to 'Génie'. This article was by Saint-Lambert but it is generally agreed that Diderot had a hand in it, since apart from stylistic similarities it sets out ideas with which Diderot was explicitly concerned and which he restated elsewhere, but which have no such connections with the other works of Saint-Lambert.[22] The article marks an important point in the changing conception of genius, a change to which Diderot made a major contribution.

Before this time genius was regarded as a quality or an attribute, it was a talent a person was gifted with or possessed. With Diderot a genius became something a person was, a special kind of person. The article 'Génie' presented genius in these terms; he was someone with 'an extreme *sensibilité*',[23] who is carried away by enthusiasm, 'swept away by a torrent of ideas',[24] and 'imagines more than he has seen, produces more than he has discovered'.[25] In the *Réfutation d'Helvétius* Diderot called the genius 'a kind of monster'.[26] Helvétius believed that having genius was a matter of education, Diderot disagreed completely; for him being a genius was a question of physical constitution, a matter of birth. In the *Éléments de physiologie* he wrote: 'genius always presupposes some disorder in the machine' (see p. 261).

The most obvious and visible sign of a genius was his being subjected to those moments of enthusiasm which Diderot depicted in the *Entretiens sur le Fils naturel* (see p. 128) or described in his article 'Eclectisme' (see p. 102). 'Those in whom the flame of Prometheus burns are consumed by it.'[27] 'Before taking up your brush you must have been made to tremble twenty times by your subject, to have lost sleep, been got up in the night and run barefoot in your nightshirt to put down your sketches on paper by the glimmering light of a candle.'[28] Helvétius' work showed that he was unfamiliar with 'the tyrannical impulse of the genius', he spoke about it 'like a blind man talking of colours'.[29] 'The moment a man of genius enters an academy it seems that he becomes an ordinary man. I see no other reason for this except that in the arts and sciences the genius only persists in the task which he gives himself. He does badly all he does through duty.'[30] The genius breaks the rules 'to fly to the sublime, the great, the *pathétique*'.[31]

Nevertheless, although subject to these impulsive and uncontrolled outbursts the genius was not acting in a random way, even less was he the vessel or recipient of some non-human force. His *sensibilité* was such that his mind was always active. As well as the visible evidence of its unusual capacity there was also an invisible aspect. Both the article 'Génie' and Diderot in his article 'Théosophes' (see p. 122) described something similar to what Keats later called 'negative capability', the unconscious observation and absorption of details, experiences and events. The mind developed 'that fine awareness (*tact fin*) which we get from the continuous observation of phenomena, and which makes us conscious of a secret liaison, a necessary interconnection'[32] between what otherwise seems unrelated. He gave a full account of this 'flair, instinct, spirit of the thing, or natural taste' in the *Salon de 1767*.[33] By means of this (usually) unconscious ability the genius was continually gathering and working over material that he would later formulate and express in his moments of enthusiasm.

Furthermore, the mind of the genius did operate according to certain rules: 'There is no science or art which does not have [its metaphysic] to which genius submits without knowing it, by instinct.'[34] This instinctive identity of the genius with the inner dynamic and logic of his subject was, of course, an identity with the workings of nature itself. 'Nature pushes the man of genius, the man of genius pushes the imitator. There is no intermediary between nature and the genius, such as always comes between nature and the imitator. The genius powerfully draws towards him everything that is found in his sphere of activity.'[35] Nature, as Diderot perceived it, was a self-creating force, like a polyp;[36] so was Homer.[37] Likewise, nature had taken Buffon and Chardin into her confidence (see p. 176). Vernet's genius was such that it could be said of him that 'he has stolen nature's secret from her';[38] 'he is like the Creator, for the speed [with which he operates], he is like nature for the truth' of his paintings.[39] In other words, a genius displayed the same creative force that animated nature.

In his article 'Encyclopédie' Diderot described the effect geniuses could have on language:

> sometimes going down into the very depths of themselves, some-times rushing outside and bringing the most attentive and penetrating observation to the [aspects of] nature which surround them, they are obliged, especially at the origin of languages, to invent signs to convey accurately and forcefully what they have been the first to discover. It is a glowing imagi-nation and profound meditation which enriches a language with new expressions.[40]

In this passage Diderot handled confidently what he had glimpsed but not formulated clearly in the *Lettre sur les sourds et muets*. He had recognized the existence and significance of man's creative faculty. Nowadays this is commonplace; at that time it was still obscure.

II

Although a genius was a law unto himself he was not isolated from the world around him. Diderot made it clear in his *Discours sur la poésie dramatique* (see p. 147) and his article 'Théosophes' (see p. 123) that the form a particular genius took, or even the very appearance of a genius, depended on the social context within which he lived. Other remarks to this effect occur in the *Salons*,[41] and in the *Réfutation d'Helvétius*: 'genius is a seed which is developed quickly by charity and which is stifled or held back by the public destitution which accompanies tyranny'.[42]

At the same time as he developed the idea of the genius as a special kind of person Diderot continued to use the word 'genius' in the way it had been used previously, as a particular attribute. In this sense genius was purely the inspired moment, the sudden insight, the eruption of an overwhelming inner force. As such, genius was regarded as meeting only some of our aesthetic needs. We also need some more ordered, regular and reliable guide in our experience of works of art; this was provided by taste. The two faculties were seen as both contradictory[43] and complementary: 'genius and good taste are two very different qualities',[44] 'whatever genius a poet may have, he needs a critic'.[45]

As he became closely acquainted with the practice of one particular art – painting – Diderot came to see that these two qualities could coexist in the same individual. Describing some paintings by Vernet, in the *Salon de 1765*, he wrote that they were 'always harmonious, vigorous and wise, like the works of those great poets, those rare men, whose judgement so perfectly balances their *verve* that they are never exaggerated or cold'.[46] And in the *Salon de 1767* he wrote: 'Every beautiful composition, every true talent in painting, sculpture, architecture, eloquence or poetry, presupposes a certain temperament of reason and enthusiasm, of judgement and *verve*; a rare and fleeting temperament, an equilibrium without which the compositions are extravagant or cold.'[47] La Tour when he painted was not carried away by emotion but on the contrary was 'calm and cool . . . He remains cold and yet his imitation is warm.'[48]

These reflections led Diderot to the view that great achievements were not purely a matter of a particular kind of *sensibilité*, as he had previously supposed. On the contrary, the man whose *sensibilité* was too susceptible or impressionable would be the victim of those impressions. Human achievement was the result of the activity of our brain which channelled, controlled and shaped the impressions it received. In *Le Rêve de d'Alembert* he maintained that greatness lay not in a quality of emotion but rather in a quality of detachment (see p. 252). Shortly after he had written this work he was asked by Grimm to review a pamphlet about Garrick and acting for the *Correspondance littéraire*. This pamphlet gave

Diderot an opportunity to develop his ideas on this subject and he took the opportunity at once. It led to 'a piece which would certainly merit being put in better order', he wrote to Grimm; 'with a bit of care it could perhaps have more *finesse* and insight than anything I have ever written. It is a fine paradox. I maintain that it is *sensibilité* which makes ordinary actors; extreme *sensibilité* limited actors; a cold head and intelligence, sublime actors.'[49]

Diderot's review, his *Observations sur une brochure intitulée Garrick ou les acteurs anglais*,[50] was published in the *Correspondance littéraire* in 1770. Over the following years he expanded and revised the piece, casting it in dialogue form and entitling it *Paradoxe sur le comédien*. The final version was more than four times as long as the original *Observations* but in widening the range of the discussion Diderot weakened its impact. The subject fascinated him but his extra work on it did not bring further insights. Nor is the dialogue form an improvement, because the speakers lack definition and character. The additional material consisted of examples, anecdotes, reflections on the state of the theatre, the extent to which the actor's profession could be reformed and so forth. There are passing references to Rousseau's arguments against the moral value of theatre, but these arguments are not tackled directly. If anything Diderot's remarks lend support to Rousseau's assertions.[51]

There were several reasons why Diderot gave such attention to the piece. For one thing the theatre always interested him. For another the subject had personal implications. In writing against *sensibilité* and the *homme sensible* he was writing against an aspect of himself, as he admitted: 'the sensitive man, like myself . . . loses his head and only finds it again at the foot of the staircase',[52] 'when I declared that *sensibilité* was the characteristic of those who have good souls but mediocre talent I was making the kind of confession you do not often hear, for if nature ever moulded a sensitive soul, it was mine'.[53] The *Paradoxe*, in other words, was an extrapolation from an essentially personal drama.

This can be seen not merely in the down-grading of *sensibilité* but in the new kind of distance Diderot saw between the actor and his role, or any artist and his material. A notable feature of his earlier writings was the importance attributed to the non-rational activities of the mind, the way truth could be discovered through delirium, frenzy or dream. In such activities the thinker or artist was not in conscious control of his thought, he was in a state of distraction (see the article 'Distraction'), enthusiasm or, a word Diderot sometimes used, *aliénation*. 'I can alienate myself,' he wrote in 1758, 'a talent without which you achieve nothing of value.'[54] An actress, he wrote in 1765, needs 'a soul which can be alienated, deeply moved, carried away'.[55] Rameau's Nephew, in his most elaborate performance is seized by 'an alienation of mind, an enthusiasm close to madness'.[56] Not only was he not in conscious control, he was unaware of anything outside himself; someone in this state was impervious to pain.[57]

There were two main features of this condition: the person was in a state of uncontrolled emotion, and he was also distant from himself, he had no sense of himself: 'outside himself he is everything that the art which dominates him wants him to be'.[58] This latter aspect was something which corresponded to both a profound tendency and a constant need in Diderot's own character. It was in forgetting himself that he stepped beyond the conventional habits and patterns of his thinking; it was in becoming *another* that he realized himself most fully, as his best dialogues brilliantly demonstrate. In the *Paradoxe* he recognized the central importance of this aspect of creative activity. The actor's achievement depended on a 'denial of himself';[59] Clairon followed a model which was not herself, she was two people, *'double'*.[60] 'It is no longer the person who acts, it is the spirit of another which dominates him.'[61] However, whereas in the earlier writings this *dédoublement* was achieved only in highly emotional states, it is now seen as the achievement of the gifted but quite consciously controlled actor or artist.

The *Paradoxe* also marked a clear development from Diderot's earlier writings on the theatre. In these he had argued for the greatest possible realism on the stage; he wanted the action in the theatre to be as close as possible to life. His *Discours sur la poésie dramatique* was criticized on these grounds by Madame Riccoboni: 'to be true in the theatre it is necessary to go a little beyond the natural'.[62] Diderot disagreed: something will be true if natural, 'false if it is a matter of convention'.[63] However, his contact with the work of painters had shown him that the artist did not make any direct, or even selective, imitation of nature; instead, he worked from an imaginary model. There was a realm of art distinct from that of nature. Art worked a kind of 'magic'[64] with the materials nature provided; a great actress, Clairon, like a great painter, was a 'magician'.[65] The actor, like the painter, worked from an 'ideal model',[66] such as he had described in the *Salon de 1767* (see p. 175). When the actor performed he wore 'the mask' of the different characters, 'nature had only given him his own [face], he adopted the others by means of art'.[67] In this way he moved from 'the limited instinct of nature to the unlimited study of art'.[68] We have here a clear break with Diderot's earlier writings. Madame Riccoboni would have been gratified to read his statement that 'the actor neither says nor does anything on the stage as in society: it is another world'.[69]

The *Paradoxe sur le comédien* is therefore an important work, even if uneven and overlong. It belongs both to an old debate about how actors operate and to a particular stage in Diderot's thinking about art. The pamphlet Grimm had asked Diderot to review had maintained that actors' ability stemmed from their highly emotional characters. Diderot, drawing on his own experience, his acquired knowledge of painting, and his acquaintance with Garrick, argued the opposite. This is not to say, however, as has sometimes been said, that he denied the place of all emotion in an actor's creation of a role. He merely insisted that that emotion must be emotion recollected in tranquillity.

Paradoxe sur le comédien

FIRST SPEAKER   . . . The important point, on which your author   306
and I have completely different views, are the main qualities which a great actor needs. For my part, I want him to have a lot of judgement; I need a man who is a cold and calm spectator. I therefore demand of him insight, but no *sensibilité*, and the art of imitating everything or, what comes to the same thing, an equal aptitude for all kinds of characters and roles.

SECOND SPEAKER   No *sensibilité*!

FIRST SPEAKER   None . . . If the actor were actually experiencing emotions, do you honestly believe he could play the same role with the same fire and the same success twice in a row? He would be bursting with ardour at the first performance, drained and cold as marble at the third. Whereas the acting of one who is an observant imitator and a thoughtful disciple of nature, the first time he presents himself upon the stage under the name of Augustus, Cinna, Orosmane, Agamemnon or Mahomet, since he is rigorously

copying what he has observed in himself and in others and continually observes our reactions – his acting, I repeat, instead of   307
growing weaker, will be progressively strengthened by the new
ideas he will have gathered. He will judge how far to raise or lower
his tone and will thus satisfy you the more. If he is himself when he
is acting, how can he can cease to be himself?

What confirms me in this opinion is the unevenness apparent in
performers who act from the heart. There is no use your expecting
any unity in their acting: it is by turns strong and weak, hot and
cold, flat and sublime. Tomorrow, they will fail in the place where
they excelled today, and the next day they will excel in the place
where they failed the day before. Whereas the actor who works
from reflection, from a study of human nature, from constant
imitation of some ideal model, from imagination, from memory,
will give uniform performances, all of them equally perfect. Everything has been measured, combined, learned, ordered in his head;
there is neither monotony nor dissonance in his delivery. His
emotions will be seen to progress, to rise and fall, to have a
beginning, a middle and an end. The accents, the gestures, the
movements are always the same; if there is any difference between
two successive performances, it will usually be to the profit of the
second. He will not vary from day to day: he is a mirror always
ready to reflect nature – and alway ready to reflect it with the same
precision, the same force and the same truth. Like the poet, he
continually goes back to replenish himself from the inexhaustible
store of nature: whereas if he depended solely on his own
resources, he would quickly see the end of them.

What acting could be more perfect than Clairon's? Yet if you
follow her performances and study her work, you will be convinced
that she knows every detail of her role as much by heart by the sixth
performance as she knows the words. Undoubtedly she has first
constructed a model for herself, to which she then tries to conform: 308
doubtless, too, she made it as noble, as great, as perfect as she was
able; but this model that she has borrowed from history or which
her imagination has created like some great ghost is not she. If the
stature of the model were no greater than that of the actress, how
feeble and petty its action would be! When, by dint of hard work,
she has come as close to that model as lies within her power, then
the job is done: to hold herself firmly at that point is purely a matter
of practice and memory . . .

Why should the actor differ from the poet, the painter, the   309 orator, the musician? It is not in the first furious impulse of inspiration that characteristic traits present themselves; it is in cool and tranquil moments, in entirely unexpected moments. We do not know where these flashes come from: they are a matter of inspiration. For the beauties of inspiration, the fortuitous flashes with which these geniuses sow their works at moments when they themselves are hung suspended between nature and their first sketch – casting alternate and attentive glances at each in turn – these beauties, which often surprise the artists themselves by their sudden appearance, are far more assured of their effect and success than any added in a moment's caprice. It is for *sang-froid* to temper the frenzy of enthusiasm.

It is not the violent man unable to control himself who moves us; that is an advantage reserved for the man in full possession of himself. The great dramatists in particular are diligent spectators of what is happening around them in both the physical and the moral spheres.

310

SECOND SPEAKER   Which are one and the same.

FIRST SPEAKER   They absorb everything that strikes them; they store it all away. And it is from these hidden stores, laid up inside them without their knowing it, that so many rare phenomena pass into their works. The emotional, violent, warm-hearted men are on the stage; they give the performance, but they are unable to enjoy it. They are the models from which the genius makes his copies. Great poets, great actors, and perhaps all the great imitators of nature generally, no matter of what kind, endowed with a fine imagination, a great deal of judgement, delicacy of touch and infallible taste, are nevertheless the least *sensible* creatures. They are fitted in equal measure for too many things; they are too busy looking, recognizing and imitating to be deeply affected by anything within themselves. I see them with their portfolios constantly on their knees, their pencils always in their hands.

We feel; they observe, study and depict. Shall I say it? Why not? Great genius is scarcely ever accompanied by *sensibilité*. A genius will love justice, but he will exercise that virtue without tasting its sweetness. It is not his heart, it is his head that does everything. Whereas the *homme sensible* loses his head even at the slightest unexpected occurrence; and will never be a great king, a great minister, a great general, a great lawyer or a great doctor. You may fill the auditorium with such moist-eyed creatures, but don't put any of them onto the stage.

Yet even if these truths were clearly proved, great actors would   311
never admit them: they are their secret. Mediocre actors or novices
would be bound to reject them and there are others of whom we
might say that they believe they feel, as one says of the superstitious
man that he believes he believes, since the latter cannot envisage
his salvation without faith, and the former cannot envisage his
without *sensibilité*.

'Come, now,' people will protest, 'do you mean to say that the   312
heart-rending, grief-stricken accents being torn from that mother's
very bowels, and so strongly affecting my own, are not being
produced by actual feelings or inspired by despair?' Not in the
slightest. And the proof is that they are being uttered in metre; that
they are all parts of a system of declamation; that if they were the
twentieth part of a quarter tone higher or lower in pitch, they would
be false; that they are subject to a law of unity; that they have been
prepared and led into just as a passage of music is; that they have
been made to satisfy all the required conditions only after long
study; that they are contributing toward the solution of a given
problem; that it was necessary to rehearse them a hundred times in
order to make them ring true; and that despite these frequent
repetitions, the intended effect is still sometimes missed . . .

The actor's whole talent consists not in feeling, as you suppose,
but in re-creating the external signs of feeling with such scrupulous
accuracy that you are taken in by them. Those grief-stricken cries
are noted down in his ear. Those despairing gestures are performed
from memory and have been rehearsed in front of a mirror. He
knows the exact moment when he will draw out his handkerchief,
the exact moment when the tears will start to flow; watch how they
come at that particular word, at that particular syllable, not a
moment sooner, not a moment later. That quiver in his voice, those
half-finished words, those muffled or long-drawn-out sounds, that
trembling of the limbs, that weakening of the knees, those swoons,
those attacks of fury – they are all pure imitation, a lesson learned
in advance, a plaintive look, a sublime piece of mimicry that the
actor remembers long after studying it, that he was aware of still
even at the moment when he was expecting it, that leaves him,
happily for the poet, spectator and himself, in full possession of his
mind, and that, like other physical exertions, makes no demand   313
except upon the resources of his body. Once the doublet and hose
have been taken off, his voice is weak, he experiences extreme
fatigue, he changes clothes, or he goes to bed – but he is left with no

worry, grief, melancholy or gloom. It is you who take all those impressions away with you. The actor is tired, and you are sad, because he has been flinging himself all over the stage without feeling a thing, and you have been feeling the emotions without moving from your seat. If it were otherwise, the actor's calling would be the most unfortunate calling in the world. But he is not the character; he plays it; and plays it so well that you take him for the character he is playing. The illusion is all on your side: the actor knows that he is not the character . . .

Reflect for a moment on what is called 'being true' in the theatre.   317
Does it mean presenting things as they are in nature? Not at all. The true, in that sense, would be merely the commonplace. What is truth on the stage, then? It is the conformity of action, speech, facial expression, voice, movements and gestures with an ideal model imagined by the author and often exaggerated by the actor. And there lies the miracle. This model does not merely influence the actor's tone of voice; it even modifies his gait, his bearing. That is why the actor on the stage and the actor in real life are two such different people that it is difficult to recognize the one in the other. The first time I saw Mlle Clairon in her own home, I exclaimed quite spontaneously, 'But, Mademoiselle, I expected you to be a whole head taller!'

Is it at the very moment when you have just lost your friend or   333
your mistress that you will compose a poem upon his or her death? No. Woe to him who can use his talents at such a moment! It is when the first great wave of grief has passed, when the extreme *sensibilité* has diminished, when the catastrophe is at a distance, that the soul is calm enough to recall the happiness that has been eclipsed, is capable of appreciating its loss, and that memory combines with imagination, the one to retrace, the other to magnify the sweetness of a time now past. Only then are we in possession of ourselves and able to speak well. We write that we are weeping, but no one weeps when he is hunting for a forceful expression that is eluding him; we write that we are weeping, but no one weeps when he is busy performing the harmony of a line. Or, if the tears do flow, then the pen drops from our fingers, we give ourselves up to our emotions, and we cease to write . . .

One is oneself by nature; one is another by imitation. The heart   358
which you imagine for yourself is not the heart you have. What then is true talent? That of having a good knowledge of the external symptoms of the soul, of directing that at the feelings of those who

hear us and see us, and of deceiving them by the imitation of these symptoms, an imitation which magnifies everything in their heads and becomes the rule of their judgement . . . So the person who has the best knowledge and conveys most perfectly these external signs based on the best-conceived ideal model is the greatest actor . . .

III

Diderot's preoccupation with how works of art came to be made, his re-evaluation of imagination, his redefinition of genius, his concern for the feelings works of art arouse in us or suggest – all these were part of a major shift of emphasis in aesthetic discussion. 'The principle of the fine arts,' he wrote in 1771, 'has too generally been applied to the imitation of nature . . . There is something inexplicable in the pleasure of our feelings', which the concept of imitation could not cover.[70] Diderot never formulated another concept to replace it but, as Herbert Dieckmann has noted, he did in effect 'substitute the question of expression for that of imitation'.[71] In this respect Diderot was a crucial pioneer of what came to be called romanticism.

Most of his insights which contributed to this change were generally adopted as the romantic attitude to art and artists merged imperceptibly into the modern pattern of thinking. On one subject, however, Diderot raised questions which to a certain extent remain unsettled: the relation of art to morality.

When he wrote, in the *Discours sur la poésie dramatique*, 'there is nothing sacred for the poet',[72] or 'poetry wants something tremendous, barbaric and wild' (p. 146); when he wrote elsewhere 'O poets, poets! Plato knew very well what he was doing when he expelled them from his republic. They do not have correct ideas about anything',[73] or 'the taste for the fine arts presupposes a certain contempt for fortune, a kind of negligence of domestic matters, a certain disorder of the brain',[74] he was not saying anything that had not been said before. Artists could not be relied on to tell the truth, and they were often a bit mad.

However, these ideas took on a completely different complexion when the criterion of truth itself changed. If the poet's 'hiero-glyphs' were more accurate representations of the truth than the philosopher's discourse, then previous values were reversed. Diderot never explicitly suggested such a reversal though the suggestions for it can occasionally be seen in his writings. One reason for the impact of *Le Neveu de Rameau* lies in this fact. But generally speaking the truth remained for him fidelity to those facts of nature which could be objectively established by a philosophical examination of the evidence.

What led him into new problems was not the re-evaluation of the truth but the attention he gave to the effects of art and the nature of the creative process. 'I have never been able to prevent myself from admiring human nature, even sometimes when it is atrocious . . . If wicked men did not have that energy in crime the good would not have the same energy in virtue.'[75] We have a completely amoral admiration of energy. Not only that, we can be *more* moved and excited by evil than by good. The kind of aesthetic pleasure that was called the sublime was stimulated more by 'the power that threatens than the power that protects . . . the tyrant rather than the king' (see p. 183). 'Crime is a beautiful thing,' he wrote in the *Salon de 1763*, 'both in history and in poetry, on canvas and in marble.'[76] Rameau's Nephew delights in shocking Diderot with his enthusiasm for the *sublime de mal* (see p. 210); Madame de la Pommeraye and Père Hudson in *Jacques le fataliste* evoke our admiration by the extreme degree to which they pursue their ruthless evil schemes.

These experiences led Diderot to see that evil could be not only aesthetically pleasurable for the viewer; it could also be aesthetic-ally fertile for the creator. 'What is harmful to moral beauty almost always increases poetic beauty. With virtue you hardly ever pro-duce anything except cold, calm paintings. It is passion and vice which give life to the compositions of the painter, the poet and the musician.'[77] The artist's morality was diametrically opposed to normal morality; his imperative was always to take things to the extreme (see p. 181).

> In Athens [he wrote in the *Salon de 1765*] surprising progress was made – at the expense of honour, good faith, virtue and morality – in matters of taste, art, the feeling of grace, in the knowledge and choice of characters, expressions and other things that accompany an art [painting] which presupposes the finest and

most delicate sense of touch, the most exquisite judgement, a certain nobility, a kind of heightened sense, [and] a multitude of fine qualities, delicious fumes which rise up from the depths of a cesspool. [78]

When he wrote these remarkable lines Diderot had travelled a long way from the assured conviction he had shared with Shaftesbury, that the ethical and aesthetic sense were essentially in harmony. It is not surprising that on certain occasions he maintained that art could corrupt. [79] But the implications of these insights were too disturbing to be acceptable, and while his later work shows awareness of a conflict between the claims of art and the demands of morality, he kept a certain distance from the problem. That distance remains, for many people, hard to travel even now.

12

Morality

I

Diderot was, as he said himself, 'a man who loves to moralize' (see p. 8); he always wanted to act morally and to promote virtue. However, in order to do this convincingly it was necessary to establish a sound intellectual basis for morality and this proved to be much harder than he imagined. The confident tone in which he advocated moral behaviour and displayed his belief that 'for the man who possesses it virtue is the greatest wealth in life'[1] could not always hide his doubts about his failure either to be virtuous himself or to work out a satisfactory moral system for others. In his last works, the play *Est-il bon? Est-il méchant?* and the semi-autobiographical commentary on Seneca, the *Essai sur les règnes de Claude et Néron*, these doubts were faced openly and, in the *Essai*, unhappily.

At the outset of his career there was no such hesitation. The *Essai sur le mérite et la vertu* breathes the confidence of someone who has found a body of ideas with which he can identify completely. Diderot agreed with Shaftesbury's separation of morality from religion, his conviction that man was naturally sociable, that virtue was true happiness, and that our moral sense was consonant with our aesthetic sense. But Shaftesbury's beliefs rested on metaphysical notions of universal harmony and order, and in his *Lettre sur les aveugles* Diderot broke decisively with these notions. There was no general universal order, only temporary patterns among continuously changing phenomena. The consequences of this break, ethically, were not moral anarchy – Saunderson, putting forward these ideas, is a man of exemplary moral conduct – but the need to base morality on purely human attributes.

Over the next few years Diderot pieced together the elements of a purely empirical moral theory. In his article 'Beau' (1752) he showed how the idea of order (which for Shaftesbury was an innate propensity in man as an integral part of a universally ordered creation) was not innate but developed gradually.

> We are born with the faculty of feeling and thinking; the first step in the faculty of thinking is to examine perceptions, to unite them, compare them, combine them, see relationships of agreement and disagreement among them, etc. We are born with needs which force us to resort to different expedients; we have often been convinced – by the effect which we expected of them, and which they did have – that there are good, bad, quick, short, complete and incomplete ones among them. Most of these expedients were a tool, a machine or some other invention of this kind. But every machine presupposes some combination, some arrangement of parts tending to one and the same purpose, etc. This then is how our needs and the most immediate exercise of our faculties work together from the moment we are born to give us ideas of order, arrangement, symmetry, mechanism, proportion, unity . . . These notions are matters of experience, like all other ideas.[2]

In his contribution to the *Apologie de l'abbé de Prades* Diderot discussed man in a state of nature, which, he explained, meant men 'considered in a herd and not in society . . . the condition under which almost all the savages live and from which one can set out when intending to discover philosophically . . . the origin and development of human knowledge'. This state was that of men who had 'come together by simple natural impulse, like monkeys, deer, crows, etc, without having formed any conventions which subjected them to duties, nor set up any authority which would constrain them to fulfil such conventions'. In this state 'the only check on injustice is resentment, this passion which nature, concerned for the preservation of creatures, has placed in each individual to make him someone to be feared by his fellow men'.[3] 'There is no moral notion which is innate', he concluded; morality arises out of 'a fairly immediate induction from physical good and evil'.[4] Out of our instinctive resentment at anything that causes displeasure, harm or pain, we construct our first moral ideas.

In the article 'Droit naturel' (1755) Diderot went a stage further. While the origins of morality may lie in the individual's reaction to and judgement on the behaviour of others, no stable morality could rest on such a purely personal foundation; an effective morality must be based on the general social practice of human beings, at all times and in all places. This general practice Diderot termed 'the general will'; and, he stated, it was the moral duty of every man to consult the general will in establishing what were his natural rights and how he should therefore behave.

In the first of the numbered paragraphs of this article Diderot made a general comment about freedom: 'It is evident that if man is not free . . . there will be neither moral good or evil, neither just nor unjust, neither obligation nor right.' He then added: 'from which it can be seen, to mention it in passing, how important it is to establish the firm reality, I do not say of the *voluntary*, but of *freedom*, which is only too commonly confused with the voluntary'.[5] This somewhat cryptic remark was a reference to a problem which was then receiving much attention, the nature of human freedom.

For Christians a belief in free will is a necessary corollary to a belief in a benevolent deity. If men were not free then they could not reasonably be punished for sin or wrongdoing; it is because they have a choice between good and evil that they can hope for a blissful place in heaven or must fear for a nasty time in hell. Furthermore, while God may be omnipotent it would be non-sensical to suppose that he is responsible for everything, since in that case he would be responsible for evil as well as good, and evil cannot be a manifestation of a benevolent God. These two ideas – that human beings have free will, and that all that humans do is not necessary – were central aspects of both Christian and deist belief in the eighteenth century. Both of them were subject to much debate.

In the small collection of essays printed in 1743 under the title *Nouvelles libertés de penser* (which included *Le Philosophe*) was a short *Traité de liberté*, then and now usually attributed to Fontenelle. It asked the question: are men in fact free? They cannot make themselves more intelligent, merely by wanting to do so, so why should they have the ability to be more or less moral? 'The soul depends entirely on the tendencies (*dispositions*) of the brain.'[6] We may feel we are free but actually 'the orders which men receive from their brains always conform to their inclination, since these orders also cause the inclination'.[7] The experience of considering possible choices is merely the result of a temporary equilibrium between two material tendencies; some physical cause then effectively tilts the balance in favour of one of them. 'Everything is comprehended in a physical order.'[8] The author did however make some exception to this deterministic outlook; most men (though not all) can be corrected by 'exhortations and examples';[9] it is possible to fortify their natural tendencies, although he did not explain how this could come about.

This work was in circulation in December 1754, for Grimm refers to a manuscript copy of it in his *Correspondance littéraire*.[10] Two months later he wrote that 'Collins's metaphysical paradoxes on freedom and necessity have just been translated from the English'.[11] This was a reference to Anthony Collins's *A Philosophical Inquiry concerning Human Liberty*, first published in 1717. Collins regarded liberty as 'both the real foundation of popular atheism and . . . the professed principle of the atheists themselves',[12] and writing as a Christian he wished to show how it was their lack of liberty that revealed men to be more perfect creatures. He maintained that when we make a judgement we are not acting freely since we must necessarily agree with what is clearly evident; we cannot refrain from thinking and our judgement necessarily follows from the presentation of the evidence. Similarly, 'we must will or prefer as things seem to us';[13] 'at all times and under all circumstances [man] is pursuing and enjoying the greatest happiness which his condition would allow';[14] man is 'a necessary agent, determined by pleasure and pain';[15] 'morality, or virtue, consists in such actions as are in their own nature pleasant'.[16] The reason Collins gives for the prevalence of immoral behaviour is that men may mistake pain for pleasure, an admission which seems to open the backdoor and allow freedom the run of the house. Grimm however was strongly impressed by Collins's argument and gave as an example of the deterministic operations of the mind the behaviour of men of genius: 'when genius acts in these divine men [Homer, Raphael, Pergolesi] a lively warmth takes hold of them . . . possessed by the strongest enthusiasm they produce necessarily and without will the things which cause the admiration of the universe'.[17]

In complete contradiction to these two works was Rousseau's *Discours sur l'inégalité*, completed in June 1754 and published in May 1755. It was precisely the human faculty of freedom, Rousseau argued, which distinguished human beings from animals.

Nature commands every animal, and the beast obeys. Man experiences the same impulse but he recognizes that he is free to go along with it or resist it; and it is above all in the awareness of this freedom that the spirituality of his soul is evident. For physics can explain in some way the mechanism of the senses and the formation of ideas, but we find nothing but purely spiritual acts, in no way explained by the laws of mechanics, in the power of willing, or rather of choosing.[18]

Diderot was at this time a close friend of Rousseau and through him had met Grimm. The issues at stake were clearly known to him, as his remark in the article 'Droit naturel' indicated. What he said there was in agreement with Rousseau; not only may we think, suppose or imagine that our actions are free, which is what he meant by voluntary, (this distinction had been made in the *Traité sur la liberté*)[19], but we are actually free in fact. However, a little over a year later he wrote a contribution for the *Correspondance littéraire* which put the matter rather differently. His comments occur in what is ostensibly a letter to a little-known playwright called Landois.* The latter, it seems, has been in need of help but has been rude and ungrateful to those who have tried to give him help. He has sent Diderot a manuscript in the hope that he would revise it and arrange to have it published. The manuscript was about morality, and its contents provoke Diderot to the following remarks:

Lettre à Landois

. . . In the eyes of the people your morality is detestable. In the eyes of a philosopher it is a small-minded morality, part true, part false, part petty. If I was a man of sermons and masses I would say to you: my virtue does not destroy my passions, it only tempers them and prevents them from transgressing the laws of right

---

* It has been suggested that the letter was aimed at Rousseau, who had left Paris two months earlier to take up residence at the Hermitage. Although there are one or two remarks which could refer to Rousseau, there are many more which do not; nor had the friendship between Rousseau and Diderot yet deteriorated to the extent that the latter would adopt such an abrasive tone.

reason. I know all the supposed advantages of a sophism and bad conduct, of a very subtle sophism and of very dark and obscure behaviour; but I find in myself an equal repugnance to reasoning badly and to doing wrong. I stand between two forces, one of which shows me the good and the other inclines me towards the evil. We must choose.

At the outset the moment of struggle is [always] cruel, but the pain grows less with time. The moment comes when the sacrifice of passion no longer costs anything. From my own experience I can even vouch for the fact that it is sweet; you derive from it, in your own eyes, so much nobility and dignity! Virtue is a mistress to whom you are attached as much for what you do for her as for the charms you believe her to have. It is your misfortune if the practise of good is unfamiliar to you and you do not have a large enough fund of good actions to be vain about them, to congratulate yourself about them continually, to intoxicate yourself with this perfume and be a fanatic about them.

You say: 'We receive virtue as a sick man receives a remedy', to which – if he was to be believed – he would prefer every other thing that would please his appetite. That is true of a stupid sick man. Nevertheless, if this sick man had had the merit of diagnosing his illness himself and of having found and prepared the remedy for himself, do you think he would have hesitated about taking it, however bitter it was, and that he would not give himself the credit for his insight and his courage?

What is a virtuous man? It is a man who is vain with this kind of vanity and no more. Everything we do is for ourselves. We look as if we are sacrificing ourselves when we are only satisfying ourselves. It only remains to know if we will give the name of wise men or idiots to those who have such an apparently bizarre way of making themselves happy as that of self-sacrifice. Why should we call them stupid, since they are happy, and their happiness is so similar to other people's happiness? Certainly they are happy; for although they pay a price for it, it is always the least price to them.

But if you want to weigh up properly the advantages they bring themselves, and above all the drawbacks which they avoid, you will find it difficult to prove that they are unreasonable. If you ever do undertake that, do not forget to make allowance for all that the consideration of others and of oneself is worth. Moreover, do not forget that a bad action is never unpunished: I say never because the first bad act you commit disposes you to a second and that to a

third, and that is how we advance little by little towards the scorn of
our fellow creatures, the greatest of all evils.

Dishonoured in one society, it will be said, I will move to another
where I will readily obtain for myself the honours of virtue. Wrong.
Does one cease to be wicked at will? After you have made yourself
wicked, is it only a question of going a hundred leagues to be good,
or only of saying to oneself: I want to be good? The fold is set; the
fabric must keep it.

It is here, my dear, that I am going to leave the tone of a preacher
to adopt, if I can, that of a philosopher. Look at it closely and you
will see that the word *liberty* is a word devoid of meaning; that there
are not, and cannot be, free beings; that we are only what agrees
with the general order, our physical constitution, education and
the chain of events. This is what invincibly disposes of us. One can
no more think of a creature acting without a motive, than of one of
the arms of a scales moving without the action of a weight, and the
motive for us is always external, foreign, attached either to a nature
or some cause which is not us. What deceives us is the prodigious
variety of our actions, combined with the habit we have acquired
since birth of confusing the voluntary with the free. We have so
often praised it, so often adopted it, that it is a very old prejudice to
think that we and others will and act freely. But if there is no liberty
there is no act that deserves praise or blame. There is neither vice
nor virtue, nothing which should be rewarded or punished. Then
what is it that distinguishes men? Doing good and doing harm. The
man who does harm is a man who should be destroyed and not
punished; doing good is a matter of good luck and not virtue. But
although the good or harmful man is not free, man is no less a
creature who is modified; it is for this reason that the man who does
harm must be destroyed in public. From this fact arises the good
effects of example, speeches, education, pleasure, grief, nobility,
poverty, etc. From this fact emerges a kind of philosophy full of
pity, which is strongly drawn to good people and which gets no
more angry with a wicked man than it does with a hurricane which
fills our eyes with dust.

There is, properly speaking, only one kind of cause: physical
causes. There is only one kind of necessity; it is the same for all
creatures, whatever distinctions it may please us to establish
between them, or that really exist. That is what reconciles me to
humankind. It is for this reason that I exhort you to philanthropy.
Adopt these principles if you find them good, or else show me that

they are bad. If you do adopt them they will also reconcile you to others and to yourself. You will not be able to be willing or reluctant to be what you are. Reproach others with nothing, repent of nothing yourself: these are the first steps to wisdom. Beyond that is prejudice, false philosophy. If we get impatient, if we swear, if we bite the stone, it is because in the best-constituted and most happily modified man there always remains a great deal of animal [instinct] before misanthropic [reaction] . . .

As for the rest. . . There is a lot of difference between separating yourself from humankind and hating them. But . . . is it the malice of [other] men which makes you sad, anxious, melancholy, resentful, restless and morose? . . . Give up these accusations and jeremiads and come nearer to the men you are complaining about, and see them as they are . . .[20]

The *Lettre à Landois* is a puzzling text. Its purpose is uncertain and its statements seem, at first sight, contradictory. It has often been taken as evidence that Diderot had adopted at this time a thoroughgoing determinism from which he was to spend the rest of his life trying to extricate himself. The passage about freedom in the second half of the *Lettre* is quoted in support of this.

There are, however, three distinct elements in the *Lettre*: there is the obscure matter of the quarrel between Diderot and Landois, which is a quarrel both about the latter's behaviour and the ideas in his manuscript, and there are the two replies Diderot makes, one speaking as 'a man of sermons and masses' and the other as 'a philosopher'. As far as the first element is concerned we cannot be certain precisely what is at issue, but Diderot's remarks do suggest that Landois' behaviour has been impulsive, unreasonable and anti-social, and his manuscript was in some way a justification of such behaviour. Diderot's initial purpose in the *Lettre* is to show that such ideas and such conduct are wrong.

The fact that he does so in the character of 'a man of sermons and masses' should not mislead us. There is no irony in the passage that follows, Diderot is quite sincere. This is obvious from the arguments he uses against Landois, which are in no way ecclesiastical arguments. On the contrary, he is advancing a straightforward and unashamed ethical naturalism: virtue is not painful but pleasurable, 'everything we do is for ourselves', and the worst of all evils is to lose the respect of our fellow men. For, as Diderot points out later in the *Lettre* these fellow men are not mean, malicious or deceitful, and their actions do not justify Landois' complaints against them. He owes it to himself and to them to think in a less confused and misanthropic way and to act more virtuously.

The remarks which Diderot then makes as a 'philosopher' are not in opposition to this advice but in support of it. Landois is not at liberty to act solely as he pleases or as he may want. How he behaves now will affect how he will be able to behave in future: as we grow older 'the fold is set [and] the fabric must keep' whatever fold that is.* Our choice is limited by a number of factors. It depends a great deal on our physical constitution, whether we have a natural inclination to do good or harm. It also depends on how we have been 'modified', that is to say, how we have been influenced by education, family upbringing, social pressures and so forth. But an element of choice exists. If it did not, Diderot's advice to Landois would be completely meaningless; if the latter could not behave in any other way than how he had been behaving, then Diderot's letter would be a waste of time. Yet it is clear that Diderot thought his letter was serving a constructive purpose.

When Diderot states that 'the word *liberty* is a word devoid of meaning' he is not denying the claims of morality or the need for virtuous conduct. He is arguing against the Christian or Cartesian or Rousseauist view that man was different from other animals. Dualism, not morality, is the enemy. Human beings as much as all other creatures are part of the natural order, they are not some kind of privileged beings who are exempt from 'the chain of events'. When he says that 'there is neither vice nor virtue' he means that morality as generally taught, by the Church in particular, is wrong in so far as it suggests that we have completely free choice about our actions. Free will in the Christian sense does not exist.

At one point in the *Lettre* Diderot suggests that human beings have no free will of any kind. When he says that 'the general order . . . *invincibly* disposes of us' and 'the motive for us is *always* external' he is denying all choice. When he goes on to say that man can be modified, and then gives advice to Landois, he draws back from this extreme position. This is only one of several shifts of emphasis which indicate not only Diderot's habit of changing direction as he discusses a subject, but evident uncertainties in his own

---

* Diderot repeated this belief in some comments about morality written in 1771.[21]

mind. The device of speaking first as a 'preacher' and then as a 'philosopher' also suggests that he is unclear how to resolve the problem of how much choice we have. It should also be noted that several passages in the *Lettre* bear a close resemblance to the *Traité sur la liberté* and that there is as well a hint of a *jeu d'esprit*, ideas being exercised for the pleasure of seeing where they lead.

All in all, a close reading of the *Lettre* does not support the view that Diderot was a convinced determinist for whom morality was merely an illusion, a façade or a social convenience. It suggests rather that he was a convinced moralist who could not see how to reconcile his moral convictions with his naturalistic principles.

II

The uncertainty evident in the *Lettre à Landois* continued to the end of Diderot's life. Over the ensuing years we find side by side the same moral convictions and the same desire to see them within a scientific context, a context which continually threatens to engulf or deny any specifically moral dimension.

The play *Le Fils naturel* revolves around the ability of the central character Dorval to make a moral choice, and in the last scene, after his success in doing so, he can proclaim with confidence: 'I am free.'[22] In the letter of dedication which preceded his next play, *Le Père de famille* (1758), he wrote of 'the notions of order, harmony, self-interest, altruism and beauty, the seeds of which we carry within us, which we are not free to resist and which are continually revealed and strengthened'.[23] The suggestion here of innateness was corrected by another remark that year, in his *Réflexions* on Helvétius' *De l'esprit*: 'it is possible to find in our natural needs, in our life, in our existence, in our physical constitution and our *sensibilité* which lays us open to suffering, an eternal foundation of the just and unjust'.[24] Another affirmation of this view comes in the *Supplément au Voyage de Bougainville*: 'at birth we bring with us only a similarity in physical constitution with other creatures, the same needs, the attraction towards the same pleasures, a common aversion to the same pain. It is that which makes man what he is and should be the basis of the morality which suits him.'[25]

In articles for the *Encyclopédie* we find an apparent denial of virtue ('Vice'); restatements of the idea that human nature can be modified ('Modification', 'Vindicatif'); and in the article 'Volonté' an admission of uncertainty: 'how difficult it is to conceive any idea at all of liberty, especially in an interconnection of causes and effects, such as that of which we are a part'.[26] In *Le Rêve de d'Alembert* the extreme position that occurs in the *Lettre à Landois* is restated (see pp. 253-4), but once again there are qualifications: habit and education have some influence (p. 251) and 'a powerful motive' can be effective in achieving self-control. The *Éléments de physiologie* contain many reflections on this subject: *'sensibilité* is more powerful than will',[27] and 'our vices and virtues relate very closely to our organs',[28] but 'every order of beings has its particular mechanism . . . that of the man is not that of his organs' (see p. 259).

In this last remark lay one solution to the problem which was troubling Diderot. Although he had never suggested that human beings were indistinguishable from animals the predominantly bio-logical and medical emphasis of his interest tended to overlook or underrate any specifically human characteristics. But he never denied that such characteristics existed. In his letter of dedication to *Le Père de famille* he had said that men were distinct from animals: 'man retains in all his acts a perspective which distin-guishes him'.[29] The development of the idea that the whole is different from the sum of the parts, in *Le Rêve de d'Alembert*, leads Bordeu to suggest that it is precisely in his detachment from his emotions that the greatness of great men lay. Yet Diderot's incli-nation was always to stress the connections between our emotional and intellectual or moral condition, not the differences. Only when he was faced with a work that took to the extreme the materialist premisses which were his own point of departure did he see the need to make a clear distinction.

This work was Helvétius' *De l'homme*, published posthumously in 1773. In it Helvétius argued that men were only moved by self-interest, the pursuit of physical pleasure and the avoidance of pain, and that all men were more or less alike; it is education that makes them different. Diderot read the book in Holland, on his way to Russia, and made a large number of notes, comments and counter-arguments. In Paris later he collected them into a single work, the *Réfutation suivie de l'ouvrage d'Helvétius intitulé L'Homme*. He admired Helvétius' book – 'an excellent work full of shrewd reflections which it is not given to everyone to discover'[30] –

and this admiration is one reason for the amplitude of his commentary. But the main reason was the fact that Helvétius indicated to him errors which he had been close to committing. As he wrote succinctly elsewhere: 'Head – organ about which Helvétius has not said a word. Yet from it [stems] the difference between the animal and the man.'[31] We differ from animals in having brains. This means that we are not entirely conditioned by our physical constitution. 'A naturally wicked man has felt by experience and by reflection the drawbacks of wickedness; he remains [naturally] wicked and [yet] he does good.'[32] Helvétius regarded the mind as the passive recipient of sensations, impressions and influences. Against this view Diderot argued forcefully.

Réfutation d'Helvétius

*To feel is to judge**

This assertion, as it is phrased, does not seem strictly true to me. A stupid man feels but does not necessarily judge. A being totally deprived of memory feels, but it does not judge: judgement presupposes the comparison of two ideas. The difficulty consists in knowing how this comparison is performed, since it presupposes the simultaneous presence of two ideas in the mind. Helvétius would have removed a terrible stumbling block if he had given a clear explanation of how we entertain two ideas simultaneously or how, if we do not entertain them simultaneously, we can nevertheless still compare them.

563

Perhaps I was in an ill humour when I read this sixth chapter, but here are my remarks on it – good or bad, I shall set them down. From the author's fundamental view there emerges the fact that judgement, or the comparison of objects with each other, presupposes some motive for comparing them. Helvétius then concludes that this motive arises necessarily from the desire for happiness, which, in its turn, arises from physical *sensibilité*. This conclusion is very far-fetched; it is more applicable to animals in general than to man. To leap suddenly from physical *sensibilité*, i.e. the fact that I am not a plant, a stone, or a metal, to the desire for happiness, from the desire for happiness to self-interest, from

564

* The italicized passages are from Helvétius.

self-interest to attention, from attention to the comparison of ideas – these are generalities I cannot accept. I am a man, and I must have causes that are appropriate to man. The author also adds that by climbing two rungs higher or descending one rung lower, he could go on from physical *sensibilité* to organization, from organization to existence and could then say, 'I exist, and I exist in this form; I feel, I judge; I wish to be happy because I feel; my self-interest leads me to compare my ideas because I have a desire for happiness.' But what possible utility can I derive from a string of consequences that is equally applicable to a dog, a weasel, an oyster, or a dromedary? . . .

Descartes said, 'I think, therefore I am.'

Helvétius wants us to say, 'I feel, therefore I wish to feel pleasantly.'

I prefer Hobbes. He claims that if we are to draw any meaningful conclusion, we must say, 'I feel, I think, I judge, therefore a portion of matter organized as I am can feel, think, and judge' . . .

Is it really true that physical pleasure and pain, which are possibly 566 the only principles of action in animals, are also the only principles of action in men?

It is certainly necessary to possess an organization like ours and to feel in order to act. But it seems to me that those are merely the essential and basic conditions, the data *sine qua non*, and that the immediate and most direct motives of our aversions and desires are something else.

Without alkali and sand, there can be no glass, but are those elements the cause of transparency?

Without uncultivated land and without a pair of arms, we cannot clear new land, but are those the motives of the farmer when he clears a stretch of forest?

To take conditions for causes is to lay oneself open to childish paralogisms and meaningless conclusions.

If I were to say: one must be in order to feel; one must feel in 567 order to be an animal or a man; one must be an animal or a man in order to be miserly, ambitious and jealous; therefore jealousy, ambition and avarice have as their primary causes organization, *sensibilité*, and existence – would you be able to refrain from laughing at me? And why? Because I would be confusing the conditions for all animal actions in general with the motives for the actions of one individual taken from one particular species of animal called man.

Admittedly I do everything I do in order to feel pleasure or in order to avoid pain, but has the word 'feel' only one connotation?

Is there only physical pleasure in possessing a beautiful woman? Is there only physical pain in losing her, either through death or through infidelity?

Is the distinction between the physical and the moral not as solid as that between the animal which feels and the animal which thinks?

Is it not true that what pertains to the feeling being and what pertains to the thinking being are sometimes united and at other times separated in almost all the actions that make for happiness or unhappiness in our lives (a happiness and an unhappiness that presupposes physical sensation as a condition); which is to say, that it is not necessary to be a cabbage?

Thus we see how important it was not to make *feeling* and *judging* two perfectly identical operations . . . *Why does one help someone who is suffering? Because one identifies with him.* But what is this honest and sublime identification? Does it relate to the physical man or the moral man? . . .

Pleasure and pain are, and always will be, the sole principles of men's actions.

I agree. And this work contains a multitude of other maxims and observations of which I should say likewise, 'I agree' – but I should then add, 'though I deny the conclusion you have drawn. You admit only corporal pleasures and pains, whereas I have experienced other kinds. And you attribute the causation of these latter to physical *sensibilité*, whereas I claim that that is only an ultimate, essential, but basic condition of such pleasures and pains. I contradict you, therefore I exist. Very well. But "I contradict you *because I exist*" is no more tenable a proposition than "I need a pistol to blow a man's brains out, therefore I am blowing a man's brains out because I have a pistol." '

There are learned men, it is said, who condemn themselves to lives spent in isolation, withdrawn from society. Now, how can we convince ourselves that the passion these men have for their work is based on the love of physical pleasures, especially on a desire for women? How are we to reconcile these irreconcilables?

The fact is that they cannot be reconciled. The objection you have made to yourself is insoluble . . .

Why not dispense with all those subtleties, which no good mind could ever accept, and believe that when Leibniz shut himself away

568

at the age of twenty and spent thirty years in his dressing-gown, buried in the deeps of geometry or lost in the dark regions of metaphysics, he was no more thinking of obtaining an appointment, or of sleeping with a woman, or of filling an old chest with gold, than he would have been if faced with imminent death. He was a thinking-machine, just as the stocking-loom is a weaving-machine. He was a being who enjoyed thinking. He was a sage or a madman, whichever you prefer, who attributed an infinite value to the praise of his fellow men and who loved the sound of applause as much as any miser ever loved the ring of gold coin . . .

'Since he is a man,' you say, 'he likes women.'

I don't know whether that's true or not.

'Since he likes women, he is using the only means at his disposal to obtain their favours.'

If that is true, then go into his room, present him with all the most beautiful women you can find, and let him enjoy them – on condition that he renounces any further attempt to solve his problem. He will not accept.

'He is ambitious for high position.'

Offer him the post of prime minister if he will throw his *Treatise on Preestablished Harmony* onto the fire. He will certainly not do so . . .

The fact is that there is a principle our author has not grasped: that man's reason is an instrument corresponding in all its variety to animal instinct; mankind includes within itself analogues of all the various kinds of animals, and it is no more possible to take a man out of his own particular subdivision that it is to take an animal out of its species – not, at least, without denaturing them both and without putting oneself to a great deal of trouble simply in order to make them into two stupid beasts. I grant that man combines ideas, just as a fish swims and a bird flies; but each man is impelled by his particular organization, character, temperament and natural aptitude to combine such and such ideas rather than such and such other ones. Chance and, to an even greater extent, the needs of life dispose of us according to their caprice. Who knows this better than I? It is the reason why, for almost thirty consecutive years, against my personal taste, I worked constantly on the *Encyclopédie* and wrote only two plays. It is the reason why talents are misplaced, why every calling in our society is filled with unhappy men performing their tasks in a mediocre fashion, why the man who might have been a great artist ends up merely a poor scholar or an

569

570

571

indifferent jurist. And that is the true story behind our lives, not all these subtle propositions, in which I can see much wisdom but no truth, charming details accompanied by absurd conclusions, and everywhere the portrait of the author presented to us as a portrait of man.

For what do we learn from all these assertions Helvétius has made? That he was born with a great deal of sensuality and that, in his wanderings through society, he has run up against a great many lackeys and swindlers.

And from all that I have just said, what conclusion should we draw? That men do not seek glory, wealth and honours merely as coin with which to pay for sensual pleasures . . .

What is the source in man of that urge to attempt something at   573
the very moment it becomes dangerous? What have you to say about all those philosophers, our friends and contemporaries, who have so boldly taken priests and even kings to task? They cannot use their names; their aim cannot be either fame, self-interest or sensual gratification, for where is the woman they wish to lie with, the appointment their ambition has singled out for them, or the flood of wealth that is to inundate their lives? We both of us know men of this kind who, though already enjoying all these advantages, disdain them because such things cannot bring them happiness and who, moreover, could be deprived of them by the slightest indiscretion on the part of their friends or the least suspicion in the minds of the civil authorities. How can you reduce this generous enthusiasm that exposes them to the loss of their personal liberty, of their fortunes, of even their honour and their lives – how, without the most pitiable abuse of words, can you in the final analysis reduce all this to mere sensual pleasures? They are outraged by our prejudices, they groan at the errors with which we make our lives such torture; from the midst of the darkness where we are all charging about, scourging one another on, their voices can be heard calling us to a better fate: that is how they satisfy their impulse to reflect and meditate, that is how they yield to their natural inclinations, which have been reinforced by education, and to the goodness ever present in their hearts – hearts weary of being merely spectators of the ills to which the wretched human race has been so cruelly and for so long subjected. They will avenge mankind; yes, they will avenge it; that is what they say to themselves.   574
And what the final goal of their intention is, I do not know, unless it be this dangerous honour itself.

I know what you will say: 'They flatter themselves that their names will someday come to be known and that their memory will be eternally honoured among men.' I agree. But what does such heroic vanity have in common with physical *sensibilité* or with the sort of abject reward that you would reduce it to?

'They are gratified in advance by hearing the sweet strains of future voices raised in concert to celebrate their glory, and their hearts leap with joy at the sound.'

'And so?'

'Does that leaping in their hearts not presuppose physical *sensibilité*?'

'Yes, since it presupposes a heart that can leap. But does a condition without which something is impossible also constitute its motive? Again and again, always the same sophistry . . . '

We are all born with good minds!   594

But what is a good mind? It is one that denies those things that ought to be denied and affirms those things that ought to be affirmed. Do we really all bring this precious gift into the world with us when we are born? And even if nature did give it to us, would it be in our power to preserve it?

However much I should like to share the opinion of Helvétius in this matter, I cannot. Why not? Why do I persist in my conviction that one of this writer's greatest inconsistencies lies in his attribu-ting the difference between man and beasts to the difference in their organizations and then excluding that same cause when it comes to explaining the difference between one man and another? Why does it seem to him to be proven that every man is equally fitted for everything and that his dull-witted porter has as much intelligence as he himself, potentially at least, when such an asser-tion seems to me the most palpable of absurdities? Why are all his subtlety, his eloquence and his arguments insufficient to make me agree with him that all our likes and dislikes may be reduced in the last analysis to a desire for or a fear of sensory and physical pain or pleasure?

Any man who has a normal physical constitution is capable of everything . . .

[But] I have not found the truth, and I have looked for it with more attributes than you say are necessary. I will say more: though I have met with problems that seemed at first glance to be rather   595 complicated, yet turned out to be quite simple when I looked into them, there have also been others, apparently quite simple at first glance, that I was subsequently forced to recognize as being beyond my powers. For example, I am convinced that even in a society as badly ordered as ours, one in which vice when it succeeds is often acclaimed and virtue when it fails is almost always mocked, I am convinced, I say, that when all is said and done, the best way of achieving happiness is to be virtuous. To my way of thinking, the most important and interesting work yet to be written is one dealing thoroughly with this subject; it is the achievement I would recall with greatest satisfaction in my last moment. It is a subject I have considered a hundred times, and with all the intellectual concentration of which I am capable. I was in possession, I believe, of all the necessary data. And yet, though I hesitate to admit it, I have never dared to take up my pen and write even so much as the first line of it. I said to myself, 'If I do not emerge victorious from this attempt, then I shall have made myself an advocate of wickedness; I shall have betrayed the cause of virtue; I shall have encouraged man to be vicious. No, I am not equal to this sublime task; even if I were to devote my whole life to it, it would be in vain.'

Would you like a simpler problem? Here it is: Should the philosopher, if summoned before a court of law, confess his true opinions at the peril of his life? Was Socrates right or wrong to stay in prison?

And think how many other subjects there are that have more to do with character than with logic! Will you dare to cast blame upon the sincere and courageous man who prefers to die rather than to retract and, by that retraction, to sully his own reputation and that of his fellow believers? If such a role is noble and beautiful in a tragedy or any other work of art, why should it be senseless or   596 ridiculous in reality?

What is the best form of government for a great empire? And what reliable precautions could we devise that would effectively limit its sovereign power?

Is there any case at all in which it is permissible for a subject to raise his hand against his king? And if perchance such a case does exist, what is it? In what circumstances may a private individual consider himself to be the interpreter of the wills of all other individuals? Is eloquence a good thing or a bad thing? Must the happiness of the present generation be sacrificed to the [uncertain] chances of a revolution for the sake of the happiness of the generation to come?

Is the savage state preferable to the civilized state?

None of these is a problem for children. Do you really believe that all men are endowed by nature with the capacity to resolve them? Without foolish modesty, I beg you to except me. They are questions that would have taxed even Montesquieu's powers to the full and taken up most of his life . . .

Helvétius says: 'Character depends entirely on circumstances.' 601
Substitute: 'I think that circumstances modify character.' *He says*: 'You can give man the temperament you want him to have, and whatever may be his natural temperament he will not have either more or less aptitude for genius.' *Substitute*: 'Temperament is not always an insuperable barrier to the progress of the mind . . . ' *He says*: 'All that proceeds from man can be reduced, in the last 602 analysis, to physical *sensibilité.*' *Substitute*: 'As condition, but not as cause . . . ' *He says*: 'Innumerable experiments have proved 611 that men everywhere are essentially the same.' *Substitute*: 'If he means one society of free and civilized men is much like another society of free and civilized men, then that is more or less true. If he means that man is everywhere a man as opposed to being a horse, then that is a platitude. If he means that in any society, one man is essentially the equal of another, then that is a mistake . . . '

It is nature, it is the physical constitution, it is purely physical 615 causes which prepare the man of genius; it is moral causes which make him blossom; it is concentrated study, acquired knowledge which leads him to fortunate conjectures; it is these conjectures verified by experiment which immortalize him . . .

The fruitful idea, however bizarre it may be, however haphazard 617 it may appear, does not resemble in any way the stone which comes loose from a roof and falls onto a head. The stone will hit indiscriminately any head which might be in the path of its fall. It is not like that with the idea . . .

We do not provide what nature has refused; perhaps we destroy what she has given. The culture of education improves her gifts . . . A natural disposition of some vice, virtue or talent, by being opposed, can be eradicated; the organ remains but it has no energy . . . The benefit of education lies in improving a natural aptitude if it is good, and stifling or diverting it if it is bad, but never in providing some aptitude which is missing . . .

III

Diderot's affirmation that there was an essentially human dimension of intellectual and moral activity has its parallel in his aesthetic writings, notably the *Salon de 1767* and the *Paradoxe sur le comédien* with their insistence on an autonomous realm of art. It is clear, though, from the final extract of the *Réfutation d'Helvétius* given above, that Diderot still regarded these activities as taking place within a generally determinist framework.

What exactly this meant remained something of a problem. In part this was due to the fact that Diderot never distinguished clearly between different kinds of causes that affect human beings – genetic, physiological, sociological, geographical, etc. – so that determinism remained for him even more loose and unwieldly an idea that it usually is. But even if he had restricted himself, as he was inclined, to physiological determinism he still faced a very difficult problem, and one that remains unsolved today. Diderot's insistence that there must be a physical correlation to any mental state was one that would now find general agreement. But that does not mean that any mental state is uniquely determined by a physical cause, and we do not yet understand the exact relation of the mind to the brain. Diderot's difficulties in this area have often been put down to conceptual confusion, an inability to distinguish between metaphysical freedom and psychological free will. In some contexts this is a fair comment. But it should also be recognized that he frequently displayed insights which show a remarkable grasp of an elusive problem.*

About one thing we can be certain. In the later years of his life Diderot saw no conflict between his ethical and scientific views. This is demonstrated clearly in another work of marginalia, now known as the *Commentaire sur Hemsterhuis*.

Hemsterhuis was a Dutch philosopher who met Diderot in Holland and asked him to comment on his *Lettre sur l'homme et ses rapports*; he provided him with a copy specially interleaved with blank pages for this purpose. The book, first published in 1772, was a short treatise setting out Christian principles in idealistic, quasi-Platonic terms. Diderot's commentary, which was only discovered

---

* Diderot's subtlety in this matter can be appreciated if his open-ended treatment – 'I do not preach or pronounce, I question'[33] – is compared with the similar but much more cut-and-dried assertions of Holbach in his *Système de la nature* (Part I, Chs. 11 and 12).

twenty years ago, throws further light on how he regarded his moral views as being securely grounded on an empirical and determinist basis, but their being no less effective for that.

Commentaire sur Hemsterhuis

No author, materialist or not, has ever set out to make the notions of vice and virtue ridiculous, or to attack the reality of moral behaviour. The materialists, rejecting the existence of God, base the ideas of just and unjust on the eternal relationships between man and man.   45

Man does nothing by himself. There is always a cause, either internal or external, that moves him.   111

I know of no movement that the animal cannot modify, that some of them do modify, and which a man may modify if he has self-control (*se possédait*).   135

There is only one single activity in man: that is to feel. That activity, which is never free, takes the form of thought, reasoning, deliberation, desire or aversion.   155

Spontaneity is nothing other than my necessary acquiescence in doing what I necessarily do in the present moment . . . The acquiescence to produce the effect which one necessarily produces, as a single cause, is nothing other than the consciousness of what one is at the moment of acting. So *I will* is synonymous with *I am such*.   157,159

This *self* wants to be happy. This constant tendency is the eternal, permanent source of all duties, even the most meticulous. Every law contrary [to this tendency] is a crime of *lèse-humanité*, an act of tyranny.   243

Instead of *soul* I say *origin of the bundle* [of fibres] or *man*. You have an unintelligible little *harpist* there, who is not in that spot, who has no organs, no kind of touch and who plucks the strings. For my part I do without him very well.   255

[Moral ideas] are sometimes stronger than physical causes.   287

Duty and virtue are synonymous, or if there is any difference it is that virtue is only duty fulfilled. We should look for the notion of duty in that of individual happiness, properly understood. A wicked man is one who wants his happiness and does the opposite of what he wants. He does not see further than his nose; he calculates badly; he makes false moves at every step. 297

We have no general idea of virtue; we have one word which we use to cover a great number of acts which have one quality in common, doing good (*bienfaisance*). 299

We cannot exist for long without conceiving ideas of order and disorder, doing good and doing harm, love and aversion, in us and in others. It is impossible that we do not judge our own actions, by comparing them with these ideas. It is impossible that we do not admit to ourselves how they agree or oppose those ideas; hence the conscience which judges. It is impossible for us to refuse the contempt which we would have for someone else who might have committed such acts; hence the origin of remorse. It is impossible that we are aware of others' detestation for those acts and those who commit them without blushing; hence [the origin of] shame. Or without the fear of being discovered and of being punished for them; hence the uneasiness of the wrongdoer. 315

I would have committed many bad deeds, perhaps even crimes, if my judgement had not tempered my *sensibilité*. 333

The idea of duty is always inseparable from that of happiness. 361

Some men are virtuous because they are naturally drawn to virtue by their character, fortified by a good education; others are virtuous as a result of experience which has taught them that, taken all in all, being a good man is a surer way to happiness in this world than being wicked. 441

Freedom is a chimera. 501

Intolerance has [caused] philosophy to put on a harlequin's costume . . . For my part I have saved myself by using the most subtly ironic tone that I could find, by being sweeping, laconic and obscure. 513

IV

In the *Réfutation d'Helvétius* Diderot declared that he had often wanted to write a book demonstrating that 'the best way of achieving happiness is to be virtuous' but he had not done so largely because of the fear that if he was unsuccessful he would have been 'an advocate of wickedness . . . and [would have] encouraged man to be vicious'. The same desire and fear occur in a letter of 1759.[34] The failure to write this work stemmed from a problem which was as fundamental to Diderot's conception of morality as the problem of freedom. It was a problem that arose from a central feature of any empirical theory, that of basing morality on pleasure.

> Wicked men have an initial impulse which is strong, but it is only good men who persevere. That is a necessary consequence of the nature of man, who loves pleasure and hates pain, of the nature of wickedness, which always gives pain, and of the nature of goodness, the practice of which is always accompanied by pleasure.[35]

Two difficulties arose from this belief. The first was that of relativism. Generally speaking, human morality existed because men were basically similar physical creatures, who derived similar pleasure from the same actions and attitudes. But while human beings could be seen as a single species, distinct from other species, there were among human beings immense differences of physical type, upbringing and so forth. 'If there is a morality appropriate to a species, perhaps within the same species there is a morality appropriate to different individuals, or at least to different groups or collections of similar individuals.'[36]

Diderot had no answer to this problem, but it only worried him intermittently. Far more serious was the second difficulty, which arose from the fact the wicked could take pleasure in their wickedness, that evil could be as emotionally satisfying as the good. This was the fear that threatened Diderot's whole moral belief and prevented him writing a moral treatise. The idea crops up continually in his writings. Not only did he find himself admitting that the moral and aesthetic impulses were quite separate, and that the morally objectionable could be aesthetically productive (see p. 280), he also found himself admiring the evildoer. In the amoral characters of Gousse[37] or Père Hudson[38] in *Jacques le fataliste*, in

the boldness and courage of Damiens, who attempted to assassin-
ate Louis XV,[39] above all in the character of Rameau's Nephew
Diderot made it vividly clear that evil could be accompanied by
pleasure. Even in the *Commentaire sur Hemsterhuis,* which is
concerned to show that atheism and materialism are no less moral
than Christianity, we find the remark: 'the wicked man sometimes
feels remorse at not having done as much evil as he could'.[40]

This problem had already been indicated by the *philosophe* La
Mettrie in his *Discours sur le bonheur* (1750), as Diderot indicated
in his *Commentaire.*[41] While Diderot was appalled by the difficulty,
La Mettrie adopted an attitude similar to the unqualified hedonism
later advocated by De Sade. The degree of unease which La
Mettrie caused Diderot is evident from the violent attack on him
that occurs in the *Essai sur les règnes de Claude et de Néron.*

> [His name is] justly denounced, [he is] an author with no judge-
> ment . . . who has not written a single good line in his *Traité du
> bonheur* . . . [where he says] that man is perverse by nature . . .
> He seems to be concerned to calm the mind of the criminal in his
> crime, and the corrupt man in his wickedness; his coarse argu-
> ments – dangerous on account of the cheerfulness with which he
> seasons them – reveal a writer who has not the first idea of the
> true foundations of morality . . . His principles, if pushed to
> their extreme consequences, would overturn every system of
> law, would absolve parents from the education of their children,
> would shut up in a madhouse the brave man who is stupidly
> struggling against his dissolute inclinations, and would ensure
> immortality to the wicked man who abandons himself without
> remorse to his inclinations . . . La Mettrie, dissolute, imperti-
> nent, idiot, flatterer, was made for a life in royal courts and the
> favour of powerful men. He died as he deserved to die,* victim
> of his greed and his madness; he was killed by ignorance of the
> art which he professed [to know].[42]

Diderot may in this final work denounce La Mettrie and extol the
moral example of Seneca, but he cannot disguise the threat which
the former posed. It is for this reason that we find a renewed
emphasis in his later works on a social dimension to morality. The
attention moves from the individual to society. 'Domestic edu-

---

* La Mettrie died after eating a large meal.

cation and . . . general morality,' he wrote in the *Essai*, 'are two moulds which alter the original form of the character.'[43] 'The true notion [of the sacred name of virtue] is based on public utility.'[44] The same idea occurs in the *Entretien d'un philosophe avec la maréchale*:

> Ensure that the good of individuals is so closely related to the general good that a citizen can hardly harm society without harming himself. Assure virtue its reward as you have assured wickedness its punishment, and make sure that . . . wherever it is found merit will lead to the highest positions in the State. You can then expect there to be no wicked people except a small number whose perverse nature leads them to wrongdoing and which nothing can correct.[45]

At the end of his life Diderot was on the verge of seeing a political or sociological dimension to morality. But that step was one he never took.

13

Sexuality

Sexuality held for Diderot a lifelong fascination. His interest took different forms. At its most exalted sexual pleasure was for him the most vivid manifestation of that *natura creatrix* which Lucretius had also praised.[1] He wrote in the article 'Animal' of 'that procreative virtue which is constantly active and never destroyed, and which is to us . . . a mystery the depths of which it seems we will never be allowed to sound;'[2] his article 'Jouissance' (see p. 115) was a notable declaration of this attitude, as was the aesthetic ideal of the inhabitants of Tahiti in the *Supplément au Voyage de Bougainville* – not a '*Vénus galante*' but a '*Vénus féconde*'[3]. At its lowest it was the occasion of some prurient writing, as in certain episodes in *Jacques le fataliste* and *Les Bijoux indiscrets*. The central theme of the latter was female sexuality, and although the overall tone and purpose of the book was light-hearted, mischievous and obscene, there was an underlying seriousness to some aspects of this subject. Naigeon was mistaken when he said that Diderot 'daily regretted having written *Les Bijoux indiscrets*',[4] for Diderot cared enough about the book to add two chapters (XVIII,XIX) to it later. These dealt with the need for marriage partners to be well matched physically, an example of the way he was also concerned to treat sexuality in a practical way. This was evident in the last section of *Le Rêve de d'Alembert*, where Bordeu speaks in favour of masturbation, or in the one unconventional aspect of Diderot's education of his daughter, his making sure she understood human anatomy in its different forms. He frequently spoke of sexual pleasure as being 'the greatest pleasure that can be imagined'.[5]

During 1770 Diderot had a brief, but on his side intense, love-affair with Madame de Maux, which seems to have provided the impetus for a series of works over the next few years, all concerned with sexuality. One feature of these works was the portrayal of women as both more elemental and more inexplicable than men. In a short essay *Sur les femmes*, written in 1772, we find an extra-ordinary mixture of views. At one moment admiring – 'when you write of women you should dip your pen in the rainbow and scatter the dust of butterfly wings on your words'[6] – the next brusque – 'ideas of justice, virtue, vice, good and evil, float superficially in [women's] souls . . . They have preserved all the energy of their natural egoism and self-interest . . . more civilized than us on the outside, they have remained true savages within, all of them more or less machiavellian. The symbol of women in general is that of the Apocalypse, on whose forehead was written: MYSTERY.'[7] At times Diderot attributes this to the physical characteristics of women, 'organized completely the opposite way'[8] to men, at other times to the way they have been treated socially: 'in almost every country the cruelty of civil laws against women has been united with the cruelty of nature. They have been treated like idiot children.'[9] At times both explanations are combined: 'inscrutable when they dissemble, cruel in revenge, steady in their plans, unscrupulous about how to achieve success, animated by a profound and secret hatred against the despotism of men, it seems that there is among them a clear plot to [win] domination, a sort of league like that which exists among priests in every country.'[10]

Another theme in these works was the inconstancy of human emotions and particularly sexual feelings.

The first oath made by two creatures of flesh was taken at the foot of a rock which was crumbling into dust; they called to witness their constancy a sky which is never for one moment the same. Everything within them and around them was in a state of transition, and they believed that their hearts were free from change[11] . . . You can be inconstant in love . . . without being devoid of honour and honesty. We are not in charge either of stopping a passion which has taken light, nor of prolonging one which has died out.[12]

The combination of these two themes, female behaviour and sexual infidelity, produced one of Diderot's most vivid and impressive pieces of fiction in the Madame de la Pommeraye episode in *Jacques le fataliste*.[13]

In the short stories *Ceci n'est pas un conte* and *Madame de la Carlière* Diderot depicted love-affairs in which there had been an unhappy disparity between the two partners' expectations. In the latter, which in its first printed version had the title *Sur l'inconséquence du jugement public de nos actions particulières*, there was a suggestion that social pressures or prejudices had distorted the lovers' feelings, that public judgement was more to blame than individual actions. 'I have my own ideas, maybe correct, certainly unusual,' concludes the narrator of the story, 'on certain acts which I regard less as vices of men than as consequences of our absurd systems of law, which produce equally absurd behaviour and a corruption which I would willingly call artificial. That is not very clear but I will perhaps make it clear some other time.'[14] The *Supplément au Voyage de Bougainville* takes up the thread where this story ends and attempts to reach a conclusion about the problems which the two stories had posed. Diderot's focus expands steadily through the three works, until in the *Supplément* he is dealing not simply with sexuality but the nature of civilization itself.

Bougainville was a French soldier, sailor, mathematician and writer who had made a journey round the world between 1766 and 1769. He had returned to France with a Tahitian, Aotourou, who had spent a year in Paris, and in 1771 his account of his journey, the *Voyage de Bougainville* was published. Like Wallis, who had discovered Tahiti just before him, and Cook, who visited the islands shortly after, Bougainville had been struck by the generous nature and especially the sexual freedom which the inhabitants displayed. Diderot wrote a review of this book (presumably for the *Correspondance littéraire*, though it was not published there), in which he enthused over the natural virtues of these people and the way their sexual freedom was part of a much broader and more profound freedom:

Ah! Monsieur de Bougainville, sail away from the shores of these innocent and fortunate Tahitians; they are happy and you can only harm their happiness. They follow the instinct of nature, and you are going to erase its noble, sacred character. Everything belongs to everyone, and you are going to bring them the fatal distinction of 'mine' and 'thine'. Their wives and daughters belong to all and you are going to set alight the furies of love and jealousy among them . . . This man whom you are grabbing like an animal or a plant is a child of nature like you. What right have you over him? Leave him his way of life, it is more upright and wise than yours. His ignorance is worth more than all your enlightenment.[15]

The following year, 1772, Diderot expanded this review into a work he called the *Supplément au Voyage de Bougainville*, and subtitled a *Dialogue between A and B on the disadvantage of attaching moral ideas to certain physical acts which have nothing to do with them.* It opens with a conversation between A and B who, we gather from the remarks which open and close the work, are the two men who discussed the story of Madame de la Carlière. B has been reading Bougainville's *Voyage* and they discuss aspects of his journey and Aotourou's reactions to life in Paris; when the latter returns to Tahiti, B maintains, the people there will think he 'is a liar rather than believe that we are so mad . . . The life of the savage is so simple, and our societies are such complex mechanisms. The Tahitian is in touch with the world as it was originally and the European is reaching the point of its old age. The distance between us is greater than that between a new-born child and a decrepit old man. He understands nothing of our customs, our laws, or he sees in them only fetters disguised in a hundred different ways, which can only provoke indignation and contempt in a creature for whom freedom is the most profound of feelings.'[16] A accuses B of wanting to make a 'fable' about Tahiti. B denies this and says that A would agree if he had read the supplement to Bougainville's account. As he has a copy of this supposed supplement to hand the two men look at it. Most of Diderot's work consists of extracts from it, framed by the dialogue between A and B. The extracts begin with a valediction spoken to Bougainville by an old inhabitant of Tahiti.

Supplément au Voyage de Bougainville

'We are innocent, we are happy; and you can only spoil our happi-   466
ness. We follow the pure instinct of nature; and you have tried to erase its character from our souls. Here everything belongs to

everybody. You have preached to us I know not what distinctions between "mine" and "thine". Our daughters and our wives are 467 common to us all. You have shared this privilege with us; and you have set alight passions in them previously unknown. They have become maddened in your arms; you have become ferocious in theirs. They have begun to hate each other; you have slain each other for them, and they have returned to us stained with your blood. We are a free people; and now you have planted in our country the title deeds of our future slavery. You are neither a god nor a demon; who are you, then, to make slaves? Orou! You understand the language of these men, tell us all, as you have told me, what they have written on this sheet of metal: "This country is ours." This country yours? And why? Because you have walked on it? If a Tahitian landed one day on your shores, and scratched on one of your rocks or on the bark of your trees: "This country belongs to the people of Tahiti", what would you think?

'The Tahitian you want to seize like an animal is your brother. 468 You are both children of nature; what right have you over him that he has not over you? When you came, did we rush upon you, did we pillage your ship? Did we seize you and expose you to the arrows of our enemies? Did we yoke you with the animals for toil in our fields? No. We respected our own likeness in you. Leave us to our ways; they are wiser and more honest than yours. We do not want to barter what you call our ignorance for your useless enlightenment. Everything that is necessary and good for us we possess. Do we deserve contempt, because we have not known how to develop superfluous needs? When we hunger, we have enough to eat; when we are cold we have what we need to clothe us. You have been in our huts; what is lacking there, in your opinion? You may pursue as far as you like what you call the comforts of life; but allow sensible people to call a halt, when they would only have obtained imaginary good from the continuation of their painful efforts. If you persuade us to exceed the narrow limits of our needs, when shall we ever finish toiling? . . .

[He contrasts the physical fitness of his people with that of the Europeans and condemns the latter for having brought venereal disease and a sense of shame to the islands:] 'the idea of crime and the threat of disease came to us through you' (470).

[After this, says B, the *Supplément* contains a conversation between the expedition's almoner and Orou, the Tahitian who had written down and translated the old man's speech. Each of

Bougainville's crew had been welcomed by an islander and taken
into his home, the almoner being taken in by Orou, his wife and
their three daughters.]

When he was about to go to bed, Orou, who had been absent   475
with his family, reappeared, and presenting to him his wife and
three daughters, all naked, said: 'You have eaten, you are young
and in good health; if you sleep alone you will sleep badly, for man
needs a companion beside him at night. There is my wife, there are
my daughters; choose the one who pleases you best. But if you wish
to oblige me you will give preference to the youngest of my
daughters, who has not yet had any children.' The mother added:
'Alas! But it's no good complaining about it; poor Thia! it is not her
fault.'

The almoner answered that his religion, his office, good morals
and decency would not allow him to accept these offers.

Orou replied: 'I do not know what this thing is that you call   476
"religion"; but I can only think ill of it, since it prevents you from
enjoying an innocent pleasure to which nature, the sovereign mistress, invites us all; which prevents you from giving existence to one
of your own kind, from doing a service which a father, mother and
children all ask of you, from doing something for a host who has
received you well, and from enriching a nation, by giving it one
more citizen. I do not know what this thing is which you call your
"office" but your first duty is to be a man and to be grateful . . .'

[The youngest daughter also asked the almoner to sleep with her.
The almoner agreed. Next day he and Orou discussed his religion.
He explains how God had decreed that sex should only take place
between two people who were lifelong partners and belonged
exclusively to one another. Orou declares these precepts to be
'opposed to nature and contrary to reason, and therefore made to
multiply crimes'. They were 'contrary to nature because they suppose that a free, thinking and feeling creature can be the property
of another creature like him or her' and they refused 'to admit that
change is part of us' (480). He continues:]

'Do you want to know what is good and what is bad in all times
and in all places? Hold fast to the nature of things and of actions;   482
to your relations with your fellows; to the influence of your conduct
on your individual usefulness and the general good. You are mad if
you believe that there is anything, high or low in the universe,
which can add to or subtract from the laws of nature. Her eternal
will is that good should be preferred to evil, and the general good to

the individual good. You may ordain the opposite but you will not be obeyed. You will multiply the number of malefactors and the wretched by fear, punishment and remorse. You will deprave consciences; you will corrupt minds. They will not know what to do or what to avoid. Disturbed in their state of innocence, at ease with crime, they will have lost their guiding star.'

[He asks: do young people not go against the law in the almoner's country. The latter admits that they do, but then public opinion punishes them. Orou is appalled; he sees how destructive such a system must be.]

'As soon as one allows oneself to dispose at pleasure of the ideas 483 of justice and ownership, to take away or to give an arbitrary character to things, to attribute or deny good or evil to certain actions, capriciously, then one can be censorious, vindictive, suspicious, tyrannical, envious, jealous, deceitful. There is spying, 484 quarrelling, cheating and lying; daughters deceive their parents, wives their husbands. Girls, yes, I don't doubt it, will strangle their infants, suspicious fathers will hate and neglect theirs, mothers will leave them and abandon them to their fates. And crime and debauchery will show themselves in all their forms. I know all that as if I had lived among you. It is so, because it must be so; and your society, of which your leader boasts because of its good order, will only be a swarm of hypocrites who secretly trample all laws under foot; or else of unfortunates who are themselves the instruments of their own suffering in submitting; or else of imbeciles in whom prejudices have quite stifled the voice of nature; or else of abnormal creatures in whom nature does not protest her rights.'

[Orou then explains the flexible arrangements in Tahiti where children are shared and no one has property rights over their offspring, where all of appropriate age are encouraged to have children, and where the advent of sexuality in puberty is a matter of general rejoicing. Incest is permitted and the only restrictions are biological, i.e. those of age or menstruation. In place of marital or parental love there is a sense of everyone's interest being best served by these arrangements. In the final section A and B discuss these conditions.]

A   What useful conclusions are to be drawn from the strange 504 manners and customs of an uncivilized people?

B   I see that as soon as some physical causes, such as, for example, the necessity for conquering the barrenness of the soil, have stimulated man's intelligence, this impetus carries him far beyond his [immediate] objective, and that when the period of need has passed, he is carried off into the limitless realm of fantasy, from which there is no coming back. May the happy people of Tahiti stay where they are! I see that except in this remote corner of our globe, there has never been morality and perhaps never will be anywhere.

A   Then what do you understand by morality?

B   I understand a general submission to, and a conduct consistent with, good or bad laws. If the laws are good, morals are good; if the laws are bad, morals are bad; if laws, good or bad, are not observed at all, which is the worst condition of a society, then there is no morality at all. Now, how can laws be observed if they contradict one another? Examine the history of various epochs and nations, both ancient and modern, and you will find men subjected   505 to three codes of law, the laws of nature, civil law and the law of religion, and constrained to infringe alternately all these codes, which have never been in agreement . . .

A   From which you conclude, no doubt, that in basing morality on the eternal relations which exist between men, the law of religion may become superfluous, and that civil law ought only to be the enunciation of the laws of nature.

B   And that, under pain of multiplying the wicked instead of making the good.

A   Or that, if it be judged necessary to keep all three codes, the last two should only be exact copies of the first, which we carry always graven in our hearts and which will always be the most powerful.

B   That's not very exact. We have at birth only a similar physical constitution with other beings, the same needs, an attraction towards the same pleasures, a common aversion for the same pains; that is what makes man as he is, and that ought to be the basis of the morality suitable for him.

A   That's not easy.

B   It is not so difficult. I would willingly believe the most primitive people on earth, a Tahitian, who has kept scrupulously to the laws of nature, nearer to a good code of laws than any civilized people.

A   Because it is easier for him to get rid of his excess of primitiveness, than for us to retrace our steps and remedy our abuses.

[They discuss differing attitudes to sex, marriage, jealousy, flirtatiousness etc.]

A   But how has it happened that an act whose end is so solemn,   509
and to which nature invites us by the most powerful attraction, that
the noblest, most delicious and most innocent of pleasures should
have become the most abundant source of our depravities and our
evils?

B   Orou explained it at least ten times to the almoner; now
listen again and try to remember it. It is by the tyranny of man, who
has converted the possession of a woman into a matter of property;
by the manners and customs which have overloaded with stipu-
lations the union of marriage; by civil laws which have subjected
marriage to an infinity of formalities; by the very nature of our
society, where the diversity of fortune and rank has instituted rules
of what is and is not done; by a peculiar contradiction common to   510
all existing societies, whereby the birth of a child, always regarded
as an increase of wealth for the nation, more often and more
certainly means an increase of poverty to the family; by the political
opinions of sovereigns who relate everything to their own interest
and security; by religious institutions which have applied the names
vices and virtues to actions which were not susceptible to any
morality.

How far we are from naturalness and happiness! The empire of
nature cannot be destroyed; you may try to thwart it with obstacles,
but it will prevail . . .

A   How short the law of nations would be, if it conformed
exactly to the law of nature! How many errors and vices would man
be spared!

B   Would you like to know the short history of almost all our
miseries? Here it is. There existed a natural man; an artificial man
was introduced within this man; and within this cavern a civil war   511
breaks out, which lasts for life. Sometimes the natural man is
stronger; sometimes he is felled by the artificial, moral man; and in
both cases the miserable monster is plagued, tortured, tormented,
stretched on the rack; ceaselessly lamenting, always wretched,
whether a false enthusiasm of glory carries him away and intoxi-
cates him, or a false shame bows him and casts him down. Nevertheless there are extreme circumstances which bring man back to
his original simplicity.

A   Want and sickness, two great exorcists.

B   You have named them. In reality, what becomes of all these
conventional virtues then? In want, a man has no remorse; and in
sickness a woman is without shame.

A   So I have observed.

B   But another phenomenon which will not have escaped you either, is that the return of the artificial and moral man follows step by step the progress from illness to convalescence, and from convalescence to a state of health. The moment when the bodily infirmity ceases is the one when the internal civil war begins again, and almost always to the disadvantage of the invader.

A   That's true. I have myself experienced in convalescence that the natural man had deadly strength against the artificial and moral man. But now tell me, must we civilize man or abandon him to his instincts?

B   Must you have a precise answer?

A   Undoubtedly.

B   If you propose to be his tyrant, then civilize him, persecute him all you are able with a morality contrary to nature; fetter him in all ways; impede his actions with a thousand obstacles; frighten him   512
with phantoms, make eternal the war in the cavern, and let the natural man be always shackled at the feet of the moral man. But do you want him to be happy and free? Then don't meddle with his affairs; plenty of unforeseen events will lead him towards enlightenment and to depravity. And always remain convinced, that it is not for your sake but for theirs that these wise lawgivers have moulded you and made you artificial like you are. I appeal to all political, civil and religious institutions; examine them deeply; and I shall be greatly deceived, if you don't find the human race bowed century after century under the yoke which a handful of scoundrels resolved to put upon it. Beware of anyone who wants to order things. To regulate is always to make oneself master of the others by restricting them.

[Townsmen have been seen to give up all and go back to the forest but 'no one has ever seen the man of the forest clothe himself and set himself up in the town' (513).]

A   What shall we do then? Shall we return to nature, or submit   515
to the laws?

B   We must speak against insane laws until they are reformed; while waiting [for that to happen], we must submit to them. Anyone who infringes a bad law by his own private authority authorizes all others to infringe the good ones. There is less inconvenience in being mad among madmen, than in being wise alone. Let us tell ourselves, let us cry out unceasingly, that shame, punishment and dishonour have been attached to actions innocent in themselves; but let us not commit these actions, because shame, punishment and dishonour are the greatest of all evils. Let us copy the good almoner, be a monk in France, a primitive man in Tahiti.

A Take the dress of the country you are going to, and keep that of the country where you are . . .

The epigraph for the *Supplément* is taken from Horace: 'How much better – and how opposed to this – is the advice that nature, rich in her own resources, gives, if only you would use it wisely and not confuse what is to be avoided with what is to be desired. Do you think it is of no consequence whether your trouble is your own fault or beyond your control?'[17] For three-quarters of the work these words are an appropriate comment and reflection. Diderot demonstrates how the Tahitians seem to follow nature's advice and lead healthy and happy lives. The people have little idea of property, 'work and harvests arc donc communally . . . the passion of love, reduced to a simple physical appetite, produces none of our disorders. The whole island offers the image of a single large family.'[18] They have stopped at a moderate level of development (*la médiocrité*), and are free from 'superfluous needs', 'imaginary goods', 'the limitless realm of fantasy'.

In the last quarter of the work, however, Diderot's perspective alters bewilderingly. Reading it is like being in a car which has gone out of control, the momentum of its previous speed carries it relentlessly forward but the driver at the wheel is helpless. The Tahitians, who have initially been shown to be 'innocent and gentle',[19] are revealed as being severe and calculating. Sexual intercourse is not accepted as a simple pleasure, but only as a means of reproduction. If women who have passed child-bearing age want sex with a man they are liable to 'exile in the north of the island or slavery';[20] the younger women of Tahiti did not sleep with Bougainville's sailors out of friendship but because they need an increase in population, 'savages though we are we too know how to be calculating'.[21] In the ensuing dialogue between A and B the latter maintains that both marriage and jealousy, both of which we had been led to believe were unknown in Tahiti, are in fact natural – 'vices and virtues, all are equally natural'.[22] B's enthusiasm for the natural, as opposed to civilized, state seems straightforward, yet twice, when A presses him on this point, he equivocates.[23] He suggests what seems like a grotesque parody of Rousseau's idea of *dénaturation* when he talks of civilizing man by tyrannizing and persecuting him with 'a morality contrary to nature', and gives the despotic government of Venice as a possible example of this.[24]* His conclusion, that 'shame, punishment and dishonour are the greatest of all evils', seems a blatant contradiction of the earlier part of the work.

The fact is that Diderot's reflections on sexuality had brought him face to face with a problem he was not able to solve. No human feeling manifested so intensely those contingent, volatile and physical qualities which always fired his imagination, and no human experience could seem more 'natural' than the sexual impulse. In the early part of the *Supplément* where he sets the uncomplicated sexual behaviour of Tahiti within its similarly uncomplicated social circumstances he seems on the verge of grasping the conceptual relation between the two, but in the last quarter of the work he wanders further and further from achieving that understanding. A possible solution to the problem lay in that historical and sociological perspective which Rousseau had outlined in his *Discours sur l'inégalité*. Rousseau had not only described the difference between 'natural man' and 'civilized man', he had also shown the process by which the one became the other, the stages in which human nature had evolved. This had not been a matter of individual decisions but the result of social and other pressures, for human behaviour is affected by social conditions in a profound way. Diderot's *Supplément* contains several reminiscences of Rousseau's ideas but the central insight eludes him.

The question continued to preoccupy him. He was powerfully attracted to a utopian condition: 'Shall I tell you a fine paradox? It is that I am convinced that the only true happiness for the human race lies in a social state in which there would be no king, no magistrate, no priest, no laws, no "mine", no "thine", no movable property, no landed property, no vices, no virtues. And this social state,' he added, 'is damnably ideal.'[26] When presented in 1769 with a social system along these lines devised by Dom Deschamps he said: 'I suddenly found myself in the world for which I was

---

* In Book One of *Emile* Rousseau wrote that 'good social institutions are those best able to denature man, to take away [the sense which natural man has of] his absolute [i.e. completely independent, amoral] existence and give him instead a [sense of] his relative existence'.[25] It is clear from the context of this passage and elsewhere (*Du contrat social*, Bk One, Ch. 8) that Rousseau did not see this *dénaturation* as being 'contrary to nature' but a positive development from nature.

born.'[27] In the *Supplément* he depicted such a world as that of man in a state of nature. But the different worlds were merely juxtaposed; there was no historical sense, no suggestion of how the one could become or had become the other.

Diderot's failure was not only due to a conceptual limitation. It arose also out of his commitment to and pleasure in his own world. While he may have wanted a different social order for himself he wanted the existing social order for his daughter. Angélique's marriage had taken place earlier in 1772 and, as Herbert Dieckmann suggests,[28] the emotions associated with this event surely contributed to the different emphasis in the last section of the work. 'Have for your husband every imaginable condescension', Diderot wrote to her[29] in a tender and moving letter four days after the wedding. 'Restrict your society and again restrict it. Where there are many people there are many vices'[30] – words which display not only paternal concern, but also that familiar phenomenon – male anxiety about female sexuality. This was one issue on which Diderot, like most of his contemporaries (and many of our contemporaries), was still to be enlightened.

14

Politics

I

Diderot's first political writing of any consequence occurred in the article 'Autorité politique' in Volume One of the *Encyclopédie* (see p. 92). There he expressed clearly the view that the only political authority which was legitimate was that based on a contract or choice or consent, that 'true and legitimate power is necessarily limited', i.e. it must be 'reasonable and moderate', and that government was a 'public possession' which essentially belonged to the people and which they entrusted to the prince. These ideas were not original; they had been developed by the natural law theorists Grotius, Pufendorf and his French translator Barbeyrac, as well as by Locke in his *Second Treatise on Government*. There were also direct borrowings in the article from the Abbé Girard's *Synonymes françaises*[1] and from Sully's *Mémoires*. Nevertheless the forthright expression of views directly opposed to the absolutist claims of the French monarchy in a work being published *avec approbation et privilège du roi* caused an immediate outcry. The article was denounced as being 'manifestly seditious', 'not only anti-monarchical but anarchic as well',[2] and these attacks were important factors in bringing about the (temporary) suspension of publication of the *Encyclopédie* after Volume Two the following year.

Despite the alarm and hostility it caused the article was not in fact as anti-monarchical as its critics liked to claim. While it attacked arbitrary or absolute rule, as existed in Turkey, it defended a legitimate monarchy, as existed in France. If there should at some future date 'by the greatest misfortune' be no male heir to the

French throne then 'the sceptre and crown would return to the nation', but until such a putative time the French people should obey their monarchs even if 'they had an unjust, ambitious and violent king'; 'all those notions which are believed to justify resistance, when closely examined, are often only subtly phrased excuses for disloyalty'. These statements in the final paragraph of the article, which seemed to mitigate the force of the earlier paragraphs, were confirmed in the Errata which prefaced Volume Three:

> We should explain our thought. We have never suggested that the authority of legitimate princes does not come from God; we have only wanted to distinguish their authority, which people are always obliged to obey, even in such prince's disgrace, from that of usurpers . . . The sign that the authority comes from God is the consent of the people; it is this irrevocable consent which has assured the crown to Hugh Capet and his descendants.[3]

There is a certain ambivalence in all these remarks, none of them denies the right of resistance, but there is no suggestion of France being ruled by any form of government except that of a limited monarchy.

The limits were those of 'the laws of nature and of the State'. In his article 'Droit naturel' in Volume Five Diderot explained what he meant by these laws. His ideas here also followed the natural law writers in supposing man to be naturally reasonable and sociable but unlike them he does not give these faculties any divine basis or sanction; that is to say, he does not explain their existence as being due to the fact that, or the manner in which, God created man. His argument for natural right is in completely human and naturalistic terms. It is based on what he calls 'the general will', which is 'a pure act of understanding which reasons when the passions are silent on what a man can demand of his fellow man and on what his fellow man is entitled to demand of him' (see p. 100). There is an emotional disposition towards this, stemming from natural feelings of 'indignation and resentment', and there is historical evidence to support it, 'in the principles of law written down by all civilized nations' and 'the social practice of savages and barbarians'. These are helpful but they are not central; the essence of natural right emerges from applying reason to human conduct considered in social, rather than individual, terms. Such an activity is natural to man since men naturally come together in social groupings and for them reason is a natural faculty – 'man is the animal who reflects'.[4] It was some years before Diderot explained exactly why social existence should be natural – his explanation lay in men having a common need to share their efforts to ensure their survival, in the face of nature's indifference or hostility – but he never wavered in his belief that society had a natural, and not a contractual, basis. For this reason natural law in his view preceded any civil law: 'laws do not give us ideas of justice, [rather] it seems to me they pre-suppose such ideas'.[5] And good civil laws were those which reflected most closely the natural laws.

Diderot wrote a number of other articles on politics for the *Encyclopédie*: 'Bourgeois', 'Cité', 'Citoyen', 'Homme' but none of them was as important as 'Autorité politique' or 'Droit naturel'. Between them these two articles laid down the principles to which Diderot adhered for the rest of his life, above all the ideas of natural law and limited monarchy. These in turn were based on a desire for individual freedom. It has sometimes been suggested that Diderot's monistic materialism led him to an equivalent poli-tical belief in absolute authority or legal despotism.[6] This view is unquestionably wrong. While Diderot's attitude to the law and authority of his time may have been obedient and submissive, he never qualified his demand for individual freedom and he never doubted the existence of political freedom as he did that of meta-physical or psychological freedom. Furthermore, in *Le Rêve de d'Alembert* the work in which he developed his materialism most fully, he made a clear distinction between 'exact sciences', like physics and mathematics, where there were 'necessary connec-tions', and 'conjectural sciences', such as politics and ethics, in which there were only 'contingent connections' (see pp. 230-1). Both the important articles in the *Encyclopédie* began with unequivocal statements on this matter, and 'the preservation of freedom' was declared to be one of 'the fertile sources of all great things and all fine actions', along with 'the observation of the laws and the love of the *patrie*' (see pp. 93-4). For similar reasons it is also wrong to say that Diderot's moral determinism is 'basically only the justification of [his] political conservatism'.[7] Diderot was not, to be sure, radical in the way Rousseau was; but neither was he conservative. (Nor would it be wholly accurate to call him liberal, since there were some hard spots in his humanitarianism.[8]) His temperament may have had its cautious sides, and his behaviour too, but he also on

occasion acted courageously and his political views were consistently in opposition to the established institutions. The fact that he
never provided any coherent or satisfactory alternative does not
detract from the validity of such opposition. His moral determinism
was first suggested in the *Lettre à Landois* in 1756; that it had no
bearing on his political outlook can be judged from the *Épître
dédicatoire* which prefaced *Le Père de famille* two years later. The
letter takes the form of the advice Diderot would give to the
children of the Princesse de Nassau-Saarbruck, to whom the play is
dedicated. It shows clearly that his belief in authority was by no
means uncritical and that there was a difference, in his eyes,
between the necessity of human-made laws and 'the necessity of
events'. The letter's combination of humanitarian concern and
moralistic tone is characteristic of much of Diderot's political
writing.

> I would not tire of saying [to the children] that a single, powerful,
> stupid or wicked man can cause a hundred thousand other men
> to weep, groan, and curse their existence. That that kind of
> wicked man who upsets the world and tyrannizes over it is the
> true author of blasphemy. That nature has not made any men
> slaves, and nobody under heaven has more authority than
> nature. That the idea of slavery was born in bloodshed and
> conquest. That men would have no need of being governed if
> they were not wicked; and that consequently the purpose of all
> authority is to make men good. That every moral system or
> political device which tends to distance man from man is bad.
> That an institution which distinguishes one man from his fellow
> by capricious means is contrary to the views of nature; it is the art
> of cancelling out real distinctions by [introducing] imaginary
> distinctions . . . That justice is the first virtue of the person who
> commands and the only virtue which checks the complaint of the
> person who obeys. That the law should be the same for the
> person who imposes it as for the person who submits to it, and
> that it is only its necessity and its universality which cause it to be
> loved. That men will submit without trouble to the person they
> recognize as being worthy to command them. That if an indi-
> vidual's virtue can be sustained without support, it is not the
> same with a people's virtue. That people of merit should be
> rewarded and industrious men encouraged, and each should be
> brought closer to the other. That the more limited a State is the

closer political authority comes to [be like] paternal power. That
if the sovereign has the qualities of a [good] sovereign, his State
will always be extensive enough, and if he does not it will always
be too extensive. That there are men of genius everywhere and it
is up to the sovereign to make them emerge.

My son, it is in prosperity that you will display your goodness,
but it is in adversity that you will show your greatness. If there is
a time when it is good to see a man calm it is when dangers are
crowding around him. If you want to know the truth, I will say to
him, go out and mix with different occupations. Look at the
countryside. Go into a cottage, speak to the person who lives
there, or rather, look at his bed, his food, his clothes, his
dwelling-place; and you will know what those who flatter you
will seek to hide from you. Do good, and think that the necessity
of events is equal for all. Submit yourself to it, and grow accustomed to looking with the same emotion at the blow which
strikes a man and knocks him down as the fall of a tree which
would destroy his statue. You are mortal like any other man, and
when you fall a little dust will cover you like anyone else.[9]

II

The crisis over the publication of the *Encyclopédie* in 1759, and the
need thereafter to continue the work clandestinely, seems to have
made Diderot reluctant to express his political views publicly, at
least until the later years of his life. But this reluctance may also
have been due to his awareness that his generalized ideas were
remote from the specific problems which France faced. As political
questions became increasingly acute his own position varied enor-
mously. At one extreme we find the pessimistic assertion that
'maybe our society is fairly badly administered, but that is the way
it is with all societies',[10] while a year later, in 1766, he consoles
himself with the fact that he gets up each morning with the hope
that the unjust will have changed, because he cannot believe in
wickedness for long.[11] He became enthusiastic over the
physiocratic ideas of Lemercier de la Rivière and sang the praise of
agriculture in the *Salon de 1767*;[12] but in the same work he admitted
the difficulty of defining public utility,[13] a doubt no good physiocrat

would ever admit, and declared his belief in a cyclical view of history: 'the fate which rules the world wants everything to pass away. The happiest condition of a man or a state has its limit. Everything carries within it a secret seed of destruction.'[14]

His enthusiasm for the ideas of the physiocrats, like his brief interest in the abstract schemes of Dom Deschamps,[15] did not last. Such general theories could never impress him or affect him to the same degree as specific and detailed facts. And a strong argument against the physiocrats was put forward by his friend the Abbé Galiani. The latter was a remarkable man who made a deep impression on Diderot; he was a Neapolitan, working as Secretary to the Ambassador of Naples in Paris, and was gifted as an economist, a literary critic, a mimic and *raconteur*, who became one of the brightest features of the social life of the homes both of the Baron d'Holbach and Madame d'Epinay. As far as politics were concerned, wrote Diderot, 'nobody had a more sovereign contempt for those people who have only seen society through the narrow neck of a bottle of abstractions'.[16] Galiani wrote an attack on the ideas of the physiocrats, his *Dialogue sur le commerce des blés*, and when he was suddenly recalled to Naples in 1769 Diderot saw the work through the press for him.

The growing sophistication of economic speculation and the increasing crisis that was overtaking France combined to make the issues at stake both significant and contentious. Broadly speaking the physiocrats maintained that if all the many barriers and controls that affected the grain trade were lifted then distribution would improve and prosperity should follow. Galiani argued that completely free trade would benefit those who were trading and supplying at the expense of those in need, and that some controls were essential. In 1770 Diderot made an extended trip to Langres and Bourbonne.[17] The restrictions on the grain trade had been lifted six years previously and that year (1770) the price of corn reached its highest level before 1787. What Diderot saw of the hard conditions endured by the peasants gave him visible confirmation of Galiani's argument that the cause of free trade in grain was mistaken. When this argument was attacked by Morellet he wrote a reply, the *Apologie de l'abbé Galiani*.

The work takes the form of impulsive and often splenetic comments on Morellet's ideas, criticizing and abusing him for being out of touch with the real world: 'you utopianize (*utopisez*)',[18] 'you do not have the first idea of what happens in times of famine';[19] 'if you want to get a proper idea you must abandon general notions and go into all the detail of fears, hope, greed';[20] 'put all your fine pages into a utopia, then they'll look good';[21] 'it is facts, existing pheno- mena, which provide rungs to climb up, and not abstract specula- tions which provide steps to go down. Before we have [individual] phenomena in our heads we have nothing.'[22] This emphasis on proceeding empirically, which runs through the *Apologie de l'abbé Galiani*, gives the work a decisive place in Diderot's developing interest in politics. Although empirical analysis alone will not be sufficient to provide a satisfactory answer to the problems he considers, from this point on he will not look to abstract or general theories to fill the gap.

The following year Diderot came to the defence of another friend, Holbach, whose *Essai sur les préjugés* had been attacked by Frederick II of Prussia. The *Essai* advocated various measures to make society less hierarchical, closed and stultified; if princes did not adopt such measures, which were put forward in a reformist spirit, then philosophers should suggest them to the people and in that way change public opinion. Frederick rejected these ideas in his *Examen de l'essai sur les préjugés* (1770) and Diderot in turn attacked Frederick in a short work that has come to be known, since its discovery in 1937, as *Pages contre un tyran*.

Frederick II had always been enamoured of French culture and had taken a keen interest in the intellectual life of France; in his court at Berlin he had received and protected a number of the leading figures of the Enlightenment. Diderot, however, always kept his distance from him. In part this may have been due to his dislike of court life generally but there were obviously other reasons as well.* In the *Pages contre un tyran* he took the monarch to task for his authoritarian views. The latter maintained that a good citizen should respect the government under which he lived.

What do you call 'respecting the form of government under which one lives'? [asked Diderot]. Do you mean that one must

---

* One reason, in later years, may have been his bad conscience over his debt to the equally autocratic Catherine II. Some such unease seems to lie beneath the curious work he wrote on his return from Russia, aimed at Frederick, the *Principes de politique des souverains* (1774). These were a series of reflections 'written by the hand of a sovereign in the margin of Tacitus'[23] which have the same kind of ambivalent fascination and horror at the ruthless use of power that is found in Machiavelli's *The Prince*.

submit to the laws of the society of which one is a member? There is no difficulty about that. Do you suggest that if these laws are bad then one must remain silent? Perhaps that is what you think, but how then will the legislator recognize the failings of his administration, and the faults of its laws, if no one dares raise his voice? And if by chance one of that society's odious laws should award the death penalty against the person who dares attack them must he bow beneath the yoke of that law? No. Let us scribble away on paper, and you scribble away yourself as much as you want.[24]

The belief that had inspired the publication of the *Encyclopédie*, that the truth must be communicated, was one about which Diderot never wavered. (That is to say, he never wavered in his belief even if he did not always communicate his ideas to the public.) The truth must always be told. 'It is the lie that is at the origin of all our disasters,' he wrote in the *Pages contre un tyran*.[25] The distinction he drew between submitting to existing laws and speaking out, if necessary, against them, was a consistent feature of his mature thought. The idea occurs in the *Salon de 1767*,[26] the *Supplément au Voyage de Bougainville* (see p. 316), the *Mémoires pour Catherine II*,[27] and it inspired many of his contributions to Raynal's *Histoire des Deux Indes*. Coupled with this was a belief in what Diderot called 'the invisible church'. He meant by this a 'certain number of sensible and just men' who are more concerned with the truth than with self-promotion and who in the long run are those 'who form the feeling of the nation'.[28] A good government, he believed, would be that of a monarch who had a 'council of critics (*censeurs*)'[29] made up of such men.

However, Diderot did not support the idea of enlightened despotism, and his condemnation of it was unequivocal. When Helvétius quoted with approval Frederick's remark that 'there is no better form of government than the arbitrary rule of a just, humane and virtuous prince', Diderot disagreed vehemently:

And it is you, Helvétius, who quote this tyrant's maxim with approval! The arbitrary rule of a just and enlightened prince is always bad. His virtues are the most dangerous and the surest form of seduction; they lull a people imperceptibly into the habit of living, respecting and serving his successor, whoever that successor may be, no matter how wicked or stupid. Such a prince deprives his people of the right to deliberate, to will or not to will, even to oppose his will when he orders what is good. But such a right of opposition, senseless though it is, is sacred; without it, subjects resemble nothing but a herd of cattle whose protests are ignored on the pretext that they are being led to fat pastures. By governing according to his own pleasure, the tyrant is committing the greatest of crimes. For what is it that characterizes the despot? Is it goodness or wickedness? Not at all; those two notions do not even enter into the definition. It is the extent of the authority he arrogates to himself, not the use to which he puts it. One of the greatest misfortunes that could happen to a nation would be two or three successive periods of rule by just, gentle, enlightened but arbitrary power; the people would be led by their happiness into complete forgetfulness of their privileges, into the most complete slavery. I do not know whether there has ever been a tyrant who, together with his children, thought to put this formidable political strategy into practice, but I have no doubt at all that it would have been successful. Woe to those subjects in whom all sense of their own freedom has been destroyed, even by the most apparently praiseworthy means. For such an appearance only makes those means the more fatal for the future. That is how a people is lulled into a sleep that may be sweet but is like death, a sleep during which patriotic feelings die out and citizens become foreigners to the government of their own State. If the English had been ruled by three Elizabeths in succession they would now be the basest slaves in all Europe.[30]

The difference in tone between the *Pages contre un tyran* and the *Réfutation d'Helvétius*, and the assertion in the latter of the 'sacred' right of opposition, was due to the acute political crisis that occurred in France. A recent verdict on these events was that 'government Louis XV style had come closer to despotism between 1771 and 1774 than French monarchy had perhaps ever done'.[31]

By the late 1760s the French economy was in severe trouble. The expense of, and defeat in, the Seven Years War (1756–63) and a rising population accentuated what had been recognized as major problems for over a hundred years. Richelieu, Colbert and Fleury had all tried to reform the archaic tax-structure and government machinery; none had succeeded. The attempt by Machault the Controller-General to introduce a new tax, the *vingtième*, had provoked a serious crisis in 1749, the focus of which was the struggle between the king and the Paris Parlement. The French Parlements were not elected assemblies but courts of law, most of whose members occupied their position through hereditary right; however, inasmuch as no edict by a monarch could be made law unless it was registered by the Parlements these bodies acted as the only institution with some positive countervailing power. (There was a host of municipal corporations, local privileges, official log-jams and petty interests which acted as a negative power.) Since the nobility, like the clergy, were exempt from direct taxation the Parlements were opposed to any new tax or tax reform, hence the vicious circle in which the government was trapped. When Maupeou replaced Choiseul as the dominant minister in 1770 he decided to revive the idea of the *vingtième*; when the Paris Parlement refused to accept it he simply exiled and dissolved that body, in January 1771, and then reconstituted it in an ineffectual form.

Diderot was no admirer of the Paris Parlement. Reviewing Voltaire's *Histoire* of it in 1769 he had written that a more serious study (than Voltaire's) would have shown how 'this body refused justice to the people and caused anarchy when it was a matter of defending imaginary rights, [but] never when it was a question of defending the people'.[32] It was 'the most violent enemy of all liberty, whether civil or religious, the slave of the powerful, the oppressor of the weak . . . constantly opposed to the good . . . devoid of any proper view of administration or public utility'.[33] However, Maupeou's action in 1771 shook him, as it did many others. He wrote in a letter:

This event has caused great emotion among all the orders of the State. Princes make representations, other courts of law make representations, all the nobility make representations; and it does not stop there. Heads are warming up and the heat is slowly spreading. The principles of liberty and independence, formerly hidden in the hearts of a few people who think, now take hold and are openly expressed. Every century has a spirit which characterizes it. The spirit of our century seems to be that of liberty. The first attack on superstition was violent, immoderate. Once men have dared in some way to attack the barrier of religion, the most formidable and most respected barrier that there is, it is impossible to stop. When they have cast a hostile glance over the majesty of heaven, they will not hesitate the next moment to cast one over earthly sovereignty. The cord that holds and binds humanity is formed of two strands; one cannot be loosened without the other breaking. Such is our current situation; and who can say where it will lead us? If the [royal] court withdraws from its position its opponents will learn to appreciate their strength and that cannot happen without leading to grave results. We are on the point of a crisis which will end in slavery or liberty.[34]

Exactly how the situation might lead to freedom Diderot did not say. His thoughts were full of foreboding:

If it is slavery it will be like that which exists in Morocco or Constantinople . . . I am convinced that it is a thousand times easier for an enlightened people to return to barbarism than for a barbarian people to take a single step towards civilization. Indeed, it does seem that every thing, the good and the evil, has its span of maturity. When the good reaches its point of perfection it begins to turn to the evil; when the evil is complete it rises towards the good.[35]

The principle enunciated in 'Autorité politique' that 'true and legitimate power is necessarily limited', had been violated by Louis XV and his ministers. The country was being ruled despotically. In such an extreme situation extreme measures were justified. In November 1771 Diderot wrote: 'I was asked one day how a nation which had lost its vigour could regain it. I replied: the same way that Medea brought youth back to her father, by cutting him up and putting him on the boil.'[36] Since this remark occurs in a letter to John Wilkes, a correspondant with whom Diderot often adopted a playful tone, it might be taken as a jest, were it not for the fact that he repeated it in the *Réfutation d'Helvétius*[37] and set out the idea soberly and seriously in a contribution to the *Correspondance littéraire* in 1772 (most of which was later printed in the 1774 and 1780 editions of the *Histoire des Deux Indes*[38]):

Subjects who come together and render justice to a bad sovereign do not merit the odious name [of a parricide]; they do not even deserve [to be called that] when they render justice to a good sovereign who would have done good against the general will. He should be punished for the single reason that he had gone beyond the limits of his rights; he would have committed the crime of *lèse-société* against the present and against the future.[39]

Nothing can justify slavery, but there is 'a principle which absolves tyrannicide',[40] and the thought of such an act recurred through Diderot's later years.

However, it was only an intermittent suggestion and there could be no assurance that it would provide a solution; fuller consideration of the problem was necessary. When he travelled to Holland and Russia in 1773 and 1774 he had an opportunity for such consideration, and the results are evident in the *Réfutation d'Helvétius* and the series of reflections, memoranda and advice he gave to Catherine II known as the *Entretiens* or *Mémoires pour Catherine II*. This latter work opens with a long *Essai historique* on French government. 'The first fault, the original sin' of the French nation had been to hand over 'all public power to the king'.[41] There should have been some body which was 'a barrier put up to defend the people against the arbitrary power of a stupid or wicked sovereign'.[42] The Paris Parlement had not been such a body because 'all its resistance to the sovereign's wishes was only play-acting; the nation's interests were always sacrificed and it only fought boldly for its own interest';[43] 'it remained gothic in its practices and opposed to all good reform . . . intolerant, bigoted and superstitious'.[44] But, continued Diderot, 'was the destruction of this body a good thing? No. It was the greatest misfortune.'[45] 'The veil had been torn away and tyranny openly showed its face';[46] 'in an instant we had jumped from a monarchical State to the most thoroughly despotic State'.[47]

The absence of effective restraint on monarchical power was not the only thing wrong with France. There was also the lack of 'a general and uniform law . . . France is condemned never to have one code [of laws]. Our law based on custom is immense.'[48]

The custom in Burgundy is different from that which operates in Normandy. The law is not the same for peasants as it is for nobles. The clergy has a particular set of rules, so do the military and the magistrates[49] . . . The person who planned the overthrow of this monstrous colossus would shake every kind of

property. He would not complete his undertaking without committing a mass of crying injustices. He would undoubtedly stir up
the different orders of the State. Yet I would do it, because I
think that you should do a great evil which lasts a moment for the
sake of a great good which will endure.[50]

Then there were the financial problems. Diderot dealt with these
in another chapter of the *Mémoires*, entitled *Du luxe* (XXVI). If he
were king he would sell the royal domains, which produced no
revenue, reduce the royal household and stables, the number of
residences and royal pensions. He would travel less; he would
secularize the monasteries and inherit their possessions. He would
get rid of the many corrupt tax-gatherers and end the tax exemption
enjoyed by the military, the nobility and the magistrates, so that
'the distribution of taxes was in relation to wealth'.[51] He would
publish the national balance sheet. Prosperity would surely follow
if the guilds were suppressed, inventors rewarded, agriculture encouraged, 'if gold were not the national god and if, by competition
for positions, merit and virtue were assured their reward'.[52] As he
considered the matter in more detail Diderot began to feel that the
situation was not beyond saving. 'Monsieur Turgot is one of the
most upright men in the kingdom and certainly, perhaps, the most
able in all spheres. He will never be promoted from his position [as
Intendant] in Limoges, [but] if he is I will let out a cry of joy,
because the spirit of our government will immediately change and
things improve in an almost miraculous way. There are small
matters which announce great events; that is one.'[53] Being in
Russia gave Diderot a new perspective. 'What a difference there is
between a man's thought in his own country and that of a man 900
leagues from his court! None of the things I have written in
St Petersburg would have come to me in Paris. How fear restricts
the head and the heart! What a remarkable effect liberty and
security have!'[54]

III

Unlike Montesquieu or Rousseau Diderot did not travel until late
in his life. His visit to Holland and Russia was his first journey

outside France. This fact, combined with the political crisis in France and the need to discuss political questions with Catherine II, led to that new sense of interest in the issues involved which is evident in the *Mémoires* and the work he wrote on his return from Russia, the *Observations sur le Nakaz*.

The *Mémoires* is a wide-ranging series of reflections about France and suggestions for change in Russia. Diderot was principally concerned with three matters. The first was the need in Russia, as much as in France, for a *commission*, some form of assembly that would act as a check on the monarch's power. Three chapters dealt with this (IX, XV, XXIV) and the last of these was forthright in its refusal to countenance any despotism, however enlightened – 'in any society of men the right of opposition seems to me a natural, sacred and inalienable right'[55] – and in its assertion that there must be some institution, the *commission*, 'a permanent, constant, physical being',[56] which would embody and enact this right. His next concern was the need to form a 'third estate' (VII), to people the towns (XXXVII), develop trade (XXIV), encourage industry and manufacture (LVI, LVII). In a contribution to the *Correspondance littéraire* in 1772 Diderot had already maintained that the first step in bringing civilization to a backward country like Russia was not to start at the top, by bringing in illustrious men, but by starting at the bottom, 'by invigorating the mechanical arts and the lower occupations. Learn how to cultivate the land, to treat skins, manufacture wool, make shoes, and in time . . . people will then be painting pictures and making statues.'[57] His other main concern in the *Mémoires* was with education (XI, XVI, XVII, XXV, XXVII, XLIII) and cultural activities – the value of theatres (VI, XX), academies (LIV) and his offer to edit another *Encyclopédie* (LXII). He also gave Catherine an account of how he went about writing, *Sur ma manière de travailler* (LIII), and the relaxed form of the work gave opportunity for many other interesting comments.

On his return from Russia he developed his ideas on education at Catherine's request into a full-length work, the *Plan d'une université pour le gouvernement de Russie*.

To instruct a nation is to civilize it; to broaden its knowledge is to lead it away from the primitive state of barbarism . . . Instruction gives man dignity. [It] softens people's characters, enlightens them about their duties, refines, stifles or masks their vices, inspires a love of order, justice and virtue, and hastens the birth of good taste in everything[58] . . . The first step in wisdom in our time has been to relate everything to the culture of the earth; the second step, which remains to be made, is to become aware of the importance of public education or the culture of the man.[59]

Diderot's scheme begins with practical matters and leads on to literary and theoretical subjects, things coming before words. He recommends books for the different courses and displays a generous breadth of interest.

More significant was the other work he wrote on his return from Russia, the *Observations sur le Nakaz*. In 1765 Catherine had drawn up a Preparatory Instruction, the *Nakaz*, to be considered by the Estates General when they were called together two years later. It set out many forward-looking ideas, drawn largely from Montesquieu and Beccaria.[60] In the event the assembly was dissolved before the document was considered, as war broke out between Russia and Turkey, but it remained on the table and was still the official version of Catherine's political intentions. The document was translated into French in 1769 and it provided Diderot with the occasion for his most developed political writing, his clearest statement of the political issues which since 1771 had become of urgent importance. Just as being distant from France had enabled him to see French affairs more incisively, so being distant from Russia put Catherine's ideas and actions in a sharper light.

Observations sur le Nakaz

I

There is no true sovereign except the nation; there can be no true legislator except the people. It is rare for a people to submit sincerely to laws which have been imposed on them; but they will love them, respect them, obey them and protect them as their own work, if they are the authors of them themselves. Then the laws are not the arbitrary wishes of one man, but those of a number of men who have consulted one another about their happiness and their security. They are vain if they do not apply equally to everyone; they are vain if there is a single member of the society who can infringe them with impunity. The first point of a code should therefore be to tell me about the precautions that have been taken to ensure that the laws have authority.

The first line of a well-made code should bind the sovereign.* It should begin thus: 'We people, and we sovereign of this people, swear conjointly [to obey] these laws by which we will be equally judged; and if it should happen that we, the sovereign, enemy of our people, should change them or infringe them, it is just that our people should be released from the oath of loyalty, (that they should pursue us, depose us and even condemn us to death if the case demands it).'† . . .

Any sovereign who refuses this oath declares himself in advance to be a despot and a tyrant.

The second law is that the representatives of the nations should assemble every five years to judge if the sovereign has conformed exactly to any law to which he has sworn, to decide on the punishment he deserves if he has infringed it, to allow him to continue, or to depose him and swear once again these laws . . .

People, if you have all authority over your sovereign, make a code; if your sovereign has all authority over you, abandon your code. You will be forging chains for yourselves alone.

II

After this preliminary, the second point on which the code should offer me a decision is about the kind of government the nation has chosen.

The Empress of Russia is certainly a despot. Is her intention to maintain the despotism and transfer it to her successors, or to abdicate it? . . . If she abdicates it, this abdication should be formal: if this abdication is sincere, she should concern herself conjointly with her nation to establish the surest way of preventing despotism from re-emerging . . .

If in reading what I have just written and in listening to her conscience her heart jumps with joy then she no longer wants [to rule over] slaves; if she trembles, feels weak and goes pale, then she has taken herself for a better person than she really is.

* In the opening paragraph Diderot uses 'sovereign' in the same way that Rousseau used the word, meaning the source of legitimate authority, which for Rousseau resided in all the people. In the second paragraph, and subsequently, Diderot uses the word in the conventional sense, meaning the monarch.
† The words in brackets were deleted from the copy sent to Catherine.

III

A question to discuss is whether the political institutions should be put under the sanction of religion. [Diderot decides against this.] Religion is a support which always ends by toppling the house. The distance between the altar and the throne can never be too great . . . Catherine and Montesquieu have opened their works with God. They would have done better to begin with the necessity of laws, foundations of the happiness of men, contract in which [conditions] are laid down for our liberty and our properties . . .

IV

*Russia is a European power.** It little matters whether it is Asiatic or European. The important point is that it should be great, flourishing and durable.

Behaviour (*moeurs*) is everywhere the result of legislation and government; it is not African or Asiatic or European. It is good or bad. One is a slave under the pole where it is very cold, one is a slave in Constantinople where it is very warm; but everywhere a people should be educated, free and virtuous. What Peter I brought to Russia, if it was good in Europe, was good everywhere . . .

[Diderot considers the problem caused by the size of Russia. He makes three suggestions.] One thing which seems to me very wise would be first of all to put the capital in the centre [of the country]. The heart is very badly situated at the end of a finger . . . The second thing would be to choose someone undistinguished either by birth or wealth, to put him in charge of a district, and make him carry out there a sensibly worked-out plan of civilization which would serve as a model for all the other districts . . . The third would be to introduce a colony of Swiss people, to place it in a suitable area, guarantee it privileges and freedom, and grant the same privileges and freedom to all those subjects who entered the same colony. The Swiss are farmers and soldiers; they are loyal . . .

VI

It is more advantageous to obey the laws under a single master than to depend on several masters.

I agree, provided that the master is the first slave of the laws. It is against this master, the most powerful and dangerous of wrong-

---

* Words in italics are quotations from the *Nakaz*.

doers, that the laws should mainly be directed. Other malefactors can trouble the social order, only he can overthrow it . . .

VII

The object and purpose of every government should be the happiness of the citizens, the strength and magnificence of the State and the glory of the sovereign . . .

[Diderot insists that despotism, even if it were by good men, would be a disaster.] For these excellent despots would accustom the nation to blind obedience; during their reigns the people would forget their inalienable rights; they would fall into a fatal security and apathy; they would no longer experience that continual alarm that is the necessary preserver of freedom . . .

VIII

. . . Good government is that in which the freedom of individuals is least restricted, and the freedom of sovereigns is as restricted as it is possible to be.

Why is Russia less well governed than France? It is because the natural freedom of the individual is there reduced to nothing and sovereign authority is unlimited. Why is France less well governed than England? It is because the sovereign authority is still too great there and natural liberty is still too restricted . . .

IX

The sovereign is the source of all political and civil power.

I do not understand that. It seems to me that it is the consent of the nation, represented by deputies or assemblied in bodies, which is the source of all political and civil power . . .

XIII

It would be pertinent to fix the rights of the intermediary powers and fix them in a way that cannot be revoked even by the legislator or his successors; if they are dependent on the supreme power they are nothing. A free people only differs from an enslaved people by the permanence of certain privileges which belong to man as man; to each order of citizens, as member of that order, and to each citizen as member of that society. Where the sovereign disposes as he pleases of rights and laws there are no rights, nor laws, nor liberty. A fair-minded legislator concerned to do good has worked in vain if the person to whom the sceptre is transferred can overturn everything. To tie one's own hands and those of one's successor, that is the height of heroism, humanity and love of the subjects, and one of the most difficult things in legislation. I only know three or four ways of doing it: public education or awareness, the brevity of the code and rules of law, education, the national oath and the periodic assembly of the Estates General; but, above all, education and the enjoyment [of rights and laws] confirmed by a long interval of time.

XIV

Fundamental laws really exist in a State wherever there are channels which convey the [common] interest and the general will to the sovereign, and where these channels cannot be flooded by gold nor broken by the sovereign. Without these preliminaries I will see nothing on the surface of the earth except slaves under different names.

XVII

What is the embodiment (depôt) of the laws? An institution which examines, authorizes, publishes and carries out the will of the sovereign. But what is the guarantee of the strength and survival of this institution? In France the body entrusted was the Parlement, but the Parlement no longer exists. In Russia it is the senate, but the senate is nothing: a voice crying in the desert. One day Herod had that head which was crying in the desert cut off and it was presented on a plate to Herodias.

XVIII

. . . *This institution checks the whims and greed of the sovereign.* Where? That does not even happen in London. The rich man buys the votes of those entrusted to him to obtain the honour of representing them; the court buys the votes of the representatives to govern more despotically . . .*

XX

The equality of citizens consists in all being submitted to the same laws. The word *equally* should be added . . . [However] there is a natural inequality between individuals. There are [also] conventional inequalities, which depend on the position the individual occupies in society. If merit has decided this position then the inequality enters the category of natural inequalities. I respect all such inequalities, it is a share of property. But I cannot allow those artificial rights or privileges attached to particular occupations as a result of which the burden of society is so unequally shared and the authority of the law is so different.

XXIII

[Diderot again considers the intermediary body] . . . What should be the prerogative of this body? To revise, approve, and disapprove the wishes of the sovereign, and to notify the people of them. Who should make up this body? Owners of large property. How should this body be given some strength? It is a matter of time, of public consideration, of its own constitution, rules, of the sanction given to these rules, of the oath taken by the members of this body, of the permanence of these members, of the privilege of naming them, of keeping itself exclusively for the sovereign, etc. . . .

LI

[Diderot lists some of the subjects Catherine has not discussed] . . . She has said nothing about taxes. She has said nothing about war . . . I would not have made slaves; on the contrary, I would have needed a third estate and it would have produced everything, I needed workers of every kind and I would have provided myself with them. I needed free men who would have taught my subjects the price of liberty and they would have known it . . .

The Empress has said nothing about the emancipation of the serfs. But that is a very important point. Does she want the nation to carry on in slavery? Does she not know that there is no true government, laws, population, agriculture, trade, wealth, science, taste or art, where liberty does not exist?

---

* Diderot's friend Holbach returned from a visit to England in 1765 with evidence of the corruption of the English system of government. John Wilkes confirmed this evidence on his visits to Paris. (Wilkes had been a fellow-student of Holbach at Leyden University and became a friend of Diderot in Paris.) These impressions contributed to that disillusion with the English system that became characteristic of Diderot's generation. This loss of a visible alternative to the French system of government undoubtedly affected and restricted Diderot's political outlook.

She has said nothing about the education of a successor to the empire [nor about education generally].

This is the list of subjects of a true system of laws: the choice of government; the sovereign, the succession; the heir to the empire and his education; the emancipation [of the serfs]; civil and criminal laws; the nobility; war; the navy; finance; the judiciary; priests; trade and agriculture; population; public education . . .

LX

. . . Whatever may be the multiplicity of the laws, regulations, decrees, it is impossible that they should be contradictory if they all relate to one fixed point; and that fixed point is given, it is liberty and property.

LXXIII

A society should first of all be happy; and it will be if liberty and property are assured; if trade is unrestricted; if all the orders of citizens are equally subjected to the laws; if the tax is supported in relation to [differing] strengths, or is well distributed; if it does not exceed the needs of the State; if virtue and talents are well rewarded . . .

[But it is not enough for man only to enjoy material well-being.] It seems to me that a being which feels is made to be happy in all his thoughts. Is there any reason to put a limit to the mind and senses and say to man: You will only think so far, you will only feel so much? I confess that that kind of philosophy tends to keep man in a kind of mindlessness and on a moderate level of enjoyments and happiness quite contrary to his nature; and all philosophy contrary to his nature is absurd, just as is any system of law where the citizen is continually forced to sacrifice his taste and happiness for the good of society. I want society to be happy but I also want the citizen to be happy, and there are as many ways of being happy as there are individuals . . .

LXXVII

There is an excellent means of preventing the revolt of the serfs against their masters; that is for there to be no serfs.

[In other articles Diderot deals with criminal and judicial procedure, the economy, taxes, the army, education and the arts. He concludes:]

CXLV

I see in Her Majesty's *Instruction* a plan for an excellent code, but not a word on the means of ensuring the stability of this code. I see in it the name of the despot abdicated, but the thing itself preserved, and despotism called monarchy.

I see no provision in it for the emancipation of the body of the nation; now without emancipation, or without liberty, there is no property; without property, no agriculture; without agriculture, no strength, greatness, prosperity, wealth.

But the Empress has a great soul, insight, enlightenment, a very extensive genius; justice, goodness, patience and firmness . . .

The *Observations* were only sent to Catherine after Diderot's death. They were not well received.

No work demonstrates more clearly Diderot's limitations as a political thinker. His opening paragraph sets out clear principles but there is no attempt to carry them through. He sees the weakness of Catherine's proposals but he has little alternative to offer. He displays a manifest inability to define clearly what will be the all-important constitutional body that will check the sovereign's power. He shows almost complete neglect of the machinery of government. He refuses to consider how conditions in Russia are different and how different solutions might be necessary. His proposals in fact lie in a no man's land between thoughtful speculation and empirical analysis. His suggestion about importing a colony of Swiss settlers to promote the spirit of liberty had first been made in the *Correspondance littéraire* in 1772, before he went to Russia.[61] The fact that he repeated it, first in the *Mémoires* during his visit, then in the *Observations*, after his return, shows a lamentable disregard for the Russian situation, quite apart from being an inept idea anyway. We must conclude that in these matters Diderot was out of his element.

IV

In 1774 Louis XV died and Louis XVI came to the throne. He dismissed Maupeou, restored the Parlements, and among the men he appointed to high office was Turgot, who was made Controller-General of finances. Diderot's hope, expressed in his *Mémoires*, was realized. Where Helvétius had written 'no salutary crisis will restore freedom to France', Diderot now replied: 'current experience proves the opposite. Let the upright people who now hold the top positions in the State keep them for only ten years and all our misfortunes will be repaired. The restoration [of the Parlements] has brought back the time of freedom.'[62]

This optimism did not last. Turgot's economic measures were largely concerned with lifting restrictions on the grain trade. This led to increased prices and serious riots which reached Paris in May 1775. Turgot was unable either to win over the Paris Parlement or keep the confidence of his ministerial colleagues and the following year he was dismissed. Two years later, in 1778, another able man highly thought of by Diderot was appointed to the same post, the Genevan banker Necker. But on top of the endemic problems of the inequitable tax-structure, bureaucratic inefficiency, and rising population, there was now the additional burden of war; that year France entered the War of American Independence. Immense sums of money had to be borrowed to pay for it. (By 1788 three-quarters of the French government revenue was being spent on servicing the national debt.) The decision to enter the war was a popular one, for it offered France an opportunity to get even with Great Britain after the defeat of the Seven Years War. But that did not obscure or override the seriousness of the economic situation. There was not, as there had been between 1771 and 1774, a sense of political crisis, but rather an increasingly sombre awareness that the country was faced with intractable problems. It was in this atmosphere that Diderot wrote most of his contributions to Raynal's *Histoire des Deux Indes*.

This work was a history of European colonization from its beginnings in the East Indies and West Indies. It describes the settlement of newly discovered lands and the ensuing development of trade, beginning with the Portuguese, Dutch, English and French in Asia and the Pacific, then the Spanish, Portuguese, French and English in South and North America. It combined historical and anthropological information, and attacks on slavery, with a firm belief in the benefits of commerce, 'this new soul of the moral world'.[63] In the *Salon de 1769* Diderot wrote that everyone was becoming 'preoccupied with administration, commerce, agriculture, imports, exports and finance . . . The Abbé Raynal can boast of having been the hero of this change.'[64] However, the humanitarian aspect of the *Histoire* was as important as the economic or historical information – the work was dedicated to 'Humanity, Truth and Liberty'[65] – and Raynal himself clearly saw the work as being in the same spirit as the *Encyclopédie*. In the background of the frontispiece featuring his portrait were some volumes of the *Encyclopédie*, and in the last book of the *Histoire* there was a fulsome tribute to that achievement.[66]

Diderot was one among several people who contributed to the work, having been asked to do so by Raynal in 1765. At first he seems to have taken no great interest in it and his contributions to the first edition, dated 1770 (though it was not published until 1772), are generally unremarkable; they are mostly concerned with the bad effects of colonization and religion, the injustice of slavery and reflections about *sauvages*. This edition was very successful and this success, as well as his growing interest in political questions, seems to have led him to become more involved in the second edition, dated 1774, for his contribution doubled in size and became more incisive in tone. This edition was also successful. Diderot now devoted a large part of his energies partly to revising but mostly to writing new material, twice as much again, for the third edition, published in 1780. According to Meister he spent 'two years occupied almost entirely' with this work,[67] and according to his daughter 'he sometimes worked fourteen hours a day and neglected no reading matter that could inform him about the subjects he was dealing with'; he wanted the work to be 'a model of eloquence'.[68] He undoubtedly saw it as an opportunity to express views which were otherwise unpublished, as Michèle Duchet has suggested,[69] and his contributions do mark a further stage in his development as a writer.

That development was not one which advocated revolution. The argument that such was the case does not stand up to close examination. The passages that have been taken as calls to revolt are either passages for which there is no firm evidence that Diderot was the author,[70] or, when looked at in their context, are in no sense revolutionary. In Book One, for example, Diderot wrote: 'No, no; sooner or later justice must be done. If it does not come I would address the populace. I would say to them: People, you whose roars have so often made your masters tremble, what are you waiting for? For what occasion do you keep your torches, and the stones which pave your streets? Tear them up.'[71] Taken in isolation this does indeed look like a call to revolt. But the injustice in question is not European, it is the renewal of the trading monopoly of the East India Company, due to expire in 1780, and monopoly was one of the worst sins in Diderot's breviary. The Europeans in India had committed appalling crimes and the East India Company's monopoly had enabled them to do so with impunity. That is the injustice Diderot wanted stopped, and which he believed would be stopped, for the passage continues: 'But the upright citizens, if some remain, will finally speak up. The spirit of monopoly will be seen to be mean and cruel; it will be seen to be incompatible with the public good',[72] and he goes on with a vehement denunciation of the 'spirit of monopoly'. In Book Eleven Diderot made a clear distinction between 'the condition of those unfortunate people' subjected to slavery and that of Europeans.[73]

Nor can the passages where Diderot writes in praise of the American Revolution be taken as establishing a general doctrine of revolution.[74] He reaffirmed his belief in the right of resistance and the right of a people to change their government, 'the legitimate exercise of a natural and inalienable right',[75] (though he no more goes into details of how people could change their government than he worked out details of the all-important *commission* in Russia). For this reason the Americans were justified in rising up against their English oppressors, and the men who fought and died for their country and the 'sacred love of liberty'[76] should be venerated. But he does not go on to suggest that English people themselves should rise up against their government. The action of the Americans should inspire them to esteem 'the price and greatness of liberty'; but it should be an inspiration for general reform not a specific example to follow. If their government became despotic the English should not rise up in revolt but rather leave England and go to America.[77]

Nor is there any development in Diderot's basic political thinking. On the strength of a passage in Book Eighteen it has been suggested that he rejected the idea of natural sociability and effected 'a complete volte-face in his views on the social compact [which he now saw as not] consecrated by reason and hallowed by nature but something purely artificial'.[78] This passage, however, was taken from Thomas Paine's *Common Sense* (1776) and Paine wrote an open *Letter to Raynal* in 1782 complaining about the plagiarism. Some of his complaint was unjustified, in so far as the idea that society arose through a struggle against nature had been a feature of Diderot's writing since at least 1772.[79] But the crucial distinction between society and government was drawn from Paine[80] and this passage makes use of Paine rather as Diderot regurgitated ideas from Montesquieu in his *Essais sur la peinture*;[81] the ideas are borrowed, not stolen.* That there was no development in his political thinking is evident from his reiteration elsewhere in the *Histoire* of the ideas of natural sociability and of no qualitative change between natural man and social man, and of his inability to explain how the intrinsic sense of sociability in the former could develop into the injustices suffered by the latter (see pp. 353-4, 356). Diderot was still trapped in his conceptual limitations, and the remarks he made in the final paragraphs of the *Histoire* (see p. 358) suggest that he was conscious of this.

Diderot did consider the possibility of something similar to what we would now call revolution during the crisis of 1771-4. It is one of the difficult questions in the *Réfutation d'Helvétius* (see p. 299). and in Russia he had come close to believing that such an upheaval could be necessary for France, as his consideration of reforming the legal system indicates (see pp. 331-2). 'There are circumstances where the extreme of evil is a good and where a palliative which perpetuates the evil is the most fatal of remedies.'[85] But this idea was not developed in the *Histoire des Deux Indes*, nor the *Essai sur les règnes de Claude et de Néron*, nor in the letters of these final years. What we do find is a forthright attack on tyranny and despotism and a clear defence of tyrannicide. This was the lesson of English history.[86] Similarly, this is what would justify the slaves killing their masters in the West Indies[87] or the serfs doing the same in Russia.[88] In the passionate defence of the *Histoire* Diderot wrote in 1781, his *Lettre apologétique de l'abbé Raynal à Monsieur Grimm*, he said:

---

* The same could be said of the passage in Book Fifteen where Diderot writes of the discovery that 'the vices of morality and legislation [only] arise with the establishment of societies' (see p. 351). This is the one place in Diderot's work, to my knowledge, where he shows an awareness of the implications of Rousseau's *Discours sur l'inégalité*. (Elsewhere in the *Histoire* it may have been Diderot who wrote, in words very similar to those used by Rousseau in his article 'Economie Politique',[82] 'men are what the government makes them',[83] but this attribution is not certain.) But these remarks were never taken up and developed in such a way that they became central to his thought. Indeed, immediately after the passages drawn from Paine he wrote 'in any society there is no class which does not devour and may not be devoured, whatever have been or may be the forms of government'.[84]

'The book I like, and which kings and their courtiers detest, is the book which causes Brutuses to be born.'[89] Brutus was not a revolutionary, he was a man who killed a tyrant;* as such he had featured in several eighteenth century works, including a play by Voltaire (*La Mort de César*), and as such he was esteemed by Diderot.[91]

For Diderot a limited monarchy remained the right form of government for France. His address to Louis XVI in Book Four is in no way anti-monarchical; in Book Seventeen he repeated his belief in the loyalty of the French towards their sovereign, 'They love him, they cherish him . . . The only sovereign they would hate would be the most wicked of sovereigns.'[92] There is no doubt that Diderot felt apprehensive about the situation in France and there are places where his forebodings can indeed be seen to prefigure the events of 1789.[93] But the purpose of his comments is always to prevent such an occurrence. In his enthusiasm for the struggle of the Americans against the English, with his call for a 'happy fanaticism, born of [a love of] politics and liberty',[94] he may sound like a revolutionary, but whenever his attention is turned to Europe or to political ideas in general it is clear that no change in his basic thinking has taken place.

Yet there was a development in Diderot's contributions to the *Histoire*. This was less a matter of ideas than of style. Political questions have taken on a new seriousness for him; his ideas may not have developed but they are more explicit, and his pleas for justice and his affirmations of liberty have a new urgency. The result is a new tone, a new rhetorical force. In previous writings, like the *Satire contre le luxe* in the *Salon de 1767* and the dithyrambic poem *Les Eleuthéromanes* (1771),[95] Diderot's denunciations of injustice had been set in a self-consciously literary framework. Now they arose from his own experience (the crisis of 1771–4, his visit to Russia), and his own anxiety about the present.*

---

* A tyrannicide kills an unjust ruler in the belief that that act will bring an end to injustice. A revolutionary will also kill an unjust ruler but he believes that greater change is necessary to end injustice than a mere change of the person at the top; he has a vision of a new order, or, at the very least, a sense that major alterations are needed to the existing order. Diderot had no such vision, and little idea of what alterations could or should be made. Unlike many of his contemporaries he even refused to imagine that a better order existed in classical times.[90] Two other obstacles to his adopting a belief in revolution (though neither was incompatible with such a belief) were his low regard for the mass of the people and his belief in a cyclical pattern of history.

The results were successful and influential. Raynal's work was one of the most frequently reprinted books in the years immediately preceding the French Revolution, and Raynal himself was invited to be a member of the Constituant Assembly in 1789. Not all the strong rhetoric in the work was by Diderot; the passage in praise of republican government in Book Nineteen[97] was more direct in its attack and more confident in the future – 'liberty will be born from the heart of oppression' – than anything Diderot wrote. But Diderot's contribution was of great significance, and his hope that he 'had contributed to the happiness of [his] fellow men and prepared, perhaps from far away, the improvement of their lot', did not turn out to be vain. The function of the *philosophe* was to speak out, to 'enlighten men about their inalienable rights';[98] by doing so he made people aware of injustice, he did indeed arouse 'indignation',[99] and that was an undoubted factor in bringing about subsequent change.

Histoire Des Deux Indes

[In Book Four Diderot addresses Louis XVI.]

The nation counts on a better use of the public revenue in the   II.162
new reign . . . Young prince, you who have been able to maintain a horror of vice and dissipation in the midst of the most dissolute court and under the most inadequate teachers, deign to listen to me with indulgence because I am a good man and one of your best subjects, [concerned only with] the happiness of the human race and the prosperity and glory of your reign . . .

What monarchy commands such patient, loyal, affectionate sub-   163
jects? What nation is more straightforward, active and industrious? Has not the whole of Europe adopted that social-minded spirit (*esprit social*) which so happily distinguishes our age from the

---

* They can also be seen to derive some of their force from his difficulty in having no effective solution; what he lacked in insight he made up for in rhetoric. (In his *Lettre apologétique* he expressed the fear that what he had written might be dismissed as no more than rhetoric.[96]) It has often been pointed out that in his mature works Diderot resolved problems for which he could find no satisfactory intellectual answer by imaginative means, by the use of dialogue, impersonation, and other such devices. The same could be said of some of his writing for the *Histoire*.

centuries which have gone before? . . . [Then Diderot describes
the country's weaknesses, both external – 'O splendour, o respect
for the French name, what has become of you?' – and internal:
there are many bankruptcies, much official corruption.] Cast your   165
eyes over the capital of your empire and you will find two classes of
citizens there. Some, wallowing in wealth, flaunt a luxury which
provokes indignation in those who are not corrupted by it. Others,
overwhelmed with need, make their situation worse by the pretence of a prosperity which they do not have. For such is the power
of gold, when it has become the god of a nation, that it takes the
place of all talent, it replaces all virtue, and you must either have
wealth or make people believe you have it . . . Look at the pro-
vinces, where all kinds of industry are dying out. You will see them
succumbing to the burden of impositions and to the many cruel
vexations of the horde of people who hang around the tax-farmer.

Then lower your eyes to the countryside and consider with a dry   166
eye, if you can, the person who makes our prosperity condemned
to die of poverty; the unfortunate labourer who scarcely has
enough straw from the land he has cultivated to cover his cottage
and make himself a bed . . . See the crowds of men who have
nothing, leaving their habitation at dawn and going on the road,
with their wives, children and animals, with no salary and no food,
to work on the highways, which benefit only those who possess
everything . . .

Know that kings have no relatives and that family pacts only last
as long as the contracting parties find them to be in their
interest . . . Know that an empire cannot endure without morals
and virtue any more than an individual family can, that dissipation
is the road to ruin, and that can only be avoided by economy . . .   167
Know that you will only escape from the abyss made by your
predecessors if you resolve to make your conduct conform to that
of a rich but debt-ridden individual who is nevertheless honest
enough to want to honour the thoughtless commitments of his
fathers and just enough to be indignant at [the thought of] all
tyrannical means and rejects them . . .

[Diderot then suggests particular indulgences that could be
avoided, economies that could be adopted, and reforms to the
tax-structure. He concludes:]

You will hear people murmur around you: 'That cannot be; and   169
if it could it would mean innovations.' Innovations! Yes, indeed.
But how many discoveries have there been in the sciences and the

arts that have not been innovations? Is the art of governing the only one that cannot be perfected? The assembly of the estates of a great nation, the restoration of original freedom, the respectable exercise of the first acts of natural justice, would these then be innovations?

[In Book Eight Diderot defends the right of colonization where a country is partly or wholly uninhabited.]

Reason and equity allow colonies. [If a country is partly inhabited IV.105 and partly deserted then] the deserted part is mine. I can take possession of it by my work . . . A country that is [entirely]   106 deserted and uninhabited is the only country that can be appropriated. The first properly noted discovery was a capture of legiti-   107 mate possession.

[In Book Eleven Diderot discusses slavery. He describes how serfdom came to an end in Europe, and] freedom became more V.275 widespread, in the greatest part of Europe, than it had been in any other country or under any other climate . . . [Classical] Athens had twenty serfs for one citizen. The disproportion was even greater in Rome . . . Since slavery has been abolished among us the people are a hundred times happier, even in the most despotic empires, than they were formerly in the best ordered democracies.

But hardly had domestic liberty been reborn in Europe than it was buried in America. The Spaniard . . . thought he had no duty to people who did not share his colour, customs or religion. He saw in them only tools for his greed, and he clapped them in irons . . . Then slaves from Africa were demanded . . . What a horrible system!   276

Liberty is the property of oneself. We can distinguish three kinds of liberty. Natural liberty, civil liberty and political liberty, that is to say, the liberty of the man, the citizen and the people. Natural liberty is the right which nature has given every man to dispose of himself as he wishes. Civil liberty is the right that the society should guarantee to each citizen to be able to do everything that is not contrary to the laws. Political liberty is the situation of a people who have not alienated their sovereignty, and who make their own laws or are partly associated in their legislation.

The first of these liberties is, after reason, the distinctive characteristic of man. We tie up and subject the animal because it has no notion of right and wrong, high and low. But in my liberty resides the principle of my vices and virtues. It is only the free man who can say *I wish* or *I do not wish* and who consequently can be worthy of praise or blame.

Without liberty, or the property of one's body and the enjoyment of one's mind, one cannot be husband, father, relative, friend. One has no *patrie*, fellow citizen, nor God . . . He who like   277
a coward abdicates his liberty gives himself up to remorse and the greatest misery that a thinking and feeling creature can experience . . . God is my father and not my master. I am his child and not his slave. How then could I grant to the political power that which I refuse to the divine almighty?

Will these eternal and unchangeable truths, the foundation of all morality, the bedrock of all reasonable government, be contested? . . .

Men or demons, whoever you are, would you dare to justify these   278
violations of my independence by the right of the strongest? . . .

[In Book Thirteen he reflects on the role of the philosopher.]

Disorder comes about through the childhood of sovereigns, the   VI.147
incapacity or pride of ministers and the patience of victims. We would be consoled for past and present evils if the future should change this fate. But that is a hope with which it is impossible to delude ourselves. And if the philosopher was asked what use was the advice which he persisted in giving nations and those who govern, and he replied with sincerity, he would say that he was satisfying an unstoppable inclination to speak the truth, in the chance of arousing indignation and even of drinking from the cup of Socrates.

[Book Fourteen opens with some remarks on England.]

England is, in modern history, the country of great political   VII.1
phenomena . . . It is there that one king, brought legally to the scaffold, and another deposed with all his line by a national decree, have given a great lesson to the earth . . .

[Diderot goes on to say that the English constitution] if not   2
perfect, if not free of faults, is at least the most well suited to the condition of the country, the most favourable to its commerce, the most appropriate to develop genius, eloquence and all the faculties of the human mind; perhaps the only one, since man lived in society, where the laws have ensured him his dignity, personal freedom and freedom of thought; where the laws have made him, in a word, a citizen, that is to say, an integral and constituent part of the state and the nation.

[He discusses the bad effects of despotism.] People think little,   9
speak not at all and are afraid to argue. They are frightened of their
own ideas. The philosopher hides his thought as the rich man hides
his wealth . . . Mistrust and terror form the basis of general
behaviour. The citizens keep themselves to themselves and the
whole nation becomes melancholy, cowardly, stupid and dumb.
These are the chains, the fatal symptoms, or the scale of misery on
which each people will know its own degree.

If you go back over the phenomena which lead [to this state of
affairs] and you imagine them being just the opposite, they will
indicate the movement of legislations which tend to liberty. It is
difficult, it is rapid, it is violent. It is a fever, more or less severe, but
always convulsive. Everything announces seditions, murders.
Everything seems to threaten a general collapse, and if the people
are not fated for the final misfortune, it is in blood that happiness is
reborn.

England experienced this in the first years of the administration
of Charles I.

[In Book Fifteen Diderot comments on the ideas derived from the   162
knowledge of primitive people brought back by travellers.]

Without doubt it is important for future generations that they do
not lose the accounts of the life and behaviour of *sauvages*. It is to
this knowledge perhaps that we owe all the progress which moral
philosophy has made among us. Up to now moralists have looked   163
for the origin and foundations of society in the societies which they
had before their eyes. People attributed crimes to man, in order to
give him figures who atoned for them; they plunged him into
blindness in order to become his guides and masters, and they
called mysterious, supernatural and heavenly that which is only the
product of time, ignorance, weakness and deceit. But since it has
been seen that social institutions did not derive either from the
needs of nature or from the dogmas of religion – because countless
numbers of people lived in a state of independence and with no
religion – the vices of morality and legislation have been seen to
arise with the establishment of societies. We have become aware
that these original evils came from founders and legislators who,
for the most part, had created social order (*la police*) for their own
use, or whose wise ideas of justice and the public good had been
perverted by the ambition of their successors and by the changes
made by time and custom. This discovery has already brought

much enlightenment but it is as yet no more than the dawn of a beautiful day for humanity. It is too opposed to established prejudices to have brought about great benefits so soon, but it will no doubt make such benefits the delight of future generations. That happy prospect should be a consolation for the present generation.

[In Book Eighteen Diderot discusses at length the revolt of the Americans against the English.]

There is no political authority, whether created yesterday or one VIII.27 thousand years ago, which cannot be abrogated in ten years or tomorrow.

No power, however respectable, however sacred it may be, is authorized to regard the state as its property. Whoever thinks otherwise is a slave . . . All authority in this world has begun with the consent of the subjects or by the strength of the master. In either case it can end up being legitimate. Nothing prescribes tyranny against liberty.

The truth of these principles is particularly essential [to realize] because all power by its nature tends to despotism, in even the nation which is quickest to take offence, among you, the English, yes, among you.

I heard it said to a Whig – fanatical words, perhaps, but words of great sense sometimes emerge from the stupid – I heard it said to him that as long as a bad sovereign, or at least a bad minister, was not led to Tyburn with as little formality, ceremonial, disturbance and surprise as the most obscure criminal the nation would not have its rights, nor the correct idea, nor the full enjoyment [of these things] appropriate to a people which dares to regard itself or call itself free . . .

Public happiness is the first law, as it is the first duty . . . Before   280 all else [governments] owe liberty and justice to the individuals who compose them. Every newborn child or every new citizen who   281 comes to breathe the air of the *patrie* which he has built for himself or which nature has given him, has the right to the greatest happiness which he can enjoy. All obligation which cannot be reconciled with that is null and void. All complaint against [such a condition] is a violation of the individual's rights . . .

God who is the principle of justice and order, hates tyrants. He   287 has printed on the heart of man this sacred love of freedom; he does not want servitude to disfigure and degrade his most beautiful work . . .

If you look at the history of republics you will see that the crowd   310
almost always is impetuous and heated in the initial moments but
that it is only in a small number of men, chosen and made to be
leaders, that dwell those vigorous and constant resolutions which
advance with a firm and assured step towards a great end, who are
never distracted from them, and struggle stubbornly against misfortunes, bad luck and hostile men . . .

[In Book Nineteen Diderot discusses the origin and development
of society.]

Men were never isolated, as they have been shown to be . . .   IX.39
They carried within them a seed of sociability which tended continually to be developed. [This instinct, it seems, should] necessarily   40
direct all moral and political laws, from which a longer and happier
existence would result for the majority of men. However, looking
at what has taken place you would say that all societies have only
had as their principle and supreme law the security of the dominant
power. Where does this remarkable contrast between the end and
the means, between the laws of nature and those of politics, come
from? It is a question which it is difficult to answer adequately
without having a proper notion of nature and the succession of
different governments; and history scarcely gives us any help on
this great subject. All the foundations of current society are lost in
the ruins of some catastrophe or physical change. Everywhere we
see men driven by the flames of the earth or the fire of war, by
floods of water or devouring insects, by scarcity or famine, to come
together in some corner of the uninhabited world or to disperse and
spread out in regions already peopled. Everywhere civilization
begins with brigandage, and order with anarchy.

But to arrive at some result which would satisfy reason we must
neglect these momentary shocks and consider nations in a stationary and peaceful condition, which leaves a free path to the
development of phenomena.

It has been said that there are two worlds, the physical and the
moral. The wider one ranges in thought and in experience, the
more convinced you will become that there is only one world, the
physical, which leads everything when it is not opposed by fortuitous causes. Without such causes we would have continually
seen the same interconnection in the most surprising moral
developments, such as the origin of religious ideas, the advances of
the human mind, the discovery of truths, the birth and continu-

ation of error, the beginning and end of prejudices, the formation of societies and the periodic order of different governments.

All civilized people have been savages; and all savage people, left to their natural impulse, were destined to become civilized. The family was the first society; and the first government was patriarchal government, founded on love, obedience and respect. The family grows and divides. Opposed interests lead to war between brothers who do not recognize one another. One people takes up arms against another. The vanquished become the slaves of the victor who divides up their fields, wives and children. The country is governed by a leader, by his lieutenants and by his soldiers, who represent the free part of the nation, while all the rest are subjected to the atrocities and humiliation of serfdom. In this anarchy, mixed with jealousy and ferocity, the peace is soon disturbed. These anxious men march against one another; they are exterminated. With time there remains only a monarch or a despot. Under the monarch there is a shadow of justice; legislation makes some advance; ideas of property develop, the name of slave is changed into that of subject. Under the supreme will of despotism there is only terror, servility, flattery, stupidity, superstition. That intolerable situation ends either by the assassination of the tyrant or the dissolution of the empire, and democracy arises on this corpse. Then for the first time the sacred name of *patrie* is heard. Then the bowed man lifts up his head and shows himself in all his dignity. Then the annals are filled with heroic deeds. Then there are fathers, mothers, children, friends, fellow citizens, public and domestic virtues. Then laws reign, genius takes wing, sciences are born, useful work is no longer held in low esteem.

Unfortunately this state of happiness is only momentary. Everywhere the revolutions in the government succeed one another with a speed that one can hardly follow. There are few countries which have not suffered them all, and there is none which, in time, does not complete this periodic movement. All will follow more or less often a regular circle of prosperity and misfortune, liberty and slavery, morality and corruption, enlightenment and ignorance, greatness and weakness; all reach every point of this fatal horizon. The law of nature, which wills that all societies gravitate towards despotism and dissolution, that empires are born and die, will not be suspended for any society . . .

[There follows a survey of European history from ancient Jewish times and classical Greece onwards. Later, in this Book, Diderot discusses political change.]

The state is a very complicated machine which one can neither   115
assemble or set in action without knowing all the pieces. One
cannot press or loosen a single one without all the others being
disturbed. Any project useful for one class of citizens, or for one
moment of crisis, can become fatal for the whole nation and
harmful for a long future . . .

All innovations should be gradual (*insensibles*), born from need,   116
inspired by a kind of public cry, or at least in accord with the
general wish. To create or destroy suddenly is to corrupt the good
and make the evil worse. To act without consulting the general will,
without collecting, so to speak, the majority of votes in public
opinion, is to alienate hearts and minds, to discredit everything,
even the upright and good . . . In the happy condition of civilization   117
and enlightenment which Europe has reached one is very aware
that the conviction of mind which produces a free, acceptable and
general obedience, can only arise from a certain demonstration of
the utility of the laws. If governments do not wish to bribe thinkers
– who would perhaps become suspect or corrupt once they were
hirelings – they should at least allow superior minds to watch over
the public good in some way. Every writer of genius is born magistrate of his country. He should enlighten it, if he can. His right is his
talent. Whether he is an obscure or a distinguished citizen, whatever his rank or his birth, if his mind is always noble he is qualified
by his intelligence. His court is the whole nation; his judge is the
public, not the despot who does not hear him, or the minister who
does not wish to listen to him.

No doubt, all truths have their limits; but it is always more
dangerous to stifle freedom of thought than to abandon it to its
inclination, to its ardour. Reason and truth triumph from the
activity of good minds, which only grow angry by being restricted
and grow irritable by being persecuted. Kings and ministers, love
the people; love men and you will be happy. You then have no
reason to fear free and disgruntled minds, nor the revolt of the
wicked. The revolt of people's hearts is much more dangerous; for
virtue grows bitter and indignant [and that leads] to atrocity. Cato
and Brutus were virtuous; they only had to choose between two
great offences (*attentats*), suicide or the death of Caesar.

Remember that the interest of the government is only that of the
nation. Whoever divides in two this simple interest has a poor
knowledge of government and can only have a bad effect on it.

Authority divides this great interest when individuals' wills are   118
substituted for the established order. The laws and the laws alone
should reign.

[Later in this book he discusses morality.]

For a long time people have looked to degrade man . . . a   290
creature who is always weak, often seduced by error, sometimes
misled by the imagination, but issuing from the hands of nature
with upright inclinations. Man is born with a seed of virtue,
although he is not born virtuous. He only reaches that sublime
condition after having studied himself, after having learnt his
duties, after having contracted the habit of fulfilling them . . .

In the court of philosophy and reason morality is in effect a   292
science, the object of which is the preservation and common happiness of the human race. It is to this twin goal that these rules should
relate. Their constant and eternal physical principle is in man
himself, in the similarity between the physical constitution of one
man and another; a similarity which entails that of the same needs,
pleasure, pains, strength and weakness; source of the necessity of
society, or of a common struggle against the common dangers
which arise from the heart of nature itself threatening man   293
from a hundred different sides. This is the origin of individual
bonds and domestic virtues; this is the origin of general bonds and
public virtues; this is the source of the notion of personal and
general utility; this is the source of all individuals' pacts and all
laws.

There is properly only one virtue, which is justice; and only one
duty which is to be happy. The virtuous man is the person who has
the most precise notions of justice and happiness and who makes
his conduct conform most rigorously to them. There are two tri-
bunals, that of nature and that of laws. One knows the offences of
man against his fellows; the other, the offences of man against
himself. The law punishes the crimes, nature punishes the vices.
The law shows the assassin the gallows, nature shows the intemperate man either dropsy or consumption.

Many writers have looked for the first principles of morality in
the feelings of friendship, tenderness, compassion, honour,
charity, because they have found them engraved on the human
heart. But do they not also find there hate, jealousy, revenge,
pride, love of domination? . . . These philosophers have felt the
necessity of morality, they have glimpsed what it ought to be; but
they have not grasped the first and fundamental principle. In fact,

the very feelings which they adopt as a foundation of morality, because they seem to them useful to the general good, could be very harmful if abandoned to themselves. How could one decide to punish the guilty man if one only listened to [the voice of] compassion? . . . All these virtues have a limit, beyond which they 294 degenerate into vices; and that limit is determined by the invariable rules of justice in its essence, or what comes to the same thing, by the common interest of men united in society, and by the constant purpose of that union.

Is it for oneself that one erects courage into a virtue? No, it is because of its usefulness for society . . .

[At the end of *Histoire* Diderot reflects sombrely on some of the consequences of the European explorations, discoveries and colonization.]

How many calamities have followed from the conquest of those 308 regions which cannot be compensated for!

[A new kind of fanaticism has developed, the search] for continents to invade, islands to plunder, peoples to despoil, subjugate and massacre.

[A new kind of savage nomad has grown up, who belongs nowhere and owes allegiance to no one, and] that insatiable thirst 309 for gold has given birth to the most infamous and atrocious of trades, the slave-trade . . .

[Then:] Will one count for nothing the complications in the government machinery that have ensued from the colonization of the two Indies? Before this era the hands ready to hold the reins of empires were extremely rare. A more burdened administration has demanded a more comprehensive genius and more profound knowledge. The concerns of sovereignty divided between citizens placed at the foot of the throne and subjects settled on the equator or near the pole, have been insufficient for both one and the other. 310 Everything has fallen into confusion. The different states have languished under the yoke of oppression, and interminable or constantly renewed wars have worn out the world and covered it with blood.

[Could anyone read this record and still wish that the Americas and the East Indies should be discovered?]

People, I have spoken to you of your greatest interests. I have put the benefits of nature and the products of industry before your eyes . . . The voice of my heart has been raised in favour of all men, with no distinction of sect or country. They have all been equal in my eyes, in relation to the same needs and the same miseries, as they are equal in the eyes of the supreme Being, in respect of their weakness to his power.

I have not been unaware that subjected to masters your fate should above all be [the object of] their work and that speaking to you of your evils was to reproach them for their errors or crimes. This reflection has not diminished my courage. I have not believed   311
that the holy respect which one owes humanity can ever not be in agreement with the respect owing to its natural protectors. In my mind I have transported myself into the council of the powers. I have spoken openly and without fear, and I have not to reproach myself for having betrayed the great cause I dared to plead. I have told the sovereigns what were their duties and your rights. I have related to them the fatal effects of the inhuman power which oppresses or the indolent and feeble power which permits oppression. I have surrounded them with pictures of your misfortunes and their hearts should tremble. I have warned them that if they turn away their eyes these accurate and frightening scenes will be engraved on the marble of their tomb . . .

But talent is not always equal to zeal. I have undoubtedly needed a great deal more of that insight which makes the means visible and that eloquence which makes the truth persuasive. Sometimes perhaps my soul has been elevated by genius; but most often I have felt myself overwhelmed by my subject and my weakness.

May writers more favoured by nature finish with their masterpieces what my attempts have begun!

May that chain of union and charity which should bring all civilized nations together extend one day, under the auspices of philosophy, from one end of the world to the other! May those nations no longer carry the example of vices and oppression to the uncivilized nations! I do not flatter myself that at the epoch of that happy revolution my name will still live.

This feeble work, which will only have the merit of having produced better works, will undoubtedly be forgotten. But at least I will be able to say to myself that I have contributed as much as I was able to the happiness of my fellow men, and prepared, perhaps   312
from afar, the improvement of their lot. This sweet thought will take the place for me of glory. It will be the charm of my old age, and the consolation of my final moments.

15

Conclusion

Thoughts about morality were never far from Diderot's mind. They took the form not only of enquiries about the basis of morality or admonitions to others, but also of reflections about himself. The gift of a new dressing-gown leads him to wonder whether he is succumbing to the corrupting hand of luxury, a doubt which was entertained and dispelled in his attractive short essay *Regrets sur ma vieille robe de chambre* (1769). Memories of his father and his family, sparked off by a visit to Langres in 1770, led to the dialogue *Entretien d'un père avec ses enfants*, in which Diderot, his father, brother and sister discuss whether or not there are cases when it is right to disobey the law. The law must always be obeyed, insists the brother; 'there are no laws for the wise man',[1] replies Diderot, 'you must listen to [the voice of] your heart'.[2] 'I would not be too angry if there were one or two people in a town like you; but I would not live there if they all thought like that,' concludes the father.[3]

In these works Diderot displayed complete confidence in his own moral standing; the problem was not whether he was a good man, but how a good man should act. But in the years following his return from Russia he began to wonder whether he really was a good man, and whether his own actions had been moral. The first product of this uncertainty was a play, first sketched in 1775, revised in 1777, and given a final form in 1781 under the title *Est-il bon? Est-il méchant?*

This play owed nothing to Diderot's ideas about reforming the theatre, put forward twenty years previously. It was a light-hearted, frivolous piece revolving around one character, Hardouin, who was an undisguised self-portrait. People come to him with various requests and, despite his complaints, he is happy to carry them out even though the only way to do so is to be dishonest in the process. He is thought to be good; the truth is otherwise – 'Me, a good man, like people say! I am not that. I was born thoroughly hard, wicked and perverse . . . Hardouin, you laugh at everything, there is nothing sacred for you. You are a downright monster.'⁴ At times he seems happy to be what he is, at other times he fears 'the reproaches of my conscience'.⁵ When, at the end of the play, his behaviour is revealed for what it is, both successful in meeting the requests made and deceitful in achieving that, the other characters pronounce judgement on him: 'Is he good? Is he bad?' 'One after the other.' 'Like you, like me, like everyone.'⁶

Although this conclusion may seem reassuring there is a constant sense of unease beneath the surface of the play. Hardouin retains throughout the action a sense of detachment and distance from the other characters, but at the same time he cannot turn away their demands; he is both uninvolved yet unable to escape. Diderot had suggested in the *Paradoxe sur le comédien* that the ability to be detached was a condition of great achievements; (and the *Paradoxe* also contains a reference to this play).⁷ But although he does achieve things Hardouin seems to derive little personal satisfaction from them. The unease does not stem from the methods used to fulfil the requests, it arises from the fact that Hardouin is ill at ease in himself. Being of use to others, winning their approval, cannot obscure this fact. This unease is even more evident in Diderot's last work, a commentary on the life and writings of Seneca. This was written at Holbach's request, to accompany a translation of Seneca's works begun by La Grange, the tutor of Holbach's children, and completed by Naigeon. It was first published as the *Essai sur la vie de Sénèque* in 1778, and then in a second longer version as the *Essai sur les règnes de Claude et de Néron* in 1782.

To some extent this unease is not unexpected in works that were so personal and autobiographical. Diderot had a pressing desire to be himself – 'I am happy nowhere except in the enjoyment of my soul, being myself, entirely myself'⁸ – and he had once suggested to Sophie Volland a 'plan of sincerity', which would involve studying himself, keeping 'an exact account of all the thoughts in his mind, all the movements of his heart, all his pleasures and pains'.⁹ But as his own life and writings continually demonstrated, Diderot only found himself through others, through working for other people, through writing as other characters. To set about self-examination in a direct personal way would inevitably bring disappointment. His own gifts were not suited to it.

But this problem, serious though it was, was only one factor behind his unease. Another factor was the continuing presence in his mind of the personality and ideas of Rousseau. The two men had had much in common and shared many experiences in their formative years together in Paris; they praised one another in their early works, Diderot in the *Pensées sur l'interprétation de la nature*[10] and the article 'Encyclopédie',[11] Rousseau in the *Discours sur l'inégalité*.[12] But then they had quarrelled and in 1758 Rousseau had broken decisively with Diderot. The differences between them were both intellectual and personal. Rousseau's fundamental insight, that the development of society (or, the character of any given society) changed man's nature, that there neither was nor could be any simple continuity between nature and culture, put him at odds with Diderot's most cherished belief: 'Everything that is can neither be outside nature nor opposed to nature.'[13] Rousseau believed in God, Diderot was an atheist. To develop his ideas Rousseau needed solitude, for his part Diderot needed company; given this temperamental difference, and the closeness of their previous friendship, it is no surprise that when the break came it was so painful. 'It may be,' wrote Rousseau in his last pleading letter, 'that the image of your dying friend will take away your peaceful nights. Diderot, think on it.'[14] A year later Diderot wrote: 'How I pity [Rousseau]! He will often be the torment of my thought.'[15] This was to be the case. As Jacques Proust has said: 'Rousseau's fundamental ideas never ceased to occupy Diderot's mind, even after the break-up of their friendship.'[16]

In 1768 it was rumoured that Rousseau was writing his memoirs. This suggestion made Diderot anxious and fretful,[17] and it led him to contribute to a malicious rewriting of the events of the 1750s, the pseudo-memoirs of Madame d'Epinay known as the *Histoire de Madame de Montbrillant*. There were various reasons for this anxiety. From the time of his quarrel with Hume Rousseau was generally regarded by the *philosophes* as being mad, bad and dangerous to know; there was no saying what unjust calumnies and unjustified insults would be thrown at them from the pages of his memoirs. Then there was the fact that Rousseau had been the spokesman for the citizens of Geneva who felt themselves to be, and were, excluded from political power and resentful of French influence. Diderot regarded these citizens as 'the mob'[18] and too close an association with Rousseau, however distant, might have been dangerous. (What Diderot thought of *Du contrat social* we do not know; his only comments were to say that it was easily available in Paris, despite the ban on its importation,[19] and a brief equivocal dismissal of it in the *Essai sur les règnes de Claude et de Néron*.)[20] Above all, there must have been the thought that for all the bewildering complexity of his character Rousseau had always made clear his refusal to accept favours from those in authority. The first recorded quarrel between the two men occurred precisely over this point. After the success of his opera *Le Devin du village* Rousseau had been offered a pension by Louis XV; his refusal to accept it made Diderot very angry.[21] This difference between them must have been hard for Diderot to bear.

In the first edition of his *Essai* Diderot inserted a short note which did not name Rousseau but was clearly aimed at him. It set out to discredit whatever remarks the latter's memoirs might contain. How could anyone trust a man whose 'life had been hidden for more than fifty years [i.e. up to the time of their quarrel] under the thickest mask of hypocrisy? Throw far away from you his squalid libel . . . Detest the ungrateful man who speaks evil of his benefactors; detest the atrocious man who does not hesitate to blacken [the reputation of] his former friends.'[22] Appearing, as it did, only a few months after Rousseau's death this note provoked widespread criticism. But Diderot was unrepentant. The critics were mistaken; they did not know Jean-Jacques as he did – 'the snake is dead but his poison is not'.[23] In the second edition he reprinted the note and then attacked his critics. 'I am not writing a satire but my vindication and that of a fairly large number of citizens who are dear to me; I am fulfilling a sacred duty.'[24] The fact was that little of Rousseau's work was original, his life had been a parade of blatant contradictions and dishonest pretence, he was wicked, perverse, mad, and worst of all 'he had become an *anti-philosophe*';[25] his fanatical followers hated priests much less than they hated the *philosophes*.

In this last accusation we can see another reason for Diderot's unease. The *philosophes* had not achieved as much as they had hoped. The intellectual differences that had separated first Rousseau and then Voltaire from Diderot and his friends had undermined the cause of enlightenment not only among *la république des lettres*, but among the public generally. The quarrels had been used to discredit all concerned. Then there had been the failure first of the reforms of Turgot, who had been dismissed in 1776, and then of the measures taken by Necker, who had resigned in 1781. Both had been at one time friends of Diderot and neither had been able to halt France's inexorable slide beyond bankruptcy into crisis.

In addition Diderot had doubts about his own achievements. During the years after his return from Russia he spent a considerable amount of time revising his manuscripts and having them copied.[26] He entered into negotiations with the Amsterdam publisher Rey for a complete edition of his works.[27] But when he reflected on the principal questions that had preoccupied him, uncertainties rose to the surface. Writing about science he said:

> it is not a matter of what has occurred in [a scientist's] head but of what occurs in nature. It is for her to explain herself; she must be questioned, and we must not answer for her. To make up for her silence by an analogy, or a conjecture, is to dream ingeniously, maybe wonderfully, but it is to dream . . . Nothing is more difficult than to observe well; nothing is more difficult than to make a good experiment; nothing is more difficult than to draw from the experiment or the observation only strict conclusions . . . Perhaps [only when] we possess a complete account of phenomena . . . will we know if movement is essential to matter, and if matter is created or not; and, created or uncreated, whether its diversity does not offend reason more than its simplicity. For it is perhaps only our ignorance that makes its unity or homogeneity so difficult to reconcile with the variety of phenomena.[28]

The insights of *Le Rêve de d'Alembert* did not rest on a solid basis of evidence. Nor had he written the moral treatise he had wanted to write; La Mettrie, the man who had shown most clearly the difficulties he faced, was bitterly attacked in the *Essai* (see p. 305). Moreover, it seemed that there was not one subject that he had really mastered: because of 'an unbridled curiosity and a small income I have never been allowed to devote myself completely to a single branch of human knowledge'.[29]

All these factors contributed to the *Essai sur les règnes de Claude et de Néron* but the major reason for the restless, uneasy, unhappy tone of the work is the anxiety Diderot felt about his own

behaviour. 'Let us wait for the last moment,' he had written in the
Réfutation d'Helvétius, 'to pronounce judgement on our lot and on
our virtue.'[30] That moment had come and the judgement was in
doubt. He had always believed in and valued posterity, but posterity looks at the life together with the works, and in his case a
major contradiction had developed over the years, his dependence
on Catherine II. Even as he was writing against tyranny in the
Histoire des Deux Indes he was asking a tyrant for money.[31] Hence
his interest in and identification with Seneca, who had been in a
comparable situation *vis-à-vis* Nero. 'We each have our saint,' he
announced in the *Essai*, 'Seneca is mine.'[32]

In his earlier works, the *Essai sur le mérite et la vertu* and the *Plan
d'une université*, Diderot had not had a high regard for Seneca.[33]
In the *Essai*, however, it became a matter of urgent importance to
him to show that the Roman philosopher's behaviour was
exemplary and, moreover, that by staying in office he achieved
good things.[34] He was 'a man of great talent and rare virtue',[35] who
had not been interested either in power or in enriching himself
(criticisms often made), and without whose beneficial influence
Nero would have done worse things and degenerated even more
rapidly. In making his case Diderot distorts the evidence[36] and
discredits the critics. His admiration for Seneca becomes
exaggerated – 'O Seneca! It is your breath which dispels the vain
phantoms of life . . . It is you who know how to speak about virtue
and inspire enthusiasm for it. You would have done more for me
than my father, my mother and my teachers'[37] – and his protests
discordant.

Nevertheless, while its detail may be inaccurate and its tone
strained, there is one theme that runs through the *Essai* which did
not suffer from these faults: the philosopher must be a man of
action.

> The philosopher who gives precepts without [himself setting an]
> example only fulfils half his task[38] . . . I will not put the person
> who reflects and the person who acts on the same line. A life in
> retirement is more agreeable, but an active life is more useful
> and honourable . . . If [a philosopher] does without the State he
> is a bad citizen; if the State does without him, the State is stupid[39]
> . . . Among Seneca's ideas I take much more pleasure in quoting
> those which show the goodness of his soul than those which show
> the beauty of his mind, because I rate the first of these qualities

more highly than the second, because I would prefer to have done a good deed than written a beautiful page; I envy Voltaire the defence of Calas, rather than the tragedy of *Mahomet*[40] . . . It is said: live first, then philosophize. It is the people who speak like that. But the wise man says: first philosophize, then live accordingly, if you can.[41]

This last comment also occurs in the *Lettre apologétique de l'abbé Raynal à Monsieur Grimm*,[42] written in March 1781, in which Diderot defended the *Histoire des Deux Indes* against the criticism Grimm had made of it. Grimm had become 'one of the most dangerous *antiphilosophes*'[43] in discarding the claims of humanity and justice. These claims must be recognized and published.

> What use is philosophy if it is silent? [he wrote in the *Essai*]. You must either speak out, or renounce the title of teacher of the human race. You will be persecuted, that is your destiny; they will make you drink hemlock, Socrates drank it before you. You will be imprisoned, exiled, your works burnt, you may even be made to climb a funeral pyre . . . You turn pale! You are gripped by fear, and you want to attack bad laws, bad behaviour, prevailing superstitions, the vices, vexations and acts of tyranny! Abandon your dignified costume, or know how to renounce a quiet life. Your state is a state of war.[44]

In the *Essai*, his first work to be published in France with his own name on the title-page since 1758, Diderot tried to live up to these principles. Not only did he hail the victory of the American rebels against the English as 'instructing those who govern about the legitimate use of their authority',[45] and for preparing a place of shelter 'to all the children of men now groaning, or who will be groaning, under the rod of civil and religious tyranny'.[46] He also spoke out directly against tyranny: 'a society of men is not a herd of animals; to treat them in the same way is to insult the human race. Peoples and their leaders owe one another a mutual respect.'[47] He spoke out against enlightened despotism;[48] he spoke up for the right of resistance;[49] he praised Raynal's *Histoire des Deux Indes*, 'a work full of research, boldness, eloquence and genius'.[50] He implied several parallels and drew one explicit parallel between Rome in Seneca's time and France in his own time: 'the conformity of our behaviour and that of [Seneca's] time is remarkable'.[51] His attitude to the possibilities of change may have been pessimistic,[52] his attitude to the people was certainly devoid of hope,[53] but nevertheless he spoke out.

Diderot was taking a considerable risk in publishing these remarks, and he was aware of the danger he faced.[54] But the *Essai* displays a stubborn persistence. The quality which had helped sustain him through the difficulties and setbacks of publishing the *Encyclopédie* was not diminished by age. This persistence does not make the *Essai* more agreeable to read; on the contrary, the relentless tone of self-defence or apology for Seneca, or the intemperate attacks on critics, make it troublesome and tiresome. But Diderot was speaking out in his own name, after years of silence. He may not have said a great deal, but what he did say was true to his conscience. As a result, when the *Essai* was published, he was threatened with arrest. He made an apology in person and there the matter ended.[55]

The *Essai* had opened with a calm, almost serene, sense of purpose:

> I do not compose, I am not an author. I read or I talk; I ask or I reply . . . This book, if it is one, is like one of my walks. Do I come to a beautiful viewpoint? I stop and enjoy it. I hurry my pace, or slow it down, according to the richness or barrenness of the sites. Always led on by my reverie, I have no other concern than to prevent the moment growing weary.[56]

As he proceeds, however, the uneasiness prevails and the mood becomes sombre. His own life had not been blameless, it had many disappointments. And the future looked grim. He wanted the book to be a summing-up, he wanted that summing-up to be favourable. But Diderot was never good at endings. Far from being an exception, the *Essai sur les règnes de Claude et de Néron* is conclusive evidence of that fact.

Nevertheless, it would be wrong to see the *Essai* purely as a reflection of Diderot's personal disappointments and limitations. For the work has a more than personal significance. Its resolute advocacy of philosophy as a *vita activa* is the final flowering of those ideas which had inspired the great achievement of the *Encyclopédie* and the equally successful *Histoire des Deux Indes*. In one of his contributions to the latter, written for the third edition at about the same time that he was working on the *Essai*, Diderot briefly outlined the intellectual history of his century: meta-physicians had given way to geometricians, 'who gave way to physicists, who gave way to naturalists and chemists'.

> [Now] the taste for natural history is on the decline. We are all preoccupied with questions of government, legislation, morality, politics and commerce. If I might be allowed to make a prediction I would declare that minds will incline more and more towards history: an immense field in which philosophy has not yet set foot . . . The moment approaches when reason, justice and truth will tear from the hands of ignorance and flattery a pen which they have held for all too long.[57]

In the light of this comment Diderot's *Essai* can be seen to reflect the changing concerns of his time. The emphasis of the *philosophe* as man of action was one example of this; the hesitations and repetitions were another. They were not merely the failings of a man grown old and weary, they were also the result of looking at and living among unwelcome problems with no easy solutions at hand. The sombre tone of the *Essai* was in its way true to the sombre mood of its time. As the closing pages of the *Histoire* made clear, Diderot believed that necessary change was a long way off and the future was dark with uncertainties. In the public realm, to which he had been increasingly drawn, he felt least at home. But that was where he belonged.

'Whoever has known Diderot only through his writings,' wrote Marmontel, 'has not known him.'[58] We should amend Marmontel's words; they should read: 'Whoever knows Diderot only through the writings published in his lifetime does not know him.' Those writings were an essential part of Diderot but only a part. Diderot's life as a writer did not end with the *Essai*, the best was yet to be revealed. In the latter half of his life he had often claimed that posterity alone would be able to give a fair judgement on his work, and that turned out to be true. Gradually and sporadically his unpublished writings came to light. They presented a bewildering assortment, a prodigal display of interests, talent and achievement – fiction admired by Stendhal, art criticism admired by Baudelaire, letters admired by Sainte-Beuve. *Le Neveu de Rameau* was praised by Marx (who once called Diderot his favourite writer) and Freud, the *Rêve de d'Alembert* was hailed as a prophetic work by material-ists, the *Paradoxe sur le comédien* was much discussed by people in the theatre. With succeeding generations, as more and more works appeared, the image and estimate of Diderot changed. In recent years, as the eighteenth century in general has come to be seen with fresh eyes and as Diderot's texts have been illuminated by scholarly attention, he has come to be seen as a figure as important as Voltaire and Rousseau. He did not have the brilliant wit of the former, nor the profound insight of the latter, but he made an equally distinct contribution to literature and the history of ideas. In his works now we meet the man so admired in his lifetime by those who knew him well. And what sort of man was that? Let us leave the last word with Marmontel: 'When in speaking he became animated and let his prolific thoughts take their course . . . and abandoned himself to the impulse of the moment, then indeed he was irresistible.'[59]

Notes

The following abbreviations are used in reference to Diderot's works:

AT   = *Oeuvres complètes* (ed. J. Assézat and M. Tourneux, Paris, 1875–77) 20 vols.

DPV   = *Oeuvres complètes* (edited under the direction of H. Dieckmann, J. Proust and J. Varloot, Paris, 1975–) 11 volumes have appeared so far.

EST   = *Oeuvres esthétiques* (ed. P. Vernière, Paris, 1959).

PHI   = *Oeuvres philosophiques* (ed. P. Vernière, Paris, 1956).

POL   = *Oeuvres politiques* (ed. P. Vernière, Paris, 1963).

ROM   = *Oeuvres romanesques* (ed. H. Bénac, Paris, 1962).

Commentaire = F. Hemsterhuis, *Lettre sur l'homme et ses rapports. Avec le commentaire inédit de Diderot* (ed. G. May, New Haven, 1964).

Éléments   = *Éléments de physiologie* (ed. J. Mayer, Paris, 1964).

Inventaire   = *Inventaire du Fonds Vandeul* (ed. H. Dieckmann, Paris, 1951).

Mémoires   = *Mémoires pour Catherine II* (ed. P. Vernière, Paris, 1966).

Neveu   = *Le Neveu de Rameau* (ed. J. Fabre, Geneva, 1950).

Raynal   = G. Raynal, *Histoire philosophique et politique du commerce et des établissements des Européens dans les deux Indes* (Neuchâtel and Geneva, 1783) 9 vols. plus one supplementary volume.

Roth   = *Correspondance* (ed. G. Roth (and J. Varloot), Paris, 1955–70) 16 vols.

Wherever possible reference is made to the most widely diffused and generally accessible modern edition, that published in the Classiques Garnier series – EST, PHI, POL and ROM. The one exception to this is *Le Neveu de Rameau*, for which the Fabre edition is used. Where the Classiques Garnier edition gives a work only in extract, as with the *Salons* or the *Réfutation d'Helvétius*, reference is made to the Assézat–Tourneux edition in brackets.

The following abbreviations are also used:

Corr. litt.	= *Correspondance littéraire, philosophique et critique par Grimm, Diderot, Raynal, Meister, etc.* (ed. M. Tourneux, Paris, 1877–82), 16 vols.
DS	= *Diderot Studies.*
ENC	= *Encyclopédie ou dictionnaire raisonné des sciences, des arts et des métiers* (Paris, 1751–65) 17 vols.
JJR	= *Oeuvres complètes de Jean-Jacques Rousseau* (edited under the direction of B. Gagnebin and M. Raymond, Paris, 1959–) 4 vols.
SVEC	= *Studies on Voltaire and the Eighteenth Century.*

1   INTRODUCTION (pp.1–21)

1. B. Willey, *The Eighteenth Century Background* (London, 1940), p. 44.
2. J. S. Mill, 'Coleridge' (1840) in *Essays on Literature and Society* (ed. J. Scheewind, New York, 1965), p.319.
3. Ibid.
4. K. Clark, *Landscape into Art* (2nd edition, London, 1976), p.105.
5. L. Stone, *New York Review of Books*, 29 May 1980, p.46.
6. E. Faguet, *Dix-huitième siècle* (Paris, 1890), p.219.
7. J. Chouillet, *L'Esthétique des lumières* (Paris, 1974), p.162.
8. JJR, I.1115.
9. Roth, IV.281.
10. AT, I.xvii–xviii.
11. Quoted in *Textes choisis* (ed. M. Roelens, Paris, 1966), p.285. Kant's remark occurs in his 1784 essay *Was ist Aufklärung?*, and was itself a quotation from Horace, *Epistles* II.2.40.
12. *Le Philosophe* (ed. H. Dieckmann, St Louis, 1948), p.46.
13. Ibid., p.44.
14. Ibid., p.56.
15. AT, III.248.
16. AT, III.221.
17. *Éléments*, p.300.
18. *Lettres philosophiques*, Ch.XXV, para.23.
19. AT, X.69.
20. A good case for attributing the work to Dumarsais is made by A. Fairbairn, SVEC, LXXVII (1972), pp. 375–95.
21. *Oeuvres* (ed. G. Schelle, Paris, 1913–23), I.215–6.
22. *De l'esprit* (Paris, 1758), I.i–ii.
23. AT, XI.93.

24. AT, III.517 (see also Roth, II.299).
25. Roth, II.225.
26. AT, III.421.
27. POL,76 (see also AT, X.162).
28. POL,112.
29. AT, III.421.
30. POL, 467 ff. (AT, II.427 ff.).
31. *Essay on Human Understanding*, IV, Ch.3, para. 20.
32. PHI, 90.
33. AT, VI.315.
34. *Mémoires*, 249 (see also EST,736).
35. AT, VI.372 ff.
36. DPV, VII.232.
37. AT, II.403.
38. Roth, III.98.
39. AT, III.524 (see also *Commentaire*, 507; Raynal, III.259).
40. EST, 433.
41. J. A. Naigeon, *Mémoires historiques et philosophiques sur la vie et les ouvrages de M. Diderot* (Paris, 1821), p.46.
42. AT, XI.133 (see also AT, XI.123–4, 133 ff. *Éléments*, 23–4; *Inventaire*, 199; PHI, 609).
43. Roth, II.207.
44. AT, VIII.206.
45. Roth, IX.204.
46. Roth, VII.62.
47. AT, II.273 (see also AT, II.251, IV.60–1, VI.384).
48. EST, 206.
49. AT, III.227.
50. AT, XII.57.
51. See 'Sur ma manière de travailler', *Mémoires*, 247–9.
52. *Commentaire*, 179. On this aspect of his work see G. May, 'Diderot, artiste et philosophe du décousu', *Europäische Aufklärung* (ed. H. Friedrich and F. Schalk, Munich, 1967), pp.165–88.
53. *Éléments*, 42.
54. PHI, 310.
55. EST, 433.
56. Roth, II.56.
57. Roth, II.283–4.
58. *Éléments*, 224.
59. *Commentaire*, 207.
60. AT, XI.127.
61. AT, II.411.
62. *Éléments*, 58.
63. AT, I.xix.

64. ROM, 67.
65. Roth, IX.154.
66. AT.VIII.231.
67. PHI, 568 (AT, II.310).
68. See *Sur la liberté de la presse* (ed. J. Proust, Paris, 1964).
69. PHI, 380.
70. PHI, 216 (see also PHI, 369).
71. PHI, 395.
72. DPV, IV.361.
73. AT, IX.203.
74. Roth, IX.205.
75. EST, 452 (AT, X.172).
76. EST, 711.
77. POL, 81.
78. AT, II.273. On this aspect of his work see R. Mortier, 'Diderot et le problème de l'expressivité', *Cahiers de l'association internationale des études françaises* XIII (1961) pp.283–98.
79. DPV, VII.328.
80. Roth, I.192.
81. *Corr. litt.*, II.67.

2 LIFE (pp.22–30)

1. ROM, 255.
2. Roth, V.191.
3. DPV, I.37.
4. EST, 540 (AT, X.349).
5. DPV, I.13.
6. AT, XI.265–6.
7. DPV, I.300.
8. AT, X.280.
9. AT, II.440.
10. *Sur la liberté de la presse* (ed. cit.), p.89.
11. EST, 362 (see also EST, 355).
12. Roth, II.39.
13. AT, X.379.
14. AT, X.237.
15. DPV, I.31.
16. POL, 345.
17. Roth, XIV.152.
18. AT, III.406.
19. DPV, I.31.
20. DPV, I.34.
21. Condorcet, *Oeuvres* (ed. A. C. O'Connor, Paris, 1847), III.67.

3   ATHEISM (pp.31–55)

Page numbers in the margin refer to PHI.

1. DPV, I.296.
2. *Characteristics* (London, 1711), II.109.
3. Ibid., II.98.
4. Ibid., II.75.
5. Ibid., II.120.
6. DPV, I.329.
7. *Characteristics* (ed. cit.), II.113–4.
8. DPV, I.313.
9. AT, II.85, n.2.
10. DPV, I.290.
11. DPV, I.353.
12. DPV, I.354.
13. DPV, II.138.
14. DPV, II.138.
15. DPV, II.131.
16. PHI, 92.
17. PHI, 93–4.
18. PHI, 88.
19. PHI, 115, 140.
20. PHI, 146.
21. See Lucretius, *De rerum natura*, I.1028, II.899–901.
22. PHI, 135.
23. PHI, 94.
24. PHI, 96.
25. Roth, I.74.
26. Roth, I.77.
27. ROM, 107–8.
28. Roth, I.55.
29. AT, II.82.
30. AT, II.84.
31. AT, X.391; *Mémoires*, 245.
32. *Mémoires*, 106.
33. AT, II.270.
34. AT, II.88n.
35. Roth, VIII.217.
36. Roth, IX.154 (see also AT, III.138).
37. *Mémoires*, 109.
38. PHI, 526.
39. PHI, 534.
40. PHI, 539.

41. PHI, 543.
42. PHI, 550.

For this chapter see A. Vartanian, 'From Deist to Atheist', DS I (1949), and the introductions and notes by P. Casini and J. S. Spink to the *Essai sur le mérite et la vertu* in DPV I, by H. Dieckmann to *La Promenade du sceptique* in DPV II, and by Y. Belaval and R. Niklaus to the *Pensées philosophiques* and the *Lettre sur les aveugles* in DPV II and IV.

4   DISCOVERY (pp.56–73)

The translation in this chapter is by D. Coltman, (except for I, III, X, XVII, XVIII, XX and XXII).

1. Naigeon, op. cit., p. 10.
2. PHI, 218.
3. PHI, 199.
4. PHI, 214.
5. PHI, 199.
6. PHI, 203.
7. EST, 666.
8. AT, X.307–8, XI.13, XI.15, XI.292–4.
9. PHI, 193.
10. PHI, 194.
11. PHI, 222.
12. PHI, 222.
13. PHI, 211.
14. PHI, 212.
15. PHI, 208.
16. PHI, 186.
17. PHI, 217.
18. J. Roger, *Les sciences de la vie dans la pensée française du XVIIIe siècle* (2nd edn. Paris, 1971), p.484.
19. PHI, 175.

5   ENCYCLOPAEDIA (pp.74–124)

Page numbers in the margin refer to DPV V (*Prospectus – Autorité politique*), DPV VI (*Beau – Croire*), DPV VII (*Délicieux – Locke*), and DPV VIII (*Malebranche – Voluptueux*).

1. Roth, I.160.
2. ENC, III.xvia.
3. Roth, I.199.
4. Roth, II.39.
5. Roth, II.150.
6. Roth, IV. 300–6.

7. DPV, VII.353.
8. DPV, VII.236.
9. DPV, VII.115.
10. ENC, III.xi.
11. ENC, III.iv.
12. ENC, VII.599b.
13. ENC, I.xliii
14. *A Diderot Pictorial Encyclopaedia of Trades and Industry* (ed. C. C. Gillispie, New York, 1959).
15. AT, III.467.
16. DPV, VII.194.
17. Roth, IV.172.
18. *Éléments*, 343.
19. Roth, III.283–8.

For this chapter see J. Proust, *L'Encyclopédie* (Paris, 1965) and J. Lough, *The Encyclopédie* (London, 1971).

6   THEATRE (pp.125–50)

Page numbers in the margin refer to EST. The translation from the *Entretiens sur le Fils naturel* is by D. Coltman, that from the first five chapters of the *Discours sur la poésie dramatique* is by J. G. Linn.

1. EST, 223.
2. ROM, 143.
3. ROM, 142.
4. EST, 81.
5. EST, 85.
6. EST, 113.
7. EST, 64.
8. EST, 79.
9. DPV, VII.192 (see also DPV, VII.257–8).
10. AT, VIII.226.
11. EST, 227.
12. EST, 241.
13. EST, 129.
14. DPV, X.65.
15. DPV, X.68.
16. Roth, XII.15–17, XII.19.
17. DPV, X.437–51.
18. Roth, III.112
19. DPV, X.549–52.
20. EST, 61.
21. *Mémoires*, 52–3, 102–4.

For this chapter see the introductions and notes by J. Chouillet in DPV X.

7   FICTION (pp.151–66)

The two extended extracts from *Jacques le fataliste* are translated by J. Robert Loy.

1. EST, 29.
2. DPV, II.130.
3. EST, 30–1.
4. EST, 35.
5. EST, 29.
6. EST, 29.
7. EST, 44.
8. EST, 33.
9. ROM, 850.
10. ROM, 851.
11. ROM, 864.
12. ROM, 866.
13. ROM, 856.
14. ROM, 281.
15. ROM, 301.
16. ROM, 310.
17. ROM, 311.
18. ROM, 342.
19. On *La Religieuse* see the introductions and notes by H. Dieckmann and G. May in DPV XI.
20. ROM, 783.
21. ROM, 792.
22. ROM, 791.
23. ROM, 789.
24. ROM, 790.
25. ROM, 793.
26. ROM, 821.
27. ROM, 833.
28. See, for example, EST, 775.
29. AT, XI.374.
30. J. Proust has edited *Quatre Contes* (Geneva, 1964) with an interesting introduction; H. Dieckmann has written several articles on the *contes*, reprinted in *Studien zur Europäischen Aufklärung* (Munich, 1974); see also R. Niklaus, 'Diderot's Moral Tales', DS VIII (1966).
31. ROM, 493–5.
32. Roth, IV.172.
33. ROM, 778.
34. P. Vernière, 'Diderot et l'invention littéraire: à propos de Jacques le fataliste', *Révue d'histoire litteraire de la France* LIX (1959), p.153.
35. PHI, 618–9 (AT, II.372–3).

36. ROM, 670.
37. ROM, 671.
38. ROM, 520.
39. See the 1796 comment cited in *Jacques le fataliste et son maître* (ed. S. Lecointre and J. Le Galliot, Paris and Geneva, 1977), p.lxxxii. This edition presents the best available text of the novel; its introduction has less to recommend it.
40. ENC, I.xxviii.
41. ROM, 504.
42. ROM, 780.
43. ROM, 579.
44. ROM, 505.
45. ROM, 731.
46. ROM, 553.
47. ROM, 544.
48. ROM, 664, 682. For Diderot's definition of an *original* see PHI, 578 (AT, II. 331).
49. ROM, 682.
50. ROM, 574.
51. ROM, 515–6.
52. ROM, 516.
53. ROM, 663–5.
54. See the remarks by E. Koehler in J. Proust, *Lectures de Diderot* (Paris, 1974), p.191.
55. See the introduction to the edition cited in note 39, pp.cxxx,clxii.
56. *Tristram Shandy*, Bk VIII, Ch 1.

Dix-huitième siècle V (1973), p.137 contains a list of articles about *Jacques le fataliste*; among them those by L. G. Crocker in DS III (1961) and S. Werner in SVEC, CXXVIII (1975) offer two contrasted and well-presented points of view.

8   PAINTING (pp.167–83)

Page numbers in the margin refer to AT XI.

1. AT, XI.394.
2. AT, XI.17 (see also Roth, V.167).
3. AT, X.226.
4. AT, X.162 (see also AT, X.200).
5. AT, X.233.
6. AT, X.237.
7. EST, 531 (AT, X.341).
8. AT, X.453.
9. AT, XI.3.

10. EST, 512 (AT, XI.22).
11. AT, X.226, XI.78.
12. AT, XI.18.
13. AT, X.160.
14. AT, X.187.
15. Roth, V.167.
16. AT, XI.288.
17. EST, 449 (AT, X.112).
18. AT, XI.57.
19. AT, XI.75.
20. AT, X.113.
21. AT, X.146.
22. EST, 723.
23. This comment by a contemporary is quoted in *Salons* (ed. J. Seznec, Oxford, 1967), IV.330.
24. AT, XII.63.
25. AT, XII.64.
26. EST, 794.
27. AT, X.418.
28. EST, 722.
29. EST, 518 (AT, X.142).
30. EST, 519 ff. (AT, X.151 ff.).
31. EST, 548 ff. (AT, X.356 ff.).
32. EST, 533 ff. (AT, X.343 ff.).
33. EST, 481 (AT, X.98).
34. EST, 484 (AT, X.194).
35. EST, 487 (AT, X.301).
36. AT, X.115, 138, 146.
37. EST, 714.
38. The borrowings are detailed by Gita May in 'Diderot and Burke', *Publications of the Modern Language Association* LXXV (December, 1960), pp.527–39.
39. AT, X.137 (see also AT, X.308).
40. AT, XI.238.
41. EST, 642–4 (AT, XI. 229).
42. AT, XI.160 ff.
43. Diderot's description of how he would like his father portrayed reads like an account of a painting by Greuze: Roth, II.195.
44. AT, X.188–9, 308; in relation to poetry, see EST, 65. (see also, on this subject, EST, 239, and AT, II.330).
45. AT, X.376 (see also AT, XI.238, 270).
46. JJR, II.133. See my *The Indispensable Rousseau* (London, 1979), pp. 92–94.
47. EST, 542–4 (AT, X.351).

48. AT, XI.246.
49. AT, XI.254.
50. EST, 484 (AT, X.194).
51. EST, 485 (AT, X.299).
52. EST, 495 (AT, XI.409).
53. AT, X.187–8.
54. AT, XI.11.
55. AT, XI.12.
56. AT, XI.12–14.
57. AT, XI.14.
58. AT, XI.15.
59. AT, XI.481.
60. AT, XI.223, 370.
61. AT, XI.411–13; Raynal, IX.266.
62. EST, 753, 796, 815.
63. AT, XI.241, III.477.
64. AT, XI.73, 107–8, 267–70.
65. AT, XI.89–94.
66. See *Salons* (ed. J. Seznec and J. Adhémar, Oxford, 1963), III.348.
67. See, for example, Roth, IX.185–6.
68. *Satires*, II.6.60.

For this chapter see the informative and excellently illustrated four volume edition of the *Salons* by J. Seznec and J. Adhémar (Oxford, 1957–67); also, the study by M. Cartwright, 'Diderot critique d'art et le problème de l'expression', DS XIII (1969), pp.99–235. The best available selection from the *Salons* is by J. Seznec, *Denis Diderot sur l'art et les artistes* (Paris, 1967).

9   RAMEAU'S NEPHEW (pp.184–218)

Page numbers in the margin refer to *Neveu*.

1. Naigeon, op. cit., p.316.
2. AT, XI.169.
3. See the Appendix to *Neveu*, pp.243–54.
4. Roth, IV.281.
5. D. O'Gorman, *Diderot the Satirist* (Toronto, 1971), pp.56 and 135.
6. R. Desné in the introduction to his edition of *Le Neveu* (Paris, 1972), pp.65 and 72.
7. Ibid., p.73.
8. J. Doolittle, *Rameau's Nephew* (Geneva, 1970), p.25.
9. Ibid., p.36.
10. AT, VI.303–16. The text is also printed in D. O'Gorman, op. cit., and R. Desné, op. cit.

11. Roth, III.292.
12. *Neveu*, 44.
13. EST, 140.
14. EST, 48.
15. See on this subject G. May, 'L'angoisse de l'échec et la genèse du *Neveu de Rameau*', DS III (1961), pp.285–307.
16. *Neveu*, 94.
17. See on this subject H. Dieckmann, *Studien zur Europäischen Aufklïung* (Munich, 1974), pp.131–2.
18. *Satires*, II.7.14.
19. Roth, III.98.
20. Roth, XI.211.
21. Roth, IV.189.

For this chapter see the studies by D. O'Gorman and J. Doolittle, cited above; also, H. Josephs, *Diderot's Dialogue of Gesture and Language* (Ohio, 1969) and *Entretiens sur le Neveu de Rameau* (ed. M. Duchet et M. Launay, Paris, 1967). The excellent edition by J. Fabre (Geneva, 1950) remains the essential starting-point for any study of the work.

10   D'ALEMBERT'S DREAM (pp.219-63)

Page numbers in the margin refer to PHI and *Éléments*. The translation of *Le Rêve de d'Alembert* is by J. Stewart and J. Kemp.

1. PHI, 242.
2. DPV, VIII.367.
3. AT, VI.407–10.
4. AT, II.272–4.
5. Roth, II.282–3.
6. *Éléments*, 299.
7. Roth, V.141.
8. AT, XI.146.
9. Roth, IX.130.
10. Roth, IX.126.
11. Roth, IX.140.
12. PHI, 280.
13. PHI, 287, 341.
14. PHI, 301.
15. *Éléments*, 261.
16. PHI, 318.
17. PHI, 276.
18. PHI, 367.
19. *Éléments*, 41; PHI, 187–8, 227.
20. *Éléments*, 5, 209; *Commentaire*, 201, 217, 503.

21. *Éléments*, 43; PHI, 308.
22. *Éléments*, 46, 50, 295; PHI, 310, 326.
23. J. Roger, op. cit., p.663 ff.
24. *Éléments*, 6.
25. *Éléments*, 60.
26. *Éléments*, 307–8.
27. PHI, 566 (AT, II.302).
28. *Éléments*, 24.
29. See on this subject R. Mortier, 'Holbach et Diderot', *Revue de l'université de Bruxelles* (1972), pp.222–36; also the comments by S. Moravia, pp.271–3.
30. PHI, 393.
31. PHI, 394.
32. PHI, 395.
33. PHI, 399.
34. PHI, 398.

For this chapter see L. G. Crocker, 'Diderot and Eighteenth Century French Transformism' in *Forerunners of Darwin, 1745–1859* (ed.H. B. Glass, Baltimore, 1959); J. Ehrard, 'Diderot et les six tentations du matérialisme des lumières' in *Studies in the French Eighteenth Century* (ed. D. J. Mossop *et al.*, Durham, 1978), H. Dieckmann, 'The Metaphoric Structure of the *Rêve de d'Alembert*' in DS XVII (1973); J. Varloot's introduction to his edition of the *Rêve* (Paris, 1971), and J. Mayer's introduction to his edition of the *Éléments* (Paris, 1964).

11   AESTHETICS (pp.264–81)

Page numbers in the margin refer to EST. The translation of the *Paradoxe sur le comédien* is by D. Coltman.

1. DPV, IV.162.
2. DPV, IV.157.
3. DPV, IV.158.
4. DPV, IV.161.
5. DPV, IV.169.
6. DPV, IV.170–1.
7. DPV, IV.182.
8. DPV, IV.207. On the *Lettre sur les sourds et muets* see the excellent edition by P. H. Meyer, DS VII (1965).
9. AT, VI.407.
10. PHI, 598 (AT, II.349).
11. PHI, 280–1.
12. AT, X.308.
13. ENC, I.xvi.

14. Roth, II.52 (see also DPV, V.314, VII.562).
15. *Éléments*, 250–7.
16. EST, 218.
17. EST, 219.
18. EST, 212.
19. EST, 308 (see also Raynal, I.340).
20. PHI, 182, 189.
21. PHI, 189.
22. See on this subject H. Dieckmann, 'Diderot's Conception of Genius', *Journal of the History of Ideas* II (1940), pp.151–82.
23. EST, 16.
24. EST, 13.
25. EST, 15.
26. PHI, 590 (AT, II.341; see also AT, II.290).
27. AT, X.430.
28. AT, X.145.
29. PHI, 591 (AT, II.341).
30. *Mémoires*, 250 (see also AT, VII.407).
31. EST, 12.
32. EST, 666.
33. AT, XI.292–4.
34. AT, X.307.
35. AT, II.411.
36. Roth, II.284.
37. AT, III.481.
38. EST, 563 (AT, X.202).
39. EST, 568 (AT, X.310).
40. DPV, VII.196.
41. See, in particular, AT, X.319–20, XI.427.
42. PHI, 591 (AT, II.342).
43. EST, 11–12.
44. DPV, VII.234.
45. EST, 233.
46. EST, 570 (AT, X.312). For a description of *verve* virtually identical to *génie*, see AT, VI.412.
47. AT, XI.177–8 (see also EST, 720).
48. AT, XI.151.
49. Roth, IX.213.
50. AT, VIII.343–59.
51. See, for example, EST, 354.
52. EST, 331.
53. EST, 362.
54. DPV, X. 445.
55. Roth, V.101.

56. *Neveu*, 83.
57. AT, VI,456; PHI, 350.
58. EST, 252.
59. EST, 318.
60. EST, 309.
61. EST, 362.
62. DPV, X. 436.
63. DPV, X. 444.
64. EST, 319.
65. EST, 357.
66. EST, 338 ff.
67. EST, 342.
68. EST, 370.
69. EST, 363.
70. AT, VIII.508.
71. *Cinq Leçons sur Diderot* (Paris, 1959), p.116.
72. EST, 252.
73. AT, VI.414.
74. AT, XI.450.
75. Roth, III.98.
76. AT, X.185.
77. Roth, IV.56.
78. AT, X.319.
79. AT, III.160, 181.

For a good discussion of several aspects of Diderot's aesthetics see D. Funt, 'Diderot and the Esthetics of the Enlightenment', DS XI (1968).

12 MORALITY (pp.282–306)

Page numbers in the margin refer to PHI and *Commentaire*. (The last three sentences of the extracts from the *Réfutation d'Helvétius* are not in PHI but AT, II.408, 410.) The translation from the *Réfutation d'Helvétius* is by D. Coltman.

1. Roth, II.108.
2. EST, 415–6.
3. DPV, IV.334.
4. DPV, IV.353.
5. POL, 30.
6. Fontenelle, *Textes choisis* (ed. cit.), p.147.
7. Ibid., p.155.
8. Ibid., p.158.
9. Ibid., p.157.
10. *Corr. litt.*, II.444.

11. *Corr. litt.*, II.480.
12. *A Philosophical Inquiry concerning Human Liberty* (London, 1717), p.61.
13. Ibid., p.41.
14. Ibid., p.71.
15. Ibid., p.86.
16. Ibid., p.89.
17. *Corr. litt.*, II.482.
18. JJR, III.141–2.
19. Fontenelle, *Textes choisis* (ed. cit.), p.152.
20. Roth, I.211–16.
21. AT, IX.463.
22. DPV, X. 76.
23. Roth, II.52.
24. AT, II.270.
25. PHI, 505 (see also AT, VI.444).
26. DPV, VIII.446.
27. *Éléments*, 21.
28. *Éléments*, 295.
29. Roth, II.57.
30. Roth, XIII.37.
31. *Inventaire*, 235. See on this subject D. Creighton, 'Man and mind in Diderot and Helvétius', *Publications of the Modern Language Association* LXXI (September, 1956), pp.705–24.
32. AT, II.296.
33. AT, II.388, 389, 396.
34. Roth, II.107.
35. AT, XI.446.
36. AT, XI.124.
37. ROM, 554, 575.
38. ROM, 673–82.
39. Roth, III.142.
40. *Commentaire*, 315.
41. *Commentaire*, 45.
42. AT, III.217–8.
43. AT, III.27.
44. AT, III.113.
45. PHI, 539.

For a different treatment of some of the issues dealt with in this chapter see C. Blum, *Diderot, The Virtue of a Philosopher* (New York, 1974).

13   SEXUALITY (pp.307–19)

Page numbers in the margin refer to PHI. The translation from the

Supplément au Voyage de Bougainville is by J. Stewart and J. Kemp.

1. *De rerum natura*, I.629, V.1362.
2. DPV, V.388.
3. PHI, 489.
4. Naigeon, op. cit., p.36.
5. PHI, 377.
6. AT, II.260.
7. AT, II.260.
8. AT, II.252.
9. AT, II.258.
10. AT, II.253.
11. ROM, 604 (see also PHI, 480).
12. ROM, 812.
13. ROM, 599–652.
14. ROM, 835.
15. AT, II.203.
16. PHI, 464.
17. *Satires*, I.2.73–7.
18. PHI, 503–4.
19. PHI, 462.
20. PHI, 498.
21. PHI, 501.
22. PHI, 507.
23. PHI, 512–3, 513–4.
24. PHI, 514.
25. JJR, IV.249.
26. AT, VI.439.
27. Roth, IX.245.
28. *Supplément au Voyage de Bougainville* (ed. H. Dieckmann, Geneva, 1955), p.cxxxii.
29. Roth, XII.123.
30. Roth, XII.125.

On the *Supplément* generally see the editions by H. Dieckmann, cited in note 28, and by G. Chinard (Paris, 1935).

14   POLITICS (pp.320–58)

Page numbers in the margin refer to Raynal.

1. These are indicated in the useful chapter on this article in J. Lough, *Essays on the Encyclopédie of Diderot and D'Alembert* (London, 1968).
2. Quoted in J. Lough, op. cit., pp.448 and 459.
3. ENC, III.xvia.

4. EST, 821 (see also *Éléments*, 33).
5. AT, II.355. On this article see R. Wokler, 'The Influence of Diderot on Rousseau', SVEC CXXXII (1975), pp.55–76.
6. See, for example, J. Proust, *Diderot et l'Encyclopédie* (Paris, 1962), p.434.
7. J. Proust, op. cit., p.324.
8. See, for example, AT, IV.65–8; also, PHI, 416.
9. Roth, II. 53–5.
10. Roth, V.173.
11. Roth, VI.336.
12. AT, XI.93.
13. AT, XI.121.
14. AT, XI.93.
15. Roth, IX.245.
16. AT, VI.443.
17. AT, XVII.333–61.
18. POL, 91.
19. POL, 84.
20. POL, 100.
21. POL, 85.
22. POL, 87.
23. POL, 155.
24. POL, 144.
25. POL, 139.
26. AT, XI.122–3.
27. *Mémoires*, 235.
28. *Inventaire*, 233.
29. Roth, III.86–7.
30. PHI, 619–20 (AT, II.381–2).
31. O. Hufton, *Europe: Privilege and Protest 1730–1789* (London, 1980), p.328.
32. AT, VI.403.
33. AT, VI.404.
34. Roth, XI,19–20.
35. Roth, XI.20–1.
36. Roth, XI.223.
37. POL, 466 (AT, II.276). It also occurs in Raynal, V.170.
38. Raynal, IX.52. The passage is abridged and less forceful in this version.
39. Diderot, *Oeuvres complètes* (ed. R. Lewinter, Paris, 1971), X.75.
40. Ibid., X.77. This sentence was not repeated in the *Histoire des Deux Indes* but the idea was, see the references given in notes 86, 87 and 88.
41. *Mémoires*, 1.
42. *Mémoires*, 24.

43. *Mémoires*, 16.
44. *Mémoires*, 18.
45. *Mémoires*, 18.
46. *Mémoires*, 20.
47. *Mémoires*, 32.
48. *Mémoires*, 3.
49. *Mémoires*, 5.
50. *Mémoires*, 3.
51. *Mémoires*, 152.
52. *Mémoires*, 155.
53. *Mémoires*, 159–60.
54. *Mémoires*, 235 (see also *Mémoires*, 44; Roth, XIV.85).
55. *Mémoires*, 117.
56. *Mémoires*, 119.
57. *Oeuvres complètes* (ed. R. Lewinter, Paris, 1971), X.103.
58. AT, III.429.
59. AT, III.520.
60. An English translation is given in *Documents of Catherine II* (ed. W. F. Reddaway, Cambridge, 1931).
61. *Oeuvres complètes* (ed. R. Lewinter, Paris, 1971), X.101–2. The idea is repeated in *Mémoires*, 199.
62. POL, 465 (AT, II.275).
63. Raynal, IX.171.
64. AT, XI.450.
65. Raynal, Frontispiece (see also Raynal, I.377).
66. Raynal, IX.287–8.
67. AT, I.xviin.
68. DPV, I.32.
69. M. Duchet, 'Diderot collaborateur de Raynal', *Revue d'histoire littéraire de la France* LX (1960), pp.543–4.
70. For example, Raynal VI.95 and IX.22.
71. Raynal, II.79.
72. Raynal, II.79.
73. Raynal, V.283–4. See also Raynal, V.256–7.
74. This is suggested by Y. Benot, *Diderot, de l'athéisme à l'anti-colonialisme* (Paris, 1970), p.194, and A. Strugnell, *Diderot's Politics* (The Hague, 1973), p.209.
75. Raynal, VIII.276.
76. Raynal, VIII.287.
77. Raynal, VIII.293.
78. A. Strugnell, op. cit., p.211.
79. At, VI.444, II.431, III.429; POL,402; *Mémoires*, 174; *Commentaire*, 421.
80. See T. Paine, *A Letter addressed to the Abbé Raynal* (Philadelphia

and London, 1782), p.58 ff. For the original passage see T. Paine, *Common Sense* (ed. I. Kramnick, Harmonsworth, 1976), p.65.

81. EST, 700.
82. JJR, III.251.
83. Raynal, IX.305. If I understand her correctly M. Duchet suggests that this sentence is by Diderot; see *Diderot et l'Histoire des Deux Indes ou l'écriture fragmentaire* (Paris, 1978), p.105. However, in both her references – to the *Observations* (POL, 372) and to the *Supplément* (PHI, 504–5) – the notion that natural laws persist in the civil State, is contrary to the idea that 'men are what the government makes them'. Another passage in the Observations (POL, 349–50) could support her suggestion, but none of these references seems to me decisive.
84 Raynal, VIII.275.
85. *Mémoires*, 4 (see also *Mémoires*, 235).
86. Raynal, VII.1, VII.277–9. For another clear statement of this principle see Raynal, I. 100–1.
87. Raynal, V.278, 288–9.
88. Raynal, IX.54.
89. PHI, 640.
90. See, for example, AT, II.393, 425, III.331, X.168.
91. See, for example, AT, III.324, IX.466.
92. Raynal, VIII.76. See on this subject H. Wolpe, *Raynal et sa machine de guerre* (Paris, 1956), pp. 97–99, 102–18.
93. Raynal, IX.241–3, IX.264–5.
94. Raynal, VIII.287.
95. AT, XI.90 ff, IX.12–19.
96. PHI, 643.
97. Raynal, IX. 133–4.
98. *Mémoires*, 235.
99. Raynal, VI.147–8. See also PHI, 640.

15   CONCLUSION (pp.359–68)

1. PHI, 443.
2. PHI, 433.
3. PHI, 443.
4. AT, VIII.202.
5. AT, VIII.180.
6. AT, VIII.244.
7. EST, 329.
8. Roth, VII.171.
9. Roth, IV.39.
10. PHI, 234.

11. DPV, VII.244.
12. JJR, III.213.
13. PHI, 380.
14. *Correspondance complète de J–J. Rousseau* (ed. R. A. Leigh, Geneva, 1967), V.48–9.
15. Roth, II.108.
16. Introduction to *Quatre Contes* (ed. cit.), p.lxiv.
17. Roth, VIII.17–18.
18. DS, III.318.
19. *Sur la liberté de la presse* (ed. cit.), p.82.
20. AT, III.95.
21. JJR, I.381.
22. AT, III.91.
23. AT, III.98. The sentence is in Italian; a quotation from an Italian opera?
24. AT, III.99.
25. AT, III.96.
26. Roth, XIV.42, XV.271–3, 279.
27. Roth, XV.50–1, 54.
28. AT, III.360–1. (See also Raynal, V.199–200).
29. AT, III.400–1.
30. PHI, 611 (AT, II.365).
31. Roth, XV.149–50. He publicly acknowledged his debt to Catherine in the *Essai*, AT, III.400.
32. AT, III.94 (see also AT, III.188).
33. DPV, I.425; AT, III.484.
34. AT, III.65, 375.
35. AT, III.373.
36. See W. Conroy, 'Diderot's *Essai sur Sénèque*', SVEC CXXXI (1975), pp.53–70.
37. AT, III.371.
38. AT, III.66.
39. AT, III.323 (see also AT, III.210, 248, 338).
40. AT, III.285 (see also AT, III.332).
41. AT, III.209.
42. PHI, 629.
43. PHI, 630.
44. AT, III.271.
45. POL, 491 (AT, III.324).
46. AT, III.393.
47. AT, III.264.
48. AT, III.265.
49. AT, III.103.
50. AT, III.394.

51. AT, III.258.
52. AT, III.33, 163.
53. AT, III. 90n, 111, 121, 164, 263.
54. Roth, XV.271–2.
55. Roth, XV.300–3.
56. AT, III.10–11.
57. Raynal, V. 200–1.
58. Marmontel, *Mémoires* (ed. M. Tourneux, Paris, 1891), II.243.
59. Ibid., II.243–4.

On *Est-il bon? Est-il méchant?* see the excellent edition by J. Undank, SVEC XVI (1961). For a comparison of the 1778 and 1782 texts of the *Essai* see *Essai sur Sénèque* (ed. H. Nakagawa, Tokyo, 1966).

Dates

Life and writings

1713   5 October, born at Langres.

1728–9   Goes to Paris to complete his education.

c.1733   Starts training to become a lawyer.

c.1734–46 Works as a tutor, translator and general hack.

1743   Marries Antoinette Champion.

1745   Publication of his translation of Shaftesbury's *Enquiry concerning virtue or merit*.

1746   Publication of *Pensées philosophiques*, condemned by the Paris Parlement.

1747   First involvement with the *Encyclopédie*. Writes on mathematical subjects and *La Promenade du sceptique*.

1748   Publication of *Les Bijoux indiscrets*.

1749   Publication of *Lettre sur les aveugles* leads to his arrest and imprisonment at Vincennes (August to November).

1750   Publication of *Prospectus* for *Encyclopédie*.

1751   Volume One of *Encyclopédie* published; also *Lettre sur les sourds et muets*.

1752   Temporary suspension of the *Encyclopédie*. Writes contribution to the *Apologie de l'abbé de Prades*.

1753   Birth of Angélique, the only child to survive.

1754   Publication of *Pensées sur l'interprétation de la nature*.

c.1755   Beginning of friendship with Sophie Volland.

1757   Publication of *Le Fils naturel* with its *Entretiens*.

1758   Break with Rousseau. Publication of *Le Père de famille* with the *Discours sur la poésie dramatique*.

1759   Death of father. Publication of the *Encyclopédie* halted. Writes first *Salon*.

1760   First work on *La Religieuse*.

1761   Writes *Éloge de Richardson* (published the next year) and second *Salon*.

1762   Publication of the first volume of plates for *Encyclopédie*. First work on *Le Neveu de Rameau* (?).

1763   Writes third *Salon*.

1764   Discovery of Le Breton's censorship of articles in the *Encyclopédie*.

1765   Sale of library to Catherine II. Writes fourth *Salon*. Publication of remaining volumes of text of the *Encyclopédie*.

1766   Writes *Essais sur la peinture*.

1767–8 Writes fifth *Salon*.

1769   Writes *Le Rêve de d'Alembert*, sixth *Salon*, first version of *Paradoxe sur le comédien*.

1770   Affair with Madame de Maux. Journey to Langres and Bourbonne. Writes *Deux Amis de Bourbonne, Entretien d'un père avec ses enfants, Apologie de l'abbé Galiani*.

1771   Writes or completes *Principes philosophiques sur la matière et le mouvement*, first version of *Jacques le fataliste, Pages contre un tyran*, seventh *Salon*.

1772   Marriage of Angélique. Writes *Madame de la Carlière, Ceci n'est pas un conte, Supplément au Voyage de Bougainville*.

1773   Leaves Paris and travels via Holland, where he works on *Réfutation d'Helvétius* and *Commentaire sur Hemsterhuis*, to St Petersberg. There he writes *Mémoires pour Catherine II*. Publication of *Deux Amis de Bourbonne, Entretien d'un père avec ses enfants* and *Regrets sur ma vieille robe de chambre*.

1774   Returns to Paris. Writes *Entretien d'un philosophe avec la maréchale, Principes de politique des souverains, Observations sur le Nakaz*.

1775   Writes eighth *Salon*, completes *Plan d'une université*.

1776   Works on *Pensées détachées sur la peinture*.

1777   Prepares complete collection of works. Publication of *Entretien d'un philosophe avec la maréchale*. Works on contributions to *Histoire des Deux Indes*.

1778   Publication of first version of *Essai sur Sénèque*. Completion of *Jacques le fataliste*.

1780   Completes second version of *Essai sur les règnes de Claude et de Néron* (published in 1782). Works on *La Religieuse*.

1781   Writes *Lettre apologétique de l'abbé Raynal à M. Grimm* and ninth *Salon*.

1782–3 Final revisions to *Est-il bon? Est-il méchant?, Jacques le fataliste, La Religieuse* and *Le Neveu de Rameau* (?).

1784   31 July, dies in Paris.

Posthumous publications

1791	*Principes philosophiques sur la matière et le mouvement.*
1795	*Salon de 1765, Essais sur la peinture, Les Éleutheromanes.*
1796	*La Religieuse, Jacques le fataliste, Supplément au Voyage de Bougainville.*
1798	*Salon de 1767, Pensées détachées sur la peinture, Madame de la Carlière, Ceci n'est pas un conte, Principes de politique des souverains.*
1805	(in German) *Le Neveu de Rameau.*
1819	*Salon de 1761.*
1821	*Le Neveu de Rameau.*
1830	*Le Rêve de d'Alembert, Paradoxe sur le comédien, Promenade du sceptique, Lettres à Sophie Volland.*
1834	*Est-il bon? Est-il méchant?*
1845	*Salon de 1759.*
1857	*Salons de 1763, 1769, 1771, 1775, 1781.*
1861	*Sur la liberté de la presse.*
1875	*Réfutation d'Helvétius, Plan d'une université, Éléments de physiologie.*
1899	*Mémoires pour Catherine II.*
1920	*Observations sur le Nakaz.*
1937	*Pages contre un tyran.*
1951	*Lettre apologétique de l'abbé Raynal à M. Grimm.*
1954	*Apologie de l'abbé Galiani.*
1964	*Commentaire sur Hemsterhuis.*
1976	*Pensées détachées* from the *Histoire des Deux Indes.*
1977	*Mélanges* from the *Histoire des Deux Indes.*
1978	Analysis of *Histoire des Deux Indes* showing all Diderot's contributions.

Further Reading

IN ENGLISH

By Diderot

Selected Writings (New York, 1966). Edited by L. G. Crocker. The most wide-ranging selection available, though the brevity of the editorial material can make some of Diderot's writings seem rather bewildering.

Diderot: Interpreter of Nature (London, 1937). Edited by J. Kemp. Contains *Le Rêve de d'Alembert, Principes philosophiques sur la matière et le mouvement* and *Entretien d'un philosophe avec la maréchale*; most of *Le Neveu de Rameau* and the *Supplément au Voyage de Bougainville*, and extracts from *Les Bijoux indiscrets, Pensées sur l'interprétation de la nature* and *Éléments de physiologie*. A useful volume, mostly concerned with Diderot's materialism.

Rameau's Nephew and Other Works (Indianopolis, 1964). The translation of *Le Neveu de Rameau* by J. Barzun is more fluent and readable than other versions. The other works, translated by R. H. Bowen, are *Le Rêve de d'Alembert, Supplément au Voyage de Bougainville, Deux Amis de Bourbonne, Entretien d'un père avec ses enfants, Regrets sur ma vieille robe de chambre* and much of the article 'Encyclopédie'. This is the best single volume of Diderot's works in English.

Early Philosophical Works (Chicago, 1916). Translated by M. Jourdain. Contains *Pensées philosophiques, Lettre sur les aveugles, Lettre sur les sourds et muets*.

Dialogues (London, 1927). Translated by F. Birrell. Contains *Le Rêve de d'Alembert, Supplément au Voyage de Bougainville, Regrets sur ma vieille robe de chambre, Entretien d'un philosophe avec la maréchale, Sur les femmes*.

Rameau's Nephew and Other Works (London, 1926). Translated by W. Jackson. The other works are the *Supplément au Voyage de Bougainville* and *Regrets sur ma vieille robe de chambre*.

Rameau's Nephew and D'Alembert's Dream (Harmondsworth, 1966). Translated by L. Tancock.

The Nun (Harmondsworth, 1974). Translated by L. Tancock.

Jacques the fatalist and his master (New York, 1959). Translated by J. Robert Loy.

Selections from the Encyclopaedia (New York, 1959). Translated by S. J. Gendzier.

The Paradox of Acting (London, 1883). Translated by W. H. Pollock.

Letters to Sophie Volland (London, 1972). Translated by P. France. An attractive selection.

D'Alembert's Preliminary Discourse (New York, 1963). Introduction by R. N. Schwab. A good edition; the third section incorporates Diderot's *Prospectus*.

Dramatic Essays of the Neoclassic Age (New York, 1950). Edited by H. H. Adams and B. Hathaway. Contains the first five chapters of the *Discours sur la poésie dramatique*.

European Theories of the Drama (London, 1929). Translated by B. Clark. Contains most of the first eleven chapters of the *Discours sur la poésie dramatique*.

French Liberalism and Education in the Eighteenth Century (London, 1932). Edited by F. De la Fontainerie. Contains most of the *Plan d'une université*.

About Diderot

The best general introduction is the thorough biography by A. M. Wilson, *Diderot* (New York, 1972). There are also good chapters in R. Niklaus, *A Literary History of France, The Eighteenth Century 1715–1789* (London, 1970), P. France, *Rhetoric and Truth in France* (Oxford, 1972), L. Spitzer, *Linguistics and Literary History* (Princeton, 1948), G. Poulet, *Studies in Human Time* (Baltimore, 1956), and by J. Barzun in *Varieties of Literary Experience* (ed. S. Burnshaw, New York, 1962).

L. G. Crocker, *Diderot's Chaotic Order* (Princeton, 1974) is a general survey of some of his leading ideas; O. Fellows, *Diderot* (New York, 1977) is a short account of the life and works. C. Sherman, *Diderot and the Art of Dialogue* (Geneva, 1976) and J. Undank, *Diderot – inside, outside and in-between* (Madison, 1979) are two studies of his literary manner.

For studies of individual works see the books and articles mentioned in the Notes. There are articles on all aspects of Diderot's achievement in *Diderot Studies* and *Studies on Voltaire and the Eighteenth Century*.

IN FRENCH

By Diderot

The new Hermann edition of the works (edited under the direction of H. Dieckmann, J. Proust and J. Varloot, Paris, 1975–) provides the best available texts and much of the critical apparatus is also good. However, it does not supersede some of the editions of individual works, such as those by J. Fabre on *Le Neveu de Rameau*, H. Dieckmann on the *Supplément au Voyage de Bougainville* or P. H. Meyer on the *Lettre sur les sourds et muets*, details of which have been given in the Notes. Readers should also consult the useful editions by P. Vernière in the Classiques Garnier series, details of which will be found in the Notes. The Roth edition of the *Correspondance* (Paris, 1955–70) is comprehensive and well presented. M. Duchet, *Diderot et l'Histoire des Deux Indes ou l'écriture fragmentaire* (Paris, 1978) provides an analysis of the *Histoire des Deux Indes* indicating Diderot's contributions; substantial selections of these have been published in two useful volumes edited by G. Goggi, *Pensées détachées* (Siena, 1976) and *Mélanges et morceaux divers* (Siena, 1977).

About Diderot

H. Dieckmann's *Cinq Leçons sur Diderot* (Paris, 1959) remains, to my mind, the best single study that has been written. F. Venturi, *Jeunesse de Diderot* (Paris, 1939) is also excellent. Among the important studies that have appeared in recent years particular attention should be paid to J. Proust, *Diderot et l'Encyclopédie* (Paris, 1962), J. Chouillet, *La Formation des idees esthétiques de Diderot 1743–1763* (Paris, 1973) and the long chapter on Diderot in J. Roger, *Les Sciences de la vie dans la pensée française de XVIIIe siècle* (Paris, 1963). J. Chouillet, *Diderot* (Paris, 1977) is an up-to-date account of the life and works. For a brief introduction see C. Guyot, *Diderot par lui-même* (Paris, 1965), R. Pomeau, *Diderot, sa vie and son oeuvre* (Paris, 1967), or J–L. Leutrat, *Diderot* (Paris, 1967). On Diderot's influence and changing reputation, see R. Mortier, *Diderot en Allemagne* (Paris, 1954) and J. Proust, *Lectures de Diderot* (Paris, 1974). *Dix-huitième siècle* contains some interesting articles and there is a comprehensive bibliography in F. A. Spear, *Bibliographie de Diderot* (Geneva, 1980).

Index